*06. AUGUST 1928 PITTSBURGH †22. FEBRUAR 1987 NEW YORK CITY

ANDY WARHOL

Andy Warhol studierte Grafikdesign in Pittsburgh, bevor er nach New York ging. Dort schlug sich der mittellose Andy als freier Werbegrafiker und Schaufensterdekorateur durch oder verkaufte auf der Straße Obst und Gemüse. Er arbeitete für Zeitschriften und Magazine, entwarf Grußkarten, Werbegeschenke und Kochbücher. Ende der 50er Jahre gehörte er zu den bestbezahltesten Grafikern der City. Zunehmend verschwammen die Grenzen zwischen Grafikdesign und Kunst. Seine erste Ausstellung 1956 im MoMA war noch die des Grafikers Warhol. Doch mit Gründung der »Factory« änderte sich dies sehr schnell. Der Inspirator und Teamarbeiter Warhol versammelt Tänzer, Schauspieler, Maler, Musiker und Filmer um sich. Dort frönte er neben der Malerei und dem Siebdrucken seiner zweiten Leidenschaft: dem Film. Außerdem förderte er die legendäre Rockformation »The Velvet Underground«. Warhol war einer der größten Pop-Artisten und fehlt heute in keiner großen oder kleinen Dauerausstellung anerkannter Museen.

[MIT FREUNDLICHER ERLAUBNIS VON: SELF PORTRAIT © 2008 THE ANDY WARHOL FOUNDATION/CORBIS]

darüber sind Kaufhäuser Art Museum.

ADVERTISING 2008

VOLUME A

ART DIRECTORS CLUB FÜR DEUTSCHLAND
VERLAG HERMANN SCHMIDT MAINZ

RALF ZILLIGEN setzt sich vehement für neue kreative Organisationsformen ein.

RALF ZILLIGEN is a passionate advocate of new and creative organisational forms.

WIE ENTSTEHT EINE IDEE?
How do ideas happen?

Seit mehr als 60 Jahren produzieren Agenturen auf mehr oder weniger dieselbe Weise: Sie sperren einen Texter und einen Art Director so lange in einen Raum, bis eine Idee herauskommt. Inzwischen wird Deutschland von einer Frau regiert, die Autoindustrie erkennt neben Benzin auch andere Treibstoffe an und das Schwenken einer Flagge bleibt nicht mehr Nazitrotteln vorbehalten – nur wir Agenturleute verhalten uns so, wie immer. Dabei machen es unsere Kunden vor: Bei Procter & Gamble entstehen Ideen inzwischen zu über 30% bei externen Mitarbeitern. An runden Tischen. Über offene Netzwerke. IBM hat ein weltweites Brainstorming mit über 150.000 Teilnehmern durchgeführt. Mit Mitarbeitern, Geschäftsfreunden und deren Familienangehörigen. Heraus kamen mehr als 46.000 Ideen innerhalb von 72 Stunden. Zur Nachahmung empfohlen? Warum nicht? Bislang sind Agenturen jedenfalls die letzten protektionistischen Zonen im Geschäft mit Ideen. Noch immer entsprechen ihre Berufsbilder denen der guten, alten Zeit. Noch immer werden lieber mittelgute Ideen aus dem eigenen Haus der Möglichkeit vorgezogen, durch moderne Technik ein weltweites Netz von Kreativen für sich einzuspannen. Und noch immer ist Kontrolle beim Herstellen von Ideen das am häufigsten eingesetzte Mittel. Der ADC ist dazu da, die besten Ideen eines Jahres zu prämieren. Auch in diesem Jahr ist das den Juroren wieder auf vorzügliche Weise gelungen. Ich bin gespannt, welche Ideen wir demnächst werden auszeichnen können, wenn endlich mehr und mehr Agenturen ihre Arbeitsweise der Zeit entsprechend angepasst haben.

Herzlichst, Ihr Ralf Zilligen

For over 60 years, ad agencies have been producing work in pretty much the same fashion: lock a copywriter and an art director together in a room and wait until an idea emerges. Today, however, Germany is governed by a woman, the car industry is recognising fuels other than petrol and flag-waving is no longer the preserve of Nazi morons – we advertising types are the only ones who haven't moved with the times. Even our clients are showing us the way; for example, Proctor & Gamble are now generating more than 30% of their ideas through external suppliers – at round tables or through open networks. IBM carried out a worldwide brainstorming session with more than 150,000 participants – staff members, business associates, family members – resulting in the creation of more than 46,000 ideas in a span of 72 hours. Should we be following their lead? Why not? Agencies have, up to now, remained the last bastion of protectionism in the ideas business. Their job descriptions still continue to hark back to the good old days. They still prefer to generate moderately good ideas in-house, rather than open themselves up to the possibility of using modern technology to put in place their own worldwide network of creative people. Equally, supervision of the generation of ideas remains the most commonly used method. The ADC exists to award prizes to the best ideas in any given year – a task the jurors accomplished in exemplary fashion once again this year. I can't wait to see what types of ideas we will have the opportunity to award in future years, once more agencies have finally adapted their work methods to suit the times.

Yours, Ralf Zilligen

INHALT
Content

004 VORWORT
    FOREWORD
010 GRAND PRIX
    GRAND PRIX

JURY 01
PUBLIKUMSANZEIGEN
CONSUMER ADVERTISEMENTS

019 Konzerthaus Dortmund – Konzertreihe ›Junge Wilde‹ Kampagne »Outstanding Talents«
020 Mercedes-Benz Kampagne »Monumente«
022 Hornbach Baumarkt Kampagne »Helden 2007«
024 BMW 1er Coupé Kampagne »Verdichtete 1ntensität«
027 VW Golf GTI-Technologie Edition 30 Kampagne »5,9 kg pro PS«
029 Hornbach Baumarkt »Women at Work«
031 Sixt – rent a car »Beauty«
032 Louis Vuitton Kampagne »Stars«
034 EXIT Deutschland »Mein Früher«
037 F.A.Z. »Dahinter steckt immer ein kluger Kopf«
039 13TH STREET Kampagne »Kopfkino«
041 DMAX Kampagne »Fernsehen für die tollsten Menschen der Welt: Männer«
042 Jeep Kampagne »Türknopf«
043 VW Golf GTI Kampagne »Männer brauchen wir nicht zu überzeugen«
044 BMW EfficientDynamics Kampagne »Tropfen«
045 Mercedes-Benz R-Klasse Kampagne »250 Sachen«
046 Mercedes-Benz Integrales Sicherheitssystem Kampagne »Ultraschall«
047 www.scheidungsanwalt.de Kampagne »Kleiner Unterschied«
048 Sixt – rent a car »Little Man«
049 Dolormin Kampagne »Keine Schmerzen«
050 Oryza Spitzenreis Kampagne »Reisfeld«
051 Hut Weber »Hitler vs. Chaplin«
052 IWC »Kampagne 2007«
053 Falk Navigationsgeräte Kampagne »Einfach Navigieren«
054 CinemaxX Kampagne »Nur im Kino«
055 Misereor Hilfswerk Kampagne »Kriegswaisen«
056 www.wikipedia.org Kampagne »Hypertext«
057 UNICEF Kampagne »ProAging«
059 Du bist Deutschland Kampagne »Eine Initiative für mehr Kinderfreundlichkeit«
060 Edding Kampagne »Fineliner«
061 STABILO BOSS ORIGINAL Kampagne »Details«
062 F.A.Z. Kampagne »Relaunch – Weiße Serie«
063 Comedy Central Kampagne »Witze«
064 STABILO Kampagne »Entdeckung«
065 IKEA »Bälleland«
066 Comedy Central Kampagne »Ernst«
066 Volkswagen Park Distance Control »Einpark-Kampagne«
066 McDonald's McCafé »Kaffee-Bohne«
066 Bosch Akkuschrauber PSR 14,4 LI-2 »Fliege«
067 Malteser Kampagne »Typo Crash«

JURY 02
FACHANZEIGEN
TRADE ADVERTISEMENTS

070 »Eigenwerbung 2007«
072 Comedy Central »Ernst-Kampagne«
074 Inlingua Kampagne »Umrisse«
076 Wieners + Wieners Werbelektorat Kampagne »Wirre Grafiken«
077 Jung von Matt »Geiziger Abschied«
078 Honda Motoren Corporate Kampagne »Motiv Kondensstreifen«
079 BIC Cristal Kampagne »More joy of writing«
080 WMF Kampagne »Schnellkochtöpfe«
081 13TH STREET Kampagne »Kopfkino«

TAGES-/WOCHENZEITUNGSANZEIGEN
ADVERTISEMENTS IN DAILY/WEEKLY NEWSPAPERS

084 adidas Football Kampagne »Der 11-Stufen Countdown zum DFB Pokal Finale«
087 Volkswagen Park Distance Control »Einpark-Kampagne«
089 Aquatimer Automatic 2000 »Fisch«
090 BURGER KING Pommes »Stellenanzeige Kartoffel«
091 Hornbach Baumarkt »Helden 2007«
093 Jeep Kampagne »Spuren«
094 Loewe Flat TV Kampagne »Unglaublich realistisch.«
095 Volkswagen Komfort-Bremsassistent Kampagne »Schreckenlos«
096 VW Golf »Horst Schlämmer Grevenbroicher Tagblatt«
096 Comedy Central »Ernst-Kampagne«
096 Konzerthaus Dortmund – Konzertreihe ›Junge Wilde‹ Kampagne »Outstanding Talents«
097 VW Golf GTI-Technologie Edition 30 Kampagne »5,9 kg pro PS«
096 BIC Cristal Kampagne »More joy of writing«

JURY 03
PLAKATE UND POSTER (INDOOR UND OUTDOOR)
BILLBOARDS AND POSTERS (INDOOR AND OUTDOOR)

- 100 Deutsche Post »Pong«
- 105 Braun Nasenhaarschneider Kampagne »Exact Series«
- 106 Tierpark Berlin Kampagne »Ich bin auch Knut«
- 108 Malteser Kampagne »Typo Crash«
- 111 McDonald's McCafé »Kaffee-Bohne«
- 112 Protefix Haft-Creme Kampagne »Nussknacker«
- 113 Thomapyrin Kopfschmerztabletten Kampagne »Paradoxien«
- 114 Deutsche Lufthansa Kampagne »Billig«
- 115 Greenpeace Kampagne »Müll«
- 116 Bosch Akkuschrauber PSR 14,4 LI-2 »Fliege«
- 117 McDonald's »Danke Schwester«
- 118 Astra Kampagne »CLPs 2007«
- 119 Naturkundemuseum Stuttgart Kampagne »Stammbaum«
- 120 PAPSTAR Aluminiumfolie Kampagne »Alufolie schützt«
- 121 neu.de Kampagne »Vorher – Nachher«
- 122 Falk Navigationsgeräte Kampagne »Einfach Navigieren«
- 123 Comedy Central »Ernst-Kampagne«
- 123 Eos Cabriolet »Schattenplakat«
- 123 Inlingua Kampagne »Umrisse«
- 123 VW Golf GTI Technologie Edition 30 Kampagne »5,9 kg pro PS«
- 124 Volkswagen Park Distance Control »Einpark-Kampagne«
- 124 Sixt – rent a car »Beauty«
- 124 BMW 1er Coupé Kampagne »Verdichtete 1ntensität«
- 124 Mercedes-Benz G-Klasse Kampagne »Sandplakat, Steinplakat«
- 125 VW Golf GTI Kampagne »Männer brauchen wir nicht zu überzeugen«
- 125 WMF Kampagne »Schnellkochtöpfe«

JURY 04
PRODUKT-/WERBEBROSCHÜREN
PRODUCT/ADVERTISING BROCHURES

- 128 Mercedes-Benz LKW Blue Tec »Geschichten in Öl«
- 130 Mercedes-Benz G-Klasse »Der Stoff aus dem die Helden sind«
- 132 Katholische Klinikseelsorge »Gebrauchsanweisung für die Seele«
- 134 MKI Matzku & Konz Industrievertretung »Gehäuse, Induktivitäten, Leiterplatten & Folientastaturen«
- 136 Mercedes-Benz Original-Service »Das lange Buch vom langen Leben«
- 137 Fanartikelkatalog »FC St Pauli 2007/08«
- 138 OHROPAX »Lauter Ruhe«
- 139 VW Golf »Horst Schlämmer Grevenbroicher Tagblatt«

TEXT
COPY

- 140 Dali Anzeigenkampagne »Die Dalimonologe«
- 142 Mercedes-Benz Anzeigen »G-Klasse Händlerkampagne«
- 144 Mercedes-Benz LKW Blue Tec Folder »Geschichten in Öl«
- 147 Volkswagen Zeitung »Horst Schlämmer Grevenbroicher Tagblatt«
- 148 MTV Masters Anzeigenkampagne »MTV Masters macht unsterblich«
- 150 Mercedes-Benz S-Klasse Anzeige »Vordermann«
- 152 Volkswagen Kampagne »Horst Schlämmer bloggt«
- 154 Zettl Katalog »Part:two«
- 156 Hornbach Baumarkt Broschüre »Women at Work«
- 157 Du bist Deutschland Anzeigenkampagne »Eine Initiative für mehr Kinderfreundlichkeit«
- 158 Tages-Anzeiger »Was, wenn...«
- 159 DMAX Anzeigenkampagne »Fernsehen für die tollsten Menschen der Welt: Männer«
- 160 Doppelherz Anzeigenkampagne »Die Gedicht-Kampagne«
- 161 Konzerthaus Dortmund – Konzertreihe Symphonie um Vier Anzeigenkampagne »Partituren«
- 162 Festspielhaus Baden-Baden Anzeige »Lang Lang in Baden-Baden«
- 163 IWC Anzeigen »Kampagne 2007«

JURY 07
VERKAUFSFÖRDERUNG
SALES PROMOTION

- 169 Greenpeace »Gletscherskulptur«
- 171 Serviceplan Hamburg »Shen International Advertising«
- 173 ASICS Europe »Triathlon«
- 175 Meister Camera/Leica D-LUX 3 »Verpixelt«
- 176 Kolle Rebbe Texterschmieden-Anzeige »Gewinnspiel«
- 177 »Schleichwerbung für Sönke Busch«
- 178 BIONADE Promotion »Stille Taten«
- 179 IKEA »Desktopmöbel«
- 180 Volkswagen Kampagne »Bologna auf Rädern«
- 181 smart »Miniatur Wunderland«
- 182 Titanic »Harry Potter stirbt auf Seite 652«
- 183 Astra »Herrenhandtasche«
- 184 Taxiruf 22456 Promotion »2,0 Promille«
- 185 Volkswagen Service Promotion »Fake Sounds Live«
- 186 Volkswagen Kampagne »Horst Schlämmer macht Führerschein«
- 186 IKEA »3D-Cover«
- 187 Olympus Unterwassergehäuse PT-029 »Unterwassergehäuse Promotion PT-029«
- 187 Eos Cabriolet »Schattenplakat«
- 187 TUI »Hawaii-Hemden«

MEDIA
MEDIA

188 Eos »Schattenplakat«
192 MTV Europe Music Awards sponsored by Sony Ericsson »Graffiti Projektionen«
194 Wissenschaftsjahr 2007 Kampagne »Die Geisteswissenschaften. Das ABC der Menschheit.«
196 Olympus Unterwassergehäuse PT-029 »Unterwassergehäuse Promotion PT-029«
199 Mercedes-Benz G-Klasse Kampagne »Sandplakat, Steinplakat«
201 SIXT »Ebay Ads«
202 jobsintown.de Promotion »Friseur-Umhang«
203 BMW 1er Coupé »160.000 x Verdichtete 1ntensität«
204 Leifheit Roll-CLP »Fensterwischer«
205 EnBW CLPs »Elektrischer Adventskranz«
206 Hornbach Baumarkt TV-Kampagne »Schnick&Schnack Ramsch«
207 Greenpeace »Bildschirmschoner«
208 Brot für die Welt Anzeigenkampagne »Worte helfen nicht mehr«
209 n-TV Promotion »Kanzleramt«
210 Mercedes-Benz LKW Blue Tec Promotion »Clean Wall«
211 Bitburger »Bierkorken«
212 TUI Promotion »Hawaii-Hemden«
213 Filmfest Hamburg CLP Strecke »Patrone«
214 BMW 1er Coupé »Verdichtete Magazintitel«
215 IKEA Promotion »3D-Cover«
215 Volkswagen Service Promotion »Fake Sounds Live«

JURY 08
TV-SPOTS
TELEVISION COMMERCIALS

221 Volkswagen Kampagne »Horst Schlämmer macht Führerschein«
223 adidas Kampagne »Impossible Is Nothing«
225 Media Markt Kampagne »Das kauf' ich Euch ab.«
226 Renault Deutschland »Ballett«
228 DEVK Versicherung »Fahrrad«
230 Dextro Energy »Hotline«
232 jobsintown.de Kampagne »Bildschirmschoner«
234 Beate Uhse »Kindersicherung«
236 Wrigley Juicy Fruit Squish »Ranch«
238 Bild am Sonntag »Tarnung«
240 Schneider Weisse »Traum«
242 Arcor Power Paket Kampagne »Gamer Spots«
243 »Du bist Deutschland«
244 Hornbach Baumarkt »Schnick&Schnack Kampagne«
245 Zürcher Kammerorchester »Achterbahn«
246 Allianz Unfall Aktiv »Extrawünsche«
247 Audi R8 »Warm-up«
248 Runners Point »Löwe«
249 ER221 Bart-/Haarschneider »Rotkehlchen«
250 IFAW »Safari«
251 Jeep »Türknopf«
252 smart fortwo cdi »Umwelt«

253 VW Golf Variant Kampagne »Der längste Golf aller Zeiten«
254 Bundesministerium für Umwelt, Naturschutz und Reaktorsicherheit/EPURON »Power of Wind«
254 Hornbach Baumarkt »Mach es fertig«
254 Mercedes-Benz 4MATIC »4matics«
255 Jeep »Ten little vehicles«
255 Konzerthaus Dortmund Saison 2007/2008 »symphony in red«
255 Sixt – rent a car »Matthias Reim«
255 Freeware.de Kampagne »Highspeed Download«
256 adidas Football »Impossible Park Football«
256 Smart »Benzinkanister Blues«
256 Hornbach Baumarkt »Screws«
257 Mercedes-Benz G-Klasse »Hindernisse«
257 Mercedes-Benz »The Race F1«

JURY 09
KINOWERBEFILME
CINEMA COMMERCIALS

260 Hornbach Baumarkt »Mach es fertig«
264 Mercedes-Benz 4MATIC »4matics«
266 Smart »Benzinkanister Blues«
268 Mercedes-Benz G-Klasse »Hindernisse«
270 Jeep »Ten little vehicles«
272 Mercedes-Benz C-Klasse T-Modell »Oper«
274 adidas Football »Impossible Park Football«
275 Hornbach Baumarkt »Screws«
276 Mercedes-Benz »The Race F1«
277 Bundesministerium für Umwelt, Naturschutz und Reaktorsicherheit/EPURON »Power of Wind«
277 Renault Deutschland »Ballett«
277 YouTube »Horst Hrubesch«
277 Runners Point »Löwe«

FILME FÜR VERKAUFSFÖRDERUNG/
UNTERNEHMENSDARSTELLUNGEN
FILMS FOR SALES PROMOTION/COMPANY
PRESENTATION

278 Konzerthaus Dortmund Saison 2007/2008 Imagefilm »symphony in red«
280 smart fortwo POS-Spot »Wendekreis«
281 mi adidas Animationsfilm »InStore Spot«
282 Maggi Würze Imagefilm »Suppen-Kaspar«
283 Volkswagen Kampagne »Horst Schlämmer macht Führerschein«
283 ASICS Europe Imagefilm »Origami«
283 Beate Uhse TV-Spot »Kindersicherung«

VIRALE FILME
VIRAL FILMS

285 adidas Football Kampagne »Impossible Park Football«
286 YouTube »Horst Hrubesch«
288 Freeware.de Kampagne »Highspeed Download«
289 Volkswagen Kampagne »Horst Schlämmer macht Führerschein«
289 Sixt – rent a car »Matthias Reim«
289 Beate Uhse »Kindersicherung«

CONTENT INHALT 009

JURY 10
TV-ON-AIR-PROMOTION
TV ON-AIR PROMOTION

292 13TH STREET Kampagne »Kopfkino«
294 Schweizer Fernsehen »SF Delikatessen«
296 Schweizer Fernsehen »Imagekampagne«
297 Blaupunkt »Car Hifi«

AUDIOVISUELLE MEDIEN: DESIGN
AUDIOVISUAL MEDIA: DESIGN

299 NICK »Winterdesign«
300 ASICS Europe »Origami«
302 Mercedes-Benz G-Klasse »Hindernisse«
303 Jeep Animationsfilm »Ten little vehicles«

JURY 11
MUSIKKOMPOSITIONEN/SOUND-DESIGN
MUSIC COMPOSITIONS/SOUND DESIGN

306 AUDI Sound-Design »Kite«
308 Tinnitus Hilfe Düsseldorf Sound-Design »Teekessel«
310 Coop Musikkomposition »Stress«
311 Mercedes-Benz C-Klasse T-Modell Sound-Design »Oper«
312 Konzerthaus Dortmund Saison 2007/2008 Musikkomposition »symphony in red«
312 Hornbach Baumarkt Sound-Design »Mach es fertig«
312 Dextro Energy Musikkomposition »Hotline«
313 Sixt – rent a car »Matthias Reim«
313 Renault Deutschland Musikkomposition »Ballett«

Und ... so weiter und so weiter. Gibt nicht mehr viel zu e
eigentlich. Weil wie das war, kann jeder ganz leicht nach
en, der einmal mühsam so einen Berg hinaufgewandert

JURY 12
FUNKSPOTS
RADIO COMMERCIALS

316 VW Polo Kampagne »Polo Podcast«
320 Arcor Spam Blocker Kampagne »Spam Blocker«
322 Mercedes-Benz Kampagne »Nanga Parbat«
324 Philharmonie Essen Kampagne »Polizeichor«
325 Feuerwehr Dresden Recruiting »Warteschleife«
326 Volkswagen Kampagne »Horst Schlämmer macht Führerschein«
328 K-Fee Kampagne »Nachrichten«
330 Comedy Central »Halloween-Kitty«
331 BIONADE Kampagne »Anrufe für eine bessere Welt«
332 VW Fox Kampagne »Kurz & Gut«
333 Volkswagen Kampagne »Original Teile«
334 Mercedes-Benz Vito Kampagne »Falscher Partner«
335 Pan Sandwiches Kampagne »Frische Zutaten«

336 Rodenstock Gleitsichtbrillen Kampagne »Golf Moderator / Formel 1 Moderator / Fußball Moderator«
337 VW Nutzfahrzeuge Caddy Maxi Kampagne »Platz«
338 Blaupunkt Radios »Funksehen«
339 Sixt – rent a car »Matthias Reim«
340 Odol-med3 Zahnseide »Nachrichten«
341 smart fortwo cdi »Wiedersehen«

JURY 13
INTEGRIERTE KAMPAGNEN
INTEGRATED CAMPAIGNS

347 Volkswagen »Horst Schlämmer macht Führerschein«
350 Sixt – rent a car »Matthias Reim«
354 adidas International »Impossible Is Nothing – Where Sport meets Art«
358 BMW 1er Coupé »Verdichtete 1ntensität«
360 ABSOLUT VODKA »In An ABSOLUT World«

JURY 14
DIALOGMARKETING
DIALOGUE MARKETING

367 VW Golf Kampagne »Horst Schlämmer macht Führerschein«
368 IKEA Katalog Promotionkampagne »3D-Cover«
370 Evangelische Kirche Frankfurt Mailing »Der Taufbrief«
373 Getty Images »Der Ideenfriedhof«
374 Naturschutzbund Deutschland Mailing »Earth Memory«
377 HDI Versicherungen Kampagne »Einkaufswagen gone wilder«
378 Renault Twingo »Teletheater«
379 OroVerde Mailing »Artenvielfalt«
380 Getty Images Sportmailing »Sportmomente«
381 Serviceplan Hamburg »Shen International Advertising«
381 Mercedes-Benz G-Klasse Broschüre »Der Stoff aus dem die Helden sind«

382 AGENTUREN
    AGENCIES
386 FIRMEN
    COMPANIES
390 PRODUKTE
    PRODUCTS
394 MACHER
    WRIGHT
408 JURYS
    JURIES
411 IMPRESSUM
    IMPRINT

ADC GRAND PRIX 2008
»POWER OF WIND«

Grand Prix: Sonderpreis, der für eine bahnbrechende, innovative Arbeit aus dem Kreis aller Goldmedaillengewinner vergeben werden kann.

Die Idee, dem Wind ein Gesicht zu geben, ist die eine Sache; einen Darsteller zu finden, der das leisten kann, eine andere. Als Guillaume den Raum betrat (der letzte Teilnehmer am letzten Tag des Castings), wusste jeder sofort, dass er es ist. Dieser unvergessliche Schauspieler macht die Geschichte des Films erst so eindrücklich.

Grand Prix: A special prize that may be awarded among the ranks of the gold medallists for innovative, pioneering work.

The idea to personify the wind is one thing. Finding an actor who can pull it off is another. When Guillaume walked into the casting session (the very last person, on the very last day) everyone knew immediately that he was the one. This unforgettable actor makes the film's message more memorable as well.

GRAND PRIX

TITLE
Bundesministerium für Umwelt, Naturschutz und Reaktorsicherheit/EPURON »Power of Wind«

CLIENT
EPURON/Bundesministerium für Umwelt, Naturschutz und Reaktorsicherheit

LEAD AGENCY
Nordpol+ Hamburg Agentur für Kommunikation GmbH

CREATIVE DIRECTION
Lars Rühmann

ART DIRECTION
Björn Rühmann, Joakim Reveman

ACCOUNT EXECUTIVE
Mathias Müller-Using

FILM PRODUCTION
Paranoid Projects Paris/
Paranoid US Los Angeles

CAMERA
Pascal Marti

MUSIC COMPOSITION
Pigalle Production

POST PRODUCTION
Mikros Images/Paris

DIRECTION
The Vikings

FILM EDITING
Basile Belkhiri

TEXT
Matthew Branning

ADDITIONAL AWARDS
GOLD
Volume Advertising page 254
TV-Spots
Television Commercials

GOLD
Volume Advertsing page 227
Kinowerbefilme
Cinema Commercials

MARLENE DIETRICH

*27. DEZEMBER 1901 SCHÖNEBERG †06. MAI 1992 PARIS

Marlene Dietrich wollte eigentlich Konzertgeigerin werden. Eine Sehnenscheidenentzündung brachte sie zum Vorsprechen bei Max Reinhardt, der sie vom Platz weg für das Deutsche Theater in Berlin engagierte. Danach folgten kleinere Filmrollen, bis Josef von Sternberg sie für die Hauptolle »Lola Lola« im ersten deutschen Tonfilm »Der blaue Engel« einsetzte. Dieser Auftritt und später die Rolle in »Marokko« verschafften ihr den internationalen Durchbruch und sie wurde für den Oscar nominiert. 1936 versuchte Josef Goebbels, sie mit hohen Gagen heim ins Reich zu locken. Sie lehnte entschieden ab und drehte lieber mit Hitchcock, Lubitsch, Welles und Wilder in den USA. Sie hasste Hitler und unterstützte nicht nur ihren Geliebten Jean Gabin und die französische Befreiungsarmee, sondern auch die amerikanischen GIs bei ihrem Vormarsch in Afrika und Europa. Nach dem Krieg stand sie meistens als Sängerin auf der Bühne. Mit Burt Bacharach kultivierte sie auf allen Bühnen der Welt ihre »One-Woman-Show«. Mit Jean Louis kreierte sie einzigartige Mäntel aus Schwanenfedern oder ein extra für sie angefertigtes Gewebe namens »Souffle«. Ihr starkes Selbstbewusstsein machte sie zu einem Idol der Frauenbewegung, ihre androgyne Ausstrahlung zu einer Ikone der Schwulen und Lesben. »Sie hatte Sex, aber kein Geschlecht.«

*27 DECEMBER 1901 SCHÖNEBERG †06 MAY 1992 PARIS

Marlene Dietrich's desire to be a concert violinist was cut short by a tendon inflammation. She auditioned as an actress for Max Reinhardt, who hired her on the spot for the Deutsche Theater in Berlin. This was followed by small film roles, after which Josef von Sternberg cast her in the lead role of "Lola Lola" in the first German sound film, *The Blue Angel*. Her performance in this film, and then in *Morocco*, led to her international breakthrough, and she was nominated for an Oscar. In 1936 Josef Goebbels tried to tempt her home to the Third Reich with the prospect of high pay. She firmly refused, choosing instead to make films in the USA with Hitchcock, Lubitsch, Welles or Wilder. She hated Hitler, and supported not only her beloved Jean Gabin and the Free French Forces but also the American GIs as they advanced across Africa and Europe. After the war she concentrated on stage performances as a singer. Working with Burt Bacharach, she presented her "One-Woman Show" at venues around the world. Together with Jean Louis she created a unique swan's down coat, plus a fabric known as "Souffle", which was manufactured especially for her. Strong and self-assured, she became an idol of the women's movement, while her androgynous aura made her a gay and lesbian icon. "She had sex, but no gender."

If I could live my life again, I would make the same mistakes.
Just a little bit earlier, so that I can enjoy them more.

WENN ICH MEIN LEBEN NOCH EINMAL LEBEN KÖNNTE, WÜRDE ICH DIE GLEICHEN FEHLER MACHEN. ABER EIN BISSCHEN FRÜHER, DAMIT ICH MEHR DAVON HABE.

CONSUMER ADVERTISEMENTS PUBLIKUMSANZEIGEN 019

SILVER

TITLE
Konzerthaus Dortmund –
Konzertreihe ›Junge Wilde‹
Kampagne »Outstanding Talents«

CLIENT
Konzerthaus Dortmund –
Philharmonie für Westfalen

MARKETING DIRECTOR
Milena Ivkovic

LEAD AGENCY
Jung von Matt AG

CREATIVE DIRECTION
Sascha Hanke, Timm Hanebeck,
Wolf Heumann (GF)

ART DIRECTION
Patrik Hartmann

CLIENT CONSULTING
Nina Gerwing, Lena Frers

PHOTOGRAPHY
Marcel Schaar

ILLUSTRATION
Wojciech Klimek

ART BUYING
Bettina Zschirnt, Karen Blome

IMAGE EDITING
Elisabeth Siegmund

POSTPRODUCTION
gloss postproduction gmbh,
Hamburg

COPY
Michael Okun

ADDITIONAL AWARDS
NOMINATION

Volume Advertising page 096
Tages-/Wochenzeitungsanzeigen
Advertisements in daily/weekly
newspapers

NOMINATION

Volume Design page 127
Kunst-/Kultur-/
Veranstaltungsplakate
Posters for arts, culture, events

NOMINATION

Volume Design page 205
Fotografie
Photography

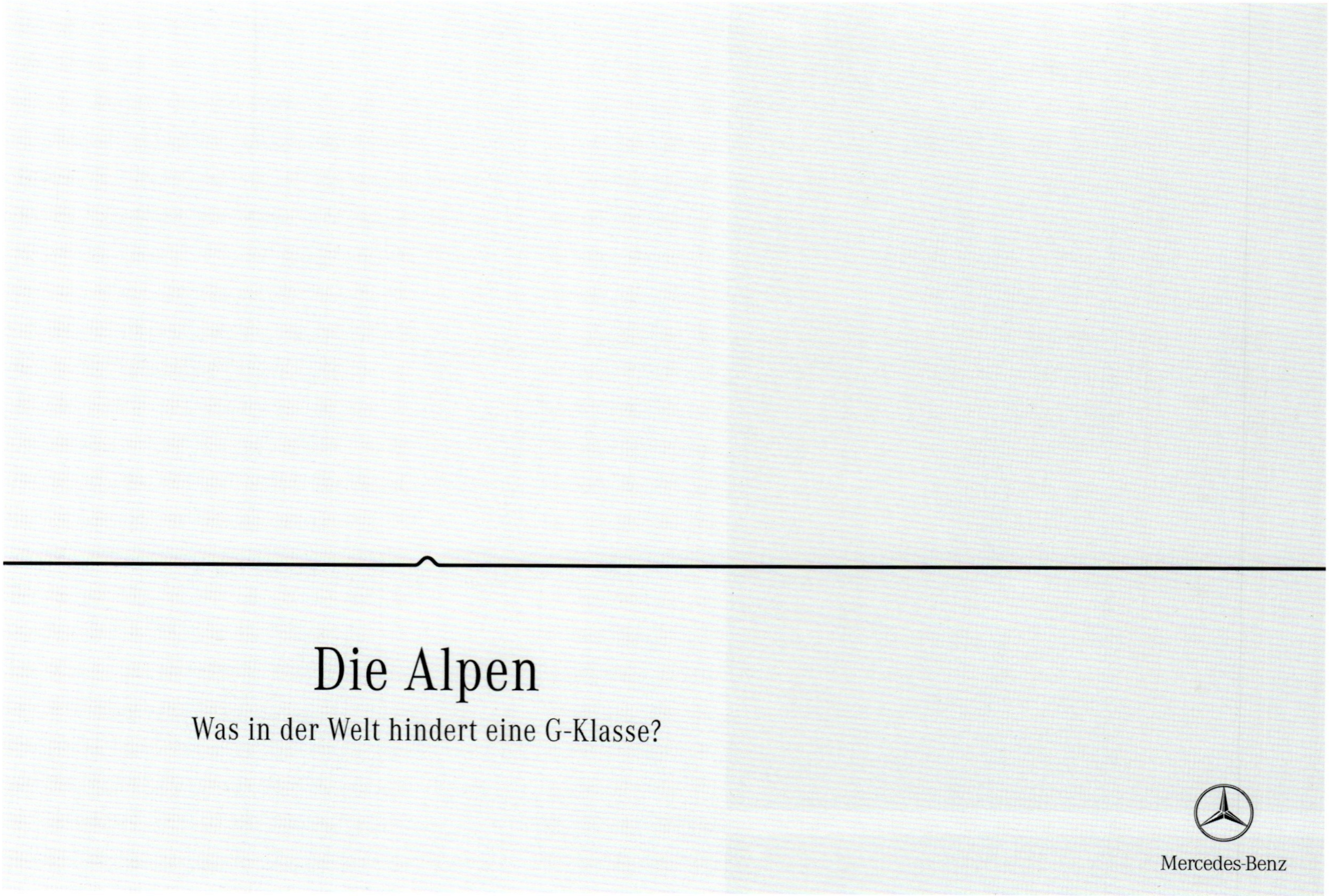

Die Alpen
Was in der Welt hindert eine G-Klasse?

SILVER

TITLE
Mercedes-Benz Kampagne
»Monumente«

CLIENT
Daimler AG

MARKETING DIRECTOR
Andreas Poulionakis

ADVERTISING DIRECTOR
Pawel Nowotny, Yvonne Emhardt,
Klaus Burghauser

LEAD AGENCY
Jung von Matt AG

CREATIVE DIRECTION
Deneke von Weltzien,
Fabian Frese, Thimoteus Wagner

ART DIRECTION
Christian Kroll

CLIENT CONSULTING
Christian Hupertz, Yves Rosengart,
Axel Müller, Johanna Hecker,
Jan Groenendijk

GRAPHIC ART
Christoph Lehmann

COPY
Peter Gocht

Niagara Fälle
Was in der Welt hindert eine G-Klasse?

Grand Canyon
Was in der Welt hindert eine G-Klasse?

Sahara
Was in der Welt hindert eine G-Klasse?

SILVER

TITLE
Hornbach Baumarkt Kampagne
»Helden 2007«

CLIENT
Hornbach Baumarkt AG

MARKETING DIRECTOR
Jürgen Schröcker

ADVERTISING DIRECTOR
Diana Koob

LEAD AGENCY
HEIMAT, Berlin

CREATIVE DIRECTION
Guido Heffels, Jürgen Vossen

ART DIRECTION
Tim Schneider, Marc Wientzek

CLIENT CONSULTING
Yves Krämer

PHOTOGRAPHY
Wolfgang Stahr

ART BUYING
Marjorie Jorrot

CONSULTING
Mark Hassan, Sammy Bohneberg

GRAPHIC ART
Michael Mackens, Joachim Zeh

MEDIA
Crossmedia GmbH, Düsseldorf

PRODUCTION
Carola Storto

COPY
Sebastian Kainz, Guido Heffels,
Till Eckel

ADDITIONAL AWARDS NOMINATION

Volume Advertising page 091
Tages-/Wochenzeitungsanzeigen
Advertisements in daily/weekly newspapers

BRONZE

TITLE
BMW 1er Coupé Kampagne
»Verdichtete 1ntensität«

CLIENT
BMW AG

MARKETING DIRECTOR
Manfred Bräunl

ADVERTISING DIRECTOR
Dr. Tobias Nickel,
Dr. Hans-Peter Ketterl

LEAD AGENCY
MAB, Berlin

CONTRIBUTING AGENCIES
Mediaplus

CREATIVE DIRECTION
Nils Haseborg, Sven Sorgatz,
Stefan Schmidt, Tomas Tulinius

ART DIRECTION
Michael Janke, Sven Sorgatz

CLIENT CONSULTING
Alexander Kerkow,
Christiane Wolters,
Leveke Lambersy,
Henning Gerstner

PHOTOGRAPHY
Mats Cordt

AGENCY PRODUCER
Lars Ebeling

ART BUYING
Martina Kersten

GRAPHIC ART
Alexander Tibelius

MEDIA
Werner Reineke,
Christian Kaessmann

POSTPRODUCTION
Zerone, Hamburg

PRODUCTION
Nowadays: Tobias Wenske;
Mats Cordt
Photography: Matthias Pretzsch

COPY
Nils Haseborg, Stefan Schmidt

ADDITIONAL AWARDS
NOMINATION
Volume Advertising page 124
Plakate und Poster
(indoor und outdoor)
Billboards and posters
(indoor and outdoor)

NOMINATION
Volume Advertising page 203, 214
Media
Media

NOMINATION
Volume Advertising page 358
Integrierte Kampagnen
Integrated campaigns

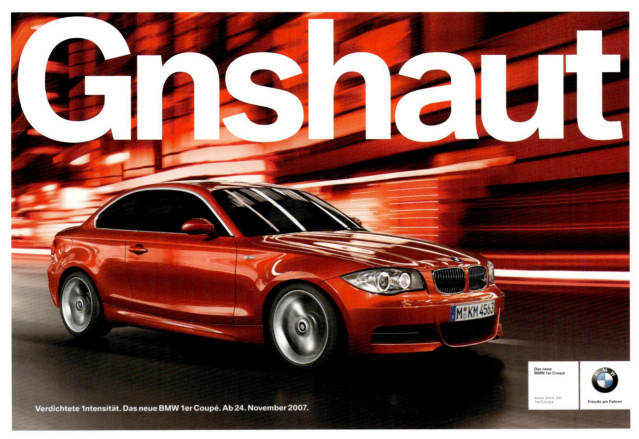

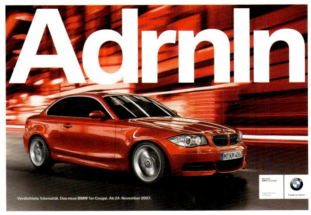

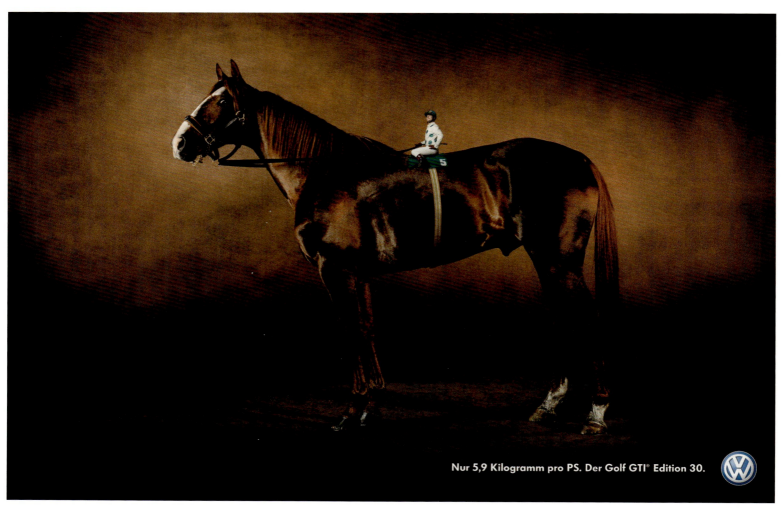

BRONZE

TITLE
VW Golf GTI-Technologie Edition 30 Kampagne »5,9 kg pro PS«

CLIENT
Volkswagen AG

MARKETING DIRECTOR
Jochen Sengpiehl

ADVERTISING DIRECTOR
Hartmut Seeger

LEAD AGENCY
DDB Germany, Berlin

CREATIVE DIRECTION
Stefan Schulte, Bert Peulecke

ART DIRECTION
Marc Wientzek

CLIENT CONSULTING
Cathleen Losch, Louisa Ibing, Silke Lagodny

PHOTOGRAPHY
Yann Arthus-Bertrand, Sven Schrader

ART BUYING
Elke Dilchert

GRAPHIC ART
Wulf Rechtacek

ARTIST
Jan Diekmann

TECHNICAL DIRECTION
Sascha Mehn

COPY
Sebastian Kainz

ADDITIONAL AWARDS
BRONZE
Volume Advertising page 123
Plakate und Poster
(indoor und outdoor)
Billboards and posters
(indoor and outdoor)

NOMINATION
Volume Advertising page 097
Tages-/Wochenzeitungsanzeigen
Advertisements in daily/weekly newspapers

BRONZE

TITLE
Hornbach Baumarkt
»Women at Work«
CLIENT
Hornbach Baumarkt AG
MARKETING DIRECTOR
Jürgen Schröcker
ADVERTISING DIRECTOR
Diana Koob
LEAD AGENCY
HEIMAT, Berlin
CREATIVE DIRECTION
Guido Heffels, Jürgen Vossen
ART DIRECTION
Danny Baarz
CLIENT CONSULTING
Yves Krämer
PHOTOGRAPHY
Christoph York Riccius
ILLUSTRATION
Ulrich Scheer
ART BUYING
Marjorie Jorrot
CONSULTING
Mark Hassan, Sammy Bohneberg
GRAPHIC ART
Jenny Kapteyn
MEDIA
Crossmedia GmbH, Düsseldorf
PRODUCTION
Carola Storto
COPY
Matthias Storath,
Siyamak Seyedasgari

ADDITIONAL AWARDS NOMINATION
Volume Advertising page 156
Text
Copy

BRONZE

TITLE
Sixt – rent a car »Beauty«

CLIENT
Sixt GmbH & Co.
Autovermietung KG

MARKETING DIRECTOR
Dr. Karsten Willrodt

ADVERTISING DIRECTOR
Daniela Erdmann

LEAD AGENCY
Jung von Matt AG

CREATIVE DIRECTION
Peter Kirchhoff, Wolf Heumann

ART DIRECTION
Vanessa Rabea Schrooten

CLIENT CONSULTING
Sandra Schymetzki, Justyna Wos

PHOTOGRAPHY
Kristian Schuller

ART BUYING
Martina Traut, Katja Sluyter

IMAGE EDITING
Peggy H.

GRAPHIC ART
Felix Taubert

PRODUCTION
Annette Hoss

COPY
Lisa Maria Hartwich

ADDITIONAL AWARDS NOMINATION

Volume Advertising page 124
Plakate und Poster
(indoor und outdoor)
Billboards and posters
(indoor and outdoor)

BRONZE

TITLE
Louis Vuitton Kampagne »Stars«

CLIENT
Louis Vuitton Malletier

MARKETING DIRECTOR
Antoine Arnoult
(Communications Director)

LEAD AGENCY
Ogilvy Paris/Ogilvy Frankfurt

CREATIVE DIRECTION
Christian Reuilly/Lars Huvart

ART DIRECTION
Antoaneta Metchanova/
Till Schaffarczyk

CLIENT CONSULTING
Shiv Sethuraman/Laurent Janneau/
Samuel Giblin/
Johannes Wilbrenninck/
Egbert Melten

STRATEGIC PLANNING
Marc-Antoine Jarry

PHOTOGRAPHY
Annie Leibovitz

COPY
Edgard Montjean/Lothar Müller

ADDITIONAL AWARDS
NOMINATION
Volume Design page 211
Fotografie
Photography

Reist man, um die Welt zu entdecken oder um sie zu verändern? Berliner Mauer. Auf dem Rückweg von einer Konferenz. Michail Gorbaschov und Louis Vuitton unterstützen das Green Cross International.

CONSUMER ADVERTISEMENTS PUBLIKUMSANZEIGEN 033

Tel. (0211) 864 70 0   www.louisvuitton.com

LOUIS VUITTON

BRONZE

TITLE
EXIT Deutschland »Mein Früher«
CLIENT
EXIT Deutschland
MARKETING DIRECTOR
Bernd Wagner
LEAD AGENCY
Grabarz & Partner
CREATIVE DIRECTION
Ralf Heuel, Ralf Nolting, Patricia Pätzold
ART DIRECTION
Fabian Klingbeil
CLIENT CONSULTING
Thomas Eickhoff, Ina Bach, Josefine Härle
GRAPHIC ART
Eduardo Inderbitzin
COPY
Oliver Heidorn, Johannes Nittmann

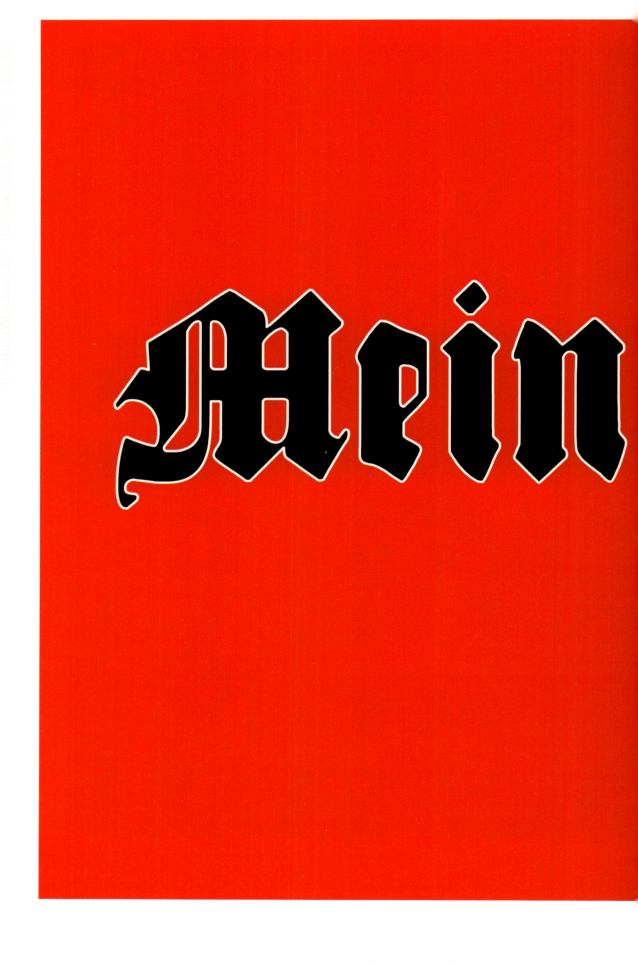

Früher

Das Aussteigerprogramm für Rechtsradikale: www.exit-deutschland.de

Andreas Gursky, Fotograf

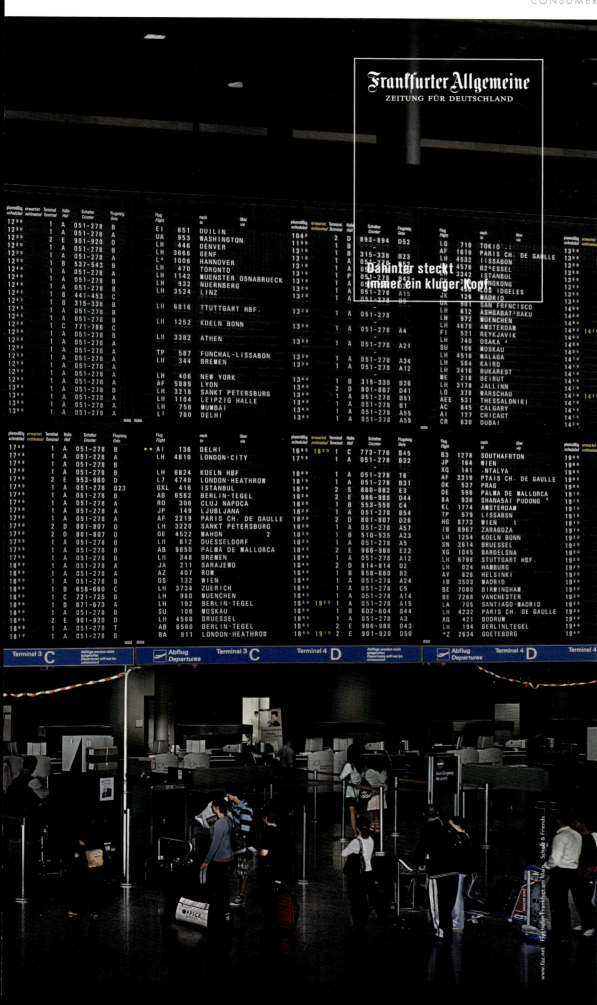

BRONZE

TITLE
F. A. Z. »Dahinter steckt immer ein kluger Kopf«

CLIENT
Frankfurter Allgemeine Zeitung GmbH

MARKETING DIRECTOR
Tobias Trevisan

ADVERTISING DIRECTOR
Marco Rühl

LEAD AGENCY
Scholz & Friends

CREATIVE DIRECTION
Oliver Handlos, Matthias Spaetgens, Sebastian Turner

ART DIRECTION
Cathrin Ciuraj

CLIENT CONSULTING
Katrin Seegers, Daniela Winkler, Katrin Voß

PHOTOGRAPHY
Andreas Gursky

IMAGE EDITING
Appel Grafik Berlin

CONSUMER ADVERTISEMENTS PUBLIKUMSANZEIGEN 039

BRONZE

TITLE
13TH STREET Kampagne
»Kopfkino«

CLIENT
NBC Universal Global Networks
Deutschland GmbH

MARKETING DIRECTOR
Sabine Kirchmair,
Andreas Lechner

ADVERTISING DIRECTOR
Nicole Pawelke

LEAD AGENCY
Jung von Matt AG

CREATIVE DIRECTION
Wolfgang Schneider,
Mathias Stiller, David Mously,
Jan Harbeck

ART DIRECTION
Andreas Böhm

CLIENT CONSULTING
Frank Lotze,
Josef Konstantin Schulte,
Helen Seiffe

PHOTOGRAPHY
Cornelius Zoch

AGENCY PRODUCER
Sven Hannemann

ART BUYING
Anne Weskamp

COPY
Max Millies

ADDITIONAL AWARDS
BRONZE
Volume Advertising page 292
TV-On-air-Promotion
TV on-air promotion

NOMINATION
Volume Advertising page 081
Fachanzeigen
Trade advertisements

CONSUMER ADVERTISEMENTS **PUBLIKUMSANZEIGEN** 041

BRONZE

TITLE
DMAX Kampagne »Fernsehen für die tollsten Menschen der Welt: Männer«

CLIENT
DMAX TV GmbH & Co. KG

MARKETING DIRECTOR
Andreas Dürr

ADVERTISING DIRECTOR
Kathrin Pawelski

LEAD AGENCY
Jung von Matt AG

CREATIVE DIRECTION
Oliver Voss, Götz Ulmer, Fabian Frese, Daniel Frericks

ART DIRECTION
Jens Paul Pfau

CLIENT CONSULTING
Karoline Huber, Jürgen Alker

GRAPHIC ART
Daniel Haschtmann, Stephanie Hotz, Tobias Völlmecke

COPY
Jan-Florian Ege, Jo Marie Farwick, Henning Robert, Tobias Grimm

ADDITIONAL AWARDS NOMINATION
Volume Advertising page 159
Text
Copy

NOMINATION

TITLE
Jeep Kampagne »Türknopf«

CLIENT
Chrysler Deutschland GmbH

MARKETING DIRECTOR
Matthias Möhler

ADVERTISING DIRECTOR
Holger Baumann

LEAD AGENCY
KNSK Werbeagentur GmbH

CREATIVE DIRECTION
Anke Winschewski, Tim Krink,
Niels Holle

ART DIRECTION
Bill Yom

CLIENT CONSULTING
Jan Isterling, Philipp Ernsting

PHOTOGRAPHY
Corbis

ART BUYING
Franziska Boyens, Julia Gaentzsch

IMAGE EDITING
ABC Digital

GRAPHIC ART
Sonja Kliem, Nathalie Krüger

COPY
Kurt Müller-Fleischer

ADDITIONAL AWARDS NOMINATION
Volume Advertising page 251
TV-Spots
Television commercials

CONSUMER ADVERTISEMENTS PUBLIKUMSANZEIGEN 043

NOMINATION

TITLE
VW Golf GTI
Kampagne »Männer brauchen wir nicht zu überzeugen«

CLIENT
Volkswagen AG

MARKETING DIRECTOR
Jochen Sengpiehl

ADVERTISING DIRECTOR
Hartmut Seeger

LEAD AGENCY
DDB Germany, Berlin

CREATIVE DIRECTION
Stefan Schulte, Bert Peulecke

ART DIRECTION
Kristoffer Heilemann,
Alexandra Sievers

CLIENT CONSULTING
Cathleen Losch, Silke Lagodny

PHOTOGRAPHY
F. A. Cesar

GRAPHIC ART
Jakob Schubert, Stephan Wege

TECHNICAL DIRECTION
Sascha Mehn

COPY
Ludwig Berndl, Philip Bolland

ADDITIONAL AWARDS
NOMINATION
Volume Advertising page 125
Plakate und Poster
(indoor und outdoor)
Billboards and posters
(indoor and outdoor)

NOMINATION

TITLE
BMW EfficientDynamics
Kampagne »Tropfen«

CLIENT
BMW AG

MARKETING DIRECTOR
Manfred Bräunl

ADVERTISING DIRECTOR
Dr. Tobias Nickel,
Dr. Hans-Peter Ketterl

LEAD AGENCY
MAB, Berlin

CONTRIBUTING AGENCIES
Mediaplus

CREATIVE DIRECTION
Nils Haseborg, Tomas Tulinius,
Sven Sorgatz

ART DIRECTION
Djamila Rabenstein, Frederick Kober

CLIENT CONSULTING
Alexander Kerkow

ILLUSTRATION
Daniel Egneus

ART BUYING
Tatjana Bilger

MEDIA
Werner Reineke,
Christian Kaessmann

COPY
Frederick Kober, Djamila Rabenstein

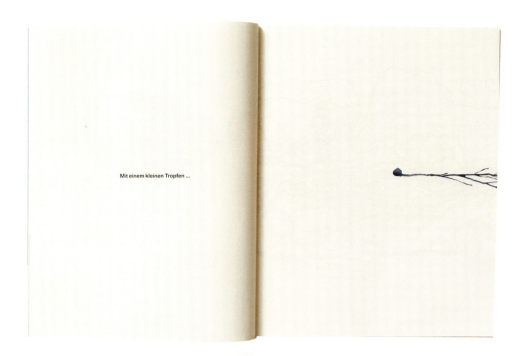

NOMINATION

TITLE
Mercedes-Benz R-Klasse
Kampagne »250 Sachen«

CLIENT
Daimler AG

MARKETING DIRECTOR
Dr. Olaf Göttgens,
Dr. Kristina Hammer

ADVERTISING DIRECTOR
Mirco Völker, Christina Freier

LEAD AGENCY
Jung von Matt AG

CREATIVE DIRECTION
Arno Lindemann, Bernhard Lukas

ART DIRECTION
Markus Kremer, Szymon Rose

CLIENT CONSULTING
Yves Rosengart, Johanna Hecker,
Jan Groenendijk, Stefanie Gombert

GRAPHIC ART
Julia Jakobi, Julia Stoffer,
Melanie Raphael

PRODUCTION
Malte Rehde, Birgit Weber

COPY
Thomas Heyen

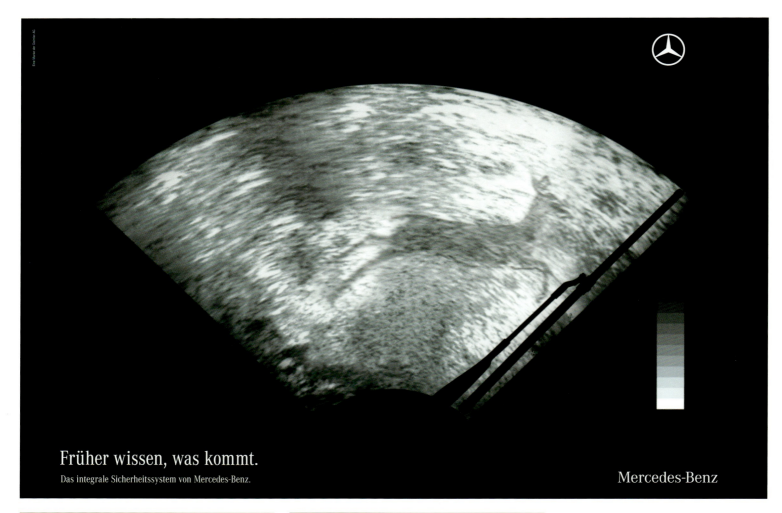
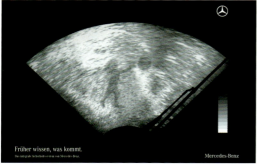
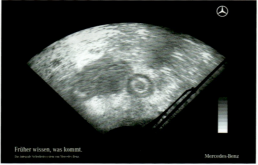

NOMINATION

TITLE
Mercedes-Benz Integrales Sicherheitssystem Kampagne »Ultraschall«

CLIENT
Daimler AG

MARKETING DIRECTOR
Dr. Olaf Göttgens, Dr. Kristina Hammer

ADVERTISING DIRECTOR
Mirco Völker, Christina Freier

LEAD AGENCY
Jung von Matt AG

CREATIVE DIRECTION
Arno Lindemann, Bernhard Lukas

ART DIRECTION
Markus Kremer

CLIENT CONSULTING
Christian Hupertz, Bastian Kuehl, Florian Schramm, Stephan Damm, Franz-Christoph Dotzler, Timon Borck

PRODUCTION
Malte Rehde, Marion Beeck, Marcus Loick, Frank Kirchhoff

COPY
Thomas Heyen

NOMINATION

TITLE
www.scheidungsanwalt.de
Kampagne »Kleiner Unterschied«

CLIENT
Anwaltsuchservice
Verlag Dr. Otto Schmidt GmbH

MARKETING DIRECTOR
Rolf Schroeder

LEAD AGENCY
Ogilvy Frankfurt

CREATIVE DIRECTION
Stephan Junghanns

ART DIRECTION
Ralf Richter

CLIENT CONSULTING
Thorsten Orth, John F. Goetze

ART BUYING
Christina Hufgard

COPY
Peter Strauss

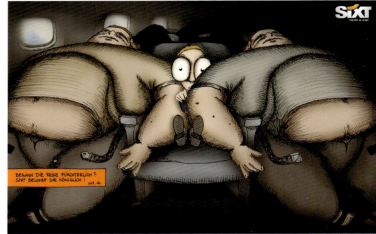

NOMINATION

TITLE
Sixt – rent a car »Little Man«

CLIENT
Sixt GmbH & Co
Autovermietung KG

MARKETING DIRECTOR
Dr. Karsten Willrodt

ADVERTISING DIRECTOR
Daniela Erdmann

LEAD AGENCY
Jung von Matt AG

CREATIVE DIRECTION
Sascha Hanke, Timm Hanebeck,
Wolf Heumann (GF)

ART DIRECTION
Patrik Hartmann

CLIENT CONSULTING
Sandra Schymetzki,
Ann-Kristin Grohsklaus

ILLUSTRATION
Sven Bommes

ART BUYING
Bianca Winter

IMAGE EDITING
Konradin Klebe, PX Group

GRAPHIC ART
Kristian Joshi

PRODUCTION
Carsten Koeslag

COPY
Moritz Grub

TYPOGRAPHY
Patrik Hartmann

NOMINATION

TITLE
Dolormin Kampagne
»Keine Schmerzen«

CLIENT
Johnson & Johnson GmbH

MARKETING DIRECTOR
Wolfgang Henkel

LEAD AGENCY
KNSK Werbeagentur GmbH

CREATIVE DIRECTION
Niels Holle, Tim Krink

ART DIRECTION
Thomas Thiele

CLIENT CONSULTING
Philipp Ernsting

PHOTOGRAPHY
Christopher Koch

IMAGE EDITING
ABC Digital

GRAPHIC ART
Sina Malosczyk

COPY
Steffen Steffens

NOMINATION

TITLE
Oryza Spitzenreis Kampagne
»Reisfeld«

CLIENT
Euryza GmbH

MARKETING DIRECTOR
Rolf Dziedek

LEAD AGENCY
Y&R Germany

CREATIVE DIRECTION
Uwe Marquardt, Christian Daul

ART DIRECTION
Natalia Richel

CLIENT CONSULTING
Berthold T. Meyer, Pia Schütz

AGENCY PRODUCER
Marion Lakatos

ART BUYING
Britta Joh

IMAGE EDITING
ORT Studios

COPY
Kai-Oliver Sass

NOMINATION

TITLE
Hut Weber »Hitler vs. Chaplin«

CLIENT
Hut Weber

MARKETING DIRECTOR
Thomas Weber

LEAD AGENCY
Serviceplan München/Hamburg

CREATIVE DIRECTION
Alexander Schill, Axel Thomsen

ART DIRECTION
Jonathan Schupp, Imke Jurok

CLIENT CONSULTING
Julia Thoemen,
Constanze Strothmann

PHOTOGRAPHY
Jo van de Loo

COPY
Francisca Maass

NOMINATION

TITLE
IWC »Kampagne 2007«

CLIENT
IWC International Watch Co. AG

MARKETING DIRECTOR
Fabian Herdieckerhoff

ADVERTISING DIRECTOR
Jacqueline Rose, Daniel Rohrer

LEAD AGENCY
Jung von Matt AG

CREATIVE DIRECTION
Daniel Frericks, Oliver Voss

ART DIRECTION
Christian Kroll, Jens Paul Pfau

CLIENT CONSULTING
Karoline Huber, Turan Tehrani

ART BUYING
Karen Blome

GRAPHIC ART
Tobias Fritschen, Lukas Hueter,
Anja von Harsdorf,
Maximilian Rieder

COPY
Philipp Barth, Jo Marie Farwick,
Peter Gocht, Tobias Grimm,
Caroline Schubiger, Henning Robert,
Samuel Wicki, Stefan Grahl

ADDITIONAL AWARDS NOMINATION

Volume Advertising page 163
Text
Copy

CONSUMER ADVERTISEMENTS **PUBLIKUMSANZEIGEN** 053

NOMINATION

TITLE
Falk Navigationsgeräte
Kampagne »Einfach Navigieren«

CLIENT
Falk Marco Polo Interactive GmbH

MARKETING DIRECTOR
Stefanie Back

LEAD AGENCY
Scholz & Friends

CREATIVE DIRECTION
Oliver Handlos, Matthias Spaetgens

ART DIRECTION
Jens-Petter Waernes, Erik Dagnell

CLIENT CONSULTING
Stefanie Littek, Sebastian Vetter,
Jeanine Wyrwoll, Eva Lipp

IMAGE EDITING
Appel Grafik Berlin

ADDITIONAL AWARDS
NOMINATION
Volume Advertising page 122
Plakate und Poster
(indoor und outdoor)
Billboards and posters
(indoor and outdoor)

NOMINATION

TITLE
CinemaxX Kampagne
»Nur im Kino«

CLIENT
CinemaxX AG

LEAD AGENCY
Jung von Matt AG

CREATIVE DIRECTION
Götz Ulmer, Fabian Frese,
Oliver Voss

ART DIRECTION
Javier Suarez Argueta,
Till Monshausen, Julia Ziegler,
Jens Paul Pfau

ILLUSTRATION
Johan Kleinjan

GRAPHIC ART
Javier Suarez Argueta

COPY
Björn Ingenleuf, Jo Marie Farwick,
Jan-Florian Ege, Tobias Grimm

ADDITIONAL AWARDS
NOMINATION
Volume Design page 220
Illustration
Illustration

NOMINATION

TITLE
Misereor Hilfswerk
Kampagne »Kriegswaisen«

CLIENT
Bischöfliches Hilfswerk
Misereor e.V.

MARKETING DIRECTOR
Michael Kleine

ADVERTISING DIRECTOR
Georg Larscheid

LEAD AGENCY
Kolle Rebbe Werbeagentur GmbH

CREATIVE DIRECTION
Sven Klohk, Lorenz Ritter

ART DIRECTION
Maik Beimdieck, Jens Lausenmeyer

CLIENT CONSULTING
Jessica Gustafsson

ILLUSTRATION
Eva Salzmann

IMAGE EDITING
Kathrin Meske

PRINTING
Digital Druck Emden

PRODUCTION
Martin Lühe

COPY
Elena Bartrina y Manns

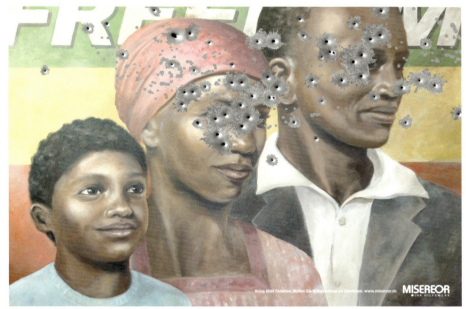

NOMINATION

TITLE
www.wikipedia.org Kampagne
»Hypertext«

CLIENT
Wikimedia e. V.

MARKETING DIRECTOR
Mathias Schindler

LEAD AGENCY
DDB Germany/Düsseldorf

CREATIVE DIRECTION
Amir Kassaei, Eric Schoeffler

ART DIRECTION
Kristine Holzhausen

CLIENT CONSULTING
Marco Diel

GRAPHIC ART
Marilyn Wolf, Markus Rittenbusch

COPY
Dennis May, Lena Reckeweg

Mit¹ Ban Ki-Moons² Amtsantritt³ wird⁴ das⁵ Weltklima⁶ zur⁷ Chefsache⁸

Barack Obamas¹ Rolle² als³ Hoffnungsträger⁴ einer⁵ ganzen⁶ Nation⁷

Stoiber¹ hinterlässt² der³ CSU⁴ ein⁵ tückisches⁶ Erbe⁷

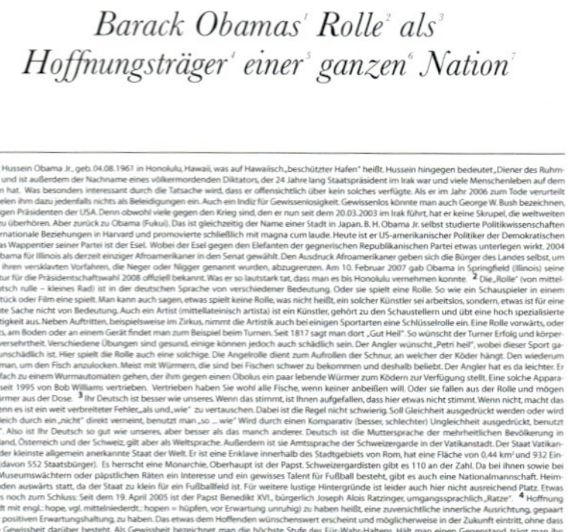

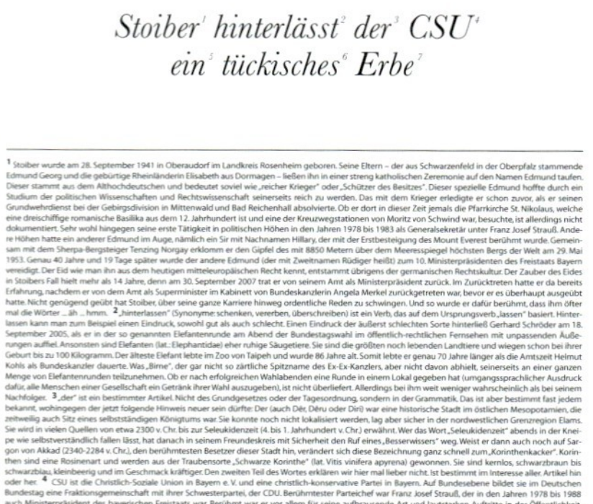

NOMINATION

TITLE
UNICEF Kampagne »ProAging«

CLIENT
UNICEF Deutschland

MARKETING DIRECTOR
Eric Mayer

LEAD AGENCY
Serviceplan München/Hamburg

CREATIVE DIRECTION
Maik Kähler, Christoph Nann, Alexander Schill, Axel Thomsen

ART DIRECTION
Amelie Graalfs, Roman Becker, Till Diestel, Maik Kähler

CLIENT CONSULTING
Robin Ruschke, Christina Franz

PHOTOGRAPHY
Beatrice Heydiri

PRODUCTION
Alphadog Hamburg

COPY
Christoph Nann

ADDITIONAL AWARDS NOMINATION
Volume Design page 234
Websites
Websites

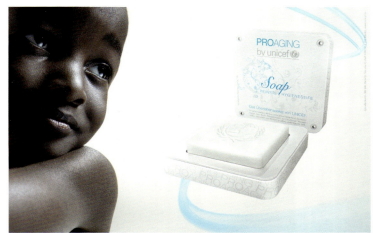

CONSUMER ADVERTISEMENTS PUBLIKUMSANZEIGEN

NOMINATION

TITLE
Du bist Deutschland Kampagne
»Eine Initiative für
mehr Kinderfreundlichkeit«

CLIENT
Du bist Deutschland GmbH

MARKETING DIRECTOR
Bernd Bauer

ADVERTISING DIRECTOR
Helge Hoffmeister

LEAD AGENCY
Jung von Matt AG,
kempertrautmann gmbh

CREATIVE DIRECTION
Oliver Voss (JvM)

ART DIRECTION
Till Monshausen (JvM)

CLIENT CONSULTING
Michael Trautmann (kt),
Andrea Bison (kt),
Franziska von Papen (kt),
Tobias Mölder (kt)

PHOTOGRAPHY
Timm Brockfeld,
Julia Baier,
Alexander Frank

CONSULTING
Julia Krömker (JvM),
Jan Rütten (JvM)

ART BUYING
Anne Weskamp (JvM)

GRAPHIC ART
Daniel Haschtmann (JvM)

POSTPRODUCTION
Malte Rehde (JvM),
Ulla Bayer (JvM)

PRODUCTION
Birgit Weber (JvM)

COPY
Jo Marie Farwick (JvM),
Robert Müller (JvM),
Ramin Schmiedekampf (JvM),
Philipp Jessen (JvM),
Willy Kaussen (JvM)

FINAL ARTWORK
Marion Beeck (JvM),
Madlen Domann (JvM)

ADDITIONAL AWARDS
NOMINATION
Volume Advertising page 157
Text
Copy

NOMINATION
Volume Advertising page 243
TV-Spots
Television commercials

NOMINATION

TITLE
Edding Kampagne »Fineliner«

CLIENT
edding international GmbH

MARKETING DIRECTOR
Angelika Schumacher

LEAD AGENCY
weigertpirouzwolf
Werbeagentur GmbH

CREATIVE DIRECTION
Kay Eichner

ART DIRECTION
Marc Leitmeyer

CLIENT CONSULTING
Christian Laur

PHOTOGRAPHY
Arne Morgenstern

ILLUSTRATION
Markus Genesius

GRAPHIC ART
Cornelius Hafemeister

COPY
Michael Rudnicki

NOMINATION

TITLE
STABILO BOSS ORIGINAL
Kampagne »Details«

CLIENT
STABILO International GmbH

MARKETING DIRECTOR
Volker Wachenfeld

LEAD AGENCY
Serviceplan München/Hamburg

CREATIVE DIRECTION
Alexander Schill, Axel Thomsen

ART DIRECTION
Jonathan Schupp

CLIENT CONSULTING
Laura Dötz, Julia Thoemen

COPY
Francisca Maass

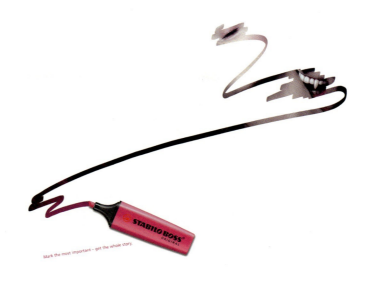

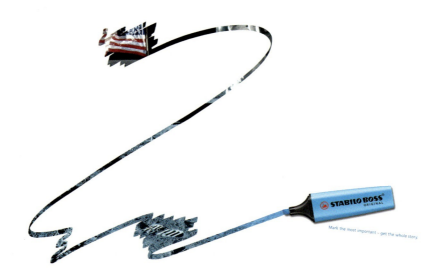

NOMINATION

TITLE
F. A. Z. Kampagne
»Relaunch – Weiße Serie«

CLIENT
Frankfurter Allgemeine Zeitung GmbH

MARKETING DIRECTOR
Tobias Trevisan

ADVERTISING DIRECTOR
Marco Rühl

LEAD AGENCY
Scholz & Friends

CREATIVE DIRECTION
Oliver Handlos, Matthias Spaetgens, Sebastian Turner

ART DIRECTION
Cathrin Ciuraj, David Fischer

CLIENT CONSULTING
Katrin Seegers, Daniela Winkler, Katrin Voß

PHOTOGRAPHY
Matthias Koslik, Christian Schmidt

IMAGE EDITING
Recom GmbH, Ostfildern

GRAPHIC ART
Michael Schmidt

COPY
Daniel Bödeker, Caspar Heuss

NOMINATION

TITLE
Comedy Central Kampagne »Witze«
CLIENT
MTV Networks Germany GmbH
MARKETING DIRECTOR
Imke Deigner (Marketing Director),
Torsten Wolf (Head of Consumer Marketing)
ADVERTISING DIRECTOR
Vivien Hucke (Junior Manager Consumer Marketing)
LEAD AGENCY
kempertrautmann gmbh
CREATIVE DIRECTION
Daniel Ernsting, Mathias Lamken
ART DIRECTION
Mathias Lamken
CLIENT CONSULTING
Peter Matz, Ilker Yilmazalp
PHOTOGRAPHY
Karsten Wegener
GRAPHIC ART
Simon Jasper Philipp
POSTPRODUCTION
Martina Huber
COPY
Daniel Ernsting, Bahador Pakravesh

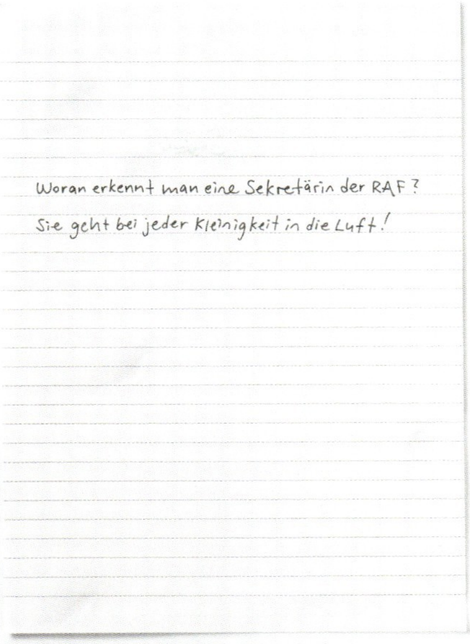

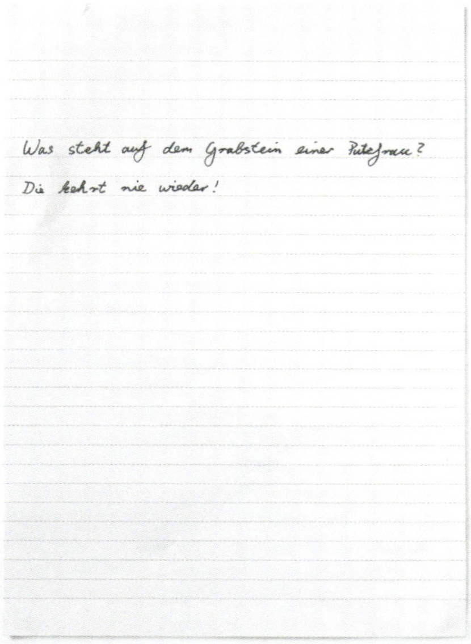

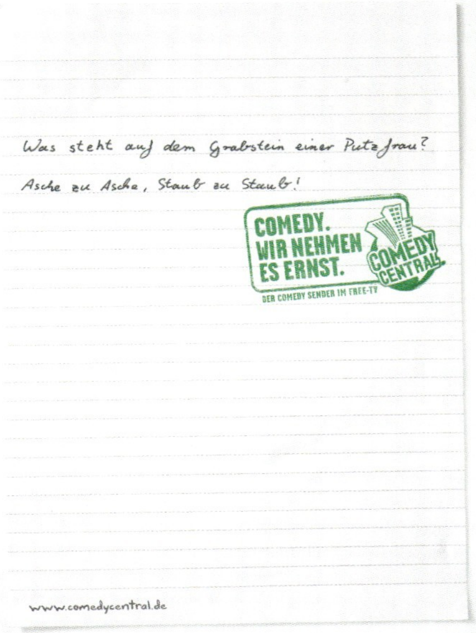

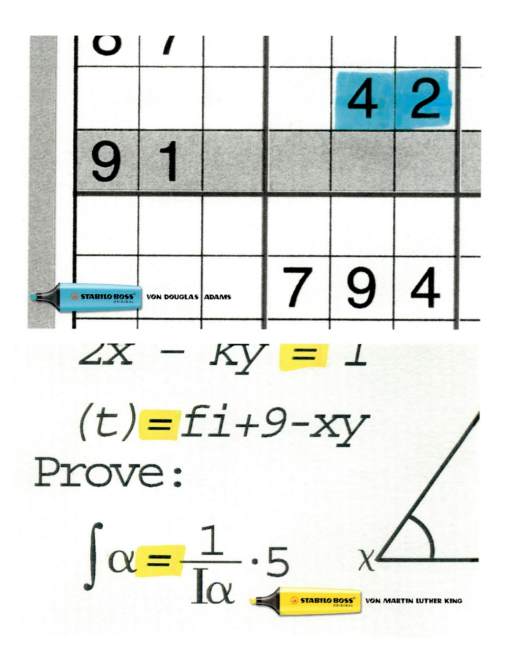

NOMINATION

TITLE
STABILO Kampagne »Entdeckung«

CLIENT
STABILO International GmbH

MARKETING DIRECTOR
Volker Wachenfeld

LEAD AGENCY
Serviceplan München/Hamburg

CREATIVE DIRECTION
Alexander Schill, Axel Thomsen,
Maik Kähler, Christoph Nann

ART DIRECTION
Till Diestel

CLIENT CONSULTING
Laura Dötz, Julia Thoemen

PHOTOGRAPHY
Till Diestel

GRAPHIC ART
Till Diestel

COPY
Rudy Novotny

CONSUMER ADVERTISEMENTS PUBLIKUMSANZEIGEN 065

NOMINATION

TITLE
IKEA »Bälleland«

CLIENT
IKEA Deutschland
GmbH & Co. KG

MARKETING DIRECTOR
Claudia Willvonseder

LEAD AGENCY
Grabarz & Partner

CREATIVE DIRECTION
Ralf Heuel, Dirk Siebenhaar

ART DIRECTION
Vanessa Iff

CLIENT CONSULTING
Denise Ewald

PHOTOGRAPHY
Christian Kerber c/o Waldmann Solar

ART BUYING
Garnet Lange

GRAPHIC ART
Nadine Kolipost

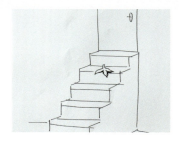   

SILVER

TITLE
Comedy Central Kampagne »Ernst«
CLIENT
MTV Networks Germany GmbH
MARKETING DIRECTOR
Imke Deigner (Marketing Director),
Torsten Wolf (Head of Consumer Marketing)
ADVERTISING DIRECTOR
Vivien Hucke (Junior Manager Consumer Marketing)
LEAD AGENCY
kempertrautmann gmbh
CREATIVE DIRECTION
Mathias Lamken
ART DIRECTION
Mathias Lamken, Tim Belser
CLIENT CONSULTING
Peter Matz, Ilker Yilmazalp
PHOTOGRAPHY
Karsten Wegener
ILLUSTRATION
Mathias Lamken
GRAPHIC ART
Simon Jasper Philipp
POSTPRODUCTION
Martina Huber
COPY
Mathias Lamken

ADDITIONAL AWARDS
SILVER
Volume Advertising page 072
Fachanzeigen
Trade advertisements

SILVER
Volume Advertising page 123
Plakate und Poster
(indoor und outdoor)
Billboards and posters
(indoor and outdoor)

BRONZE
Volume Advertising page 096
Tages-/Wochenzeitungsanzeigen
Advertisements in daily/weekly newspapers

BRONZE

TITLE
Volkswagen Park Distance Control »Einpark-Kampagne«
CLIENT
Volkswagen AG
MARKETING DIRECTOR
Jochen Sengpiehl
ADVERTISING DIRECTOR
Hartmut Seeger
LEAD AGENCY
DDB Germany, Berlin
CREATIVE DIRECTION
Bert Peulecke, Stefan Schulte
ART DIRECTION
Gen Sadakane, Tim Stübane
CLIENT CONSULTING
Mia Drexl-Schegg, Cathleen Losch,
Silke Lagodny, Marie-Louise Jakob
PHOTOGRAPHY
David Cuenca
IMAGE EDITING
PX1
TECHNICAL DIRECTION
Sascha Mehn
COPY
Jan Hendrik Ott

ADDITIONAL AWARDS
SILVER
Volume Advertising page 087
Tages-/Wochenzeitungsanzeigen
Advertisements in daily/weekly newspapers

BRONZE
Volume Advertising page 124
Plakate und Poster
(indoor und outdoor)
Billboards and posters
(indoor and outdoor)

BRONZE

TITLE
McDonald's McCafé »Kaffee-Bohne«
CLIENT
McDonald's Deutschland Inc
MARKETING DIRECTOR
Gerhard R. Schöps
ADVERTISING DIRECTOR
Vorbereitung: Susan Schmidt
LEAD AGENCY
Heye, Group GmbH
CREATIVE DIRECTION
Norbert Herold, Helmut Huschka
ART DIRECTION
Stefan Ellenberger, Sebastian Hackelsperger
CLIENT CONSULTING
Manuela Kunze
PHOTOGRAPHY
Camillo Büchelmeier
ART BUYING
Rosina Bischur
IMAGE EDITING
Christian Schulze, Therese Zisselsberger
PRODUCTION
Carsten Horn, Rüdiger Biskoping
COPY
Stefan Amtmann

ADDITIONAL AWARDS
BRONZE
Volume Advertising page 111
Plakate und Poster
(indoor und outdoor)
Billboards and posters
(indoor and outdoor)

NOMINATION

TITLE
Bosch Akkuschrauber PSR 14,4 LI-2 »Fliege«
CLIENT
Robert Bosch GmbH
ADVERTISING DIRECTOR
Claus von Berg
LEAD AGENCY
Jung von Matt AG
CREATIVE DIRECTION
Sascha Hanke, Timm Hanebeck, Wolf Heumann (GF)
ART DIRECTION
Kathrin Seupel
CLIENT CONSULTING
Inga Gerckens
PHOTOGRAPHY
Annika Rose, Andreas Mock
IMAGE EDITING
Marius Schwiegk
PRODUCTION
Philipp Wenhold

ADDITIONAL AWARDS
NOMINATION
Volume Advertising page 116
Plakate und Poster
(indoor und outdoor)
Billboards and posters
(indoor and outdoor)

NOMINATION

TITLE
Malteser Kampagne »Typo Crash«

CLIENT
Malteser Hilfsdienst e.V.

MARKETING DIRECTOR
Josef Dorfner

LEAD AGENCY
Ogilvy Frankfurt

CREATIVE DIRECTION
Christian Mommertz,
Dr. Stephan Vogel

ART DIRECTION
Christian Mommertz

CLIENT CONSULTING
John F. Goetze, Thorsten Orth

PHOTOGRAPHY
Jo Bacherl

ART BUYING
Christina Hufgard

COPY
Dr. Stephan Vogel

TYPOGRAPHY
Sabina Hesse, Sabrina Belger,
Andrea Trott/Art Support:
Daniel de Leuw

ADDITIONAL AWARDS
BRONZE
Volume Advertising page 108
Plakate und Poster
(indoor und outdoor)
Billboards and posters
(indoor and outdoor)

BRONZE
Volume Design page 244
Digitale Werbung
Digital advertising

*18. DEZEMBER 1913 LÜBECK †08. OKTOBER 1992 UNKEL AM RHEIN

Der kleine Herbert war gerade zwölf Lenze alt, als er Mitglied einer sozialistischen Kindergruppe in Lübeck wurde. Mit 13 veröffentlichte er seinen ersten Artikel im *Lübecker Volksboten*. Mit 20 kämpfte er bereits im Untergrund gegen die Nazis. Herbert Frahm emigrierte nach Norwegen und kämpfte als Parteiaktivist und Journalist mit Wort und Tat gegen die Naziherrschaft. Dort nahm er auch den Decknamen Willy Brandt an. Nach dem Krieg wurde er Mitglied des Berliner Abgeordnetenhauses. 1957 wählten ihn die Berliner zum Regierenden Bürgermeister. 1966 wurde er Außenminister und Vizekanzler. 1969 wählte der Deutsche Bundestag Brandt zum Bundeskanzler. Kaum ein anderer Politiker hat Deutschland so nachhaltig beeinflusst wie Willy Brandt. Er war der Kopf der »Neuen Ostpolitik« und leitete die Ostverträge zwischen Polen und der Sowjetunion ein. Ohne seine Entspannungspolitik wäre das wiedervereinigte Deutschland von heute nicht denkbar. 1971 erhielt er für diese Politik den Friedensnobelpreis.

*18 DECEMBER 1913 LÜBECK †08 OCTOBER 1992 UNKEL AM RHEIN

As a boy, Herbert Frahm was just 12 years old when he joined a socialist children's group in Lübeck, and 13 when his first article was published in the *Lübecker Volksbote*. At the age of 20 he was already a member of the underground, fighting against the Nazis. Herbert immigrated to Norway, continuing to oppose Nazi supremacy in word and deed as a party activist and a journalist. It was here, too, that he adopted the pseudonym Willy Brandt. After the war, he became a member of the Berlin House of Representatives. In 1957 he was elected governing mayor by the people of West Berlin, and in 1966 he became Foreign Minister and Vice Chancellor. In 1969, the German Bundestag voted Brandt as Federal Chancellor. Few other politicians have had as long-lasting an effect on Germany as Willy Brandt. He was the main proponent of the "New Ostpolitik", initiating the Warsaw and Moscow Agreements – political, social and economic agreements made between West Germany and, respectively, Poland and the Soviet Union. Without his policy of détente, today's reunified Germany would not have been conceivable. In 1971 he was awarded the Nobel Peace Prize for this policy.

The best speeches are the ones that are never delivered, the second-best are the biting ones, the third-best are the short ones.

DIE BESTEN REDEN SIND DIE, DIE NICHT GEHALTEN WERDEN, DIE ZWEITBESTEN SIND DIE SCHARFEN, DIE DRITTBESTEN DIE KURZEN.

"don't feel sorry for these bums, they might not have the newest skin cream, but think of who will survive one of those global nuclear power hits, these middle-of-nowhere-guys have good chances to be the intelligencia of the new world. good. now you wanna be an inbred boy from patagonia"

for more images go to duettmann.com and if you like people to kai zastrow.com

SILVER

TITLE
»Eigenwerbung 2007«

CLIENT
Uwe Duettmann

LEAD AGENCY
kaishaprojects

ART DIRECTION
Kai Zastrow

PHOTOGRAPHY
Uwe Duettmann

TRADE ADVERTISEMENTS FACHANZEIGEN 071

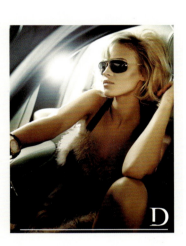

here's my lifestory A. i grew up as the prince of siam, with a skin of alabaster, than i got born and slapped by the fat hands of a nurse, making me shout for the first time.

here's my lifestory B. i came from a very poor family. they couldn't afford to have children, so our neighbour had me.

richard p.

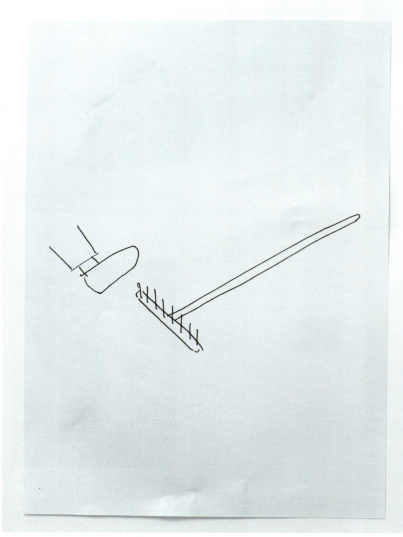

SILVER

TITLE
Comedy Central »Ernst-Kampagne«

CLIENT
MTV Networks Germany GmbH

MARKETING DIRECTOR
Imke Deigner (Marketing Director), Torsten Wolf (Head of Consumer Marketing)

ADVERTISING DIRECTOR
Vivien Hucke (Junior Manager Consumer Marketing)

LEAD AGENCY
kempertrautmann gmbh

CREATIVE DIRECTION
Mathias Lamken

ART DIRECTION
Mathias Lamken, Tim Belser

CLIENT CONSULTING
Peter Matz, Ilker Yilmazalp

PHOTOGRAPHY
Karsten Wegener

ILLUSTRATION
Mathias Lamken

GRAPHIC ART
Simon Jasper Philipp

POSTPRODUCTION
Martina Huber

COPY
Mathias Lamken

ADDITIONAL AWARDS
SILVER
Volume Advertising page 066
Publikumsanzeigen
Consumer advertisements

SILVER
Volume Advertising page 123
Plakate und Poster
(indoor und outdoor)
Billboards and posters
(indoor and outdoor)

BRONZE
Volume Advertising page 096
Tages-/Wochenzeitungsanzeigen
Advertisements in daily/weekly newspapers

TRADE ADVERTISEMENTS **FACHANZEIGEN** 073

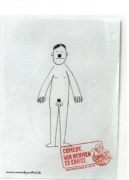

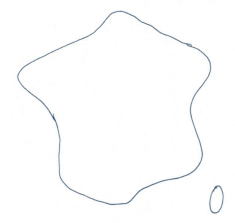

BRONZE

TITLE
Inlingua Kampagne »Umrisse«

CLIENT
Inlingua Freiburg

MARKETING DIRECTOR
Daniel Wilmsen

LEAD AGENCY
Kolle Rebbe Werbeagentur GmbH

CREATIVE DIRECTION
Ulrich Zünkeler/Rolf Leger/
Stefan Wübbe

ART DIRECTION
Florian Schmucker

CLIENT CONSULTING
Stefanie Karrer, Manuela Maurer

GRAPHIC ART
Florian Schmucker

COPY
Florian Ludwig

FINAL ARTWORK
Maik Spreen

ADDITIONAL AWARDS
BRONZE

Volume Advertising page 123
Plakate und Poster
(indoor und outdoor)
Billboards and posters
(indoor and outdoor)

TRADE ADVERTISEMENTS **FACHANZEIGEN** 075

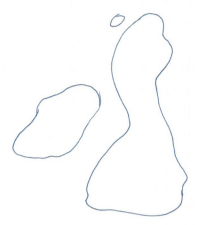

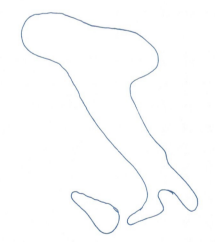

NOMINATION

TITLE
Wieners + Wieners Werbelektorat
Kampagne »Wirre Grafiken«

CLIENT
Wieners + Wieners Werbelektorats
GmbH

MARKETING DIRECTOR
Ralf Wieners, Wolfgang Bruch

ADVERTISING DIRECTOR
Ralf Wieners, Wolfgang Bruch

LEAD AGENCY
Grabarz & Partner

CREATIVE DIRECTION
Ralf Heuel, Dirk Siebenhaar

ART DIRECTION
Sebastian Hahn

CLIENT CONSULTING
Thomas Eickhoff, Ina Bach

GRAPHIC ART
Tim Hartwig, Benjamin Busse,
Hannes von Döhren

COPY
Heike Frank

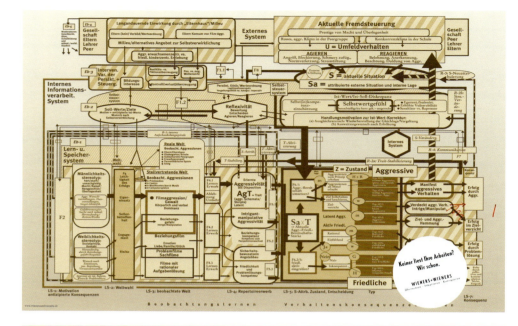

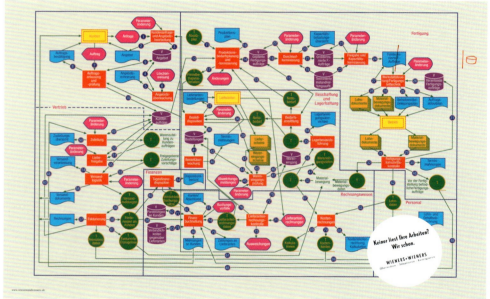

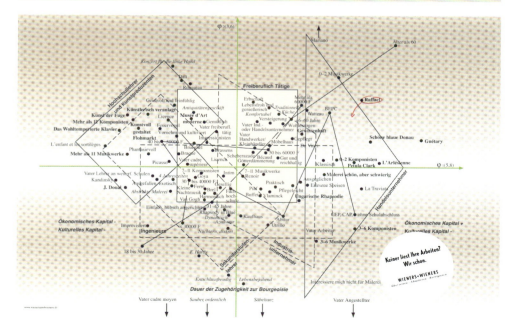

NOMINATION

TITLE
Jung von Matt »Geiziger Abschied«

CLIENT
Jung von Matt/Fleet GmbH

LEAD AGENCY
Jung von Matt AG

CREATIVE DIRECTION
Arno Lindemann, Bernhard Lukas

ART DIRECTION
Jonas Keller

CLIENT CONSULTING
Frauke Stürmer

IDEA
Jonas Keller, David Leinweber

COPY
David Leinweber

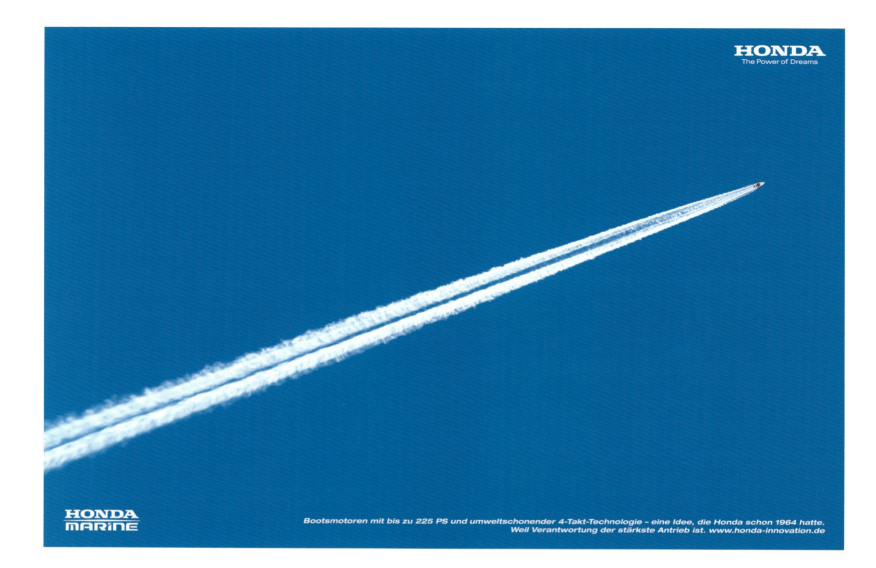

NOMINATION

TITLE
Honda Motoren Corporate Kampagne »Motiv Kondensstreifen«

CLIENT
Honda Motor Europe (North) GmbH

ADVERTISING DIRECTOR
Jürgen Höpker, Jürgen Krantz

LEAD AGENCY
Scholz & Friends

CREATIVE DIRECTION
Tobias Holland, Matthias Schmidt, Stefan Setzkorn

ART DIRECTION
P. Sydow, S. Janssen

CLIENT CONSULTING
Frank-Michael Trau, Sarah Schulte-Herbrüggen, Sven Horrer

STRATEGIC PLANNING
Holger Schneider, Sabine Moll

ART BUYING
Kerstin Mende, Chantal Mene, Angela Barilaro

IMAGE EDITING
Metagate GmbH, Hamburg; Zerone

GRAPHIC ART
David Müller-Kähmann

COPY
Marc Kittel

NOMINATION

TITLE
BIC Cristal Kampagne
»More joy of writing«

CLIENT
BIC Deutschland GmbH & Co. OHG

MARKETING DIRECTOR
Susanne Franken, Claire Gerard

LEAD AGENCY
Jung von Matt AG

CREATIVE DIRECTION
Wolfgang Schneider, Mathias Stiller,
David Mously, Jan Harbeck

ART DIRECTION
Duc Nguyen

CLIENT CONSULTING
Frank Lotze, Frauke Schmidt,
Jan Hendrik Oelckers

PHOTOGRAPHY
Dan Zoubek, Berlin

AGENCY PRODUCER
Sven Hannemann

ART BUYING
Martina Traut

GRAPHIC ART
Duc Nguyen, Oskar Strauß

POSTPRODUCTION
PX 1

COPY
Nicolas Linde

ADDITIONAL AWARDS NOMINATION

Volume Advertising page 097
Tages-/Wochenzeitungsanzeigen
Advertisements in daily/weekly
newspapers

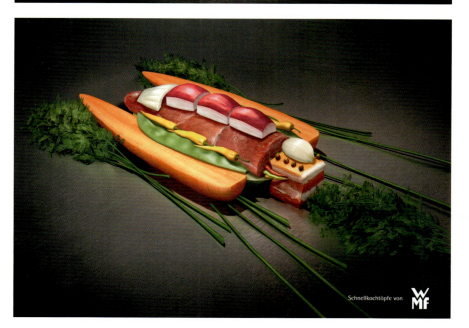

NOMINATION

TITLE
WMF Kampagne
»Schnellkochtöpfe«

CLIENT
WMF AG

ADVERTISING DIRECTOR
Wolfgang Dalferth

LEAD AGENCY
KNSK Werbeagentur GmbH

CREATIVE DIRECTION
Anke Winschewski, Tim Krink,
Niels Holle

ART DIRECTION
Bill Yom

CLIENT CONSULTING
Kirsten Kohls

ILLUSTRATION
ABC Digital

IMAGE EDITING
ABC Digital

COMPUTER ANIMATION
ABC Digital

GRAPHIC ART
Sonja Kliem, Nathalie Krüger

COPY
Kurt Müller-Fleischer

ADDITIONAL AWARDS NOMINATION
Volume Advertising page 125
Plakate und Poster
(indoor und outdoor)
Billboards and posters
(indoor and outdoor)

TRADE ADVERTISEMENTS FACHANZEIGEN 081

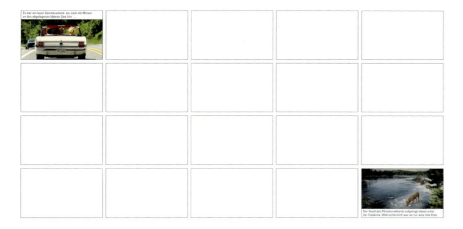

NOMINATION

TITLE
13TH STREET Kampagne
»Kopfkino«

CLIENT
NBC Universal Global Networks
Deutschland GmbH

MARKETING DIRECTOR
Sabine Kirchmair, Andreas Lechner

ADVERTISING DIRECTOR
Nicole Pawelke

LEAD AGENCY
Jung von Matt AG

CREATIVE DIRECTION
Mathias Stiller, Wolfgang Schneider,
David Mously, Jan Harbeck

ART DIRECTION
Andreas Böhm

CLIENT CONSULTING
Frank Lotze,
Josef Konstantin Schulte,
Helen Seiffe

PHOTOGRAPHY
Cornelius Zoch

AGENCY PRODUCER
Sven Hannemann

ART BUYING
Anne Weskamp

COPY
Max Millies

ADDITIONAL AWARDS
BRONZE
Volume Advertising page 039
Publikumsanzeigen
Consumer advertisements

BRONZE
Volume Advertising page 292
TV-On-air-Promotion
TV on-air promotion

SILVER

Hintergrund: Nach 1982 stand Nürnberg wieder im Pokalfinale.

Aufgabe: Spieler und Fans des 1. FCN inspirieren und mobilisieren.

Lösung: Statt hinterher eine Glückwunschanzeige zu schalten, erzählen wir im Vorfeld die Geschichten der Spieler von damals und heute. In der lokalen BILD mit direktem, redaktionellen Bezug. So wurden aus 11 Eckfeldern 11 ganze Seiten. Und aus Fußballern Pokalsieger.

Background: For the first time since 1982, Nuremberg's football club reached the German Cup Final.

Task: Inspire and activate players and fans of Nuremberg's football club.

Solution: Instead of running a congratulation ad afterwards, we told the stories of current and former Nuremberg players prior to the Cup Final – in the local edition of the daily newspaper BILD, directly within the editorial environment. This way, 11 corner ads became 11 full-pages. And football players became cup winners.

TITLE
adidas Football Kampagne »Der 11-Stufen Countdown zum DFB Pokal Finale«

CLIENT
adidas AG

MARKETING DIRECTOR
Markus Rachals

ADVERTISING DIRECTOR
Sven Schindler

LEAD AGENCY
TBWA\ Deutschland (180/TBWA), Berlin

CREATIVE DIRECTION
Stefan Schmidt

ART DIRECTION
Erik Gonan, Leila El-Kayem, Stephan Spieske

CLIENT CONSULTING
Kerstin Gold, David Barton

STRATEGIC PLANNING
Moritz Kiechle

ILLUSTRATION
Harald Renkel, Gussi Kim, Jutta Kuss, Klaus Cordeiro

AGENCY PRODUCER
Katrin Dettmann

IMAGE EDITING
Anne Döring

DESIGN
Harald Renkel

GRAPHIC ART
Gussi Kim, Jutta Kuss, Klaus Cordeiro

COPY
Markus Ewertz, Daniel Solbach

FINAL ARTWORK
Anne Döring, Sören Grochau

ADVERTISEMENTS IN DAILY/WEEKLY NEWSPAPERS TAGES-/WOCHENZEITUNGSANZEIGEN

Einparken leicht gemacht.
Der Golf Variant mit Park Distance Control.

Einparken leicht gemacht.
Der Touran mit Park Distance Control.

**Einparken leicht gemacht.
Der Golf mit Park Distance Control.**

Das Auto.

SILVER

TITLE
Volkswagen Park Distance Control
»Einpark-Kampagne«

CLIENT
Volkswagen AG

MARKETING DIRECTOR
Jochen Sengpiehl

ADVERTISING DIRECTOR
Hartmut Seeger

LEAD AGENCY
DDB Germany, Berlin

CREATIVE DIRECTION
Bert Peulecke, Stefan Schulte

ART DIRECTION
Gen Sadakane, Tim Stübane

CLIENT CONSULTING
Mia Drexl-Schegg, Cathleen Losch,
Silke Lagodny, Marie-Louise Jakob

PHOTOGRAPHY
David Cuenca

IMAGE EDITING
PX1

TECHNICAL DIRECTION
Sascha Mehn

COPY
Jan Hendrik Ott

ADDITIONAL AWARDS
BRONZE
Volume Advertising page 066
Publikumsanzeigen
Consumer advertisements

BRONZE
Volume Advertising page 124
Plakate und Poster
(indoor und outdoor)
Billboards and posters
(indoor and outdoor)

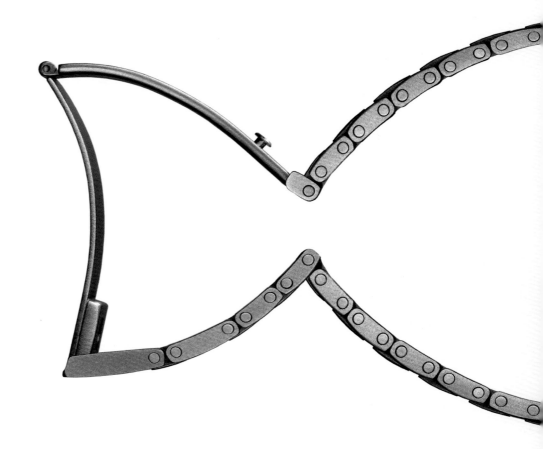

Wasserdicht bis 2000 m.
Die Aquatimer Automatic 2000.

BRONZE

TITLE
Aquatimer Automatic 2000 »Fisch«
CLIENT
IWC Schaffhausen
MARKETING DIRECTOR
Fabian Herdieckerhoff
LEAD AGENCY
Jung von Matt AG
CREATIVE DIRECTION
Dirk Haeusermann, Wolf Heumann
ART DIRECTION
Alexander Hansen
CLIENT CONSULTING
Verena Giesler, Karoline Huber, Florian Mika
PHOTOGRAPHY
Stephan Försterling
ART BUYING
Anne Weskamp
IMAGE EDITING
Marius Schwiegk
GRAPHIC ART
Lars Borker
PRODUCTION
Philipp Wenhold
COPY
Alexander Hansen

IWC
SCHAFFHAUSEN
SINCE 1868

NOMINATION

TITLE
BURGER KING Pommes
»Stellenanzeige Kartoffel«

CLIENT
BURGER KING GMBH

MARKETING DIRECTOR
Dirk Hildenbrand

LEAD AGENCY
.start GmbH

CREATIVE DIRECTION
Marco Mehrwald, Thomas Pakull

ART DIRECTION
Roland Raith

CLIENT CONSULTING
Katharina Aschauer, Tony Bergmann

GRAPHIC ART
Nina Zinnhobler

COPY
Bernd Nagenrauft

SIE MÖCHTEN BEI UNS KARRIERE MACHEN?
MACHEN SIE SICH VOM ACKER.

BURGER KING® gehört zu den führenden Quick Service Unternehmen weltweit. Mit über 11.200 Restaurants setzen wir täglich neue Maßstäbe bei Qualität und Geschmack. Kommen auch Sie in unser Team und wachsen Sie mit den Herausforderungen.

Wir suchen zum nächstmöglichen Zeitpunkt eine

KARTOFFEL (m/w)

IHR PROFIL:

Sie sind eine Kartoffel (m/w) jüngeren Alters von hervorragender Herkunft. Sie gehören zu den Jahrgangsbesten, möchten Karriere in einem global tätigen Unternehmen machen und von unserem Nachwuchsprogramm *Top of the Crop Scholarship* profitieren. Sie sind neugierig und präsentationsstark. Sie denken nicht in Schubladen wie weich- oder festkochend. Und Sie arbeiten gerne mit ebenso dynamischen wie sympathischen Kollegen zusammen. Sie zählen sich zu den High Potentials unseres Landes.

WAS SIE BEI UNS ERWARTET:

Sie gehen einer höher strebenden Tätigkeit nach, mit allen gebotenen Chancen in dieser Top-Position. Bereits nach kurzer, praxisorientierter Trainee-Zeit (ca. 5 Minuten) steigen Sie auf zur KING Pommes und tragen somit den Titel TESTSIEGER (lt. Stiftung Warentest).

MS Office- und Englischkenntnisse sind nicht erforderlich. Führerscheinklasse III von Vorteil, aber nicht Bedingung. Dienstwagen mit priv. Nutzung ist Verhandlungssache.

Sie möchten unser Team baldmöglichst verstärken und bringen o.g. Voraussetzungen mit? Dann bewerben Sie sich mit Lichtbild (bitte nicht in Freizeitkleidung, nicht älter als zum Zeitpunkt der Ernte) bei:

BURGER KING® GmbH
VR (Veg. Ressources)
Werner-Eckert-Str. 16-18
81829 München

 HAVE IT YOUR WAY®

NOMINATION

TITLE
Hornbach Baumarkt »Helden 2007«

CLIENT
Hornbach Baumarkt AG

MARKETING DIRECTOR
Jürgen Schröcker

ADVERTISING DIRECTOR
Diana Koob

LEAD AGENCY
HEIMAT, Berlin

CREATIVE DIRECTION
Guido Heffels, Jürgen Vossen

ART DIRECTION
Tim Schneider, Marc Wientzek

CLIENT CONSULTING
Yves Krämer

PHOTOGRAPHY
Wolfgang Stahr

ART BUYING
Marjorie Jorrot

CONSULTING
Mark Hassan, Sammy Bohneberg

GRAPHIC ART
Michael Mackens, Joachim Zeh

MEDIA
Crossmedia GmbH, Düsseldorf

PRODUCTION
Carola Storto

COPY
Sebastian Kainz, Guido Heffels, Till Eckel

ADDITIONAL AWARDS
SILVER
Volume Advertising page 022
Publikumsanzeigen
Consumer advertisements

NOMINATION

TITLE
Jeep Kampagne »Spuren«

CLIENT
Chrysler Deutschland GmbH

MARKETING DIRECTOR
Matthias Möhler

ADVERTISING DIRECTOR
Holger Baumann

LEAD AGENCY
KNSK Werbeagentur GmbH

CREATIVE DIRECTION
Anke Winschewski, Tim Krink, Niels Holle

ART DIRECTION
Bill Yom, Wiebke Bethke

CLIENT CONSULTING
Jan Isterling, Philipp Ernsting

ART BUYING
Franziska Boyens, Julia Gaentzsch

CONSULTING
ABC Digital

GRAPHIC ART
Sonja Kliem, Nathalie Krüger

COPY
Kurt Müller-Fleischer

NOMINATION

TITLE
Loewe Flat TV Kampagne
»Unglaublich realistisch.«

CLIENT
Loewe Opta GmbH

MARKETING DIRECTOR
Henrik Rutenbach

ADVERTISING DIRECTOR
Silke Kämpfer

LEAD AGENCY
Scholz & Friends

CREATIVE DIRECTION
Constantin Kaloff, Julia Schmidt,
Bastian Engbert, James Cruickshank

ART DIRECTION
Cornelia Pflüger

CLIENT CONSULTING
Karsten Lübke, Sebastian Neumann,
Jasper von Hardenberg

PHOTOGRAPHY
Frank Aschermann,
Sebastian Greuner

ART BUYING
Dominique Steiner, Kirsten Rendtel

GRAPHIC ART
Argentina Sanchez

COPY
Gerald Meilicke, Stuart Kummer

NOMINATION

TITLE
Volkswagen Komfort-Bremsassistent
Kampagne »Schreckenlos«

CLIENT
Volkswagen AG

MARKETING DIRECTOR
Jochen Sengpiehl

ADVERTISING DIRECTOR
Hartmut Seeger, Veronika Ziegaus

LEAD AGENCY
Grabarz & Partner

CREATIVE DIRECTION
Ralf Nolting,
Patricia Pätzold, Ralf Heuel

ART DIRECTION
Oliver Zboralski

CLIENT CONSULTING
Peter Ströh, Jasmin Schwarzinger

ILLUSTRATION
Sugar Power c/o
Margarethe Hubauer GmbH

GRAPHIC ART
Julia Elles

COPY
Constantin Sossidi

SILVER

TITLE
VW Golf »Horst Schlämmer Grevenbroicher Tagblatt«
CLIENT
Volkswagen AG
MARKETING DIRECTOR
Jochen Sengpiehl
ADVERTISING DIRECTOR
Ralf Maltzen, Hartmut Seeger
LEAD AGENCY
DDB Germany, Berlin
CREATIVE DIRECTION
Amir Kassaei, Stefan Schulte, Bert Peulecke
ART DIRECTION
Kristoffer Heilemann, Tim Schmitt
CLIENT CONSULTING
Cathleen Losch, Silke Lagodny
PHOTOGRAPHY
Markus Bachmann, F. A. Cesar, Sven Schrader
AGENCY PRODUCER
Peter Stumpe
ART BUYING
Elke Dilchert
GRAPHIC ART
Peter Mayer, Sarah Pöhlmann
ARTIST
Hape Kerkeling
TECHNICAL DIRECTION
Sascha Mehn
COPY
Ludwig Berndl, Philip Bolland, Ulrike Schumann

ADDITIONAL AWARDS
GOLD
Volume Advertising page 186
Verkaufsförderung
Sales promotion
GOLD
Volume Advertising page 221
TV-Spots
Television commercials
GOLD
Volume Advertising page 283
Filme für Verkaufsförderung/Unternehmensdarstellungen
Films for sales promotion/company presentation
GOLD
Volume Advertising page 289
Virale Filme
Viral films
GOLD
Volume Advertising page 347
Integrierte Kampagnen
Integrated campaigns
GOLD
Volume Advertising page 367
Dialogmarketing
Dialogue marketing
GOLD
Volume Design page 242
Digitale Werbung
Digital advertising
SILVER
Volume Advertising page 139
Produkt-/Werbebroschüren
Product/advertising brochures
SILVER
Volume Advertising page 147
Text
Copy
SILVER
Volume Design page 259
Digitale Medien: Viral
Digital media: Viral
BRONZE
Volume Advertising page 152
Text
Copy
BRONZE
Volume Advertising page 326
Funkspots
Radio commercials
NOMINATION
Volume Design page 095
Informationsmedien
Information media
NOMINATION
Volume Design page 235
Websites
Websites

BRONZE

TITLE
Comedy Central »Ernst-Kampagne«
CLIENT
MTV Networks Germany GmbH
MARKETING DIRECTOR
Imke Deigner (Marketing Director), Torsten Wolf (Head of Consumer Marketing)
ADVERTISING DIRECTOR
Vivien Hucke (Junior Manager Consumer Marketing)
LEAD AGENCY
kempertrautmann gmbh
CREATIVE DIRECTION
Mathias Lamken
ART DIRECTION
Mathias Lamken, Tim Belser
CLIENT CONSULTING
Peter Matz, Ilker Yilmazalp
PHOTOGRAPHY
Karsten Wegener
ILLUSTRATION
Mathias Lamken
GRAPHIC ART
Simon Jasper Philipp
POSTPRODUCTION
Martina Huber
COPY
Mathias Lamken

ADDITIONAL AWARDS
SILVER
Volume Advertising page 066
Publikumsanzeigen
Consumer advertisements
SILVER
Volume Advertising page 072
Fachanzeigen
Trade advertisements
SILVER
Volume Advertising page 123
Plakate und Poster (indoor und outdoor)
Billboards and posters (indoor and outdoor)

NOMINATION

TITLE
Konzerthaus Dortmund – Konzertreihe ›Junge Wilde‹ Kampagne »Outstanding Talents«
CLIENT
Konzerthaus Dortmund – Philharmonie für Westfalen
MARKETING DIRECTOR
Milena Ivkovic
LEAD AGENCY
Jung von Matt AG
CREATIVE DIRECTION
Sascha Hanke, Timm Hanebeck, Wolf Heumann (GF)
ART DIRECTION
Patrik Hartmann
CLIENT CONSULTING
Nina Gerwing, Lena Frers
PHOTOGRAPHY
Marcel Schaar
ILLUSTRATION
Wojciech Klimek
ART BUYING
Bettina Zschirnt, Karen Blome
IMAGE EDITING
Elisabeth Siegmund
POSTPRODUCTION
gloss postproduction gmbh, Hamburg
COPY
Michael Okun

ADDITIONAL AWARDS
SILVER
Volume Advertising page 019
Publikumsanzeigen
Consumer advertisements
NOMINATION
Volume Design page 127
Kunst-/Kultur-/Veranstaltungsplakate
Posters for arts, culture, events
NOMINATION
Volume Design page 205
Fotografie
Photography

NOMINATION

TITLE
VW Golf GTI-Technologie
Edition 30 Kampagne
»5,9 kg pro PS«

CLIENT
Volkswagen AG

MARKETING DIRECTOR
Jochen Sengpiehl

ADVERTISING DIRECTOR
Hartmut Seeger

LEAD AGENCY
DDB Germany, Berlin

CREATIVE DIRECTION
Stefan Schulte, Bert Peulecke

ART DIRECTION
Marc Wientzek

CLIENT CONSULTING
Cathleen Losch, Louisa Ibing,
Silke Lagodny

PHOTOGRAPHY
Yann Arthus-Bertrand,
Sven Schrader

ART BUYING
Elke Dilchert

GRAPHIC ART
Wulf Rechtacek

ARTIST
Jan Diekmann

TECHNICAL DIRECTION
Sascha Mehn

COPY
Sebastian Kainz

ADDITIONAL AWARDS
BRONZE
Volume Advertising page 027
Publikumsanzeigen
Consumer advertisements

BRONZE
Volume Advertising page 123
Plakate und Poster
(indoor und outdoor)
Billboards and posters
(indoor and outdoor)

NOMINATION

TITLE
BIC Cristal Kampagne
»More joy of writing«

CLIENT
BIC Deutschland
GmbH & Co. OHG

MARKETING DIRECTOR
Susanne Franken, Claire Gerard

LEAD AGENCY
Jung von Matt AG

CREATIVE DIRECTION
Mathias Stiller,
Wolfgang Schneider,
Jan Harbeck, David Mously

ART DIRECTION
Duc Nguyen

CLIENT CONSULTING
Frank Lotze, Frauke Schmidt,
Jan Hendrik Oelckers

PHOTOGRAPHY
Dan Zoubek, Berlin

AGENCY PRODUCER
Sven Hannemann

ART BUYING
Martina Traut

GRAPHIC ART
Duc Nguyen, Oskar Strauß

POSTPRODUCTION
PX 1

COPY
Nicolas Linde

ADDITIONAL AWARDS
NOMINATION
Volume Advertising page 079
Fachanzeigen
Trade advertisements

* 22 JULY 1882 NYACK/NEW YORK   † 15 MAY 1967 NEW YORK CITY

From 1905 on, Edward Hopper earned his daily bread as an illustrator for one of the first American advertising agencies. Despite this, he attached great importance to the distinction between advertising and art. Customers at the beginning of the advertising era were, in all likelihood, no more broad-minded than they are today. Edward Hopper's influence on photography may well have been more significant than his influence on painting. It is no accident that Alfred Hitchcock, Ridley Scott and Wim Wenders can be shown to have made use of Hopper's melancholy, understated scenarios. Specific paintings by Hopper, and his uniquely dreamlike style, served as the inspiration for individual settings in films like *Psycho*, *Blade Runner* and *The Million Dollar Hotel*.

EDWARD HOPPER

If you could say it in words there would be no reason to paint.

SILVER

TITLE
Deutsche Post »Pong«

CLIENT
Deutsche Post AG

MARKETING DIRECTOR
Axel Wursthorn

ADVERTISING DIRECTOR
Sylvia Flügen

LEAD AGENCY
Jung von Matt AG

CREATIVE DIRECTION
Wolfgang Schneider, Mathias Stiller,
Jan Harbeck, David Mously

ART DIRECTION
Marius Lohmann

CLIENT CONSULTING
Frank Lotze, Ilan Schäfer,
Frauke Schmidt,
Jan Hendrik Oelckers

AGENCY PRODUCER
Sven Hannemann

COPY
Christopher Ruckwied

FINAL ARTWORK
Christoph von Bartkowski

BRONZE

TITLE
Braun Nasenhaarschneider
Kampagne »Exact Series«

CLIENT
Braun GmbH

MARKETING DIRECTOR
Jose Carlos Gonzalez Hurtado
(General Manager)

ADVERTISING DIRECTOR
Alexandra Messerschmidt
(Associate Director)

LEAD AGENCY
BBDO Düsseldorf GmbH

CREATIVE DIRECTION
Toygar Bazarkaya

ART DIRECTION
Daniel Aykurt

CLIENT CONSULTING
Adam Kennedy, Silke Joosten,
Jacqueline Standt

PHOTOGRAPHY
Ralf Gellert

ART BUYING
Birgit Paulat

BRONZE

TITLE
Tierpark Berlin Kampagne
»Ich bin auch Knut«

CLIENT
Tierpark Berlin-Friedrichsfelde
GmbH

MARKETING DIRECTOR
Dr. Gerald R. Uhlich

ADVERTISING DIRECTOR
Annika Tietke

LEAD AGENCY
Scholz & Friends

CREATIVE DIRECTION
Matthias Spaetgens,
Michael Winterhagen, Joerg Jahn

ART DIRECTION
Marc Ebenwaldner

CLIENT CONSULTING
Eva Lipp, Björn Krämer

PHOTOGRAPHY
Matthias Koslik

AGENCY PRODUCER
Søren Gessat, Karolin Posselt

ART BUYING
Adriana Meneses von Arnim

GRAPHIC ART
Gregor Hackner, Walter Ziegler

COPY
Johannes Vogl, Alexander Schierl

BRONZE

TITLE
Malteser Kampagne
»Typo Crash«

CLIENT
Malteser Hilfsdienst e.V.

MARKETING DIRECTOR
Josef Dorfner

LEAD AGENCY
Ogilvy Frankfurt

CREATIVE DIRECTION
Dr. Stephan Vogel,
Christian Mommertz

ART DIRECTION
Christian Mommertz

CLIENT CONSULTING
John F. Goetze, Thorsten Orth

PHOTOGRAPHY
Jo Bacherl

ART BUYING
Christina Hufgard

COPY
Dr. Stephan Vogel

TYPOGRAPHY
Sabina Hesse, Sabrina Belger,
Andrea Trott/
Art Support: Daniel de Leuw

ADDITIONAL AWARDS
BRONZE
Volume Design page 244
Digitale Werbung
Digital advertising

NOMINATION
Volume Advertising page 067
Publikumsanzeigen
Consumer advertisements

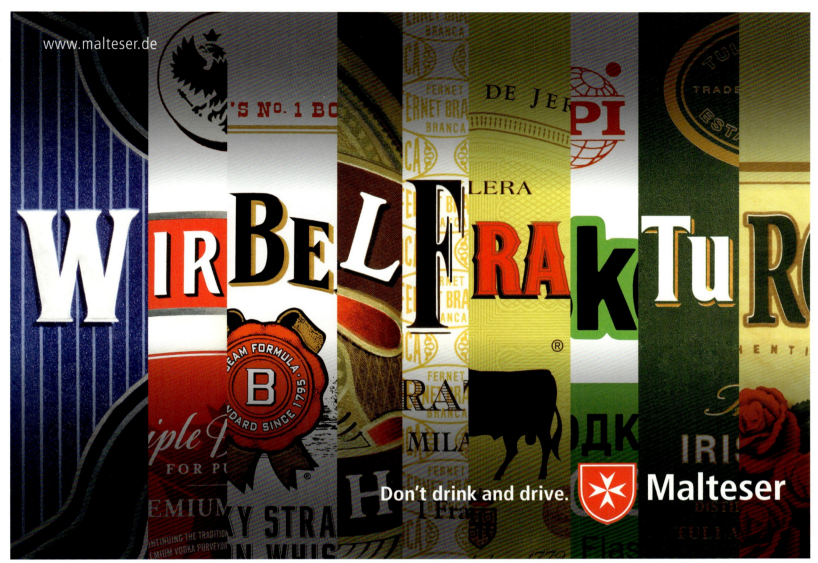

BRONZE

TITLE
McDonald's McCafé »Kaffee-Bohne«
CLIENT
McDonald's Deutschland Inc
MARKETING DIRECTOR
Gerhard R. Schöps
ADVERTISING DIRECTOR
Vorbereitung: Susan Schmidt
LEAD AGENCY
Heye, Group GmbH
CREATIVE DIRECTION
Norbert Herold, Helmut Huschka
ART DIRECTION
Stefan Ellenberger,
Sebastian Hackelsperger
CLIENT CONSULTING
Manuela Kunze
PHOTOGRAPHY
Camillo Büchelmeier
ART BUYING
Rosina Bischur
IMAGE EDITING
Christian Schulze,
Therese Zisselsberger
PRODUCTION
Carsten Horn, Rüdiger Biskoping

ADDITIONAL AWARDS
BRONZE
Volume Advertising page 066
Publikumsanzeigen
Consumer advertisements

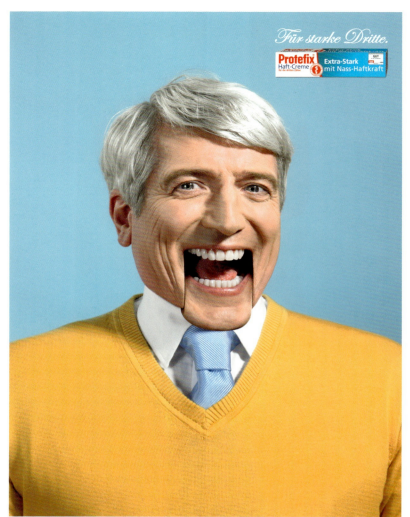
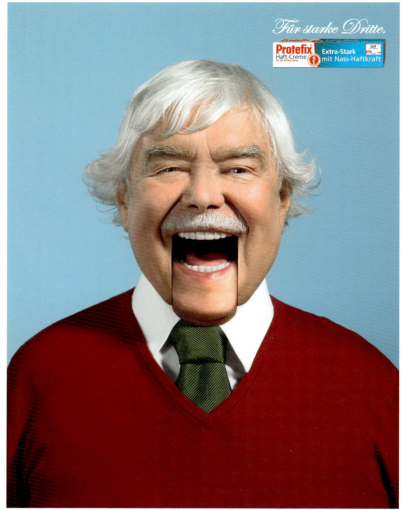

NOMINATION

TITLE
Protefix Haft-Creme Kampagne
»Nussknacker«

CLIENT
Queisser Pharma GmbH & Co. KG

MARKETING DIRECTOR
Jan K. Kuskowski

ADVERTISING DIRECTOR
Claudia Harding

LEAD AGENCY
Scholz & Friends

CREATIVE DIRECTION
Tobias Holland, Stefan Setzkorn,
Matthias Schmidt

ART DIRECTION
Pedro Sydow, Sven Janssen

CLIENT CONSULTING
Raphael Brinkert,
Sabine Hiersemann

PHOTOGRAPHY
Rainer Elstermann

ART BUYING
Chantal Mene

IMAGE EDITING
Metagate GmbH, Hamburg

GRAPHIC ART
Wolf Lang

COPY
Marc-Philipp Kittel

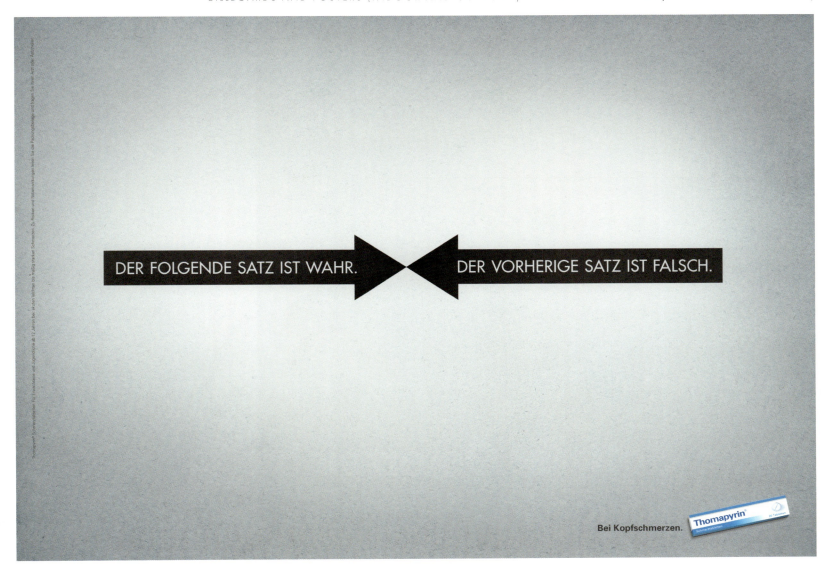

NOMINATION

TITLE
Thomapyrin Kopfschmerztabletten
Kampagne »Paradoxien«

CLIENT
Boehringer Ingelheim Pharma
GmbH & Co. KG

MARKETING DIRECTOR
Silke Schäfer

LEAD AGENCY
Euro RSCG Düsseldorf

CREATIVE DIRECTION
Felix Glauner, Florian Meimberg,
Torsten Pollmann, Martin Breuer

ART DIRECTION
Jörg Sachtleben, Désirée Rose,
Jean-Pierre Gregor

CLIENT CONSULTING
Alexander Weng

AGENCY PRODUCER
Detlef Stuhldreier

IMAGE EDITING
Peter Holzportz

NOMINATION

TITLE
Deutsche Lufthansa Kampagne »Billig«

CLIENT
Lufthansa AG

MARKETING DIRECTOR
Nicola Lange

ADVERTISING DIRECTOR
Peter Görzel

LEAD AGENCY
M.E.C.H. The Communications House Berlin GmbH

CREATIVE DIRECTION
Thorsten Adenauer, Daniel Henning

ART DIRECTION
Thorsten Adenauer

CLIENT CONSULTING
Katja Metz, Beate van den Berg

PHOTOGRAPHY
Stockbilder, PX1 at Medien GmbH

ART BUYING
Franziska Möck

IMAGE EDITING
PX1 at Medien GmbH

GRAPHIC ART
Catherina Paschke, Taro B. Wichowski

COPY
Daniel Henning

FINAL ARTWORK
PX1 at Medien GmbH

NOMINATION

TITLE
Greenpeace Kampagne »Müll«

CLIENT
Greenpeace

MARKETING DIRECTOR
Roland Hipp (Geschäftsführer)

ADVERTISING DIRECTOR
Kirsten Hagemann

LEAD AGENCY
Jung von Matt AG

CREATIVE DIRECTION
Arno Lindemann, Bernhard Lukas

ART DIRECTION
Florian Pack

CLIENT CONSULTING
Nic Heimann

PHOTOGRAPHY
Philipp Ruh

IDEA
Florian Pack, Teja Fischer

COPY
Teja Fischer

NOMINATION

TITLE
Bosch Akkuschrauber
PSR 14,4 LI-2 »Fliege«

CLIENT
Robert Bosch GmbH

ADVERTISING DIRECTOR
Claus von Berg

LEAD AGENCY
Jung von Matt AG

CREATIVE DIRECTION
Sascha Hanke,
Timm Hanebeck,
Wolf Heumann (GF)

ART DIRECTION
Kathrin Seupel

CLIENT CONSULTING
Inga Gerckens

PHOTOGRAPHY
Annika Rose, Andreas Mock

IMAGE EDITING
Marius Schwiegk

PRODUCTION
Philipp Wenhold

ADDITIONAL AWARDS NOMINATION

Volume Advertising page 066
Publikumsanzeigen
Consumer advertisements

NOMINATION

TITLE
McDonald's »Danke Schwester«

CLIENT
McDonald's Austria

MARKETING DIRECTOR
Andreas Schmidlechner

LEAD AGENCY
CCP, Heye Werbeagentur GmbH

CREATIVE DIRECTION
Werner Celand, Peter Czerny

ART DIRECTION
Dietmar Kreil

CLIENT CONSULTING
Philipp Krumpel,
Elena Wohlmuther

PHOTOGRAPHY
Thomas Hannich

IMAGE EDITING
Blaupapier, Wien

COPY
Viola Gangl

NOMINATION

TITLE
Astra Kampagne »CLPs 2007«

CLIENT
Holsten-Brauerei AG

MARKETING DIRECTOR
Hermann Crux

ADVERTISING DIRECTOR
Nicola Weiß

LEAD AGENCY
Philipp und Keuntje GmbH

CREATIVE DIRECTION
Hans Esders, Jana Liebig

ART DIRECTION
Maren Burrichter, Jan Berg,
Philipp Dörner

CLIENT CONSULTING
Andreas Müller-Horn,
Sandra Fiebranz

PHOTOGRAPHY
Christopher Koch

AGENCY PRODUCER
Stephan Gerlach

GRAPHIC ART
Jan Berg

COPY
Oliver Kohtz, Jan Berg, Aleš Polcar

NOMINATION

TITLE
Naturkundemuseum Stuttgart
Kampagne »Stammbaum«

CLIENT
Staatliches Museum für Naturkunde Stuttgart

MARKETING DIRECTOR
Tobias Wilhelm

LEAD AGENCY
Scholz & Friends

CREATIVE DIRECTION
Matthias Spaetgens, Oliver Handlos

ART DIRECTION
Mathias Rebmann

CLIENT CONSULTING
Eva Lipp, Björn Krämer

ILLUSTRATION
Johann Brandstetter

AGENCY PRODUCER
Adriana Meneses von Armin

IMAGE EDITING
Appel Grafik Berlin

GRAPHIC ART
Stephanie Wiehle, Katharina Hanel

COPY
Florian Schwalme

ADDITIONAL AWARDS NOMINATION
Volume Design page 128
Kunst-/Kultur-/Veranstaltungsplakate
Posters for arts, culture, events

NOMINATION

TITLE
PAPSTAR Aluminiumfolie
Kampagne »Alufolie schützt«

CLIENT
PAPSTAR Vertriebsgesellschaft
mbH & Co. KG

MARKETING DIRECTOR
Wolfgang Küpper

LEAD AGENCY
Scholz & Friends

CREATIVE DIRECTION
Timm Weber, Matthias Schmidt,
Stefan Setzkorn

ART DIRECTION
Sebastian Kaufmann

CLIENT CONSULTING
Alexander Yazdi, Leonie Plate,
Laura Becker

ILLUSTRATION
Torsten Wolber

ART BUYING
Chantal Mene

IMAGE EDITING
Metagate GmbH, Hamburg

COPY
Mathias Brückner

NOMINATION

TITLE
neu.de Kampagne
»Vorher – Nachher«

CLIENT
neu.de

MARKETING DIRECTOR
Isabelle Wagner

LEAD AGENCY
Saatchi & Saatchi

CREATIVE DIRECTION
Eberhard Kirchhoff

ART DIRECTION
Petra Sievers

CLIENT CONSULTING
Ronja Schütt

PHOTOGRAPHY
Christiane Gundlach

COPY
Michael Muck

NOMINATION

TITLE
Falk Navigationsgeräte Kampagne
»Einfach Navigieren«

CLIENT
Falk Marco Polo Interactive GmbH

MARKETING DIRECTOR
Stefanie Back

LEAD AGENCY
Scholz & Friends

CREATIVE DIRECTION
Oliver Handlos, Matthias Spaetgens

ART DIRECTION
Jens-Petter Waernes, Erik Dagnell

CLIENT CONSULTING
Stefanie Littek, Sebastian Vetter,
Jeanine Wyrwoll, Eva Lipp

IMAGE EDITING
Appel Grafik Berlin

ADDITIONAL AWARDS
NOMINATION
Volume Advertising page 053
Publikumsanzeigen
Consumer advertisements

SILVER

TITLE
Comedy Central »Ernst-Kampagne«
CLIENT
MTV Networks Germany GmbH
MARKETING DIRECTOR
Imke Deigner (Marketing Director), Torsten Wolf (Head of Consumer Marketing)
ADVERTISING DIRECTOR
Vivien Hucke (Junior Manager Consumer Marketing)
LEAD AGENCY
kempertrautmann gmbh
CREATIVE DIRECTION
Mathias Lamken
ART DIRECTION
Mathias Lamken, Tim Belser
CLIENT CONSULTING
Peter Matz, Ilker Yilmazalp
PHOTOGRAPHY
Karsten Wegener
ILLUSTRATION
Mathias Lamken
GRAPHIC ART
Simon Jasper Philipp
POSTPRODUCTION
Martina Huber
COPY
Mathias Lamken

ADDITIONAL AWARDS
SILVER
Volume Advertising page 066
Publikumsanzeigen
Consumer advertisements

SILVER
Volume Advertising page 072
Fachanzeigen
Trade advertisements

BRONZE
Volume Advertising page 096
Tages-/Wochenzeitungsanzeigen
Advertisements in daily/weekly newspapers

SILVER

TITLE
Eos Cabriolet »Schattenplakat«
CLIENT
Volkswagen AG
ADVERTISING DIRECTOR
Hartmut Seeger
LEAD AGENCY
DDB Germany/Düsseldorf
CREATIVE DIRECTION
Amir Kassaei, Eric Schoeffler, Heiko Freyland, Raphael Milczarek
ART DIRECTION
Fabian Kirner, Michael Kittel
CLIENT CONSULTING
Silke Lagodny
STRATEGIC PLANNING
Wiebke Dreyer, Christian Bihn
AGENCY PRODUCER
Michael Frixe
COPY
Felix Lemcke, Jan Propach

ADDITIONAL AWARDS
SILVER
Volume Advertising page 188
Media
Media

BRONZE
Volume Advertising page 187
Verkaufsförderung
Sales promotion

BRONZE

TITLE
Inlingua Kampagne »Umrisse«
CLIENT
Inlingua Freiburg
MARKETING DIRECTOR
Daniel Wilmsen
LEAD AGENCY
Kolle Rebbe Werbeagentur GmbH
CREATIVE DIRECTION
Ulrich Zünkeler/Rolf Leger/Stefan Wübbe
ART DIRECTION
Florian Schmucker
CLIENT CONSULTING
Stefanie Karrer, Manuela Maurer
GRAPHIC ART
Florian Schmucker
COPY
Florian Ludwig
FINAL ARTWORK
Maik Spreen

ADDITIONAL AWARDS
BRONZE
Volume Advertising page 074
Fachanzeigen
Trade advertisements

BRONZE

TITLE
VW Golf GTI Technologie Edition 30 Kampagne »5,9 kg pro PS«
CLIENT
Volkswagen AG
MARKETING DIRECTOR
Jochen Sengpiehl
ADVERTISING DIRECTOR
Hartmut Seeger
LEAD AGENCY
DDB Germany, Berlin
CREATIVE DIRECTION
Stefan Schulte, Bert Peulecke
ART DIRECTION
Marc Wientzek
CLIENT CONSULTING
Cathleen Losch, Louisa Ibing, Silke Lagodny
PHOTOGRAPHY
Yann Arthus-Bertrand, Sven Schrader
ART BUYING
Elke Dilchert
GRAPHIC ART
Wulf Rechtacek
ARTIST
Jan Diekmann
TECHNICAL DIRECTION
Sascha Mehn
COPY
Sebastian Kainz

ADDITIONAL AWARDS
BRONZE
Volume Advertising page 027
Publikumsanzeigen
Consumer advertisements

NOMINATION
Volume Advertising page 097
Tages-/Wochenzeitungsanzeigen
Advertisements in daily/weekly newspapers

BRONZE	**NOMINATION**	**NOMINATION**	**NOMINATION**

BRONZE

TITLE
Volkswagen Park Distance Control »Einpark-Kampagne«

CLIENT
Volkswagen AG

MARKETING DIRECTOR
Jochen Sengpiehl

ADVERTISING DIRECTOR
Hartmut Seeger

LEAD AGENCY
DDB Germany, Berlin

CREATIVE DIRECTION
Bert Peulecke, Stefan Schulte

ART DIRECTION
Gen Sadakane, Tim Stübane

CLIENT CONSULTING
Mia Drexl-Schegg, Cathleen Losch, Silke Lagodny, Marie-Louise Jakob

PHOTOGRAPHY
David Cuenca

IMAGE EDITING
PX1

TECHNICAL DIRECTION
Sascha Mehn

COPY
Jan Hendrik Ott

ADDITIONAL AWARDS
SILVER
Volume Advertising page 087
Tages-/Wochenzeitungsanzeigen
Advertisements in daily/weekly newspapers

BRONZE
Volume Advertising page 066
Publikumsanzeigen
Consumer advertisements

NOMINATION

TITLE
Sixt – rent a car »Beauty«

CLIENT
Sixt GmbH & Co. Autovermietung KG

MARKETING DIRECTOR
Dr. Karsten Willrodt

ADVERTISING DIRECTOR
Daniela Erdmann

LEAD AGENCY
Jung von Matt AG

CREATIVE DIRECTION
Peter Kirchhoff, Wolf Heumann

ART DIRECTION
Vanessa Rabea Schrooten

CLIENT CONSULTING
Sandra Schymetzki, Justyna Wos

PHOTOGRAPHY
Kristian Schuller

ART BUYING
Martina Traut, Katja Sluyter

IMAGE EDITING
Peggy H.

GRAPHIC ART
Felix Taubert

PRODUCTION
Annette Hoss

COPY
Lisa Maria Hartwich

ADDITIONAL AWARDS
BRONZE
Volume Advertising page 031
Publikumsanzeigen
Consumer advertisements

NOMINATION

TITLE
BMW 1er Coupé Kampagne »Verdichtete 1ntensität«

CLIENT
BMW AG

MARKETING DIRECTOR
Manfred Bräunl

ADVERTISING DIRECTOR
Dr. Tobias Nickel, Dr. Hans-Peter Ketterl

LEAD AGENCY
MAB, Berlin

CONTRIBUTING AGENCIES
Mediaplus

CREATIVE DIRECTION
Nils Haseborg, Sven Sorgatz, Stefan Schmidt, Tomas Tulinius

ART DIRECTION
Michael Janke, Sven Sorgatz

CLIENT CONSULTING
Alexander Kerkow, Christiane Wolters

PHOTOGRAPHY
Mats Cordt

AGENCY PRODUCER
Lars Ebeling

ART BUYING
Martina Kersten

GRAPHIC ART
Alexander Tibelius

MEDIA
Werner Reineke, Christian Kaessmann

POSTPRODUCTION
Zerone, Hamburg

PRODUCTION
Nowadays: Tobias Wenske; Mats Cordt Photography: Matthias Pretzsch

COPY
Stefan Schmidt

ADDITIONAL AWARDS
BRONZE
Volume Advertising page 024
Publikumsanzeigen
Consumer advertisements

NOMINATION
Volume Advertising page 203, 214
Media
Media

NOMINATION
Volume Advertising page 358
Integrierte Kampagnen
Integrated campaigns

NOMINATION

TITLE
Mercedes-Benz G-Klasse Kampagne »Sandplakat, Steinplakat«

CLIENT
Daimler AG

ADVERTISING DIRECTOR
Mirco Völker

LEAD AGENCY
Jung von Matt AG

CREATIVE DIRECTION
Dörte Spengler-Ahrens, Jan Rexhausen

ART DIRECTION
Hisham Kharma

CLIENT CONSULTING
Yves Rosengart, Johanna Hecker, Jan Groenendijk

ILLUSTRATION
Materialschlachten: Claudia Schildt, Fabian Zell

ART BUYING
Bettina Zschirnt

ARTIST
Claudia Schildt, Fabian Zell

PRODUCTION
Philipp Wenhold

COPY
Sergio Penzo

ADDITIONAL AWARDS
BRONZE
Volume Advertising page 199
Media
Media

BRONZE
Volume Design page 151
Grafische Einzelarbeiten
Single works of graphic art

NOMINATION

TITLE
VW Golf GTI Kampagne
»Männer brauchen wir
nicht zu überzeugen«
CLIENT
Volkswagen AG
MARKETING DIRECTOR
Jochen Sengpiehl
ADVERTISING DIRECTOR
Hartmut Seeger
LEAD AGENCY
DDB Germany, Berlin
CREATIVE DIRECTION
Stefan Schulte, Bert Peulecke
ART DIRECTION
Kristoffer Heilemann,
Alexandra Sievers
CLIENT CONSULTING
Cathleen Losch, Silke Lagodny
PHOTOGRAPHY
F. A. Cesar
GRAPHIC ART
Jakob Schubert, Stephan Wege
TECHNICAL DIRECTION
Sascha Mehn
COPY
Ludwig Berndl, Philip Bolland

ADDITIONAL AWARDS
NOMINATION
Volume Advertising page 043
Publikumsanzeigen
Consumer advertisements

NOMINATION

TITLE
WMF Kampagne
»Schnellkochtöpfe«
CLIENT
WMF AG
ADVERTISING DIRECTOR
Wolfgang Dalferth
LEAD AGENCY
KNSK Werbeagentur GmbH
CREATIVE DIRECTION
Anke Winschewski, Tim Krink,
Niels Holle
ART DIRECTION
Bill Yom
CLIENT CONSULTING
Kirsten Kohls
ILLUSTRATION
ABC Digital
IMAGE EDITING
ABC Digital
COMPUTER ANIMATION
ABC Digital
GRAPHIC ART
Sonja Kliem, Nathalie Krüger
COPY
Kurt Müller-Fleischer

ADDITIONAL AWARDS
NOMINATION
Volume Advertising page 080
Fachanzeigen
Trade advertisements

*18. OKTOBER 1926 DANZIG
†23. NOVEMBER 1991 LAGUNITAS/KALIFORNIEN

Nach eigenem Bekunden schlug er sich, bevor er 1944 eingezogen wurde, in Berlin als Schuhputzer, Laufjunge und Leichenwäscher durch. Seine ersten Theaterrollen spielte er in britischer Gefangenschaft auf selbst gezimmerten Bühnen. Obwohl er nie eine entsprechende Ausbildung dazu genossen hat, spielte er nach dem Krieg auf Anhieb in erstklassigen Häusern. Aber Kinski war schwierig. Seine Engagements hielten nie sehr lange. Allzu oft gebärdete er sich als Wüterich, schlug Scheiben ein oder zertrümmerte Mobiliar. Nicht von ungefähr füllte er das Fach »psychopathisch, getriebener Charakter« wie kaum ein anderer überzeugend aus.

*18 OCTOBER 1926 DANZIG
†23 NOVEMBER 1991 LAGUNITAS/CALIFORNIA

According to Kinski himself, he worked in Berlin as a shoeshine boy, an errand boy and a corpse washer to make ends meet before being drafted in 1944. His first theatrical roles came in a British POW camp, on stages he himself constructed. Despite never having had any training in his profession, the years following the war very quickly saw him playing in first-class theatres. But Kinski was a difficult character, and his engagements never lasted very long. All too often he would behave brutishly, breaking windows or demolishing furniture. Hardly surprising, then, that few others have ever given such convincing performances when portraying psychopathic, driven personalities.

KLAUS KINSKI

I decide who offends me.

WER MICH BELEIDIGT, ENTSCHEIDE ICH.

SILVER

TITLE
Mercedes-Benz LKW Blue Tec
»Geschichten in Öl«

CLIENT
Mercedes-Benz LKW;
Vertriebsorganisation Deutschland

MARKETING DIRECTOR
Andreas Burkhart

ADVERTISING DIRECTOR
Sascha Thieme

LEAD AGENCY
BBDO Stuttgart GmbH

CREATIVE DIRECTION
Armin Jochum, Friedrich Tromm

ART DIRECTION
Sebastian Gaissert, Stefan Nagel,
Marcus Widmann

CLIENT CONSULTING
Caroline Schäufele,
Andreas Rauscher

ILLUSTRATION
Sebastian Gaissert

AGENCY PRODUCER
Wolfgang Schif

PRODUCTION
Netzwerk P, Berlin

COPY
Friedrich Tromm, Armin Jochum,
Wolf-Peter Camphausen,
Achim Szymanski

ADDITIONAL AWARDS
SILVER
Volume Advertising page 144
Text
Copy

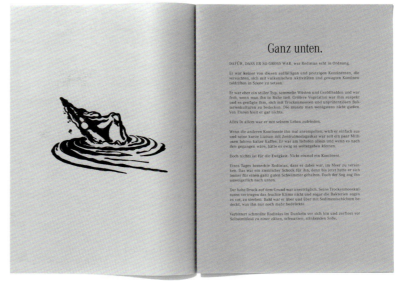

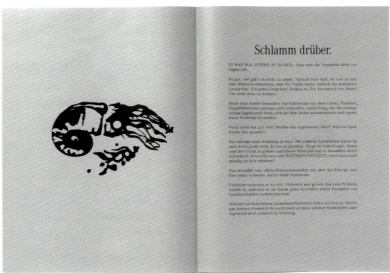

BRONZE

TITLE
Mercedes-Benz G-Klasse
»Der Stoff aus dem die Helden sind«

CLIENT
Daimler AG, MBVD

MARKETING DIRECTOR
Michael Dietz

ADVERTISING DIRECTOR
Peer Näher

LEAD AGENCY
Scholz & Friends

CREATIVE DIRECTION
Constantin Kaloff

ART DIRECTION
Jens Stein, Robert Bilz

CLIENT CONSULTING
Stephan Braun, Nadja Richter,
Ulf Cerning

AGENCY PRODUCER
Sabine Bäsler

COPY
Philipp Wöhler, Christian Brandes,
Felix Heine

ADDITIONAL AWARDS
BRONZE
Volume Advertising page 381
Dialogmarketing
Dialogue marketing

NOMINATION
Volume Design page 101
Informationsmedien
Information media

NOMINATION
Volume Design page 157
Grafische Einzelarbeiten
Single works of graphic art

BRONZE

TITLE
Katholische Klinikseelsorge
»Gebrauchsanweisung für die Seele«
CLIENT
Katholische Klinikseelsorge
ADVERTISING DIRECTOR
Heribert Dölle
LEAD AGENCY
Bargfeld Scheer
CONTRIBUTING AGENCIES
gerhardschmal.de
CREATIVE DIRECTION
Stefan Scheer, Gerhard Schmal
ART DIRECTION
Nadine Redlich, Gerhard Schmal
ILLUSTRATION
Nadine Redlich
PRINTING
Druckerei Dehl
COPY
Stefan Scheer, Tim Turiak

Die Seele ist eines der wichtigsten Bauteile des Menschen. Diese Gebrauchsanweisung liefert viele nützliche Anwendungsbeispiele.

 MAN WEISS NICHT, OB DIE SEELE REINE ENERGIE, UNSTERBLICH ODER TEIL DES GEHIRNS IST.

 ES IST JEDOCH BEKANNT, DASS DIE REGELMÄSSIGE PFLEGE DER SEELE ÜBERAUS WICHTIG IST.

WER DIES BEACHTET, WIRD IN SEINER SEELE IMMER EINEN HILFREICHEN BEGLEITER HABEN.

DIE SEELE BIETET DEM NUTZER VIELE ENTSCHEIDENDE VORTEILE IM TÄGLICHEN GEBRAUCH. ZUM BEISPIEL:

1] DANK SEELE SIND WIR NIE ALLEIN – ZUDEM IST SIE DISKRET UND UNSICHTBAR.

2] DIE SEELE MACHT UNS EINZIGARTIG – GANZ OHNE TEURE FRISEURBESUCHE.

3] DIE SEELE IST IN STÄNDIGER VERBINDUNG – OB MIT GOTT ODER MIT ANDEREN SEELEN.

Die Seele ist für viele Funktionen des Menschen zuständig. Darum ist es sehr wichtig, sie regelmäßig zu trainieren!

MAN ACHTE MAL DARAUF: DIE SEELE FÜHLT SICH INTERESSANT AN.

ACHTUNG: DIES ERFORDERT EIN BISSCHEN PHANTASIE, IST ABER ÜBERRASCHEND!

EINFACH SUPER DRAUF SEIN. DANK SEELE.

HINWEIS: FÜR DIESE ÜBUNG BITTE KEINE WEITEREN ANSPRÜCHE AN DIE SEELE STELLEN!

DIE SEELE KANN PHANTASIEN IN ECHTZEIT REALISIEREN.

VORSICHT: BEI DIESER ÜBUNG IMMER OFFEN FÜR WUNDER SEIN!

WELTWEIT SCHÄTZEN ÄRZTE DIE HEILKRÄFTE DER SEELE.

ACHTUNG: HIER BITTE SEHR GENAU AUF DIE SEELE HÖREN UND ZEIT MITBRINGEN!

WENN MAN SIE LÄSST, ERLERNT DIE SEELE KNIFFLIGE KULTURTECHNIKEN, Z.B. RECHNEN.

TIPP: DIE SEELE AUCH MAL SELBST ENTSCHEIDEN LASSEN, WAS SIE LERNEN WILL!

Sie können diese Coupons bequem und einfach einlösen. Bitte lassen Sie uns benachrichtigen (siehe Rückseite!).

GUTSCHEIN für offene OHREN

COUPON für 100% Aufmerksamkeit

GUTSCHEIN für ein Gespräch über ÄRGER

GUTSCHEIN für ein Gespräch über ANGST

·COUPON· für einen SEGEN

GUTSCHEIN für ein Gebet

GUTSCHEIN für ein Gespräch über Trauer

Gutschein für einen WITZ erzählt bekommen ha haha

BRONZE

TITLE
MKI Matzku & Konz
Industrievertretung
»Gehäuse, Induktivitäten,
Leiterplatten & Folientastaturen«

CLIENT
MKI Matzku & Konz
Industrievertretung GmbH

MARKETING DIRECTOR
Stephan Konz

LEAD AGENCY
Dorten Bauer

CREATIVE DIRECTION
Jörg Bauer

ART DIRECTION
Jörg Bauer

PHOTOGRAPHY
Jörg Schieferecke

PRINTING
Raff GmbH

IDEA
Jörg Bauer

CONCEPT
Jörg Bauer

POSTPRODUCTION
Raff Digital GmbH

COPY
Christian Schwarm

ADDITIONAL AWARDS
SILVER
Volume Design page 088
Informationsmedien
Information media

NOMINATION
Volume Design page 158
Grafische Einzelarbeiten
Single works of graphic art

PRODUCT/ADVERTISING BROCHURES **PRODUKT-/WERBEBROSCHÜREN** 135

Das lange Buch vom langen Leben.

Der Elefant. Er ist der größte Landbewohner unseres Planeten: bis zu 4 Meter hoch und mit einer Masse von bis zu 5 Tonnen so schwer wie ein Rudel von 20 Löwen. Um diese einzigartigen Ausmaße zu erreichen, gab die Natur dem Elefanten eine lange Lebenszeit. Die braucht er auch, um sich fortzupflanzen. Allein die Schwangerschaft dauert 22 Monate und es vergehen viele weitere Jahre, bis die Jungen zum ausgewachsenen Dickhäuter werden. Ihre Haut kann bis zu 3 Zentimeter stark werden – hinter den Ohren, um die Augen, an Bauch, Brust und Achseln ist sie aber dünn wie Papier.

Der Olivenbaum. 2000 Jahre zählt das älteste bekannte Exemplar Europas. Schon seit dem 4. Jahrtausend vor Christus wird der Ölbaum als Nutzpflanze kultiviert. Seine Wurzeln reichen weit zurück in die Geschichte – und ins Erdreich: Aus bis zu 6 Meter Tiefe holt er sich das lebenswichtige Wasser. Seine Früchte, die Oliven, bestehen zur Hälfte daraus. Außerdem enthalten sie viel Zucker und das begehrte Öl. Die Produkte des Olivenbaumes kann man sich aber nicht nur schmecken, sondern sie können sich auch hören lassen: Aus seinem edlen Holz werden unter anderem Musikinstrumente hergestellt.

Die Schildkröte. Es gab sie schon Millionen Jahre vor den Dinosauriern und noch heute findet man sie auf allen Erdteilen. Zum Beispiel die bis zu 2,50 Meter lange und 900 Kilogramm schwere Lederschildkröte oder die Südafrikanische Flachschildkröte, die nur 6 bis 10 Zentimeter groß wird. In 250 Millionen Jahren Entwicklungszeit haben einige Exemplare offenbar auch das Geheimnis der ewigen Jugend entdeckt: So lebte von 1830 bis 2006 die Riesenschildkröte Harriet. Darwin brachte sie einst von den Galapagosinseln mit und nutzte sie als lebendes Anschauungsobjekt für seine Evolutionstheorie.

Der Mercedes. Das Automobil, das es am längsten auf unserer Erde gibt, hat auch eine außergewöhnlich lange Lebenserwartung. Weil in jedem Mercedes Exemplar das Erbgut aus mehr als 120 Jahren Forschungs- und Entwicklungsarbeit steckt. Weil nur die besten Ideen seine Evolution bestimmen. Und vor allem, weil es Menschen gibt, die dafür sorgen, dass er jung bleibt. Mit ihrem ganzen Können, ihrer Leidenschaft und ihrer Liebe zum Detail. Und mit Erfahrung, die jahrzehntelang gewachsen ist. Der Mercedes-Benz Original-Service. Denn was einem am Herzen liegt, gibt man nur in die besten Hände.

NOMINATION

TITLE
Mercedes-Benz Original-Service »Das lange Buch vom langen Leben«

CLIENT
Daimler AG, Mercedes-Benz Vertriebsorganisation Dtld. Marketing Kommunikation Service, MBVD/VSP

MARKETING DIRECTOR
Stefan Sonntag

ADVERTISING DIRECTOR
Tim Steinküller

LEAD AGENCY
SHANGHAI DGM

CREATIVE DIRECTION
Stefan Karl/Heiner Baptist Rogge

ART DIRECTION
Franziska Räther

CLIENT CONSULTING
Frank Büchin

ILLUSTRATION
Heinz Wolf

IMAGE EDITING
Lars Menze

GRAPHIC ART
Lars Menze, Dörthe Gössler

PRODUCTION
Netzwerk P

COPY
Michael Spilker

TYPOGRAPHY
Lars Menze

PRODUCT/ADVERTISING BROCHURES PRODUKT-/WERBEBROSCHÜREN 137

NOMINATION

TITLE
Fanartikelkatalog
»FC St Pauli 2007/08«

CLIENT
Upsolut Merchandising
GmbH & Co. KG

MARKETING DIRECTOR
Christian Tötzke

ADVERTISING DIRECTOR
Hendrik Lüttmer

LEAD AGENCY
annaundbenne.gbr

CREATIVE DIRECTION
Anna Clea Skoluda

ART DIRECTION
Anna Clea Skoluda

PHOTOGRAPHY
Benne Ochs

AGENCY PRODUCER
Produktionsbüro
Romey von Malottky GmbH

IMAGE EDITING
Filestyle Medienproduktion GmbH

DESIGN
Anna Clea Skoluda

DESIGN AGENCY
www.anna-clea.de

GRAPHIC ART
Jan-Christoph Prilop

IDEA
Anna Clea Skoluda/Benne Ochs

STYLING
Jac Ziesmer

COPY
Moritz Piehler

FINAL ARTWORK
Sabine Keller

NOMINATION

TITLE
OHROPAX »Lauter Ruhe«

CLIENT
OHROPAX GmbH

MARKETING DIRECTOR
Michael Negwer

LEAD AGENCY
Scheufele
Kommunikationsagentur GmbH

CREATIVE DIRECTION
Oliver Hesse

ART DIRECTION
Nicola Sunderdiek

CLIENT CONSULTING
Silke Asbrand, Beate Scheufele

ILLUSTRATION
Nicola Sunderdiek

IMAGE EDITING
6/0/7er Druckvorlagen GmbH

DESIGN
Nicola Sunderdiek

PRINTING
Thomas-Grafische Veredelung
GmbH & Co. KG

GRAPHIC ART
Nicola Sunderdiek

IDEA
Oliver Hesse, Nicola Sunderdiek

CONCEPT
Oliver Hesse, Nicola Sunderdiek

COPY
Oliver Hesse, Roland Müller

FINAL ARTWORK
Peggy Belles

ADDITIONAL AWARDS NOMINATION
Volume Design page 100
Informationsmedien
Information media

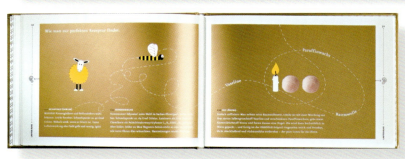

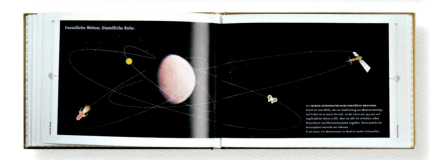

PRODUCT/ADVERTISING BROCHURES PRODUKT-/WERBEBROSCHÜREN 139

SILVER

TITLE
VW Golf »Horst Schlämmer Grevenbroicher Tagblatt«

CLIENT
Volkswagen AG

MARKETING DIRECTOR
Jochen Sengpiehl

ADVERTISING DIRECTOR
Ralf Maltzen, Hartmut Seeger

LEAD AGENCY
DDB Germany, Berlin

CREATIVE DIRECTION
Amir Kassaei, Stefan Schulte, Bert Peulecke

ART DIRECTION
Kristoffer Heilemann, Tim Schmitt

CLIENT CONSULTING
Cathleen Losch, Silke Lagodny

PHOTOGRAPHY
Markus Bachmann, F. A. Cesar, Sven Schrader

AGENCY PRODUCER
Peter Stumpe

ART BUYING
Elke Dilchert

GRAPHIC ART
Peter Mayer, Sarah Pöhlmann

TECHNICAL DIRECTION
Sascha Mehn

COPY
Ludwig Berndl, Philip Bolland, Ulrike Schumann

ADDITIONAL AWARDS
GOLD
Volume Advertising page 186
Verkaufsförderung
Sales promotion

GOLD
Volume Advertising page 221
TV-Spots
Television commercials

GOLD
Volume Advertising page 283
Filme für Verkaufsförderung/
Unternehmensdarstellungen
Films for sales promotion/
company presentation

GOLD
Volume Advertising page 289
Virale Filme
Viral films

GOLD
Volume Advertising page 347
Integrierte Kampagnen
Integrated campaigns

GOLD
Volume Advertising page 367
Dialogmarketing
Dialogue marketing

GOLD
Volume Design page 242
Digitale Werbung
Digital advertising

SILVER
Volume Advertising page 096
Tages-/Wochenzeitungsanzeigen
Advertisements in daily/weekly newspapers

SILVER
Volume Advertising page 147
Text
Copy

SILVER
Volume Design page 259
Digitale Medien: Viral
Digital media: Viral

BRONZE
Volume Advertising page 152
Text
Copy

BRONZE
Volume Advertising page 326
Funkspots
Radio commercials

NOMINATION
Volume Design page 095
Informationsmedien
Information media

NOMINATION
Volume Design page 235
Websites
Websites

SILVER

TITLE
Dali Anzeigenkampagne
»Die Dalimonologe«
CLIENT
Dali a/s, Nørager
MARKETING DIRECTOR
Mona Nielsen (ML)
ADVERTISING DIRECTOR
Lars Worre (CEO)
LEAD AGENCY
Geschke/Pufe
CREATIVE DIRECTION
Jan Geschke, Stefan Pufe
ART DIRECTION
Stefan Pufe
CLIENT CONSULTING
Geschke/Pufe
STRATEGIC PLANNING
Geschke/Pufe
PHOTOGRAPHY
Jan Geschke
COPY
Jan Geschke
TYPOGRAPHY
Stefan Pufe

Blech. Natürlich kann er mit seinem Geld machen, was er will, jedenfalls mit den 39% davon, die Einkommensteuer, Mehrwertsteuer, Verpulverungszuschlag, Heiligendammgrenzzaunabgabe und Sektsteuer übriglassen, und ja, es ist immer wieder lustig, mit einem Auto (Kraftstoffsteuer, Geldwertervorteilabzug), das eigentlich 280 fährt, im Stau zu stehen, während hinten die Tochter fragt Sind wir schon da? und der Sohn würgende Geräusche macht weil er gleich speiben wird, nämlich kotzen auf österreichisch, und man kann nicht anhalten, obwohl man schon angehalten wird, weil, wer anhält, wird ja sofort abgeschleppt, und eine Zigarette kann man auch nicht mehr rauchen,  weil, das ist jetzt eine rauchfreie Standspur hier, da fragt man sich langsam, ob man nicht besser zu Haus geblieben wär mit einer Flasche Tocai Friulano, nicht über 5°, und der Gefährtin bessrer Tage auf dem schon etwas zerliebten Ledersofa, um dem überirdisch subtil phrasierten Walzer op. 69 No. 1, Chopin, wer sonst, eine frühe Michelangeli-Aufnahme, zu lauschen, wie er aus den Dali Lautsprechern kommt, die man sich in einem Anfall von Wahnsinn letztes Jahr gekauft hat obwohl eh keiner mehr wirklich Musik hört, außer die kastrierte Version aufm Taschenspieler, und das von Hand ganz weit oben (56°42'27" Nord, 9°37'43" Ost, vielleicht sollte man da mal hinfahren) am Skagerrak geschreinerte Kirschholzgehäuse und die ganze dänische Präzision da drin weiß doch eh keiner zu würdigen, außer eventuell Michelangeli selbst, und der ist tot, schade, also, wennmandanurrechtzeitigdraufgekommenwär, vielleicht weil man das Dali-Buch gelesen hätt letztes Wochenende, das einem Dali um nix schickt, e-mail genügt, lars@dali.dk, und eine Dali CD gibt's teils auch dazu, weil die schier nicht aushalten, daß keiner mehr weiß, wie sich Musik eigentlich anfühlt, dann hätte das noch ein wunderbarer Tag werden können statt dieser verlausten Drecksversion von einem Tag wie die meisten Leute ihn meistens haben.

Danish Audiophile Loudspeaker Industries, since 1983, www.dali.dk/de

WIENERS+WIENERS
Übersetzen · Adaptieren · Korrigieren

Man darf gar nicht drüber nachdenken, u ja irre, wie die Leute zum Inneren pilgern nix findet, macht hundertfünfzig Euro, hert, weil der eh nix findet und seine drei h erst recht nicht, gehen sie zum Homöo- m Osteopathen und zum Psychopathen, in der Mitte kurz unterm Schlüsselbein, daß einem was Essentielles fehlt irgendwie, eibt, als ob man keine Crème Catalan mehr mmer, je, dabei müßt man sich nur so ein er Dalis ins Wohnzimmer stellen und seine r Miles hören, täglich, und trotz der ganzen  Misere, oder vielleicht wegen, ist da auf einmal wieder ein Funken Leben in einem, und ja, der Blutdruck geht gefühlt auch senkrecht südwärts, irgendwas mit dem vegetativen Nervensystem, und diese paar Töne, diese hergerotzten und rausgeseufzten, abgelebten Töne, aufgenommen 1956 im von Rudy van Gelder in Hackensack New einzigen verschissnen Mikrophon, machen daß es hüpft wie ein junges Zicklein, tief as von Hand ganz weit oben am Skagerrak rd, 9°37'43" Ost) liebevollst geschreinerte use und die ganze kassenpatientenrahmen- ische Technik da drin ist einem völlig egal, ndaseinerrechtzeitiggesagthätt, und wenn Buch gelesen hätt in den Herbstferien, das nix schickt, email genügt, lars@dali.dk, CD gibt's, wenn sie noch da ist, auch dazu, quasi missionarisches Sendungsbewußtsein tt man eine fabelhafte Antwort gehabt auf e Frage, Warum?, keine allgemeingültige eine die hilft.

KATEGORIE TEXT *präsentiert von*
CATEGORY COPY *presented by*

udiophile Loudspeaker Industries, since 1983, www.dali.dk/de

SILVER

TITLE
Mercedes-Benz Anzeigen
»G-Klasse Händlerkampagne«

CLIENT
Daimler AG

MARKETING DIRECTOR
Pawel Nowotny,
Andreas Poulionakis

ADVERTISING DIRECTOR
Yvonne Emhardt

LEAD AGENCY
Jung von Matt AG

CREATIVE DIRECTION
Deneke von Weltzien, Fabian Frese,
Thimoteus Wagner

ART DIRECTION
Christian Kroll, Bill Yom

CLIENT CONSULTING
Christian Hupertz,
Klaus Burghauser, Stephan Damm,
Yves Rosengart, Johanna Hecker,
Jan Groenendijk

GRAPHIC ART
Christoph Lehmann

COPY
Kurt Müller-Fleischer, Peter Gocht

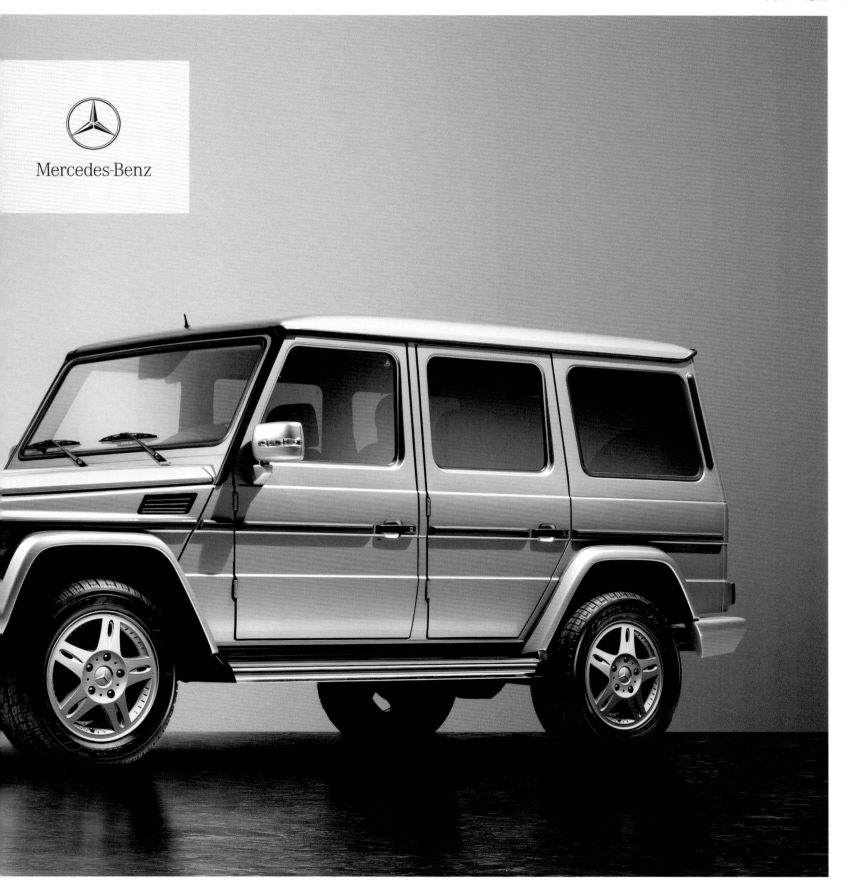

SILVER

TITLE
Mercedes-Benz LKW Blue Tec
Folder »Geschichten in Öl«

CLIENT
Mercedes-Benz LKW;
Vertriebsorganisation Deutschland

MARKETING DIRECTOR
Andreas Burkhart

ADVERTISING DIRECTOR
Sascha Thieme

LEAD AGENCY
BBDO Stuttgart GmbH

CREATIVE DIRECTION
Armin Jochum, Friedrich Tromm

ART DIRECTION
Sebastian Gaissert, Stefan Nagel,
Marcus Widmann

CLIENT CONSULTING
Caroline Schäufele,
Andreas Rauscher

ILLUSTRATION
Sebastian Gaissert

AGENCY PRODUCER
Wolfgang Schif

PRODUCTION
Netzwerk P, Berlin

COPY
Friedrich Tromm, Armin Jochum,
Wolf-Peter Camphausen,
Achim Szymanski

ADDITIONAL AWARDS
SILVER
Volume Advertising page 128
Produkt-/Werbebroschüren
Product/advertising brochures

Geschichten in Öl.

Mercedes-Benz

Ganz unten.

DAFÜR, DASS ER SO GROSS WAR, war Rodinias echt in Ordnung.

Er war keiner von diesen auffälligen und protzigen Kontinenten, die versuchten, sich mit vulkanischen Aktivitäten und gewagten Kontinentaldriften in Szene zu setzen.

Er war eher ein stiller Typ, sammelte Wüsten und Geröllhalden und war froh, wenn man ihn in Ruhe ließ. Größere Vegetation war ihm suspekt und es genügte ihm, sich mit Trockenmoosen und unprätentiösen Bakterienkulturen zu bedecken. Die musste man wenigstens nicht gießen. Von Tieren hielt er gar nichts.

Alles in allem war er mit seinem Leben zufrieden.

Wenn die anderen Kontinente ihn mal anrempelten, wich er einfach aus und seine kurze Liaison mit Zentralmadagaskar war seit ein paar Millionen Jahren kalter Kaffee. Er war am liebsten allein und wenn es nach ihm gegangen wäre, hätte er ewig so weitergehen können.

Doch nichts ist für die Ewigkeit. Nicht einmal ein Kontinent.

Eines Tages bemerkte Rodinias, dass er dabei war, im Meer zu versinken. Das war ein ziemlicher Schock für ihn, denn bis jetzt hatte er sich immer für einen ganz guten Schwimmer gehalten. Doch der Sog zog ihn unweigerlich nach unten.

Der hohe Druck auf dem Grund war unerträglich. Seine Trockenmooskulturen vertrugen das feuchte Klima nicht und sogar die Bakterien zogen es vor, zu sterben. Bald war er über und über mit Sedimentschichten bedeckt, was ihn nur noch mehr bedrückte.

Verbittert schmollte Rodinias im Dunkeln vor sich hin und zerfloss vor Selbstmitleid zu einer zähen, schwarzen, stinkenden Soße.

La Dolce Vita.

ICH HABE EIN PROBLEM. Ich werde sterben. Bald.

Vorher muss ich Ihnen aber noch etwas sagen und ich möchte, dass Sie genau zuhören, denn beim Sterben ist es wie beim Leben: Man kann die Szene nicht wiederholen, wenn man sie beim ersten Mal verpatzt hat.

Sehen Sie, ich bin viel rumgekommen, hab einiges gesehen. Man kann über das Präkambrium sagen, was man will, aber hier ist immer was los. Ich hab die sieben Urozeane durchkreuzt, hatte in jedem Hafen eine Braut, wenn Sie verstehen, was ich meine.

Klar, es war nicht immer einfach. Es gab auch Stürme und mehr als einmal hing mein Leben am seidenen Faden. Aber wo ich auch war und was auch geschah, ich wusste immer, dass meine Existenz einen Sinn hat und dass ich Teil war von etwas, das größer ist als ich selbst.

Ziemlich große Worte für eine Amöbe, sagen Sie? Früher hätte ich Ihnen für so einen Spruch meine zwei Trillionen Brüder auf den Hals gehetzt, aber meine Zeit läuft ab und ich will keinen Ärger.

Ich will bloß, dass Sie begreifen, wie schön das Leben ist, wenn man ein paar einfache Grundregeln beherzigt.

Respektieren Sie Ihren Schwarm.

Schützen Sie das Meer. Es ist die einzige Welt, die wir haben.

Fangen Sie nie eine Beziehung mit Plankton an. Ich habe schon einige gute Amöben daran zerbrechen sehen.

Vor allem aber, genießen Sie Ihr Leben.

Schlamm drüber.

ES WAR MAL WIEDER SO DUNKEL, dass man die Tentakeln nicht vor Augen sah.

Na gut, viel gab's eh nicht zu sehen. Typisch Trias halt. Ab und zu mal eine Röhrenwurmkolonie, aber die Typen waren einfach nur komplette Langweiler. Ein gutes Gespräch? Vergiss es. Ein Austausch von Ideen? Gar nicht dran zu denken.

Heute kam wieder besonders viel Kleinkram von oben runter, Plankton, Pantoffeltierchen und was nicht noch alles. Lauter Zeug, das die unangenehme Eigenschaft hatte, sich auf dem Boden anzusammeln und irgendwann furchtbar zu stinken.

Wozu sollte das gut sein? Machte das irgendeinen Sinn? Welches Spiel wurde hier gespielt?

Das Geistige kam eindeutig zu kurz. Die anderen Ammoniten waren da auch keine große Hilfe. Er war es gewohnt, Dinge zu hinterfragen, ihnen »auf den Grund zu gehen« (auf dieses Wortspiel war er besonders stolz). Schließlich: Wie sollte man sich WEITERENTWICKELN, wenn man nicht ständig an sich arbeitete?

Ihm schwebte eine offene Diskussionskultur vor, aber das Einzige, was hier unten schwebte, waren blöde Sedimente.

Vielleicht verlangte er zu viel. Vielleicht war gerade das sein Problem, dachte er, während er an einem ganz besonders üblen Exemplar von Schlammhaufen vorbeischwamm.

Schauen wir dem kleinen Ammoniten hinterher! Rufen wir ihm zu: Mach's gut, kleiner Ammonit! Du warst zwar ein ganz schöner Stinkstiefel, aber eigentlich auch ziemlich in Ordnung.

Flug 0001.

SCHON SEIT EINER GANZEN WEILE spielte das Wetter einfach nur noch verrückt. Das war nicht mehr das gemütliche Jura, das alle kannten, das tendierte schon schwer in Richtung Kreidezeit.

Überall lagen die Nerven blank.

Wenn es nicht gerade Schwefel regnete, regnete es Bimssteine, oder es regnete Schwefel UND Bimssteine, und das trieb selbst die gutmütigsten Dinosaurier auf Dauer in den Wahnsinn oder die innere Emigration.

Und dann fielen auch noch ständig irgendwelche Bäume um.

Archie hatte nie viel mit den anderen am Hut gehabt – als Archäopteryx schwebte er ganz einfach über den Dingen. Außerdem hatte er Wichtigeres zu tun, als sich von der allgemeinen schlechten Laune anstecken zu lassen.

Archie war im Training.

Was nutzte es, wenn man fliegen konnte, aber dafür jedes Mal zuerst auf einen Baum klettern musste? Das, fand Archie, machte so gar keinen Sinn. Wenn schon, denn schon. Einfach nur schnell genug rennen und dann vom Boden abheben ... das wär's doch, dachte Archie.

Viele schnelle Schritte für ihn, ein ganz großer für die Evolution.

Archie verlagerte sein Körpergewicht und ließ sich nach vorne fallen. Ein Baum auch.

Und während Archie, unter dem Baum zerquetscht, sich vom weiteren Verlauf der Geschichte verabschiedet, trommelt Bimsstein auf die Erde, beginnt es zu regnen, immer stärker, immer mehr, und Baum, Archie, Landschaft und der Rest versinken tiefer und tiefer bis auf den Grund eines neuen Meeres, wo sich alles in eine stinkende, schwarze Masse verwandelt. Für Archie war das Jura gelaufen.

Jeder Tropfen Kraftstoff erzählt eine Geschichte.
Darum gehen wir besonders verantwortungsvoll damit um.

BlueTec®. Die sauberste Dieseltechnologie der Welt.
Jetzt in allen Lkw von Mercedes-Benz.

www.mercedes-benz.de/bluetec

Grevenbroicher Tagblatt

Zeitung für Grevenbroich und die Region

Montag, den 02.04.07   Nr. 1, Woche 14, kostenlos

SONDERAUSGABE

LEITARTIKEL

Freunde,
Kannten Sie mich bisher nur als „stellvertretender Chefredakteur", so darf ich Sie und Ihnen in dieser Sonderausgabe das vertrauliche „Herr Chefredakteur" anbieten.

Denn Umstände erfordern offensives Handeln: Ja, ich bin nach wie vor Single. Und das, obwohl ich Führerschein gemacht habe, zur Steigerung meiner Attraktivität. Da die Bekanntmachung dieser Tatsache – bisher nur in Online, Funk und Fernsehen – offensichtlich nicht ausreichend war, muss nun schwarz auf weiß gedruckt werden. Und was könnte Frauenherzen noch zuverlässiger erobern als Führerschein? Beruflicher Aufstieg. Es gilt, Chefredakteur zu werden! Vorliegende Sonderausgabe ist dorthin ein erster Schritt. Und außerdem sicher nicht weniger als ein Meilenstein der Journalistik. Eher mehr, meine ich.

Aber ganz oben ist es einsam. Ich muss alles selbst machen, vom – derzeitigen – Chefredakteur ist Hilfe nicht zu erwarten. Geschweige denn finanziell. Hier muss Reklame die Bresche schlagen:

Diese Sonderausgabe wird Ihnen präsentiert von: **VW**

Mitgemacht hat nur Praktikantin Valerie (da habe ich nämlich auch ein Wörtchen mitzureden, in Sachen Festanstellung).

Sei's drum: Die Zukunft kann – und wird – kommen. Denn, Freunde, gerade wenn man Rücken hat, ist der Sessel des Chefredakteurs auf lange Sicht besser gepolstert. Da wisst ihr Bescheid.

Euer *Horst Schlämmer*

HEUTE IM TAGBLATT:

Innenpolitik 2
Die Große Reportage 3
Kfz-Wesen 4-5
Medien, Kultur & Feuilleton ... 6
Bekanntschaften 7
Horoskop 7
Blick in die Welt 8
Wetter 8

SPRUCH DES TAGES:

Grevenbroich ist zum Parken die schwierigste Stadt in ganz Westdeutschland.

Horst Schlämmer

Horst Schlämmer hat jetzt Führerschein!

Grevenbroicher Prominenter besteht bravourös Fahrprüfung

Glanz und Gloria: Mit dem Erwerb der Fahrerlaubnis vollendet Horst Schlämmer den Weg zur Unwiderstehlichkeit.   Foto: Markus B.

EIGENER BERICHT

Grevenbroich – Ganz Grevenbroich ist in Feierlaune: Einer der beliebtesten Bürger der Stadt – Horst Schlämmer – hat es geschafft, die Fahrerlaubnis zu erlangen.
Und das nach einem Weg, den der stellvertretende Chefredakteur (und alleinverantwortliche Chefredakteur dieser Sonderausgabe) als „steinig, mühsam, aber auch schwer" bezeichnet. So muss dieser Erfolg – ein Ergebnis von Beharrlichkeit, Fleiß und Willenskraft – auch weit über regionale und nationale Grenzen hinaus als positives Aufbruchsignal in allgemein ohnehin eher schwierigen Zeiten gewertet werden. Der Dank des glücklichen Führerschein-Neulings geht an die Fahrschule Hoffmann, den Kfz-Hersteller Volkswagen und nicht zuletzt an Dieter S., den Schwager des Fahrprüfers, der maßgeblich einen erfolgreichen Ausgang der Unternehmung gewährleistete. Horst Schlämmer verspricht sich von seiner neu errungenen Fähigkeit u. a. globalen Aufschwung, Brückenbau im Generationenkonflikt und mehr Erfolg „bei den Hasen".

HINTERGRUND

Warum im besten Alter noch Führerschein machen?

Je mehr Führerschein, desto weniger Single! Das ist statistisch.

Der Golf im Rampenlicht

Beleuchtet von Horst Schlämmer

Der Golf, hier nur als Foto. Mit dem passenden Text erst auf Seite 4.   Foto: Alex R.

Prominente in der Reklame

Hier gilt die Hypothese: Ja oder Nein?

Wolfsburg – Soll und kann eine bekannte Persönlichkeit Reklame machen? Noch dazu im kommerziellen Bereich?
Betrachten wir ein hypothetisches Beispiel: Angenommen ein, möglicherweise im journalistischen Bereich tätiger, Prominenter würde – eventuell – Führerschein machen wollen. Wäre es akzeptant, wenn ein, sagen wir, Kfz-Unternehmen dieses Vorhaben – theoretisch – unterstützen würde?
Ich meine, ich bin doch nicht bescheuert! Wenn die mir das anbieten! Weißte! Da musst du schließlich auch sehen, wo du bleibst, mit 3000 brutto. Schließlich gilt letztendlich zweierlei: Euer Horst muss rollen. Und der Rubel auch. Auch wenn das jetzt Euro heißt.

Horst Schlämmer mit Schlüssel: „Ich bereue nichts!"   Foto: MB

SILVER

TITLE
Volkswagen Zeitung
»Horst Schlämmer
Grevenbroicher Tagblatt«

CLIENT
Volkswagen AG

MARKETING DIRECTOR
Jochen Sengpiehl

ADVERTISING DIRECTOR
Ralf Maltzen, Hartmut Seeger

LEAD AGENCY
DDB Germany, Berlin

CREATIVE DIRECTION
Amir Kassaei, Stefan Schulte,
Bert Peulecke

ART DIRECTION
Kristoffer Heilemann, Tim Schmitt

CLIENT CONSULTING
Cathleen Losch, Silke Lagodny

PHOTOGRAPHY
Markus Bachmann, F.A. Cesar,
Sven Schrader

AGENCY PRODUCER
Peter Stumpe

ART BUYING
Elke Dilchert

GRAPHIC ART
Peter Mayer, Sarah Pöhlmann

TECHNICAL DIRECTION
Sascha Mehn

COPY
Ludwig Berndl, Philip Bolland,
Ulrike Schumann

ADDITIONAL AWARDS
GOLD
Volume Advertising page 186
Verkaufsförderung
Sales promotion

GOLD
Volume Advertising page 221
TV-Spots
Television commercials

GOLD
Volume Advertising page 283
Filme für Verkaufsförderung/
Unternehmensdarstellungen
Films for sales promotion/
company presentation

GOLD
Volume Advertising page 289
Virale Filme
Viral films

GOLD
Volume Advertising page 347
Integrierte Kampagnen
Integrated campaigns

GOLD
Volume Advertising page 367
Dialogmarketing
Dialogue marketing

GOLD
Volume Design page 242
Digitale Werbung
Digital advertising

SILVER
Volume Advertising page 096
Tages-/Wochenzeitungsanzeigen
Advertisements in daily/weekly
newspapers

SILVER
Volume Advertising page 139
Produkt-/Werbebroschüren
Product/advertising brochures

SILVER
Volume Design page 259
Digitale Medien: Viral
Digital media: Viral

BRONZE
Volume Advertising page 152
Text
Copy

BRONZE
Volume Advertising page 326
Funkspots
Radio commercials

NOMINATION
Volume Design page 095
Informationsmedien
Information media

NOMINATION
Volume Design page 235
Websites
Websites

BRONZE

TITLE
MTV Masters Anzeigenkampagne
»MTV Masters macht unsterblich«

CLIENT
MTV Networks GmbH & Co. OHG

MARKETING DIRECTOR
Imke Deigner

ADVERTISING DIRECTOR
Torsten Wolf, Verena Piltz

LEAD AGENCY
BBDO Stuttgart GmbH

CREATIVE DIRECTION
Armin Jochum, Friedrich Tromm

ART DIRECTION
Sven Gareis

CLIENT CONSULTING
Andreas Rauscher,
Caroline Schäufele

ILLUSTRATION
Sven Gareis

AGENCY PRODUCER
Wolfgang Schif

PRODUCTION
Cicero Werkstudio
für Schriftgestaltung

COPY
Georg Baur, Torben Otten

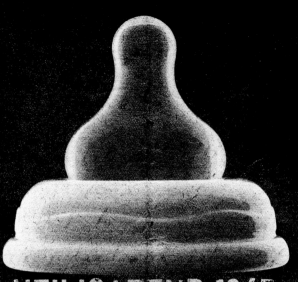

BRONZE

TITLE
Mercedes-Benz S-Klasse Anzeige
»Vordermann«

CLIENT
Daimler AG

MARKETING DIRECTOR
Dr. Olaf Göttgens, Lothar Korn

ADVERTISING DIRECTOR
Mirco Völker, Paula Picareta

LEAD AGENCY
Jung von Matt AG

CREATIVE DIRECTION
Arno Lindemann, Bernhard Lukas

ART DIRECTION
Szymon Rose

CLIENT CONSULTING
Vittal Wagner, Christoph Neuhaus

COPY
Daniel Schäfer

Erst entwickeln wir ein System, das den Abstand zum Vordermann regelt. Und dann ist da keiner.

Die S-Klasse ist Luxus-Limousine des Jahres bei der ams-Leserwahl. Vielen Dank für Ihr Vertrauen.

BRONZE

TITLE
Volkswagen Kampagne
»Horst Schlämmer bloggt«

CLIENT
Volkswagen AG

MARKETING DIRECTOR
Jochen Sengpiehl

ADVERTISING DIRECTOR
Ralf Maltzen, Hartmut Seeger

LEAD AGENCY
DDB Germany, Berlin

CONTRIBUTING AGENCIES
Tribal DDB, Hamburg

CREATIVE DIRECTION
Amir Kassaei, Stefan Schulte,
Bert Peulecke,
Friedrich von Zitzewitz

ART DIRECTION
Thomas Bober, Torben Cording,
Kristoffer Heilemann

CLIENT CONSULTING
Benjamin Reininger,
Niklas Feuerle, Kathrin Lamm,
Mirco Lange, Marc Baumann, Silke
Lagodny, C. Losch

PHOTOGRAPHY
Markus Bachmann, Sven Schrader

ART BUYING
Elke Dilchert

CONSULTING
Künstlervermittlung:
Special Key –
Christian Biedermann,
Sven Zander

ARTIST
Hape Kerkeling

PROGRAMMING
Marc Hitzmann,
Sascha Hertel, Gregory Jacoby,
André Wischnewski

TECHNICAL DIRECTION
Sascha Mehn

COPY
Ludwig Berndl, Jan Hertel,
Angela Gillmann,
Catherina Hauernherm

ADDITIONAL AWARDS

GOLD
Volume Advertising page 186
Verkaufsförderung
Sales promotion

GOLD
Volume Advertising page 221
TV-Spots
Television commercials

GOLD
Volume Advertising page 283
Filme für Verkaufsförderung/
Unternehmensdarstellungen
Films for sales promotion/
company presentation

GOLD
Volume Advertising page 289
Virale Filme
Viral films

GOLD
Volume Advertising page 347
Integrierte Kampagnen
Integrated campaigns

GOLD
Volume Advertising page 367
Dialogmarketing
Dialogue marketing

GOLD
Volume Design page 242
Digitale Werbung
Digital advertising

SILVER
Volume Advertising page 096
Tages-/Wochenzeitungsanzeigen
Advertisements in daily/weekly newspapers

SILVER
Volume Advertising page 139
Produkt-/Werbebroschüren
Product/advertising brochures

SILVER
Volume Advertising page 147
Text
Copy

SILVER
Volume Design page 259
Digitale Medien: Viral
Digital media: Viral

BRONZE
Volume Advertising page 326
Funkspots
Radio commercials

NOMINATION
Volume Design page 095
Informationsmedien
Information media

NOMINATION
Volume Design page 235
Websites
Websites

22. Januar 2007

So, Freunde.
Veröffentlicht in So, Freunde am 22. Januar 2007
122 Kommentare »
Diesen Artikel einem Freund senden »

Ihr wisst, im Horst schlummert ein Tiger. Und der schlummert leider immer noch alleine. Schwer zu glauben, aber wahr: ich bin Single. So wurde eine gründliche, rationäre Ursachenforschung unumstößlich. Ja, da muss man auch mal knallhart bei sich selber nachfragen, keine Frage. Schließlich konnte selbst bei mir ein Mangel sich feststellen: Ich habe keinen Führerschein.
Denn wie immer gilt: je mehr Führerschein, desto weniger Single. Das ist statistisch. Beziehungsweise, wer den richtigen Wagen hat, kriegt auch die richtigen Hasen. Ihr wisst, was ich meine. Man muss seine PS auch auf die Straße bringen.
Ich ende an dieser Stelle mit einem Fazit: Euer Horst macht jetzt Führerschein, und ihr seid dokumental live dabei, in Ton und Bild und Wort. Denn ich habe euch, Freunde, dafür extra das Internet gebloggt. Wisst ihr Bescheid.

Euer Horst Schlämmer

26. Januar 2007

Meine erste Theoriestunde
Veröffentlicht in Fahrschulfilme am 26. Januar 2007
77 Kommentare »
Diesen Artikel einem Freund senden »

Freunde,

selbst Konfuzius weiß: Auch der längste Weg ist steinig. Ich hingegen habe den ersten Schritt vollbracht und in der Fahrschule knallhart nachgefragt. Ihr glaubt nicht, was ein Führerschein heutzutage kostet! Das ist eine Unverfrorenheit. Ich ziehe das dennoch durch, die Entscheidung steht. Und zwar nicht zur Debatte. Wer Erfolg haben will, auch bei den Damen, muss schließlich tief in die Tasche investieren.
Aber macht euch nichts vor, so eine Theoriestunde ist tendentiös langweilig. An den Mitschülerinnen hat es nicht gelegen, das waren alles lecker Hasen. Und wie die ihre hübschen Öhrchen spitzen, wenn der Fahrlehrer etwas sagt. Das muss ein besonders erfüllender Beruf sein. Vielleicht werde ich nicht Fahrschüler, sondern Fahrlehrer. Aber selbst dafür braucht man Führerschein, meine ich. So gesehen gehe ich morgen wieder hin. Von nichts kommt nichts. Wisst Ihr Bescheid.

Euer Horst

31. Januar 2007

Ich fahre!
Veröffentlicht in Fahrschulfilme am 31. Januar 2007
82 Kommentare »
Diesen Artikel einem Freund senden »

Freunde,

mir geht immer noch die Pumpe, ihr glaubt es nicht. Das erste Mal hinterm Steuer. Die Autofahrer unter Euch wissen, was man da durchmacht: eine Odyssee. Man wird ja rein geschmissen wie ein Fisch ins Wasser. Aber ich kann auch sagen: ich bin begabt! Das Fahren war für mich keinerlei Problematik. Die Prüfung entpuppt sich da mehr und mehr als Formalie, meine ich. Dann kann es ja doch nicht so teuer werden.
Jetzt brauche ich also nur noch einen Wagen, da führt kein Weg zurück. Morgen fange ich an zu suchen. Was würde euch – so als Frau – denn beeindrucken?

Apropos: beeindrucken. Ab sofort könnt ihr meine Filme bevoten. Damit ich weiß, welche euch am besten gefallen. Das ist statistisch.

Euer Horst

7. Februar 2007
Knallhart angehalten
Veröffentlicht in Fahrschulfilme am 7. Februar 2007
53 Kommentare »
Diesen Artikel einem Freund senden »

Freunde,

ich habe Füße. Mit laufen ist da auf die Dauer nix mehr. Anhalter ist eine Alternative, aber die Zeiten sind – wie überall – hart. Die Leute fahren Autos, das ist eine Zumutung, möchte ich sagen. Da muss man wie ein alter Haudegen an der Ampel sondieren können, denn es gilt auch hier: wie man fährt, so kommt man an. Ich habe Rücken, ich steige nicht in jedes Auto. Ja, auch als Schnorrer muss man einen gewissen Standard setzen.

Aber ich wiederhole es noch mal: ich habe Füße. Da kann ich bewiesenermaßen nicht immer warten, bis die richtige Fahrgelegenheit kommt. Diesbezüglich lässt sich also ein eindeutiges Dilemma registrieren: ich brauche den Führerschein, Freunde! So schwer es auch sein mag, aufgeben ist keine Devise.

Euer Horst

9. Februar 2007
Ich fahre wieder
Veröffentlicht in Fahrschulfilme am 9. Februar 2007
42 Kommentare »
Diesen Artikel einem Freund senden »

Freunde,

Aufgeben, das sagte ich bereits, ist keine Devise. Der Lappen muss her! Ich habe also den Stier bei den Hufen gepackt. Ein Mann, ein Wort – ich war sofort wieder bei der Fahrstunde.
Und es ist doch gar nicht schwer, man muss sich nur eines merken: links und Gas und weniger. Mit Gas fährt so ein Auto praktisch von alleine.
Man soll jedoch beim Fahren nach vorne sehen. Denn Gefahr, Freunde, ist immer im Vollzug, auch mittig auf der Strasse. Ich meine hier – ganz offen – beispielsweise Fußgängerinnen, die die Straße nicht sachgerecht nutzen.
Mein Fahrlehrer hingegen, der Markus, hat mir schon wieder oft ins Lenkrad gefasst. Und das mehrmals. Ich weiß nicht, was es für ein Ende nehmen soll, mit uns beiden. Freunde, ich weiß es wirklich nicht. Man darf sich schließlich weder ein X noch ein U vormachen lassen.

Euer Horst

20. Februar 2007
Klarstellung betr. Volkswagen
Veröffentlicht in Knallhart getestet am 20. Februar 2007
117 Kommentare »
Diesen Artikel einem Freund senden »

Freunde,

Es sind Vermutungen aufgetaucht! Ja, es wird geradezu diskutiert, ob mir jemand den Führerschein bezahlt hat. Ich muss sagen, es bleibt euch nichts verborgen, ihr seid nicht vom Kopf gefallen. Von meiner Person her war Diskretion bisher die Zierde der Könige. Doch jetzt wird eine Position erforderlich, auch öffentlich. Damit Ihr, Freunde, es als erste erfahrt.

Also passt auf: Die Situation ist ernst – ich brauche Führerschein. Aber mit einem Brutto-Gehalt muss man sehen, wo man bleibt. Die Lösung heißt: Jeder Tunnel hat ein Licht. Besonders in der Öffentlichkeit. Ich bin stellvertretender Chefredakteur und deutschlandweit Grevenbroicher Prominenter. Daher finden mich wirtschaftliche Kreise interessant am Punkto Öffentlichkeitsarbeit. Das wurde von einem Ergebnis gekrönt: Volkswagen übernimmt faktisch meinen Führerschein. Und sorgt auch dafür, dass Ihr, Freunde, dokumental live dabei sein könnt. Das schaffe ich doch nicht alleine!

Schließlich gilt letztendlich zweierlei: euer Horst muss rollen. Und der Rubel auch. Auch wenn das jetzt Euro heißt.

Da wisst Ihr Bescheid.

Euer Horst

P.S.:

Zum Beweis ist hier ein Film dokumentiert, der einwandfrei zeigt: ich mache trotzdem meinen Job. Es wird weiterhin knallhart nachgefragt!

1. März 2007
Drückt mir den Daumen
Veröffentlicht in So, Freunde am 1. März 2007
40 Kommentare »
Diesen Artikel einem Freund senden »

Freunde,

mir geht die Pumpe, schon vom Gemüt her. Morgen ist der Tag, mit dem zu rechnen war! Morgen wird alles sich entscheiden: Wohl oder Wehe, Glanz oder Gloria, oder sogar noch mehr. Denn morgen mache ich Fahrprüfung! Ja, es lässt sich nicht länger aufschieben. Ich habe Blutdruck, ich habe Kreislauf, ich habe Rücken und selbst im Steiß, meine ich, hat ein Unwohlsein vermehrt zugenommen.
Schon jetzt aber ziehe ich bereits folgende Prognose: ich muss bestehen. Als Grevenbroicher Prominenter und stellvertretender Chefredakteur ist ein Ruf schließlich gerecht zu werden.
Die Vorbereitungen für einen erfolgreichen Abschluss laufen auf höchsten Touren, Valerie ist bezüglich dessen schon mit Spezialaufgaben vertraut. Ich harre auf morgen, denn: Vor Gott und vor dem Fahrprüfer sind alle Menschen gleich.

Euer Horst

2. März 2007
Prüfung!
Veröffentlicht in Fahrschulfilme am 2. März 2007
68 Kommentare »
Diesen Artikel einem Freund senden »

Freunde,

Mir geht immer noch die Pumpe.

Euer Horst

4. März 2007
Führerschein
Veröffentlicht in So, Freunde am 4. März 2007
57 Kommentare »
Diesen Artikel einem Freund senden »

Da isser! Ich hab immer noch einen dicken Kopp, Freunde.

14. März 2007
Willkommen zum Abschied
Veröffentlicht in So, Freunde am 14. März 2007
180 Kommentare »
Diesen Artikel einem Freund senden »

Freunde,

Ich weiß gar nicht, wie ich es sagen soll. Vielleicht so: Es ist vorbei, darüber führt kein Weg hinweg. Ich habe endgültig Führerschein und muss mich nun – und das hauptsächlich vermehrt – anderen Dingen widmen. Der Ruf des Weibes ist beispielhaft zu nennen. Doch jeder Abschied verinnerlicht auch einen Anfang: Ich werde zwar an dieser Stelle keine Führerscheinberichte mehr haben, jedoch eine neue Homepage mit radikal unbekanntem Material! Und zwar morgen oder sogar schon übermorgen. Dort steht ein dokumentaler Charakter meiner Erlebnisse übersichtlich im Mittelgrund.

Freunde, ich sage euch: Mir ist das Herz schwer! Und das Gemüt auch. Und in den Ohren werden mir noch lange viele Namen klingeln wie Musik (manche auch ein bisschen komisch, meine ich): Tante Alma, Cecile, kroetengruen, volksvan-de, Kleinbea, Cassarah, downtempo, Rapido, Netty, Meany, Lady D, tumirmalzweiteilchen, Erdge Schoss, Chefredakteur, horst schlaemmert, Onkel Hotte, Tomo Graf Kernspin, Freddy01... Nein, so geht es nicht! Ich meine, ich tippe mir jetzt hier einen Wolf, weißte, und dann kommt am Ende noch jemand um die Ecke und beschwert sich, dass er nicht dabei ist. Ich bin ja nicht bescheuert!

Es ist doch so: Ich habe Euch allen zu danken für die Unterstützung. Und ich habe Euch alle im Herzen. Immer.

Euer Horst

P.S.:

Hier ist weiter geöffnet für Eure Meinung. Was meint Ihr? Ich meine: Ihr braucht auch

BRONZE

TITLE
Zettl Katalog »Part:two«

CLIENT
Zettl GmbH

MARKETING DIRECTOR
Brigitta Zettl

LEAD AGENCY
Rosa Haider

ART DIRECTION
Sigi Mayer

CLIENT CONSULTING
Rosa Haider

GRAPHIC ART
Sigi Mayer

CONCEPT
Rosa Haider, Sigi Mayer

COPY
Rosa Haider

Der Friede hat seinen Preis

Eines musst du wissen.

Wenn es eine Art Friedensnobelpreis für den kleinen Mann gäbe, wäre die Brigitta Zettl ganz vorn dabei. Weil

„Alles Große beginnt im Kleinen"

hat schon für so manches Poesiealbum herhalten müssen.

Und nicht von ungefähr.

Was die Brigitta Zettl schon Leuten für eine Freude gemacht hat. Indirekt natürlich. Weil Absender immer wer anders. Keinen Geburtstag vergessen. Nie das Paket zu spät angekommen. Immer genau das Richtige zum richtigen Zeitpunkt, und, und, und.

Jetzt, wenn es diesen Zettl Katalog nicht gäbe, wüsste doch kein Mensch nie nicht, was er dem anderen schon wieder schenken soll.

Geburtstag, was schenken.

Gold Medaille gewonnen, wie gratulieren.

Hochzeit,

Baby da,

geschweige denn Weihnachten da.

Kommt wie das Amen im Gebet.
Und immer dann, wenn man selber Null Zeit hat. Und zu Weihnachten sind die Leute eh immer ein bisschen dings. Und sind weiß Gott wie beleidigt, wenn sie wieder leer ausgehen.

Ist ja auch eine Schweinerei.

Wenn man unterm Weihnachtsbaum steht und rein gar nichts heuer. Kein Zettl Lachs, keine Wenschitz Trüffel, kein Lubinger Engel, kein Fuzerl Kaviar, kein Drappier Champagner, kein gar nichts. Aber, halt. Ein winziges Zettl Kisterl. Und er, blind vor Enttäuschung wieder fast nicht gesehen. Da haben wir es. Ein Lachsgutschein von Brigitta Zettl. Und jetzt er schon wieder blind, weil Freudentränen.

Wenn man unterm Weihnachtsbaum steht und rein gar nichts heuer.

Kein Zettl Lachs,

keine Wenschitz Trüffel,

kein Lubinger Engel,

kein Fuzerl Kaviar,

kein Drappier Champagner,

kein gar nichts.

Aber, halt.

Ein winziges Zettl Kisterl. Und er, blind vor Enttäuschung wieder fast nicht gesehen. Da haben wir es.

Ein Lachsgutschein von Brigitta Zettl. Und jetzt er schon wieder blind, weil Freudentränen.

Die Entscheidungshilfe

Immer wenn du glaubst, es geht nicht mehr

Kommt von irgendwo eine Zettl Kiste her

Du machst sie auf, du schaust hinein

Für mich, von wem, das kann nicht sein

Ich war mein Lebtag nur gemein

Und trotzdem Speck, Pâté und Wein

Das muss ein kolossaler Irrtum sein

Aha, von einem gewissen Soundso

den kenn ich doch von irgendwo

Jetzt schickt mir der die ganzen Sachen

Dann muss ich wohl mit dem das machen

Aber danke sag ich sicher nicht

Weil auf Bestechung reagier ich nicht.

Aus dem Poesiealbum eines potentiellen Auftraggebers

Feuerholz

Feuerholz
Holzkassette 17x17x7cm

Weihnachtskaffee 100 g · Eigenröstung
alter Apfelbrand 100 ml in Flachmann ·
Schiefermüller
Haselnuss-Gianduja-Konfekt 5 Stück ·
X-MAS · Maître chocolatier Wenschitz
Best.Nr. 0713 / € 18,00

Lebemann

Lebemann
Holzkassette 17x17x7cm

Lebkuchen Krampus ·
Maître chocolatier Wenschitz
Whisky 100 ml in Flachmann
Anisterne
Best.Nr.0714 / € 13,00

Sparziel

Sparziel
Holzkassette 36x18x10cm

Keramik Teedose · Ass
handgeschöpfte Schokolade 70 g ·
Schokoladenmanufaktur Zotter
Trinkschokolade am Stiel 2 Stück ·
Maître Chocolatier Wenschitz
Lebkuchen Engel · Lebzelter Lubinger
Espressokaffee 250 g Eigenröstung
Best. Nr. 0715 / € 25,00

Globalisierungs-befürworter

Jetzt noch ein Wort zum Vinobles Arbeau Rosé Pecquer.
Ausgerechnet
(das war das Wort).
Du musst wissen, dieser Rosé aus Südfrankreich wird bei sehr niedriger Temperatur vinifiziert, sprich saukalt. Und, fragen Sie nicht warum, aber es wirkt sich irgendwie positiv auf sein Aroma aus. Er duftet nach Kirsch, Himbeeren und Frühlingsblumen, und, und, und. Jetzt eignet sich dieser ausgezeichnete Rosé ausgerechnet als Aperitif oder von mir aus zu Salaten und Vorspeisen. Ausgerechnet sag ich deshalb, weil er ist ziemlich schnell aus, damit muss man rechnen.

Globalisierungsbefürworter
Holzkassette 60x20x13 cm

Merlot Candle · Kerze mit Aroma · Napa Valley
Kürbiskernrohwurst ca. 350 g · Pfeifer
Preiselbeer mit rosa Pfeffer 212 ml · Trauners Genusswerkstatt
Baukrut eingelegt 210 ml · Monger Indonesia 125 g · Cafés Knopes
Preparation à base de vinagre et de pulpe de figue 200 ml ·
A l'Olivier · Feigenessig
Preiselbeerschmalz 200 ml · Haudum
Olives noires de Nice 370 g · A l'Olivier
handgemachtes Veilchenkonfekt 5 Stück ·
Maître Chocolatier Wenschitz
Rosé Pecquer 0,75 l · Vinobles Arbeau
Best.Nr. 0776 / € 87,00

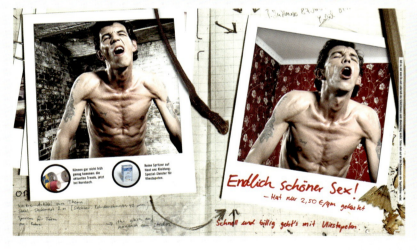

NOMINATION

TITLE
Hornbach Baumarkt Broschüre
»Women at Work«

CLIENT
Hornbach Baumarkt AG

MARKETING DIRECTOR
Jürgen Schröcker

ADVERTISING DIRECTOR
Diana Koob

LEAD AGENCY
HEIMAT, Berlin

CREATIVE DIRECTION
Guido Heffels, Jürgen Vossen

ART DIRECTION
Danny Baarz

CLIENT CONSULTING
Yves Krämer

PHOTOGRAPHY
Christoph York Riccius

ILLUSTRATION
Ulrich Scheer

ART BUYING
Marjorie Jorrot

CONSULTING
Mark Hassan, Sammy Bohneberg

GRAPHIC ART
Jenny Kapteyn

PRODUCTION
Carola Storto

COPY
Matthias Storath,
Siyamak Seyedasgari

ADDITIONAL AWARDS
BRONZE
Volume Advertising page 029
Publikumsanzeigen
Consumer advertisements

NOMINATION

TITLE
Du bist Deutschland
Anzeigenkampagne »Eine Initiative
für mehr Kinderfreundlichkeit«

CLIENT
Du bist Deutschland GmbH

MARKETING DIRECTOR
Bernd Bauer

ADVERTISING DIRECTOR
Helge Hoffmeister

LEAD AGENCY
Jung von Matt AG,
kempertrautmann gmbh

CREATIVE DIRECTION
Oliver Voss (JvM)

ART DIRECTION
Till Monshausen (JvM)

CLIENT CONSULTING
Michael Trautmann (kt),
Andrea Bison (kt),
Franziska von Papen (kt),
Tobias Mölder (kt)

PHOTOGRAPHY
Timm Brockfeld, Julia Baier,
Alexander Frank

ART BUYING
Anne Weskamp (JvM)

CONSULTING
Julia Krömker (JvM),
Jan Rütten (JvM)

GRAPHIC ART
Daniel Haschtmann (JvM)

POSTPRODUCTION
Malte Rehde (JvM), Ulla Bayer (JvM)

PRODUCTION
Birgit Weber (JvM)

COPY
Jo Marie Farwick (JvM),
Robert Müller (JvM),
Ramin Schmiedekampf (JvM),
Philipp Jessen (JvM),
Willy Kaussen (JvM)

FINAL ARTWORK
Marion Beeck (JvM),
Madlen Domann (JvM)

ADDITIONAL AWARDS NOMINATION
Volume Advertising page 059
Publikumsanzeigen
Consumer advertisements

NOMINATION
Volume Advertising page 243
TV-Spots
Television commercials

NOMINATION

TITLE
Tages-Anzeiger »Was, wenn...«

CLIENT
Tamedia AG, Verlag Tages-Anzeiger

MARKETING DIRECTOR
Dominique von Albertini

LEAD AGENCY
Spillmann/Felser/Leo Burnett

CREATIVE DIRECTION
Martin Spillmann/Peter Brönnimann

ART DIRECTION
Katja Puccio

CLIENT CONSULTING
Simone Saner/Andy Stäheli

COPY
Maren Beck/Peter Brönnimann/
Cyrill Wirz/Patrick Suter/
Martin Arnold/Diana Rossi

Was, wenn das Bienensterben in den USA weitergeht? Wird der FCZ dann nicht Meister?

Was, wenn die Bienenvölker in den USA weiterhin in Massen sterben? Werden dann viel weniger Obstbäume bestäubt? Und entsprechend viel weniger Äpfel, Birnen, Pflaumen, Pfirsiche und Aprikosen geerntet? Steigen in den USA die Preise für Früchte massiv an? Wird Obst zum Luxus? Schlucken die Amerikaner plötzlich nur noch Vitaminpräparate? Kauft Roche dann die vor 5 Jahren an DSM verkaufte Vitaminsparte wieder zurück? Steigt deswegen der Roche-Gewinn sprunghaft an? Wird mehr Dividende an die Aktionäre ausgeschüttet? Auch an die Roche-Erbin Gigi Oeri? Schiesst sie mehr Geld ins Spielerkader des FC Basel ein? Hat der FCB plötzlich die Mittel, um Lionel Messi von Barcelona zu übernehmen? Und gleich auch noch Schewtschenko von Chelsea? Gewinnt der FCB fortan alle Super-League-Spiele? Wird der FCZ dann nicht Meister? **Dranbleiben. Tages-Anzeiger**

Was, wenn Kate Moss schwanger wird? Fehlt dann dem FC Bayern der Nachwuchs?

Was, wenn Kate Moss schwanger wird? Wird sie dann immer noch als Model gebucht? Sogar noch öfter? Bleibt sie auch als Schwangere eine Stilikone? Setzt sie damit sogar einen neuen Trend? Wollen mehr und mehr modebewusste Frauen einen Kugelbauch? Gibts einen weltweiten Schwangerschafts-Boom? Steigt dadurch die Nachfrage nach sauren Gurken massiv? Muss deshalb das grösste europäische Anbaugebiet in Niederbayern ausgeweitet werden? Auf ganz Bayern? Bepflanzt man jeden Zentimeter Grün mit Gurken? Sogar die Fussballfelder? Können die bayerischen Buben deshalb nicht mehr Fussball spielen? Fehlt dem FC Bayern dann der Nachwuchs? **Dranbleiben. Tages-Anzeiger**

Was, wenn die Stadt Zürich die Steuern senkt? Steigt dann in China die Zahl der Analphabeten?

Was, wenn die Stadt Zürich die Steuern senkt? Werden die Stadtbewohner plötzlich viel konsumfreudiger? Verbringen sie jede freie Minute in den Einkaufsstrassen? Verfallen immer mehr Zürcher dem Kaufrausch? Sind die Regale in den Geschäften der Bahnhofstrasse und von Sihlcity plötzlich leer? Brauchen die Kaufhäuser mehr Nachschub? Sind die Bestellungen der Warenhäuser gross? Kann man gar sagen, riesig? Müssen die verschiedenen Hersteller mehr Leute einstellen? Betrifft das vor allem China? Brechen dann noch mehr junge Chinesen ihre Schulausbildung vorzeitig ab, um in diesen Firmen zu arbeiten? Lernen sie weder richtig lesen noch schreiben? Gibt es dann in China bald noch mehr als 116 Millionen Analphabeten? **Dranbleiben. Tages-Anzeiger**

Was, wenn die Millionensaläre der Topmanager weiter steigen? Sterben dann die Schweinsohren aus?

Was, wenn Schweizer Topmanager immer astronomischere Summen verdienen? Nimmt dann die Kritik an den Millionensalären weiter zu? Protestieren plötzlich auch Inhaber von grossen Aktienpaketen? Stimmen Pensionskassen und ihre Stiftungen gegen die Empfehlungen der Firmenverantwortlichen? Reklamiert das Volk und ruft zum Boykott von Produkten auf? Leidet das Image der Unternehmen? So sehr, dass die Verwaltungsräte Massnahmen ergreifen müssen? Entlassen sie ihre teuren Chefs und stellen chinesische Billig-CEO's ein? Umgeben sich diese wiederum mit Kaderleuten aus China? Gehen diese an den Wochenenden auf Pilzsuche in den Schweizer Wäldern? Reissen sie sich um den von ihnen geliebten Gomphus Clavatus? Sterben dann die auch als Schweinsohren bekannten Pilze aus? **Dranbleiben. Tages-Anzeiger**

Was, wenn sich das Klima weiter erwärmt? Sinken dann die Krankenkassenprämien?

Was, wenn sich das Klima weiter erwärmt? Können die Bauern in den höheren Regionen dann dreimal pro Jahr heuen? Werden deshalb ihre Kühe dicker? Und geben viel mehr Milch? Gibt es erneut eine Milchschwemme in der Schweiz? Wird man, um diese einzudämmen, die Pausenmilch in den Schulen wieder einführen? Bekommen unsere Kinder dann stärkere Knochen? Gibt es viel weniger Knochenbrüche? Sinken dann die Krankenkassenprämien? **Dranbleiben. Tages-Anzeiger**

NOMINATION

TITLE
DMAX Anzeigenkampagne
»Fernsehen für die tollsten
Menschen der Welt: Männer«

CLIENT
DMAX TV GmbH & Co. KG

MARKETING DIRECTOR
Andreas Dürr

ADVERTISING DIRECTOR
Kathrin Pawelski

LEAD AGENCY
Jung von Matt AG

CREATIVE DIRECTION
Oliver Voss, Götz Ulmer,
Fabian Frese, Daniel Frericks

ART DIRECTION
Jens Paul Pfau

CLIENT CONSULTING
Karoline Huber, Jürgen Alker

COPY
Tobias Grimm, Henning Robert,
Jan-Florian Ege, Jo Marie Farwick

ADDITIONAL AWARDS
BRONZE
Volume Advertising page 041
Publikumsanzeigen
Consumer advertisements

NOMINATION

TITLE
Doppelherz Anzeigenkampagne
»Die Gedicht-Kampagne«

CLIENT
Queisser Pharma GmbH & Co. KG

MARKETING DIRECTOR
Jan K. Kuskowski

ADVERTISING DIRECTOR
Jürgen Hennings

LEAD AGENCY
Scholz & Friends

CREATIVE DIRECTION
Christian Vosshagen,
Stefanie Zimmermann,
Matthias Schmidt, Stefan Setzkorn

ART DIRECTION
Leif Joneck

CLIENT CONSULTING
Raphael Brinkert,
Angela Hissen-Laux,
Sabine Hiersemann

COPY
Simon Urban

Vom Fett

Ich wär so gerne der, der einst den Schmand erfand.
Und hoffe, dass ich mal auf Feta throne.
Und dass mir aller Rahm gehört, im ganzen Land.
Und ich in einem Haus aus Mascarpone wohne.

Und meine Badewanne soll voll Sahne sein.
Ich fülle sie aus tausend kleinen Flaschen.
Und Mozzarella kauend steige ich hinein,
um mir das Haar mit Parmesan zu waschen.

Und in Crème double leg ich mich zur Ruh.
Und träum von meinem Butterberg bei Bremen.
Und bin mir sicher, ich nehm niemals zu.
Und bitte nur, mir das auch abzunehmen.

Reimt sich nicht, hilft aber:

Doppelherz Artischocke.
Fördert die Fettverdauung.

Amouröse Amnesie

Ach, meine Liebe, sag mir doch
mal eben schnell: Wie heißt du noch?
Und wie war das mit unsern Söhnen –
gehn die zur Uni? Oder dröhnen
auch weiter Funk und Soul durchs Haus?
Ach so: Und wie sieht unser Haus gleich aus ...?
Und: Wer ist dieser junge Mann,
mit dem du neulich in Pjöngjang
gewesen bist? Und in Katar?
Ich weiß: Du heißt Veronika ...!
Nee, doch nicht ... Was wollt ich grad sagen ...
... dass wir auf unsrer Fahrt nach Hagen ...
... oder dass die Zucchini-Preise ...
... oder dass ich neulich Paul Heyse ...
... egal. Ach – bring doch Entrecôte
vom Metzger mit. Zum Abendbrot.
Vergiss das nicht! Schön zart! Nicht zäh!
Also, bis nachher dann!

Dein ... äh ...

Reimt sich nicht, hilft aber:

Doppelherz Lecithin.
Stärkt das Gedächtnis.

Papa muss Pipi

Es pinkelt sich so gut auf der Akropolis.
(Ich weiß, für Klassikfans ist das zum Heulen.
Und überall die Hinweisschilder: Please don't piss!)
Jedoch, ich musste – und es gab so viele Säulen ...

Ich kann auch die verbot'ne Stadt empfehlen.
Sehr schön verwinkelt, voller Gassen, Kanten, Ecken.
Es muss nur schnell gehn, das will ich nicht verhehlen –
dieses Kung-Fu gibt ziemlich blaue Flecken.

Im Petersdom rat ich zu der Empore.
Im Taj Mahal kann man sich auf das Dach bequemen.
Die Zeche Zollverein hat eine Rettungslore.
Im Weißen Haus würde ich die Toilette nehmen.

Der Eiffelturm, das ist ein harter Brocken:
an jeder Ecke Vater, Mutter, Kind.
Man kann sich höchstens ans Geländer hocken.
Doch, bitte: Achten Sie auf Gegenwind!

Reimt sich nicht, hilft aber:

Doppelherz Kürbiskern-Kapseln.
Stärken die Blase und vermindern den Harndrang.

NOMINATION

TITLE
Konzerthaus Dortmund –
Konzertreihe Symphonie um Vier
Anzeigenkampagne »Partituren«

CLIENT
Konzerthaus Dortmund –
Philharmonie für Westfalen

MARKETING DIRECTOR
Milena Ivkovic

LEAD AGENCY
Jung von Matt AG

CREATIVE DIRECTION
Sascha Hanke, Timm Hanebeck,
Wolf Heumann (GF)

ART DIRECTION
Patrik Hartmann

CLIENT CONSULTING
Nina Gerwing, Lena Frers

GRAPHIC ART
Kristian Joshi, Nadya Innamorato,
William Ahrend

COPY
Michael Okun

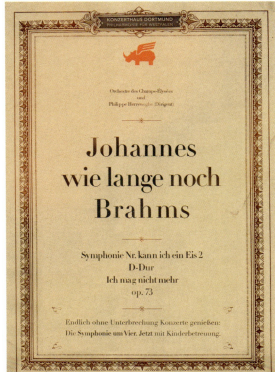
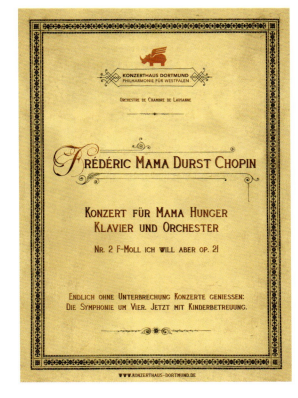

NOMINATION

TITLE
Festspielhaus Baden-Baden Anzeige
»Lang Lang in Baden-Baden«

CLIENT
Festspielhaus und
Festspiele Baden-Baden gGmbH

MARKETING DIRECTOR
Michael Drautz

ADVERTISING DIRECTOR
Ulrike Siebert

LEAD AGENCY
Scholz & Friends

CREATIVE DIRECTION
Joerg Jahn, Michael Winterhagen

ART DIRECTION
Marc Ebenwaldner

CLIENT CONSULTING
Michael Jaeger, Mandy Tschöpe

IMAGE EDITING
Appel Grafik Berlin

GRAPHIC ART
Walter Ziegler

COPY
Alexander Schierl, Alescha Lechner

NOMINATION

TITLE
IWC Anzeigen »Kampagne 2007«

CLIENT
IWC International Watch Co. AG

MARKETING DIRECTOR
Fabian Herdieckerhoff

ADVERTISING DIRECTOR
Jacqueline Rose, Daniel Rohrer

LEAD AGENCY
Jung von Matt AG

CREATIVE DIRECTION
Daniel Frericks, Oliver Voss

ART DIRECTION
Christian Kroll, Jens Paul Pfau

CLIENT CONSULTING
Karoline Huber, Turan Tehrani

ART BUYING
Karen Blome

GRAPHIC ART
Tobias Fritschen, Lukas Hueter,
Anja von Harsdorf,
Maximilian Rieder

COPY
Philipp Barth, Jo Marie Farwick,
Peter Gocht, Tobias Grimm,
Caroline Schubiger, Henning Robert,
Samuel Wicki, Stefan Grahl

ADDITIONAL AWARDS
NOMINATION
Volume Advertising page 052
Publikumsanzeigen
Consumer advertisements

Wenn diese Uhr einmal von den Bordinstrumenten abweicht, kaufen Sie sich ein neues Flugzeug.

Mit dieser Uhr können Sie die Kochzeit von zwei verschiedenen Frühstückseiern stoppen. Und das direkt im Topf.

COCO CHANEL

*19. AUGUST 1883 SAUMUR †10. JANUAR 1971 PARIS

*19 AUGUST 1883 SAUMUR †10 JANUARY 1971 PARIS

Ihr Weg beginnt ganz unten. Unehelich geboren, kam sie als Elfjährige nach dem Tod ihrer Mutter in ein katholisches Waisenhaus. Sie lernte dort Näherin. Doch danach ging es nur noch steil nach oben. Bereits als Angestellte in einem Babyartikelgeschäft nahm sie privat Schneideraufträge an. Nebenbei trat sie als Chanson-Sängerin im »Rotonde« auf. Dort angelte sie sich auch Etienne Balsan, der sie in die vornehme Pariser Gesellschaft einführte. Mit diesen neugewonnenen Kontakten eröffnete sie als erstes ein Hutgeschäft. Dann ging es Schlag auf Schlag. Bald besaß sie mehrere Modehäuser in Paris und Biarritz. Aber sie war nicht nur eine famos erfolgreiche Unternehmerin, sondern hat auch die Frauenmode revolutioniert. Mit Klarheit und Eleganz befreite sie die Frauen von Korsett und Plüsch. Das kleine Schwarze, Hosenanzüge, synthetische Düfte und vieles mehr sind ihre Erfindung.

Coco Chanel began all the way at the bottom. Born out of wedlock, she was sent to a Catholic orphanage at the age of 11 following the death of her mother. There, she trained as a seamstress. Following this, however, her ascent was meteoric. She worked in a baby clothing shop, but was already taking on private dressmaking commissions. Meanwhile, she was also appearing as a singer of chansons at *La Rotonde*. It was here, too, that she hooked and reeled in Etienne Balsan, who introduced her into Parisian high society. Using these new-found contacts, she started by opening a millinery shop. After that, things began happening fast, and soon she owned several fashion boutiques in Paris und Biarritz. But she was more than a fabulously successful businesswoman. She revolutionised women's fashion, liberating her customers from corsets and plush through lucid, elegant design. Her inventions included the little black dress, the trouser suit, synthetic perfumes and much more.

The most courageous act is still to think for yourself. Aloud.

DIE MUTIGSTE TAT IST IMMER NOCH DIE, SELBSTSTÄNDIG ZU DENKEN. UND ZWAR LAUT.

FILME DIESER KATEGORIE FINDEN SIE UNTER WWW.ADC.DE FOR FILMS FROM THIS CATEGORY VISIT WWW.ADC.DE

GLOBAL WARMING WILL NOT ONLY MELT AWAY THE ICE. ACT NOW.

GREENPEACE

GOLD

Am 18. August posierten hunderte Männer und Frauen nackt auf dem Aletschgletscher. Mit dieser »lebenden Skulptur« brachten der US-Künstler Spencer Tunick und die Agentur die Verletzlichkeit des schwindenden Gletschers symbolisch mit uns Menschen in Verbindung und wiesen auf die Gefahren des Klimawandels für uns alle hin. Die Promotion löste weltweit eine immense Medienreaktion aus.

On August 18, 2007 hundreds of men and women posed naked on Switzerland's Aletsch Glacier to foster awareness for the need to protect the climate. With this "living sculpture", US installation artist Spencer Tunick and the agency created a symbolic link between the fragility of the receding glacier and that of human beings. The promotion caused an enormous echo in the media through- out the world.

TITLE
Greenpeace »Gletscherskulptur«

CLIENT
Greenpeace

MARKETING DIRECTOR
Markus Allemann

LEAD AGENCY
Euro RSCG Zürich

CREATIVE DIRECTION
Frank Bodin, Jürg Aemmer, Claude Catsky

ART DIRECTION
Charles Blunier

CLIENT CONSULTING
Sebastian Zeuner

STRATEGIC PLANNING
Peter Schäfer

GRAPHIC ART
Régine Cavicchioli, Barney Rees

ARTIST
Spencer Tunick

FILME DIESER KATEGORIE FINDEN SIE UNTER WWW.ADC.DE FOR FILMS FROM THIS CATEGORY VISIT WWW.ADC.DE

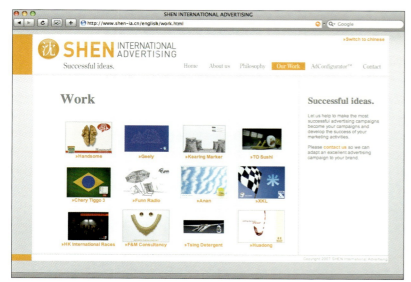
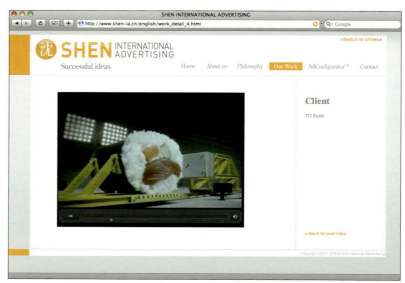
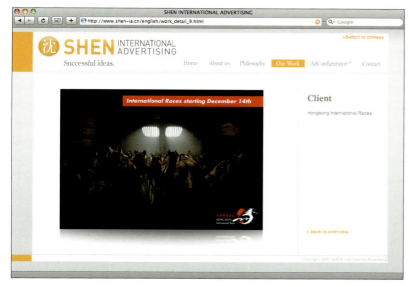
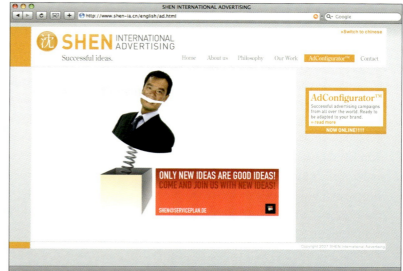

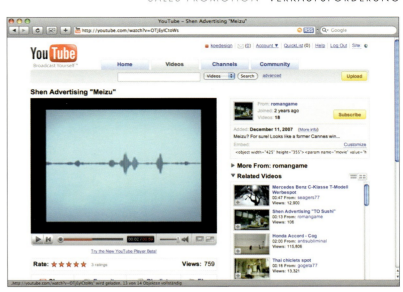
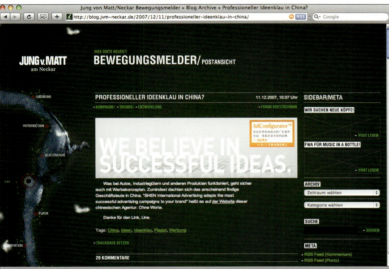

SILVER

Um die Aufmerksamkeit kreativer Köpfe zu bekommen haben wir die fiktive Chinesische Agentur »Shen International Advertising« (www.shen-ia.cn) gegründet. Sie stiehlt bekannte Kampagnen für ihre Kunden. Das Ergebnis: Shen löste große Empörung in der Werbewelt aus. Dann kam die Auflösung: »Nur neue Ideen sind gute Ideen. Bewirb dich mit deinen Ideen bei Serviceplan.«

To catch creatives' attention, we "founded" the fiktive Chinese agency "Shen International Advertising" (www.shenia.cn), which steels famous campaigns for their clients. Result: Shen became talk-of-the-town in the online advertising community. At the peak of excitement, we announced our real intention: "Only new ideas are good ideas. Come and join Serviceplan with yours."

TITLE
Serviceplan Hamburg
»Shen International Advertising«

CLIENT
Serviceplan Hamburg

MARKETING DIRECTOR
Alexander Schill

LEAD AGENCY
Serviceplan München/Hamburg

CONTRIBUTING AGENCIES
Plan.Net

CREATIVE DIRECTION
Alexander Schill, Axel Thomsen, Maik Kähler, Christoph Nann, Friedrich v. Zitzewitz, Daniel Könnecke

ART DIRECTION
Till Diestel

PROGRAMMING
Arne Kanese, André Wischnewski

SCREEN DESIGN
Dennis Fritz

COPY
Marietta Mandt-Merck, Frances Rohde

ADDITIONAL AWARDS
BRONZE
Volume Advertising page 381
Dialogmarketing
Dialogue marketing

NOMINATION
Volume Design page 257
Digitale Medien: Viral
Digital media: Viral

FILME DIESER KATEGORIE FINDEN SIE UNTER WWW.ADC.DE   FOR FILMS FROM THIS CATEGORY VISIT WWW.ADC.DE

BRONZE

Im Sommer 2007 fand zum ersten Mal in Deutschland die Triathlon-WM statt. ASICS schickte drei Promotion-Runner ins Rennen. Anstatt zu schwimmen liefen sie in aufblasbaren Laufkugeln über die Alster. Anstatt normaler Rennräder benutzten sie Fahrräder mit Laufschuhen anstelle der Reifen. Ihre Botschaft: Am Ende entscheidet die letzte Disziplin. In the end it's about running. ASICS Kernkompetenz.

In summer 2007, the Triathlon World Championships took place in Germany for the first time. Three promotion runners from ASICS took part. Instead of swimming they ran across the Alster using inflatable running balls. In place of racing bikes they used bikes with running shoes instead of tyres. The message: The last discipline is decisive. In the end, it's about running. ASICS core competence.

TITLE
ASICS Europe »Triathlon«

CLIENT
ASICS Europe B.V.

ADVERTISING DIRECTOR
Remco Rietvink

LEAD AGENCY
Nordpol+ Hamburg Agentur für Kommunikation GmbH

CREATIVE DIRECTION
Lars Rühmann

ART DIRECTION
Tim Schierwater, Sean Kirby

CLIENT CONSULTING
Mathias Müller-Using,
Niklas Franke, Axel Schüler-Bredt

FILM PRODUCTION
element e

DESIGN
Jan Schierwater

MUSIC COMPOSITION
Marini Brös

DIRECTION
Thorsten Kirves

COPY
Ingmar Bartels, Sebastian Behrendt

BRONZE

Wie verdeutlicht man, dass die Leica D-Lux 3 von Meister Camera extrem detaillierte Aufnahmen ermöglicht? Indem man zeigt, wie grob Objekte erscheinen, wenn man sie mit einer Billigkamera knipst. Dazu wurde ein gebauter 3-D-Hund vor dem Fotogeschäft platziert. Der Clou: Er setzte sich aus Tausenden von Pixeln zusammen. Ein Poster klärte den Betrachter auf: See it more detailed. Leica D-Lux 3.

How do you show people that the Leica D-Lux 3 from Meister Camera takes extremely detailed pictures? By showing them just how pixelated objects look when using a second-rate digital camera. To do this, we put a 3-D dog in front of the photo shop. The key is that the dog was completely made up of little wooden pixels. All was explained by a poster: See it more detailed. Leica D-Lux 3.

TITLE
Meister Camera/Leica D-LUX 3 »Verpixelt«
CLIENT
Meister Camera, Hamburg
MARKETING DIRECTOR
Martin Meister

LEAD AGENCY
Philipp und Keuntje GmbH
CREATIVE DIRECTION
Diether Kerner, Oliver Ramm
ART DIRECTION
Sönke Schmidt

CLIENT CONSULTING
Fedja Burmeister
AGENCY PRODUCER
Jörg Nagel
GRAPHIC ART
Sönke Schmidt, Alexander Rötterink

IDEA
Sönke Schmidt, Daniel Hoffmann
PRODUCTION
Thomas Beecken, Realisations KG
COPY
Daniel Hoffmann

FILME DIESER KATEGORIE FINDEN SIE UNTER WWW.ADC.DE FOR FILMS FROM THIS CATEGORY VISIT WWW.ADC.DE

NOMINATION

Guter Texternachwuchs ist rar. Deshalb müssen Agenturen frühzeitig auf sich aufmerksam machen. Zum Beispiel mit einer Anzeige im Vorlesungsverzeichnis der Texterschmiede. Das ist mittlerweile auch jedes Jahr voll mit wirklich guten Inseraten. Um da herauszustechen, veranstaltete Kolle Rebbe ein Gewinnspiel. Der Sieger konnte sich quasi schon mal auf seine Karriere in der Speicherstadt vorbereiten.

Talented young writers are rare. This is why agencies have to call attention to themselves early on. For example with an advertisement in the Texterschmiede's schedule of lectures, which by now is full of really good advertisements. In order to stand out there, Kolle Rebbe arranged a contest. The winner could practically prepare for a career in the Speicherstadt.

TITLE
Kolle Rebbe Texterschmieden-Anzeige »Gewinnspiel«

CLIENT
Kolle Rebbe Werbeagentur GmbH

LEAD AGENCY
Kolle Rebbe Werbeagentur GmbH

CREATIVE DIRECTION
Ulrich Zünkeler/Ingo Müller

ART DIRECTION
Petra Cremer

CLIENT CONSULTING
Thomas Stritz/Cissy Walde

PHOTOGRAPHY
Alexander Schmid

GRAPHIC ART
Alexander Schmid

PRODUCTION
Marc Schecker

COPY
Thomas Rendel

SALES PROMOTION   VERKAUFSFÖRDERUNG   177

NOMINATION

Beim ADC 2007 sorgten lebende Schnecken auf den Tischen der Jurymitglieder für Aufmerksamkeit.

During the Awardshow in 2007 living snails drew the attention.

TITLE
»Schleichwerbung für Sönke Busch«

CLIENT
Sönke Busch

LEAD AGENCY
www.buschwork.com

PRODUCTION
Optix Digital Pictures

STYLING
Arndt v. Hoff

FILME DIESER KATEGORIE FINDEN SIE UNTER WWW.ADC.DE FOR FILMS FROM THIS CATEGORY VISIT WWW.ADC.DE

NOMINATION

BIONADE ruft im Internet die Initiative »Stille Taten« ins Leben. Stille Taten sind anonyme gute Taten, die von der neuen Community ausgeführt werden. Alles, was die freiwilligen BIONADE-Unterstützer zurücklassen, ist eine Karte, die wiederum auf die Homepage der Initiative hinweist.

BIONADE created the "Silent Deeds" initiative on the internet. Silent deeds are anonymous good deeds, carried out by the new community. All that volunteer BIONADE supporters leave behind is a card, with the link to the initiative's home page.

TITLE
BIONADE Promotion »Stille Taten«

CLIENT
BIONADE GmbH

MARKETING DIRECTOR
Wolfgang Blum

LEAD AGENCY
Kolle Rebbe Werbeagentur GmbH

CREATIVE DIRECTION
Ulrich Zünkeler/Rolf Leger/Stefan Wübbe

ART DIRECTION
Lai-Sha Chan/Pia Kortemeier

CLIENT CONSULTING
Katharina Lechelt/Tamara Klien/Birgit Heikamp

STRATEGIC PLANNING
Domonic Veken

PHOTOGRAPHY
Oliver Schwarzwald

RADIO PRODUCTION
Studio Funk

ILLUSTRATION
Tina Berning

ART BUYING
Katja Werner

IMAGE EDITING
gloss, Hamburg

GRAPHIC ART
Florian Schmucker

MEDIA
Pilot Media GmbH & Co. KG

PRODUCTION
Finn Gnoycke

EDITING
Philipp Feit

SOUND DESIGN
Philipp Feit

SPEAKER
Matthias Strzoda

COPY
Florian Ludwig/Danny Fröhlich/Ingo Müller/Matthias Strzoda/Stefan Wübbe/Simon Kämper

SOUND ENGINEER
Philipp Feit

INTERACTIVE PRODUCER
Tobias Böhning

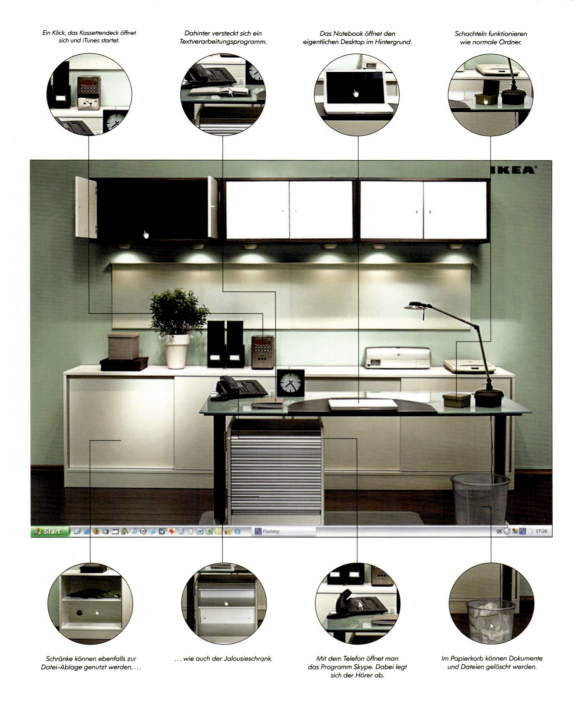

NOMINATION

IKEA Family Kunden fanden eine CD-ROM in ihrem Briefkasten. Darauf war ein PC-Programm, das den Desktop vollständig in eine IKEA-Bürolandschaft verwandelte und für Ordnung sorgte. Dabei besaß jedes Möbel- und Einrichtungsstück eine echte Computerfunktion.

IKEA Family members found a CD-ROM in their mail box. On it, they found a program that converts their computer-desktop into a real IKEA office environment and tidies things up. Thereby every piece of furniture has some real computer-functions.

TITLE
IKEA »Desktopmöbel«

CLIENT
IKEA Deutschland GmbH & Co. KG

MARKETING DIRECTOR
Benni Hermansson

ADVERTISING DIRECTOR
Pia Madison

LEAD AGENCY
Jung von Matt AG

CREATIVE DIRECTION
Fabian Frese, Götz Ulmer, Tom Hauser

ART DIRECTION
Julia Ziegler

CLIENT CONSULTING
Nicole Drabsch, Jascha Oevermann, Alexandra Beck

PHOTOGRAPHY
Stefan Försterling

GRAPHIC ART
Frank Hose

PROGRAMMING
Grimm Gallun Holtappels, Benedikt Holtappels, Ole Warns

COPY
Jan-Florian Ege

FILME DIESER KATEGORIE FINDEN SIE UNTER WWW.ADC.DE FOR FILMS FROM THIS CATEGORY VISIT WWW.ADC.DE

NOMINATION

Um zur Bologna Motor Show 2007 einzuladen, machte Volkswagen sich die bolognesische Architektur zunutze: unzählige Rundbögen. Daran wurden Nachbildungen von Volkswagen-Rädern so platziert, dass sich daraus die Form eines New Beetle ergab. Zusätzlich wurden Aufkleber verteilt, die zur Kreation eines eigenen New Beetle aufriefen. Für jedes Foto gab's am Messestand einen Probefahrt-Gutschein.

To attract visitors to their stand at the Bologna Motor Show 2007 Volkswagen took advantage of Bologna's typical architecture: countless archways. Imitations of Volkswagen wheels where attached to these arches to create the form of a New Beetle. Additionally stickers were handed out that encouraged people to create their own New Beetle. At the Motor Show each photo received a test drive voucher.

TITLE
Volkswagen Kampagne »Bologna auf Rädern«

CLIENT
Volkswagen AG

MARKETING DIRECTOR
Jochen Sengpiehl

ADVERTISING DIRECTOR
Hartmut Seeger

LEAD AGENCY
DDB Germany, Berlin

CREATIVE DIRECTION
Bert Peulecke, Stefan Schulte

ART DIRECTION
Lisa Berger, Johannes Hicks, Marc Isken

CLIENT CONSULTING
Cathleen Losch, Silke Lagodny

TECHNICAL DIRECTION
Sascha Mehn

COPY
Nina Faulhaber, Marian Götz, Kai Abd-El Salam

 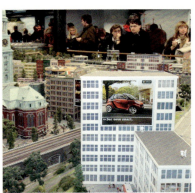

NOMINATION

Wo und wie also kann man mit einer VKF-Aktion heute überhaupt noch überraschen? Zum Beispiel, indem man da eine Kampagne startet, wo bisher noch keine Marke werben durfte: im Miniaturwunderland, der größten Modelleisenbahn der Welt. Mit einer detailgetreuen 1:80-Version der echten Launchkampagne für den neuen smart fortwo. Von Outdoor über Spots in Openair-Kinos bis hin zu POS-Events.

How and where can you surprise people these days with a sales promotion? For example, by starting a campaign where, until now, no brand has managed to start a campaign before: in the MiniaturWunderland, the world's largest model railway. With an exact replica 1:80 scale version of the real new smart fortwo launch campaign. From posters to spots at open air cinemas and events at the POS.

TITLE
smart »Miniatur Wunderland«

CLIENT
Mercedes-Benz
Vertriebsorganisation Deutschland

ADVERTISING DIRECTOR
Markus Gammert

LEAD AGENCY
BBDO Düsseldorf GmbH

CREATIVE DIRECTION
Matthias Eickmeyer, Ton Hollander,
Toygar Bazarkaya,
Sebastian Hardieck, Ralf Zilligen

ART DIRECTION
Pia Niehues, Stephan Eichler

CLIENT CONSULTING
Dirk Spakowski, Thanh Vu Tran,
Sebastian Schlosser

AGENCY PRODUCER
Steffen Gentis, Silke Rochow,
Katja Kohnen

IMAGE EDITING
VCC Perfect Pictures AG,
Düsseldorf

PRODUCTION
Tonproduktion:
Sprachlabor Audioproduktionen
GmbH, Düsseldorf

EDITING
Nina Stangl

SPEAKER
Florian Seigerschmidt

COPY
Dietmar Neumann, Kai Hoffmann,
Markus Steinkemper

SOUND ENGINEER
Eike Steffen

FILME DIESER KATEGORIE FINDEN SIE UNTER WWW.ADC.DE FOR FILMS FROM THIS CATEGORY VISIT WWW.ADC.DE

NOMINATION

Am 27.10.2007, am Erscheinungstag des letzten Harry-Potter-Bandes, fragte sich alle Welt: Wird Harry sterben? Die Titanic, Deutschlands schnellstes Nachrichtenmagazin, sah es als ihre journalistische Pflicht, das Volk zu informieren. Dank einer umfassenden Aufklärungskampagne wurden in Deutschland nachweislich (!) 17 Bücher weniger verkauft. Das ist Journalismus! Das ist schneller informiert!

On 27.10.2007, the day the last Harry Potter book was released, the whole world was asking themselves: will Harry die? We at Titanic, Germany's infamous satire magazine, saw it as our journalistic duty to inform the people. Thanks to our comprehensive educational campaign, a grand total of 17 consumers decided not to buy the book. That's journalism! That's being first with the news!

TITLE
Titanic
»Harry Potter stirbt auf Seite 652«
CLIENT
TITANIC-Verlag GmbH & Co. KG
MARKETING DIRECTOR
Thomas Gsella

LEAD AGENCY
Scholz & Friends
CREATIVE DIRECTION
Suze Barrett, Matthias Schmidt, Stefan Setzkorn

ART DIRECTION
Marcin Baba
CLIENT CONSULTING
Raphael Brinkert, Dennis Schneider, Louisa Wimmer

DIRECTION
Lars Colin Steinmeyer
COPY
Dennis Lück

NOMINATION

Wenn ein besonderes Bier wie Astra ein Sixpack auf den Markt bringt, dann muss das auch außergewöhnlich aussehen. Deshalb haben wir die Astra Herrenhandtasche entworfen. Und seitdem tragen selbst die härtesten Kerle vom Kiez gerne Handtaschen!

When an unusual brewery such as Astra launches a sixpack, it has to look unusual too. So we designed the Astra men's handbag – and ever since, even the toughest men can be seen with handbags on a night out!

TITLE
Astra »Herrenhandtasche«
CLIENT
Holsten-Brauerei AG
MARKETING DIRECTOR
Hermann Crux

ADVERTISING DIRECTOR
Nicola Weiß
LEAD AGENCY
Philipp und Keuntje GmbH
CREATIVE DIRECTION
Hans Esders

ART DIRECTION
Maren Burrichter, Jan Berg
CLIENT CONSULTING
Andreas Müller-Horn,
Sandra Fiebranz

AGENCY PRODUCER
Stephan Gerlach
GRAPHIC ART
Jan Berg
COPY
Oliver Kohtz, Aleš Polcar

FILME DIESER KATEGORIE FINDEN SIE UNTER WWW.ADC.DE   FOR FILMS FROM THIS CATEGORY VISIT WWW.ADC.DE

NOMINATION

Wer die eineiigen Zwillinge in der Disko beobachtete, musste meinen, zu viel getrunken zu haben. Denn die beiden glichen sich nicht nur aufs Haar, sondern bewegten sich auch identisch: Sie liefen, tanzten und flirteten synchron. Und wer doppelt sieht, sollte den Heimweg besser in einem Taxi antreten.

Everyone who looked at the identical twins at the disco must have come to the conclusion that he drank too much. Not only they looked exactly alike, but also moved in identical ways: they walked, danced and flirted in a perfect synch. And whoever sees double should call a cab to get home.

TITLE
Taxiruf 22456 Promotion
»2,0 Promille«

CLIENT
Taxiruf 22456/aperto move GmbH

MARKETING DIRECTOR
Jan Gessenhardt

LEAD AGENCY
Scholz & Friends

CREATIVE DIRECTION
Matthias Spaetgens, Jan Leube,
Oliver Handlos

ART DIRECTION
Mathias Rebmann

CLIENT CONSULTING
Wiebke Lorenz

AGENCY PRODUCER
Diana Wuttge

GRAPHIC ART
Katharina Hanel,
Stephanie Wiehle

CAMERA
Dirk Morgenstern

DIRECTION
Mathias Rebmann

EDITING
Daniel Klessig

COPY
Florian Schwalme

NOMINATION

Wer sich nicht für Volkswagen Original Teile, sondern für billigere Ersatzteile entscheidet, verringert den Wert seines Volkswagen erheblich. Da man das seinem Volkswagen aber leider nicht gleich ansieht, haben wir den Qualitätsunterschied »hörbar« gemacht. Wir ließen Volkswagen Fahrzeuge mit absurden Fahrgeräuschen durch Deutschlands Großstädte fahren.

The decision for cheap spares instead of Volkswagen Original parts, considerably decreases the worth of your Volkswagen. Because the difference in quality unfortunately doesn't show right away, we made it "hearable". We put Volkswagen cars giving out absurd driving noises onto the streets of Germany's major cities.

TITLE
Volkswagen Service Promotion »Fake Sounds Live«
CLIENT
Volkswagen AG
MARKETING DIRECTOR
Michael Scharnau
ADVERTISING DIRECTOR
Philipp Benzler

LEAD AGENCY
DDB Germany, Berlin
CREATIVE DIRECTION
Bert Peulecke, Stefan Schulte
ART DIRECTION
Tim Stübane

CLIENT CONSULTING
Ulrich Klenke, Nadja Richter, Silke Lagodny
AGENCY PRODUCER
Patrick Scharf, Hendrik Raufmann
GRAPHIC ART
Jussi Jääskeläinen
TECHNICAL DIRECTION
Sascha Mehn

COPY
Birgit van den Valentyn

ADDITIONAL AWARDS NOMINATION
Volume Advertising page 215
Media
Media

FILME DIESER KATEGORIE FINDEN SIE UNTER WWW.ADC.DE   FOR FILMS FROM THIS CATEGORY VISIT WWW.ADC.DE

GOLD

TITLE
Volkswagen Kampagne »Horst Schlämmer macht Führerschein«

CLIENT
Volkswagen AG

MARKETING DIRECTOR
Jochen Sengpiehl

ADVERTISING DIRECTOR
Ralf Maltzen, Hartmut Seeger

LEAD AGENCY
DDB Germany, Berlin

CREATIVE DIRECTION
Amir Kassaei, Stefan Schulte,
Bert Peulecke

ART DIRECTION
Kristoffer Heilemann,
Tim Schmitt, Alexandra Sievers

CLIENT CONSULTING
Benjamin Reininger,
Niklas Feuerle, Cathleen Losch,
Silke Lagodny

FILM PRODUCTION
Telemaz Commercials Berlin

PHOTOGRAPHY
Markus Bachmann, Sven Schrader

RADIO PRODUCTION
Hastings Audio Network Berlin

AGENCY PRODUCER
Boris Schepker

ART BUYING
Elke Dilchert

CONSULTING
Künstlervermittlung:
Special Key –
Christian Biedermann,
Sven Zander

GRAPHIC ART
Sarah Pöhlmann, Peter Mayer

ARTIST
Hape Kerkeling

POSTPRODUCTION
Condor digital media Berlin

PRODUCTION
Barbara Kranz, Frank Hasselbach

DIRECTION
Gerald Grabowski

EDITING
Kathrin Schmoll

TECHNICAL DIRECTION
Sascha Mehn

COPY
Ludwig Berndl, Philip Bolland,
Ulrike Schumann, Christian Fries

SOUND ENGINEER
Lars Gelhausen

URL
http://www.entry-hamburg-hafen.de/89/

ADDITIONAL AWARDS
GOLD
Volume Advertising page 221
TV-Spots
Television commercials

GOLD
Volume Advertising page 283
Filme für Verkaufsförderung/
Unternehmensdarstellungen
Films for sales promotion/
company presentation

GOLD
Volume Advertising page 289
Virale Filme
Viral films

GOLD
Volume Advertising page 347
Integrierte Kampagnen
Integrated campaigns

GOLD
Volume Advertising page 367
Dialogmarketing
Dialogue marketing

GOLD
Volume Design page 242
Digitale Werbung
Digital advertising

SILVER
Volume Advertising page 096
Tages-/Wochenzeitungsanzeigen
Advertisements in daily/weekly
newspapers

SILVER
Volume Advertising page 139
Produkt-/Werbebroschüren
Product/advertising brochures

SILVER
Volume Advertising page 147
Text
Copy

SILVER
Volume Design page 259
Digitale Medien: Viral
Digital media: Viral

BRONZE
Volume Advertising page 152
Text
Copy

BRONZE
Volume Advertising page 326
Funkspots
Radio commercials

NOMINATION
Volume Design page 095
Informationsmedien
Information media

NOMINATION
Volume Design page 235
Websites
Websites

SILVER

TITLE
IKEA »3D-Cover«

CLIENT
IKEA Deutschland GmbH

MARKETING DIRECTOR
Claudia Willvonseder

ADVERTISING DIRECTOR
Jens Helfrich, Gerrit Kaminski

LEAD AGENCY
Jung von Matt AG

CONTRIBUTING AGENCIES
Act Agency Hamburg,
Stein Promotions

CREATIVE DIRECTION
Arno Lindemann,
Bernhard Lukas, Tom Hauser,
Sören Porst

ART DIRECTION
Joanna Swistowski

CLIENT CONSULTING
Nicole Drabsch, Nic Heimann

COMPUTER ANIMATION
Sven Schoenmann

PRINTING
Gerstenberg Druck &
Direktwerbung

GRAPHIC ART
Matthias Grundner, Julia Jakobi

CAMERA
Justus Becker, Ingo Dannecker

MUSIC COMPOSITION
Malte Hagemeister

EDITING
Justus Becker

TECHNICAL IMPLEMENTATION
Birgit Ballhause,
Philipp Mokrohs

COPY
Caroline Ellert, Tom Hauser

ADDITIONAL AWARDS
SILVER
Volume Advertising page 215
Media
Media

SILVER
Volume Advertising page 368
Dialogmarketing
Dialogue marketing

NOMINATION
Volume Design page 319
Events
Events

SALES PROMOTION VERKAUFSFÖRDERUNG 187

BRONZE

TITLE
Olympus Unterwassergehäuse PT-029 »Unterwassergehäuse Promotion PT-029«
CLIENT
OLYMPUS EUROPA GmbH
MARKETING DIRECTOR
Uwe Lüssem
ADVERTISING DIRECTOR
Sabine Siehl
LEAD AGENCY
Springer & Jacoby Werbeagentur GmbH & Co. KG
CREATIVE DIRECTION
Dirk Haeusermann, Matthias Harbeck
ART DIRECTION
John Gloeden
CLIENT CONSULTING
Amelie Hoffmann
FILM PRODUCTION
Corinna Nugent, Fedja Burmeister
EDITOR
Johannes Kollender
FILM ANIMATION
Johannes Kollender
POSTPRODUCTION
optix Digital Pictures GmbH
PRODUCTION
Steffi Beck
SOUND DESIGN
MassiveMusic Amsterdam
COPY
Eskil Puhl, Stefan Meske

ADDITIONAL AWARDS
BRONZE
Volume Advertising page 196
Media
Media

BRONZE

TITLE
Eos Cabriolet »Schattenplakat«
CLIENT
Volkswagen AG
MARKETING DIRECTOR
Jochen Sengpiehl
ADVERTISING DIRECTOR
Hartmut Seeger
LEAD AGENCY
DDB Germany/Düsseldorf
CREATIVE DIRECTION
Amir Kassaei/Eric Schoeffler/ Heiko Freyland/ Raphael Milczarek
ART DIRECTION
Fabian Kirner/Michael Kittel
CLIENT CONSULTING
Silke Lagodny
STRATEGIC PLANNING
Wiebke Dreyer/Christian Bihn
AGENCY PRODUCER
Michael Frixe
COPY
Felix Lemcke/Jan Propach

ADDITIONAL AWARDS
SILVER
Volume Advertising page 123
Plakate und Poster (indoor und outdoor)
Billboards and posters (indoor and outdoor)

SILVER
Volume Advertising page 188
Media
Media

NOMINATION

TITLE
TUI »Hawaii-Hemden«
CLIENT
TUI AG
MARKETING DIRECTOR
Michael Lambertz
ADVERTISING DIRECTOR
Jutta Lage-Weiland, Nils Behrens, Julia Schlegl
LEAD AGENCY
Jung von Matt AG
CREATIVE DIRECTION
Arno Lindemann, Bernhard Lukas
ART DIRECTION
Ole Kleinhans, Markus Kremer
CLIENT CONSULTING
Nic Heimann, Nina Sophie Scheller
ILLUSTRATION
Sunny Clayton
COPY
Thomas Heyen

ADDITIONAL AWARDS
NOMINATION
Volume Advertising page 212
Media
Media

FILME DIESER KATEGORIE FINDEN SIE UNTER WWW.ADC.DE   FOR FILMS FROM THIS CATEGORY VISIT WWW.ADC.DE

SILVER

Wer ist besser geeignet, für ein Cabriolet zu werben, als die Sonne selbst? Deshalb brachten wir sie dazu, unsere Zielgruppe zu einer Probefahrt mit dem Volkswagen Eos einzuladen. Indem sie durch das erste Schattenplakat der Welt schien. Und jeden daran erinnerte, dass gerade perfektes Wetter für eine Probefahrt war.

Who is more qualified for advertising a convertible than the sun itself? Therefore we got the sun to invite people for a test drive by shining through the world's first shadow poster. In this way people were reminded that a sunny day is a perfect day for a ride with our Volkswagen Eos convertible.

TITLE
Eos »Schattenplakat«
CLIENT
Volkswagen AG
MARKETING DIRECTOR
Jochen Sengpiehl
ADVERTISING DIRECTOR
Hartmut Seeger
LEAD AGENCY
DDB Germany/Düsseldorf

CREATIVE DIRECTION
Amir Kassaei/Eric Schoeffler/
Heiko Freyland/Raphael Milczarek
ART DIRECTION
Fabian Kirner/Michael Kittel
CLIENT CONSULTING
Silke Lagodny
STRATEGIC PLANNING
Wiebke Dreyer/Christian Bihn
AGENCY PRODUCER
Michael Frixe

COPY
Felix Lemcke/Jan Propach
ADDITIONAL AWARDS
SILVER
Volume Advertising page 123
Plakate und Poster
(indoor und outdoor)
Billboards and posters
(indoor and outdoor)

BRONZE
Volume Advertising page 187
Verkaufsförderung
Sales promotion

FILME DIESER KATEGORIE FINDEN SIE UNTER WWW.ADC.DE FOR FILMS FROM THIS CATEGORY VISIT WWW.ADC.DE

SILVER

Sony Ericsson war einer der Hauptsponsoren der MTV EuropeMusicAwards 2007. Mehrere Nächte vor den EMAs projizierten wir Filme auf über 50 Münchner Wahrzeichen. Diese Filme zeigten einen Graffiti-Künstler beim Sprayen riesiger Kunstwerke. Die Graffitis brandete er dann mit dem MTV- und dem Sony Ericsson-Logo. Das Ergebnis war so echt, dass Passanten sogar die Polizei alarmierten.

Sony Ericsson was one of the main sponsors of the MTV EuropeMusicAwards 2007. For several nights before the EMAs, we projected films onto over 50 Munich landmarks. These films showed a graffiti artist spraying huge works of art. And branding them with the MTV and the Sony Ericsson logos! The result was so convincing that some passers-by actually alarmed the police.

TITLE
MTV Europe Music Awards sponsored by Sony Ericsson »Graffiti Projektionen«

CLIENT
Sony Ericsson Mobile Communications International AB

MARKETING DIRECTOR
Alexandra Wulff

LEAD AGENCY
Serviceplan Power of Sales München/Hamburg

CONTRIBUTING AGENCIES
Mediaedge:cia

CREATIVE DIRECTION
Karsten Gessulat

ART DIRECTION
Ryan McManus

CLIENT CONSULTING
Diana Günder

ILLUSTRATION
Loomit

AGENCY PRODUCER
Niels van Hoek, Ryan McManus

GRAPHIC ART
Ryan McManus, Bona Pfeiffer

POSTPRODUCTION
Westparkstudios

PRODUCTION
Magnus Augustin, Helmut Hartl NERDFILMS a division of Embassy of Dreams Filmproduktion GmbH

DIRECTION
Niels van Hoek, Ryan McManus

COPY
Niels van Hoek, Susanna Schreibauer

VISUAL EFFECTS
WEDIA Visuelle Großflächenwerbung

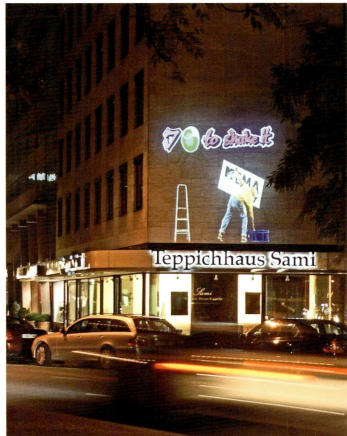

FILME DIESER KATEGORIE FINDEN SIE UNTER WWW.ADC.DE   FOR FILMS FROM THIS CATEGORY VISIT WWW.ADC.DE

SILVER

Für die Kunstinstallationen im Jahr der Geisteswissenschaften 2007 wurden in ganz Deutschland riesige Buchstaben an symbolträchtigen Gebäuden angebracht. So ist das größte ABC Deutschlands entstanden – Architektur und Design machten die Geisteswissenschaften anschaulich.

In Germany, the focus in 2007 is on the Humanities. To make the abstract "Year of the Humanities" as visible as possible in public space gigantic letters were attached to highly symbolic locations. The result was Germany's largest alphabet – architecture and design made the Humanities visible.

TITLE
Wissenschaftsjahr 2007 Kampagne »Die Geisteswissenschaften. Das ABC der Menschheit.«

CLIENT
Bundesministerium für Bildung und Forschung

MARKETING DIRECTOR
Hartmut Grübel

ADVERTISING DIRECTOR
Monika Bürvenich,
Dr. Franka Ostertag

LEAD AGENCY
Scholz & Friends Identify

CREATIVE DIRECTION
Wolf Schneider, Tobias Wolff

ART DIRECTION
Nicole Algieri, Frederik Hofmann, Jürgen Krugsperger, Gito Lima, Olivier Nowak, Christian Rühe

CLIENT CONSULTING
Dr. Christof Biggeleben,
Bettina Prange,
Penelope Winterhager

STRATEGIC PLANNING
Stefan Wegner

FILM PRODUCTION
Nele Jürgens, Daniel Klessig,
Anke Landmark,
Lars Colin Steinmayer,

PHOTOGRAPHY
Sebastian Greuner

RADIO PRODUCTION
Hastings Berlin

ARCHITECTURAL OFFICE
Scholz & Friends Identify

DESIGN
Wolf Schneider

DESIGN AGENCY
Scholz & Friends Identify

GRAPHIC ART
Jinhi Kim

LIGHTING DESIGN
Skudi Optics, Daniel Margraf

SPEAKER
Simon Jäger

TECHNICAL INSTALLATION
Nawrocki Alpin, Holger Nawrocki

COPY
Jens Daum, Mirko Derpmann,
Dr. Philipp Mehne, Hans Selge

ADDITIONAL AWARDS
SILVER
Volume Design page 164
Typografie
Typography

SILVER
Volume Design page 190
Public Areas
Public areas

FILME DIESER KATEGORIE FINDEN SIE UNTER WWW.ADC.DE FOR FILMS FROM THIS CATEGORY VISIT WWW.ADC.DE

BRONZE

Frischgebackene Besitzer einer neuen OLYMPUS mju 600 compact Kamera sollten auf das zur Kamera passende Unterwasser-Gehäuse aufmerksam gemacht werden und es direkt bestellen können. Hierzu wurde ein Film auf der Kamera vorinstalliert. Sobald die Kamera zum ersten Mal in Betrieb genommen wurde, erschien der Film auf dem Monitor.

New owners of the OLYMPUS mju 600 compact camera were to be made aware of the PT-029 underwater case for their new camera so that they could order it directly. We took the most direct way to reach OLYMPUS mju 600 owners: a film which was installed on each new OLYMPUS mju 600. When the camera is switched on for the first time, the film appears on the screen.

TITLE
Olympus Unterwassergehäuse PT-029 »Unterwassergehäuse Promotion PT-029«

CLIENT
OLYMPUS EUROPA GmbH

MARKETING DIRECTOR
Uwe Lüssem

ADVERTISING DIRECTOR
Sabine Siehl

LEAD AGENCY
Springer & Jacoby Werbeagentur GmbH & Co. KG

CREATIVE DIRECTION
Dirk Haeusermann,
Matthias Harbeck

ART DIRECTION
John Gloeden

CLIENT CONSULTING
Amelie Hoffmann

FILM PRODUCTION
Corinna Nugent, Fedja Burmeister

EDITOR
Johannes Kollender

FILM ANIMATION
Johannes Kollender

POSTPRODUCTION
optix Digital Pictures GmbH

PRODUCTION
Steffi Beck

SOUND DESIGN
MassiveMusic Amsterdam

COPY
Eskil Puhl, Stefan Meske

ADDITIONAL AWARDS
BRONZE
Volume Advertising page 187
Verkaufsförderung
Sales promotion

Machen Sie ihre mju wasserdicht

Das PT-029 Unterwasser-Gehäuse.

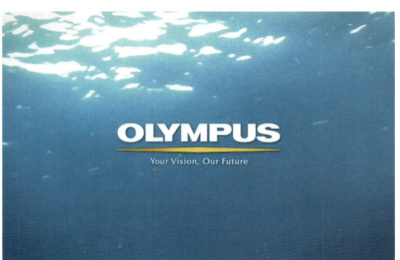

Jetzt bestellen:
Tel. 00800-65 96 78 73
(gebührenfrei Mo.-Fr. 9-18 Uhr)

OLYMPUS
Your Vision, Our Future

FILME DIESER KATEGORIE FINDEN SIE UNTER WWW.ADC.DE   FOR FILMS FROM THIS CATEGORY VISIT WWW.ADC.DE

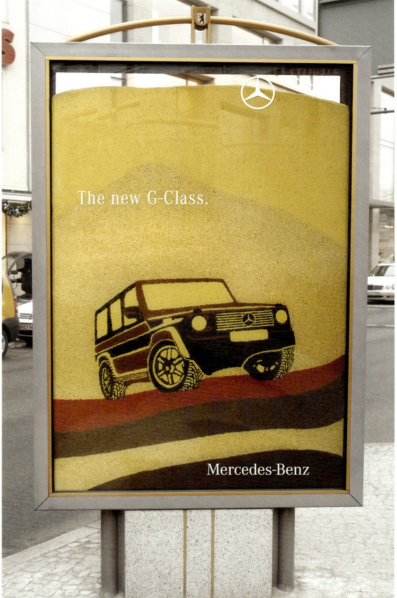

BRONZE

Die neue Mercedes-Benz G-Klasse steht für perfekte Performance im Gelände. Um das zu dramatisieren, ließen wir die G-Klasse »eins mit dem Gelände« werden. Mit einer neuen Art »CLP-Plakate«, die nur aus Sand und Stein gemacht waren.

In 2007 Mercedes-Benz launched the new generation G-Class. Our task was to create a campaign that shows that the G-Class is capable of mastering even the most challenging terrains. It could be said that the G-Class is one with the terrain. We brought this notion to life with unique posters made out of real sand and stones, placed in city light posters.

TITLE
Mercedes-Benz G-Klasse Kampagne »Sandplakat, Steinplakat«

CLIENT
Daimler AG

ADVERTISING DIRECTOR
Mirco Völker

LEAD AGENCY
Jung von Matt AG

CREATIVE DIRECTION
Jan Rexhausen,
Dörte Spengler-Ahrens

ART DIRECTION
Hisham Kharma

CLIENT CONSULTING
Yves Rosengart, Johanna Hecker,
Jan Groenendijk

ILLUSTRATION
Materialschlachten:
Claudia Schildt, Fabian Zell

ART BUYING
Bettina Zschirnt

ARTIST
Claudia Schildt, Fabian Zell

PRODUCTION
Philipp Wenhold

COPY
Sergio Penzo

ADDITIONAL AWARDS
BRONZE
Volume Design page 151
Grafische Einzelarbeiten
Single works of graphic art

NOMINATION
Volume Advertising page 124
Plakate und Poster
(indoor und outdoor)
Billboards and posters
(indoor and outdoor)

FILME DIESER KATEGORIE FINDEN SIE UNTER WWW.ADC.DE FOR FILMS FROM THIS CATEGORY VISIT WWW.ADC.DE

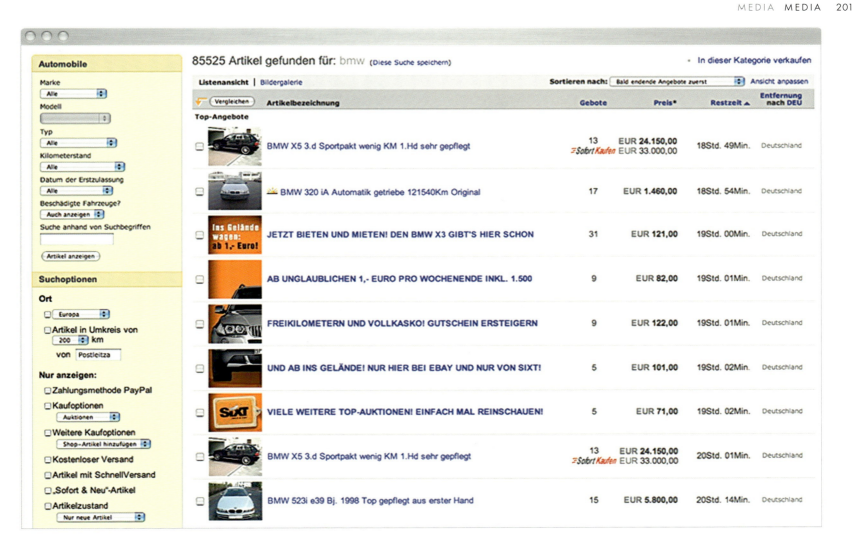

BRONZE

Wir werben für Sixt auf eBay. Allerdings nicht mit den vorhandenen Media-Formaten, sondern mit einer neuen Media-Idee direkt in den Suchergebnissen. Je fünf Einzelauktionen bilden, direkt hintereinander eingestellt, eine große, zusammenhängende Anzeige mit Bild und durchlaufender Copy. Und ein uniques Werbeformat, das Interessenten an einem Autotyp ganz gezielt auf die Angebote von SIXT anspricht.

We advertise Sixt on eBay. Not using the banners offered on the site, however, but with a new media idea directly in the search results. Five single auctions in succession form one large ad with one picture and a continuous copy. An unique advertising format, that drew the attention in a highly targeted way of prospects interested in a particular type of vehicle to SIXT's rental offering.

TITLE
SIXT »Ebay Ads«

CLIENT
SIXT GmbH & Co.
Autovermietung KG

MARKETING DIRECTOR
Karsten Willrodt

LEAD AGENCY
Jung von Matt AG

CREATIVE DIRECTION
Holger Oehrlich, Michael Ohanian

CLIENT CONSULTING
Martin Wenk, Judith Holzäpfel

DESIGN
Holger Oehrlich, Aline Neumann

EDITOR
Robert Jedam

IDEA
Holger Oehrlich

COPY
Oliver Flohrs, Lennart Frank

FILME DIESER KATEGORIE FINDEN SIE UNTER WWW.ADC.DE   FOR FILMS FROM THIS CATEGORY VISIT WWW.ADC.DE

NOMINATION

Handelsübliche Friseurumhänge wurden bedruckt und kostenlos an ausgewählte Salons geliefert. Ein Blick in den Spiegel und die Menschen konnten am eigenen Leib erfahren, wie es ist, im falschen Job zu stecken. Eine Erfahrung, die viele auf humorvolle Art dazu bewegte, ernsthaft ihren Jobwechsel mit Jobsintown.de zu planen.

Standard barber's capes were imprinted and issued for free to shops throughout Germany. One look in the mirror and people discovered how it really feels to be in the wrong job. A true insight that animated them in a funny way to think seriously about a job change with jobsintown.de.

TITLE
jobsintown.de Promotion
»Friseur-Umhang«

CLIENT
jobsintown.de GmbH

MARKETING DIRECTOR
Stefan Kraft

LEAD AGENCY
Scholz & Friends

CREATIVE DIRECTION
Oliver Handlos, Matthias Spaetgens

ART DIRECTION
Claudia Trippel, Jens-Petter Waernes

CLIENT CONSULTING
Katrin Voß, Sascha Kruse

PHOTOGRAPHY
Peter Bajer

AGENCY PRODUCER
Sören Gessat

GRAPHIC ART
Annika Stierl, Christina Gassner, Raluca Munteanu, Jennifer Schumacher

STYLING
Anna Röhrig, Catia Amato

COPY
Farid Baslam

NOMINATION

Zum Launch des neuen BMW 1er Coupé konnte man im ganzen Land Fahrfreude in ihrer intensivsten Form erleben. Und das, ohne in einem BMW zu sitzen. Die Dezemberausgabe des Politikmagazins Cicero erschien – weltweit einmalig – mit 160.000 individuellen Titelseiten. Dadurch bot sich BMW die Möglichkeit, auf der Rückseite 160.000 verschiedene Anzeigenmotive zu schalten. Auf ihnen erlebte ganz Deutschland verdichtete 1ntensität. Jede Stadt wurde auf ihre Essenz verdichtet. Aus Berlin wurde Brln. Aus Hamburg Hmbrg …

The launch of the new BMW 1 Series Coupé allowed people throughout the country to experience driving pleasure in its most intense form – without anyone having to get into a BMW. The December issue of the political magazine "Cicero" was published with – a world's first – 160,000 different title pages. This made it possible for BMW to place 160,000 different advertisement motifs on the back cover on which all of Germany was able to experience condensed intensity. Every city was Condensed into its essence. Berlin became Brln. Hamburg became Hmbrg …

TITLE
BMW 1er Coupé
»160.000 x Verdichtete Intensität«

CLIENT
BMW AG

MARKETING DIRECTOR
Manfred Bräunl

ADVERTISING DIRECTOR
Dr. Tobias Nickel,
Dr. Hans-Peter Ketterl

LEAD AGENCY
MAB, Berlin

CONTRIBUTING AGENCIES
Mediaplus

CREATIVE DIRECTION
Nils Haseborg, Tomas Tulinius

ART DIRECTION
Michael Janke

CLIENT CONSULTING
Henning Gerstner,
Leveke Lambersy,
Alexander Kerkow

STRATEGIC PLANNING
Moritz Kiechle, Till Buchner

PHOTOGRAPHY
Mats Cordt

PUBLISHING HOUSE
Ringier Publishing GmbH

AGENCY PRODUCER
Lars Ebeling

ART BUYING
Martina Kersten

GRAPHIC ART
Sandra Mithöfer

MEDIA
Werner Reineke,
Christian Kaessmann

POSTPRODUCTION
Zerone, Hamburg

PRODUCTION
Nowadays: Tobias Wenske;
Mats Cordt Photography:
Matthias Pretzsch

COPY
Ilja Schmuschkowitsch

FINAL ARTWORK
Gordon Gohde

ADDITIONAL AWARDS
BRONZE
Volume Advertising page 024
Publikumsanzeigen
Consumer advertisements

NOMINATION
Volume Advertising page 124
Plakate und Poster
(indoor und outdoor)
Billboards and posters
(indoor and outdoor)

NOMINATION
Volume Advertising page 214
Media
Media

NOMINATION
Volume Advertising page 358
Integrierte Kampagnen
Integrated campaigns

FILME DIESER KATEGORIE FINDEN SIE UNTER WWW.ADC.DE FOR FILMS FROM THIS CATEGORY VISIT WWW.ADC.DE

NOMINATION

Anhand der Rollbewegung eines City Light Plakats wird die Stärke der Leifheit Wischer gezeigt: Mit einer Handbewegung werden Glasscheiben wieder sauber.

The strength of the Leifheit cleaner is illustrated by means of the illuminated poster's scrolling movement: glass panes are cleaned with a flick of the wrist.

TITLE
Leifheit Roll-CLP »Fensterwischer«

CLIENT
Leifheit AG

MARKETING DIRECTOR
Katrin Lauer

LEAD AGENCY
kempertrautmann gmbh

CREATIVE DIRECTION
Gerrit Zinke, Jens Theil

CLIENT CONSULTING
Nils Möller, Isabel Uhlig

STRATEGIC PLANNING
Nils Wollny

PHOTOGRAPHY
Patrice Lange

ART BUYING
Susi Kastner-Linke

GRAPHIC ART
Julia Wolk, Bastian Adam

NOMINATION

Der erste elektrische Adventskranz als weihnachtlicher Gruß des Stromversorgers EnBW. Für die Plakataktion wurden City-Light-Plakate in der Stuttgarter Innenstadt gebucht. Während der vier Adventswochen vor Weihnachten wurde wie bei einem normalen Adventskranz jede Woche eine Kerze bzw. Leuchtstoffröhre mehr »angezündet«.

The first electric Advent wreath as a seasonal greeting. For EnBW, one of Germany's largest energy companies we turned backlit, stationary posters into electric Advent wreaths. The idea was put into practice in December using backlit poster displays with four neon tubes in the center of Stuttgart. Every week the passers-by could see more candles burning.

TITLE
EnBW CLPs
»Elektrischer Adventskranz«

CLIENT
EnBW Energie Baden-Württemberg AG

ADVERTISING DIRECTOR
Holger Busch

LEAD AGENCY
Jung von Matt AG

CREATIVE DIRECTION
Tanja Mann-Wisniowski,
Susanne Ostertag

ART DIRECTION
Stefanie Veihl

CLIENT CONSULTING
Christine Seelig, Jens Wages,
Katja Best

AGENCY PRODUCER
Anja Geib

GRAPHIC ART
Ralph Burkhardt

MEDIA
Un-über-Seh-Bar

PRODUCTION
FOKINA Produktions- und
Dienstleitungs GmbH

COPY
Susanne Ostertag

FILME DIESER KATEGORIE FINDEN SIE UNTER WWW.ADC.DE FOR FILMS FROM THIS CATEGORY VISIT WWW.ADC.DE

NOMINATION

Bevor Schnick & Schnack in den TV-Spots ihr Unwesen trieben, lungerten sie in Schnick & Schnack affinen TV-Umfeldern herum. Mit Verkaufslegende Walter Freiwald im RTL Shop und der überaus freizügigen Cheyenne Lacroix beim DSF Sportquiz. So schafften es Schnick & Schnack im Vorfeld in die Köpfe, Gazetten und Blogs der Republik. Sie wurden Teil der Ramschkultur. Die Hauptkampagne konnte beginnen.

Before Schnick & Schnack unleashed their mischief in TV commercials, they hung around Schnick & Schnack-friendly TV environments. With sales legend Walter Freiwald in the RTL and with the extremely lovely Cheyenne Lacroix of the DSF Sportquiz. This is how Schnick & Schnack entered the minds, media and blogs of the republic. They became part of trash culture. The main campaign could begin.

TITLE
Hornbach Baumarkt TV-Kampagne »Schnick&Schnack Ramsch«

CLIENT
Hornbach Baumarkt AG

MARKETING DIRECTOR
Jürgen Schröcker

ADVERTISING DIRECTOR
Diana Koob

LEAD AGENCY
HEIMAT, Berlin

CREATIVE DIRECTION
Guido Heffels, Jürgen Vossen

ART DIRECTION
Danny Baarz

CLIENT CONSULTING
Yves Krämer

FILM PRODUCTION
Markenfilm, Berlin

AGENCY PRODUCER
Kerstin Breuer

CONSULTING
Mark Hassan, Sammy Bohneberg

GRAPHIC ART
Jenny Kapteyn

CAMERA
Thomas Kiennast

MEDIA
Crossmedia Düsseldorf

MUSIC COMPOSITION
Thomas Süß, audioforce Berlin

DIRECTION
John Fernseher (TV-Spots),
Danny Baarz,
Matthias Storath (Zusatzspots)

EDITING
Steffen Schmidt, Arthur Heiseler (VCC)

SOUND DESIGN
Thomas Süß, audioforce Berlin

SPEAKER
John Fernseher

COPY
Matthias Storath

ADDITIONAL AWARDS NOMINATION
Volume Advertising page 244
TV-Spots
Television commercials

NOMINATION

Um Greenpeace bei ihrem Kampf gegen CO_2, den Klimakiller, zu unterstützen, wurde ein Screensaver produziert. Er ging per E-Mail an alle Mitglieder und stand auch als Download auf der Greenpeace Homepage. Sobald er angeht, zeigt sich zunächst ein bekanntes Bild: animierte Fische im Meer. Kehrt der User jedoch erst nach einigen Minuten zurück zum Screen, ist plötzlich jegliches Leben erloschen.

To support Greenpeace in their fight against CO_2, the climate killer, a screensaver was produced. It was sent by e-mail to all members and furthermore was downloadable from the Greenpeace website. When activated a familiar picture appears: animated fish in the sea. But when the user returns to the screen after a couple of minutes, a completely different sight awaits him: all life has gone.

TITLE
Greenpeace »Bildschirmschoner«

CLIENT
Greenpeace Österreich

LEAD AGENCY
Demner, Merlicek & Bergmann

CREATIVE DIRECTION
Marc Wientzek, Sebastian Kainz

CLIENT CONSULTING
Christin Herrnberger, Lilli Gerlich

ILLUSTRATION
Pixelpartners.com

AGENCY PRODUCER
Walter Krichbaumer

DESIGN
Robert Wimberger

GRAPHIC ART
Marion Schlipfinger

CONCEPT
Alistair Thompson

PROGRAMMING
Pixelpartners.com

COPY
Alistair Thompson

FILME DIESER KATEGORIE FINDEN SIE UNTER WWW.ADC.DE FOR FILMS FROM THIS CATEGORY VISIT WWW.ADC.DE

NOMINATION

Eine Kampagne, die auf überflüssige Inhalte, Worte und Bilder verzichtet. Ausschließlich ein dramatisches Foto soll für Brot für die Welt Spenden generieren – die Botschaft in der Bildunterschrift löst auf: Worte allein helfen nicht.

A campaign that dispenses with superfluous content, words, and images. Just one single eloquent shot will work to move people to donate to the "Bread for the World" charity. Then the message fades in as a caption: Words don't help.

TITLE
Brot für die Welt Anzeigenkampagne
»Worte helfen nicht mehr«

CLIENT
Brot für die Welt

MARKETING DIRECTOR
Barbara Temminghoff

ADVERTISING DIRECTOR
Jens Barthen

LEAD AGENCY
Jung von Matt AG

CREATIVE DIRECTION
Tobias Eichinger, Till Hohmann

ART DIRECTION
Dominik Kentner

CLIENT CONSULTING
Daniel Adolph, Stefanie Siegl

PHOTOGRAPHY
Archiv Brot für die Welt

MEDIA
Mediaplus Hamburg

COPY
Tassilo Gutscher

FINAL ARTWORK
Frederick Neff

NOMINATION

Die Idee war, im Rahmen der Kampagne »Schärfen Sie Ihren Blick« ein Münzfernglas vor dem Kanzleramt in Berlin aufzustellen und direkt auf das Büro von Kanzlerin Merkel auszurichten. Warf man einen Blick hindurch, erkannte man tatsächlich die Kanzlerin in ihrem Büro. Und zwar so, wie man sie noch nie gesehen hat...

The idea was to post a big binocular in front of the german chancellery. If someone looked through the binocular, he could witness the german chancellor Angela Merkel in a way no one has seen her before...

TITLE
n-TV Promotion »Kanzleramt«

CLIENT
n-tv Nachrichtenfernsehen GmbH & Co. KG

MARKETING DIRECTOR
Christoph Hammerschmidt

LEAD AGENCY
Euro RSCG Düsseldorf

CREATIVE DIRECTION
Felix Glauner, Martin Breuer

ART DIRECTION
Ingmar Krannich

CLIENT CONSULTING
Cornelia Sanders

AGENCY PRODUCER
Detlef Stuhldreier

COMPUTER ANIMATION
Armin Müller

GRAPHIC ART
Anne Westhoff

EDITING
Peter Georgi

COPY
Martin Venn, Kajo Titus Strauch

FILME DIESER KATEGORIE FINDEN SIE UNTER WWW.ADC.DE FOR FILMS FROM THIS CATEGORY VISIT WWW.ADC.DE

NOMINATION

Verdreckte Mauern in den Städten wurden gereinigt, so dass die Form eines Atego entstand. Ziel war es, auf möglichst plakative Weise darzustellen, welchen wichtigen Beitrag Mercedes-Benz leistet, um die Feinstaubbelastung zu senken. Und wie unsere Städte aussehen könnten, wenn alle Lkw mit der bahnbrechenden Dieseltechnologie »BlueTec« ausgerüstet wären.

Dirty walls in cities were cleaned up such that they revealed the shape of an Atego. The objective was, in as striking a way as possible, to portray the important part Mercedes-Benz is playing in reducing the pollution by fine particles. And what our cities could look like if all trucks were to be fitted with the ground-breaking "BlueTec" diesel technology.

TITLE
Mercedes-Benz LKW Blue Tec Promotion »Clean Wall«

CLIENT
Mercedes-Benz LKW, Vertriebsorganisation Deutschland

MARKETING DIRECTOR
Andreas Burkhart

ADVERTISING DIRECTOR
Sascha Thieme

LEAD AGENCY
BBDO Stuttgart GmbH

CREATIVE DIRECTION
Wolf-Peter Camphausen, Armin Jochum

ART DIRECTION
Claudia Dechant, Sven Gareis, Anne Seltmann

CLIENT CONSULTING
Caroline Schäufele, Andreas Rauscher, Sabrina Ott

PRODUCTION
Netzwerk P, M.A.R.K.13, Floridan Studios GmbH

COPY
Christian Stamp, Wolf-Peter Camphausen

NOMINATION

In Zusammenarbeit mit dem Weingut Graf-Müller haben wir deren Weinflaschen mit unseren Bitburger Korken verkorkt. Öffnete ein Weintrinker schließlich zu Hause seine Flasche Wein, staunte dieser nicht schlecht, als er beim Riechen am Korken unsere Botschaften las.

In cooperation with the vineyard Graf-Mueller we corked their wine bottles with our special Bitburger corks. So, wine drinkers were very surprised to read our messages when they opened one of our wine bottles.

TITLE
Bitburger »Bierkorken«

CLIENT
Bitburger Braugruppe GmbH

MARKETING DIRECTOR
Gerald Wüst, Henner Höper, Andreas Keuter

ADVERTISING DIRECTOR
Hans Joachim Meyer

LEAD AGENCY
Jung von Matt AG

CREATIVE DIRECTION
Fabian Frese, Götz Ulmer

ART DIRECTION
Julia Ziegler

CLIENT CONSULTING
Axel Müller, Anke Göbber, Marco Köditz, Alexandra Beck, Stefanie Struzyna

COPY
Jan-Florian Ege

FILME DIESER KATEGORIE FINDEN SIE UNTER WWW.ADC.DE FOR FILMS FROM THIS CATEGORY VISIT WWW.ADC.DE

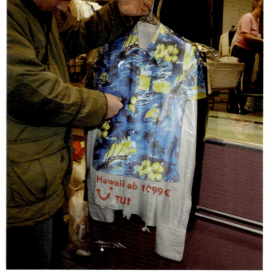

NOMINATION

Eine zahlungskräftige Zielgruppe sollte auf die TUI-Reiseangebote nach Hawaii aufmerksam gemacht werden. In Zusammenarbeit mit Reinigungen wurden die Schutzfolien der gereinigten Hemden mit bunten Mustern von Hawaii-Hemden bedruckt. So wurden die edlen Business-Oberteile zum schrillen Hawaii-Look und sorgten bei der Abholung für Verwunderung und eine Menge Fernweh.

Brief: To call the attention of a solvent target group for the TUI travel offers to Hawaii.
Solution: Working in cooperation with dry-cleaners floral Hawaiian-Shirts were printed on the protective plastic covers. This surprisingly aroused the attention of potential consumers when they picked up their business shirts, which become a brightly-coloured holiday dress.

TITLE
TUI Promotion »Hawaii-Hemden«
CLIENT
TUI AG
MARKETING DIRECTOR
Michael Lambertz

ADVERTISING DIRECTOR
Jutta Lage-Weiland, Nils Behrens, Julia Schlegl
LEAD AGENCY
Jung von Matt AG
CREATIVE DIRECTION
Arno Lindemann, Bernhard Lukas

ART DIRECTION
Ole Kleinhans, Markus Kremer
CLIENT CONSULTING
Nic Heimann, Nina Sophie Scheller
ILLUSTRATION
Sunny Clayton

COPY
Thomas Heyen

ADDITIONAL AWARDS NOMINATION
Volume Advertising page 187
Verkaufsförderung
Sales promotion

NOMINATION

Um das Interesse am »Filmfest Hamburg« zu steigern, übertrugen wir das Medium Film auf das Medium Citylight. 16 Citylights wurden hintereinander aufgestellt und durch eine spezielle Belichtungstechnik miteinander verbunden. Alle paar Sekunden konnte so ein »Kurzfilm« gezeigt werden: Eine Patrone fliegt rasend schnell durch die Nacht, um schließlich das »Filmfest Hamburg«-Plakat zu durchschlagen.

To increase the interest in the "Filmfest Hamburg" we applied the media movie to the media citylight. 16 citylights were put up one behind the other and connected by a special lighting system. This way a "short movie" could be shown: Every few seconds a bullet flys tearingly through the night and finally brake through the "Filmfest Hamburg" placard.

TITLE
Filmfest Hamburg CLP Strecke »Patrone«

CLIENT
Filmfest Hamburg GmbH

MARKETING DIRECTOR
Sven Schwarz

ADVERTISING DIRECTOR
Sven Schwarz

LEAD AGENCY
VASATA | SCHRÖDER
Werbeagentur GmbH

CREATIVE DIRECTION
Jürgen Florenz

ART DIRECTION
Boris Suchatzky

CONSULTING
Dominique Bremer

GRAPHIC ART
Christopher Ernst

PRODUCTION
Susanna Dübbers

COPY
Claus Berg

FILME DIESER KATEGORIE FINDEN SIE UNTER WWW.ADC.DE FOR FILMS FROM THIS CATEGORY VISIT WWW.ADC.DE

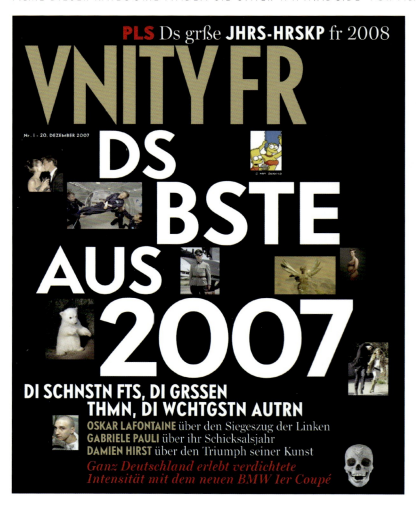

NOMINATION

Zum Launch des neuen BMW 1er Coupé konnte man im ganzen Land Fahrfreude in ihrer intensivsten Form erleben. Und das, ohne in einem BMW zu sitzen. Denn bei der Kampagne ging es weniger darum, den Menschen zu erklären, was technisch in diesem Fahrzeug steckt, als vielmehr darum, deutlich zu machen, wie es sich anfühlt, es zu fahren: das neue BMW 1er Coupé – verdichtete 1ntensität. Nicht einmal Magazintitel konnten sich der verdichteten 1ntensität entziehen.

The launch of the new BMW 1 Series Coupe allowed people throughout the country to experience driving pleasure in its most intense form – without anyone having to get into a BMW. This is because the primary purpose of this campaign was not to explain the technical components within this car, but rather to show what it feels like to drive it: The new BMW 1 Series Coupe – Condensed intensity. Not even magazine titles were able to escape this condensed intensity.

TITLE
BMW 1er Coupé
»Verdichtete Magazintitel«
CLIENT
BMW AG
MARKETING DIRECTOR
Manfred Bräunl
ADVERTISING DIRECTOR
Dr. Tobias Nickel,
Dr. Hans-Peter Ketterl
LEAD AGENCY
MAB, Berlin
CONTRIBUTING AGENCIES
Mediaplus
CREATIVE DIRECTION
Nils Haseborg, Tomas Tulinius

ART DIRECTION
Michael Janke
CLIENT CONSULTING
Henning Gerstner,
Leveke Lambersy
STRATEGIC PLANNING
Moritz Kiechle, Till Buchner
PUBLISHING HOUSE
Gruner & Jahr, Condé Nast
AGENCY PRODUCER
Lars Ebeling
GRAPHIC ART
Sandra Mithöfer
MEDIA
Werner Reineke,
Christian Kaessmann

COPY
Ilja Schmuschkowitsch
FINAL ARTWORK
Gordon Gohde

ADDITIONAL AWARDS
BRONZE
Volume Advertising page 024
Publikumsanzeigen
Consumer advertisements

NOMINATION
Volume Advertising page 124
Plakate und Poster
(indoor und outdoor)
Billboards and posters
(indoor and outdoor)

NOMINATION
Volume Advertising page 203
Media
Media

NOMINATION
Volume Advertising page 358
Integrierte Kampagnen
Integrated campaigns

SILVER

TITLE
IKEA Promotion »3D-Cover«
CLIENT
IKEA Deutschland GmbH
MARKETING DIRECTOR
Claudia Willvonseder
ADVERTISING DIRECTOR
Jens Helfrich, Gerrit Kaminski
LEAD AGENCY
Jung von Matt AG
CONTRIBUTING AGENCIES
Act Agency Hamburg,
Stein Promotions
CREATIVE DIRECTION
Arno Lindemann,
Bernhard Lukas, Tom Hauser,
Sören Porst
ART DIRECTION
Joanna Swistowski
CLIENT CONSULTING
Nicole Drabsch, Nic Heimann
COMPUTER ANIMATION
Sven Schoenmann
PRINTING
Gerstenberg Druck &
Direktwerbung
GRAPHIC ART
Matthias Grundner, Julia Jakobi
CAMERA
Justus Becker, Ingo Dannecker
MUSIC COMPOSITION
Malte Hagemeister
EDITING
Justus Becker
TECHNICAL IMPLEMENTATION
Birgit Ballhause,
Philipp Mokrohs
COPY
Caroline Ellert, Tom Hauser

ADDITIONAL AWARDS
SILVER
Volume Advertising page 186
Verkaufsförderung
Sales promotion

SILVER
Volume Advertising page 368
Dialogmarketing
Dialogue marketing

NOMINATION
Volume Design page 319
Events
Events

NOMINATION

TITLE
Volkswagen Service Promotion
»Fake Sounds Live«
CLIENT
Volkswagen AG
MARKETING DIRECTOR
Michael Scharnau
ADVERTISING DIRECTOR
Philipp Benzler
LEAD AGENCY
DDB Germany, Berlin
CREATIVE DIRECTION
Bert Peulecke, Stefan Schulte
ART DIRECTION
Tim Stübane
CLIENT CONSULTING
Ulrich Klenke, Nadja Richter,
Silke Lagodny
AGENCY PRODUCER
Patrick Scharf, Hendrik
Raufmann
GRAPHIC ART
Jussi Jääskeläinen
TECHNICAL DIRECTION
Sascha Mehn
COPY
Birgit van den Valentyn

ADDITIONAL AWARDS
NOMINATION
Volume Advertising page 185
Verkaufsförderung
Sales promotion

ALFRED HITCHCOCK

*13. AUGUST 1899 LEYTONSTONE/LONDON
†29. APRIL 1980 LOS ANGELES

Als kleiner dicklicher Katholik im anglikanischen London fand Alfred Hitchcock als Schüler keine Freunde. Er blieb ein Einzelgänger und vergrub sich zunehmend in Romane. Statt Fußball zu spielen, saß er im Theater und Kino oder verfolgte Mordprozesse am Old-Bailey-Gerichtshof. Nebenbei besuchte er Kurse in technischem Zeichnen. Die waren auch die Voraussetzung für seinen Einstieg in die Filmgeschichte. Als Zwanzigjähriger illustrierte er für Paramount in London Zwischentitel für Stummfilme. Außerdem entwarf er Szenenbilder, Dekorationen und Kostüme. Dann machte er mit Überarbeitungen von Drehbüchern auf sich aufmerksam. Bereits 1922 bewies er sich erstmalig als Regisseur. So richtig ins Rollen kam seine Karriere allerdings erst mit dem Tonfilm. Ende der 30er Jahre wurde Hollywood auf den expressionistischen Kontrollfreak aufmerksam. Hitchcock biss sich durch. Er erkämpfte sich bei den Film-Tycoons die absolute künstlerische Freiheit und drehte stilistisch einflussreiche Filme wie »Das Fenster zum Hof«, »Der Mann, der zu viel wusste«, »Der unsichtbare Dritte«, »Psycho«, »Die Vögel« und »Frenzy«.

*13 AUGUST 1899 LEYTONSTONE/LONDON
†29 APRIL 1980 LOS ANGELES

A small, podgy Catholic in Anglican London, Alfred Hitchcock had no friends as a child. He remained a loner, increasingly immersing himself in novels. Instead of playing football he sat in theatres and cinemas, or followed murder trials at the Old Bailey. Along the way, he attended courses in technical drawing, which would also in turn be the factor that led to him taking his place the history of the cinema. At the age of twenty, he designed captions for silent films for Paramount in London. He also designed scenery, decorations and costumes. He then drew attention to himself through his revisions of screenplays, going on to prove his ability as a director as early as 1922. However, it was with the advent of sound that his career really began to pick up momentum. At the end of the 30s, the expressionist control freak got the attention of Hollywood. Hitchcock fought his way through, wresting total artistic freedom from the movie moguls and directing his most stylistically influential films, such as *Rear Window*, *The Man Who Knew Too Much*, *North by Northwest*, *Psycho*, *The Birds* and *Frenzy*.

In feature films the director is God;
in documentary films God is the director.

IN SPIELFILMEN IST DER REGISSEUR GOTT;
IN DOKUMENTARFILMEN IST GOTT DER REGISSEUR.

FILME DIESER KATEGORIE FINDEN SIE UNTER WWW.ADC.DE FOR FILMS FROM THIS CATEGORY VISIT WWW.ADC.DE

Zu dieser Kampagne gehört noch ein weiterer Spot: »Drossard«.

One further spot is part of this campaign: "Drossard".

GOLD

Horst Schlämmer macht Führerschein. Er meistert die erste Fahrstunde mit Bravour, sucht nach dem richtigen Auto, recherchiert knallhart, besteht die Fahrprüfung und präsentiert sich schließlich der Damenwelt: mit neuem Golf und damit noch unwiderstehlicher als je zuvor.

Horst Schlämmer gets his driving licence: he struggles through the first driving lesson, looks for the right car, does some serious research, passes the driving test and proudly presents himself to the ladies: with his new Golf, which makes him even more irresistible.

TITLE
Volkswagen Kampagne »Horst Schlämmer macht Führerschein«
CLIENT
Volkswagen AG
MARKETING DIRECTOR
Jochen Sengpiehl
ADVERTISING DIRECTOR
Ralf Maltzen, Hartmut Seeger
LEAD AGENCY
DDB Germany, Berlin
CREATIVE DIRECTION
Amir Kassaei, Stefan Schulte, Bert Peulecke
ART DIRECTION
Kristoffer Heilemann
CLIENT CONSULTING
Benjamin Reininger, Niklas Feuerle, Cathleen Losch, Silke Lagodny
FILM PRODUCTION
Telemaz Commercials Berlin
RADIO PRODUCTION
Hastings Audio Network Berlin
AGENCY PRODUCER
Boris Schepker
CONSULTING
Künstlervermittlung: Special Key – Christian Biedermann, Sven Zander
CAMERA
Xaver Schweyer, Detlef Camp

ARTIST
Hape Kerkeling
POSTPRODUCTION
Condor digital media Berlin
PRODUCTION
Barbara Kranz, Frank Hasselbach, Kjell Kunde
EDITOR
Uli Langguth
DIRECTION
Gerald Grabowski
EDITING
Kathrin Schmoll
STYLING
Brigitte Remmert
TECHNICAL DIRECTION
Sascha Mehn
COPY
Ludwig Berndl, Philip Bolland, Christian Fries
SOUND ENGINEER
Lars Gelhausen

ADDITIONAL AWARDS
GOLD
Volume Advertising page 186
Verkaufsförderung
Sales promotion

GOLD
Volume Advertising page 283
Filme für Verkaufsförderung/ Unternehmensdarstellungen
Films for sales promotion/ company presentation

GOLD
Volume Advertising page 289
Virale Filme
Viral films

GOLD
Volume Advertising page 347
Integrierte Kampagnen
Integrated campaigns

GOLD
Volume Advertising page 367
Dialogmarketing
Dialogue marketing

GOLD
Volume Design page 242
Digitale Werbung
Digital advertising

SILVER
Volume Advertising page 096
Tages-/Wochenzeitungsanzeigen
Advertisements in daily/weekly newspapers

SILVER
Volume Advertising page 139
Produkt-/Werbebroschüren
Product/advertising brochures

SILVER
Volume Advertising page 147
Text
Copy

SILVER
Volume Design page 259
Digitale Medien: Viral
Digital media: Viral

BRONZE
Volume Advertising page 152
Text
Copy

BRONZE
Volume Advertising page 326
Funkspots
Radio commercials

NOMINATION
Volume Design page 095
Informationsmedien
Information media

NOMINATION
Volume Design page 235
Websites
Websites

  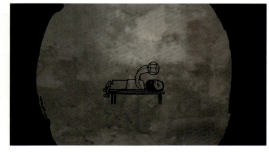
  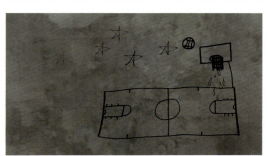

SILVER

Über 30 Ausnahmeathleten verraten in Zeichnungen, Gemälden und Skulpturen, wie sie die Schwierigkeiten auf dem Weg zur Weltspitze überwunden haben. Das Projekt erzählt von den Wendepunkten im Leben dieser Sportler – u. a. von David Beckham, Jonah Lomu und Gilbert Arenas. Die Kunstwerke schaffen eine Authentizität, wie sie im Hochleistungssport selten zu finden ist.

The world's greatest athletes inspire us in adidas' Impossible is Nothing 2007 global brand campaign with their real "impossible stories", using their own words and artwork. The athletes describe and illustrate defining moments in their lives. Their stories present a truth and honesty rarely seen in advertising.

TITLE
adidas Kampagne »Impossible Is Nothing«
CLIENT
adidas International
MARKETING DIRECTOR
Eric Liedtke
ADVERTISING DIRECTOR
Andrew Lux
LEAD AGENCY
180 Amsterdam (180\TBWA)
CONTRIBUTING AGENCIES
TBWA
CREATIVE DIRECTION
Sean Thompson, Dean Maryon
ART DIRECTION
Dean Maryon

CLIENT CONSULTING
Mark Schermers/
Nicolas Kettelhake/
Frank Persyn
FILM PRODUCTION
Passion Pictures
RADIO PRODUCTION
Grand Central Studios
AGENCY PRODUCER
Tony Stearns/Kate Morrison
EDITOR
Jamie Foord & Peter Haddon
FILM ANIMATION
Yu Sato, Jerry Fordher, Dave Burns
CAMERA
Alex Melman, Brandon Galvin

CONCEPT
Sean Thompson, Dean Maryon
MUSIC COMPOSITION
Max Richter/Badly Drawn Boy
POSTPRODUCTION
Passion Pictures
PRODUCTION
Russell Mclean
DIRECTION
Sean Thompson, Dean Maryon, Dan Gordon
SOUND DESIGN
Christopher Wilson
COPY
Sean Thompson
VISUAL EFFECTS
Dan Sumich

ADDITIONAL AWARDS
GOLD
Volume Design page 111
Bücher, Verlagsobjekte
Books, publishing house products

SILVER
Volume Advertising page 354
Integrierte Kampagnen
Integrated campaigns

SILVER

Er spielt sie alle! Olli Dittrich schlüpft in acht verschiedene Rollen und spielt die härtesten Kunden, die jemals im Media Markt eingekauft haben: Mal den schwulen Bankvorstand, der schärfer auf den Verkäufer als auf das Gerät ist. Mal ein Spießer-Ehepaar, das sich nie einigen kann. Am Ende verdient sich der Media Markt Verkäufer immer ein »Das kauf ich Euch ab!«

He plays them all! Olli Dittrich takes on eight different roles, impersonating the toughest customers who have ever shopped at Media Markt: now the gay bank director who is more interested in the salesman than the product, then the bourgeois couple who can never agree on anything. In the end, the Media Markt salesman always hears an "I'm buying that!"

TITLE
Media Markt Kampagne »Das kauf' ich Euch ab.«
CLIENT
redblue marketing GmbH
ADVERTISING DIRECTOR
Klaus Wäcker
LEAD AGENCY
kempertrautmann gmbh
ART DIRECTION
Florian Weber

CLIENT CONSULTING
Boris Malvinsky, Nils Möller, Hendrik Heine
FILM PRODUCTION
Markenfilm
FILM ANIMATION
Steady Cam: Felix Storp
GRAPHIC ART
Sharon Jessen

MUSIC COMPOSITION
nhb
POSTPRODUCTION
Markenfilm Video, Optix Digital
DIRECTION
Otto Alexander Jahrreiss
EDITING
Annett Kiener und Arthur Jagodda
SCREEN DESIGN
Optix Digital

SOUND DESIGN
nhb
COPY
Filiz Tasdan, Willy Kaussen, Michael Ohanian
SOUND ENGINEER
Wenke Kleine-Benne
INTERACTIVE PRODUCER
DOP: Martin Ruhe

SILVER

Acht Renaults fahren zu Ballett-Musik Formationen auf einem ausgetrockneten Salzsee. Es sieht aus, als würden sie tanzen. Hochästhetische Aufnahmen. Aber nach und nach crashen alle Fahrzeuge perfekt choreografiert gegeneinander. Am Ende sind alle Wagen demoliert. Aber noch in der Lage zu fahren. Sie verneigen sich zum Packshot. Die Botschaft: Das sicherste Ensemble der Welt.

Eight Renaults are driving to ballet music, creating formations on a dried salt lake. It looks like they are dancing. Highly aesthetic shots. But gradually all the cars begin to crash against one another in perfect choreography. In the end, all cars are demolished. But they are still capable of driving and line up for their packshot. Dissolve: The safest car range there is.

TITLE
Renault Deutschland »Ballett«

CLIENT
Renault Deutschland AG

MARKETING DIRECTOR
Jörg-Alexander Ellhof

LEAD AGENCY
Nordpol+ Hamburg Agentur für Kommunikation GmbH

CREATIVE DIRECTION
Lars Rühmann

ART DIRECTION
Tim Schierwater,
Christoph Bielefeldt

CLIENT CONSULTING
Mathias Müller-Using

FILM PRODUCTION
element e

MUSIC COMPOSITION
Jacques Offenbach;
Additional composing:
Steve Patuta@audioforce

POSTPRODUCTION
Deli Pictures

PRODUCTION
Jürgen Joppen

DIRECTION
Silvio Helbig

EDITING
Sabine Panek

SOUND DESIGN
Loft Tonstudios, GmbH

COPY
Sebastian Behrendt

SOUND ENGINEER
Sascha Heiny, Stefan Apell

ADDITIONAL AWARDS
SILVER
Volume Advertising page 277
Kinowerbefilme
Cinema commercials

NOMINATION
Volume Advertising page 313
Musikkompositionen/
Sound-Design
Music compositions/sound design

BRONZE

Ein Fahrradfahrer wird von einem brüllenden mittelalterlichen Ritter attackiert. Erschrocken hält er an. Der Ritter hat es auf das Rad abgesehen. Es kommt zu einer Kraftprobe, die der Ritter gewinnt. Brüllend rennt er mit dem Rad weg. Der Radfahrer kann ihm nur fassungslos hinterhersehen.
Wie erklären Sie das Ihrer Versicherung?
Einfach anrufen!
DEVK Versicherungen. Persönlich, preiswert, nah.

A man is riding a bike when suddenly a roaring medieval knight starts running towards him. Shocked them an tops. The knight is clearly after the bike. A test of strength between him and the cyclist starts which the knight wins. Roaring he flees with the bike. The cyclist stunned looks after him.
How do you explain this to your insurance?
Just call!
DEVK Insurances. Personal. Economical. Close.

TITLE
DEVK Versicherung »Fahrrad«

CLIENT
DEVK Versicherung

MARKETING DIRECTOR
Michael Knaup

ADVERTISING DIRECTOR
Christiane Niehaus

LEAD AGENCY
Grabarz & Partner

CREATIVE DIRECTION
Ralf Heuel, Dirk Siebenhaar

ART DIRECTION
Djik Ouchiian

FILM PRODUCTION
Big Fish Filmproduktion GmbH

AGENCY PRODUCER
Patrick Cahill

CONSULTING
Thomas Eickhoff, Julia Wilhelm

CAMERA
Pascal Walder

DIRECTION
Andreas Hoffmann

COPY
Martin Graß

DEVK VERSICHERUNGEN

PERSÖNLICH, PREISWERT, NAH.

BRONZE

Ein TV-Spot im typischen Werbeumfeld für Klingeltöne, der ebenfalls für eine Hotline wirbt. Allerdings ist die gesungene Telefonnummer so unendlich lang, dass man schon Dextro Energy dabeihaben muss, um sie sich merken zu können.

A TV commercial set in the typical ringtone advertising environment, which advertises for a hotline, too. However, the telephone number, which is sung, is so long that you need to have Dextro Energy with you in order to remember the number.

TITLE
Dextro Energy »Hotline«

CLIENT
Dextro Energy

MARKETING DIRECTOR
Viola Ehrenbeck

LEAD AGENCY
kempertrautmann gmbh

CREATIVE DIRECTION
Willy Kaussen, Frank Bannöhr

ART DIRECTION
Frank Bannöhr

CLIENT CONSULTING
Hendrik Heine, Nils Möller, Jacqueline Koch

FILM PRODUCTION
Tempomedia

GRAPHIC ART
Christoph Zapletal

CAMERA
Eduard Schneidermeier

MUSIC COMPOSITION
Thomas Kisser »Wake-Up-Music«, Hastings Audio Network

PRODUCTION
Alexander Schildt, Stefan Vollmert, Daniela Dreyer

DIRECTION
Andreas Link

EDITING
Christoph Zapletal, Jörn Falldorf

COPY
Willy Kaussen

ADDITIONAL AWARDS
BRONZE
Volume Advertising page 312
Musikkompositionen/
Sound-Design
Music compositions/sound design

TELEVISION COMMERCIALS TV-SPOTS

BLEIB KONZENTRIERT.

BRONZE

Der jobsintown.de TV-Spot ist der überraschende Beweis: Selbst hinter einem bekannten Bildschirmschoner kann ziemlich harte Arbeit stecken. Anstatt des erwarteten Programms, muss ein Mensch den Bildschirmschoner-Effekt wie eine Laterne durch einen großen dunklen Raum tragen. Und besonders wenn dabei etwas schiefgeht, wird deutlich: »Das Leben ist einfach zu kurz für den falschen Job.«

The TV ad of jobsintown.de proves it in a surprising way: Even a well known screensaver could be hard work. Instead of the expected program, a man has to carry the visual effect on a lantern across the room. And especially if something goes wrong it is getting more than obvious: "Life's simply too short for the wrong job."

TITLE
jobsintown.de Kampagne »Bildschirmschoner«

CLIENT
jobsintown.de GmbH

MARKETING DIRECTOR
Stefan Kraft

LEAD AGENCY
Scholz & Friends

CREATIVE DIRECTION
Matthias Spaetgens, Oliver Handlos, Jan Leube

ART DIRECTION
David Fischer

CLIENT CONSULTING
Katrin Voß, Sascha Kruse

FILM PRODUCTION
Nic Niemann, Entspanntfilm

AGENCY PRODUCER
Anke Landmark

GRAPHIC ART
Tabea Rauscher

STYLING
Stefanie Granitza

COPY
Daniel Bödeker

VISUAL EFFECTS
Sascha Haber

ADDITIONAL AWARDS
SILVER
Volume Design page 256
Digitale Medien: Viral
Digital media: Viral

TELEVISION COMMERCIALS TV-SPOTS

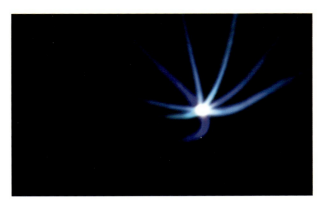

FILME DIESER KATEGORIE FINDEN SIE UNTER WWW.ADC.DE FOR FILMS FROM THIS CATEGORY VISIT WWW.ADC.DE

BRONZE

Im Bild eines süßen Vogels ist eine Frau mit gespreizten Beinen versteckt, in einem Reiterbild eine explizite Liebesszene und in einem Schneemann ein Penis – vor unseren Augen verwandeln sich Genitalien in harmlose Kinderbilder. Der Abbinder klärt uns auf: »Sie werden es sehen. Ihre Kinder nicht. Beate Uhse Erotic TV mit Kindersicherung.«

A woman with spread legs is hidden in the picture of a cute bird, an explicit love scene in a picture of a horseback rider, and a penis in a snowman – genitals are transformed into harmless children's pictures before our very eyes. The tag line explains it all: "You will see it. Your children won't. Beate Uhse Erotic TV with parental control."

TITLE
Beate Uhse »Kindersicherung«
CLIENT
Beate Uhse TV
MARKETING DIRECTOR
Stefanie Eisenschenk
LEAD AGENCY
kempertrautmann gmbh
CREATIVE DIRECTION
Gerrit Zinke, Jens Theil
ART DIRECTION
Florian Schimmer
CLIENT CONSULTING
Hendrik Heine
FILM PRODUCTION
Markenfilm
ILLUSTRATION
Jost Keller
MUSIC COMPOSITION
Thomas Kisser
POSTPRODUCTION
Markenfilm

PRODUCTION
Acki Heldens, Jannik Endemann
DIRECTION
Neels Feil
EDITING
Neels Feil
COPY
Michael Götz, Stefan Förster

ADDITIONAL AWARDS
NOMINATION
Volume Advertising page 283
Filme für Verkaufsförderung/
Unternehmensdarstellungen
Films for sales promotion/
company presentation

NOMINATION
Volume Advertising page 289
Virale Filme
Viral films

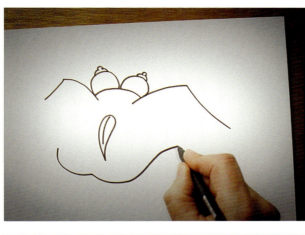

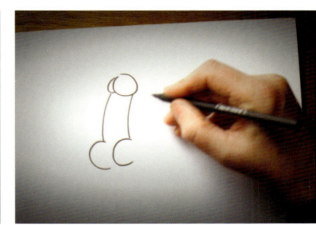

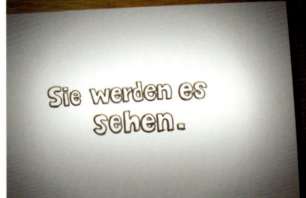

BRONZE

Wir haben es immer gewusst: Kaugummi besteht zu 100% aus Hasenzähnen. Damit der neue Juicy Fruit Squish seine fruchtige Füllung erhält, knabbern die Hasen auf der Juicy Fruit Ranch ausschließlich Obst. Unter der Aufsicht von Stallknecht Alexej und Juniorchefin Betsy wird hier der neue Juicy Fruit Squish produziert und anschließend fachmännisch geerntet. Was macht der Hase? Juicy Fruit Squish.

Essentially, we've always known it: gum is made of 100% rabbit teeth. In order to give Juicy Fruit Squish its fruity filling, the rabbits on the Juicy Fruit Ranch eat only fruit. Under the careful supervision of stableman Alexej and assistant manager Betsy, the new Juicy Fruit Squish is produced and expertly harvested. What does a rabbit do? Juicy Fruit Squish.

TITLE
Wrigley Juicy Fruit Squish »Ranch«

CLIENT
Wrigley GmbH

MARKETING DIRECTOR
Dominic Thiele (Marketing Director)

ADVERTISING DIRECTOR
Dagmar Thöner (Marketing Manager)
Sonja Voss (Jun. Brand Manager)

LEAD AGENCY
Heye, Group GmbH

CREATIVE DIRECTION
Andreas Forberger

ART DIRECTION
Anna Wolff

CLIENT CONSULTING
Ulrike Münchenberg,
Kirsten Schellberg,
Marie Hesel

STRATEGIC PLANNING
Carsten Schneider

FILM PRODUCTION
Stillking, Prag

PHOTOGRAPHY
Oliver Gast

AGENCY PRODUCER
Simon Sieverts

ART BUYING
Kim Bianchi

IDEA
Anna Wolff, Tom Meifert,
Jenny Sanden

CAMERA
Martin Matiasek

MUSIC COMPOSITION
Franco Micalizzi

POSTPRODUCTION
Rasto Simocko, UPP, Prag

DIRECTION
Wolfberg

EDITING
Filip Malasek, Robota, Prag

SOUND DESIGN
Giesing Team

SPEAKER
Thomas Albus, Benny Weber,
Uta Kienemann

COPY
Jenny Sanden, Tom Meifert

SOUND ENGINEER
Wolfgang Lechenmayer

BRONZE

Der BamS Sonntagshändler klingelt bei Frau Schneider. Als sie öffnet und sich mit verstellter Stimme als »ein Freund« ausgibt, klärt der nette Mann sie auf, dass sie mit dem »Bild am Sonntag nach Hause«-Service doch keine Verpflichtung hat, die Zeitung abzunehmen, die Maskerade also vollkommen überfüssig ist. Unbeirrt erwidert sie mit tiefer Stimme: »Das werde ich der Frau Schneider ausrichten.«

A BamS Sunday deliverer rings Frau Schneider's doorbell. She opens the door and puts on a deep voice, explaining that she's "a friend". The nice man tells her that with the Bild am Sonntag home delivery service there's no obligation to take the paper and so her pretence is unnecessary. Unperturbed, she replies in a deep voice: "I'll give Frau Schneider the message."

TITLE
Bild am Sonntag »Tarnung«

CLIENT
Axel Springer AG,
Zeitungsgruppe: Bild/BamS

MARKETING DIRECTOR
Dr. Dietrich von Kläden

ADVERTISING DIRECTOR
Stephanie Sauter

LEAD AGENCY
santamaria

CREATIVE DIRECTION
Niels Alzen, Holger Bultmann,
Norman Störl

CLIENT CONSULTING
Joachim Fuchs, Lina Burchardt

FILM PRODUCTION
Markenfilm Hamburg
GmbH & Co. KG

AGENCY PRODUCER
Nina Svechtarov

IMAGE EDITING
Ingo Behrends

EDITOR
Alexander Jurkat

CAMERA
Holger Diener

MEDIA
Universal McCann Frankfurt,
Medialeitung: Änne Laake,
Axel Springer AG

MUSIC COMPOSITION
SIZZER Music & Sound
Amsterdam

POSTPRODUCTION
Optix Digital Pictures GmbH

DIRECTION
Marc Schölermann

SPEAKER
Clemens Gerhard

STYLING
Susanne Fiedler

COPY
Niels Alzen, Caroline Schmidt

SOUND ENGINEER
Mikis Meyer

Bequem und ohne Verpflichtung.

01805 - 72 72 73
(0,14 €/Min. aus dem dt. Festnetz)

FILME DIESER KATEGORIE FINDEN SIE UNTER WWW.ADC.DE FOR FILMS FROM THIS CATEGORY VISIT WWW.ADC.DE

BRONZE

Schneider Weisse ist der Traum eines jeden Weißbiertrinkers, ein Bier, zu dem man immer wieder zurückkehrt.

Schneider Weisse is a dream of a beer, you always will return to. And it never gets empty …

TITLE
Schneider Weisse »Traum«
CLIENT
Private Weissbierbrauerei
G. Schneider & Sohn GmbH
ADVERTISING DIRECTOR
Sandra Sollinger
LEAD AGENCY
trio-group
CONTRIBUTING AGENCIES
trio-westag-bsb
CREATIVE DIRECTION
Stefan Schneider, Felix Bruchmann
ART DIRECTION
Stefan Schneider
CLIENT CONSULTING
Dr. Jürgen Kütemeyer
FILM PRODUCTION
Vogelsänger Film GmbH

AGENCY PRODUCER
Claus-Michael Sierp
CAMERA
Tim Fabian
ARTIST
Juan Carlos Lopez
POSTPRODUCTION
Jenny Menz, Frank Radermacher
DIRECTION
Alexander Ellendt
SOUND DESIGN
3klang, Sebastian Steiner
STYLING
Angie Neis,
Caroline Schlehbusch
COPY
Felix Bruchmann
VISUAL EFFECTS
Peter Schillings

TELEVISION COMMERCIALS TV-SPOTS 241

KEIN BIER. EIN TRAUM.
SCHNEIDER WEISSE.
DAS ORIGINAL.

FILME DIESER KATEGORIE FINDEN SIE UNTER WWW.ADC.DE FOR FILMS FROM THIS CATEGORY VISIT WWW.ADC.DE

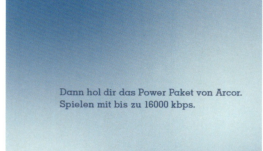

NOMINATION

Online-Spiele sind oft mit langen Ladezeiten verbunden – wenn man die falsche Internetverbindung hat. Was machen eigentlich die Spielfiguren in diesen Wartezeiten? Wir zeigen Computerspielcharaktere, die sich langweilen, die belanglosen Smalltalk führen, die sich anschweigen oder die langsam ungeduldig werden. Anschließend weisen wir auf die Lösung des Problems hin: das Power Paket von Arcor.

Online gaming is often plagued by long loading times – especially if you have the wrong Internet connection. Just what do the game's characters get up to during these loading times? We showed computer game characters who kill time with idle smalltalk, who stare at each other in awkward silence or who get ever more impatient. We ended off with a solution to the problem: the Arcor Power Package.

TITLE
Arcor Power Paket Kampagne
»Gamer Spots«

CLIENT
Arcor AG & Co. KG

ADVERTISING DIRECTOR
Jörg Quehl

LEAD AGENCY
Grabarz & Partner

CREATIVE DIRECTION
Ralf Heuel

ART DIRECTION
Fedja Kehl

CLIENT CONSULTING
Colin Garbers

FILM PRODUCTION
VCC Perfect Pictures AG/
Slaughterhouse GmbH

AGENCY PRODUCER
Patrick Cahill

PRODUCTION
Studio Funk KG

COPY
Paul von Mühlendahl

SOUND ENGINEER
Philipp Feit

NOMINATION

TITLE
»Du bist Deutschland«

CLIENT
Du bist Deutschland GmbH

MARKETING DIRECTOR
Bernd Bauer

ADVERTISING DIRECTOR
Helge Hoffmeister

LEAD AGENCY
Jung von Matt AG,
kempertrautmann gmbh

CREATIVE DIRECTION
Oliver Voss (JvM), Götz Ulmer (JvM)

ART DIRECTION
Till Monshausen (JvM)

CLIENT CONSULTING
Michael Trautmann (kt),
Andrea Bison (kt),
Franziska von Papen (kt),
Tobias Mölder (kt)

FILM PRODUCTION
Markenfilm Hamburg

PHOTOGRAPHY
Timm Brockfeld, Julia Baier,
Alexander Frank

AGENCY PRODUCER
Bey-Bey Chen (JvM)

ART BUYING
Anne Weskamp (JvM)

CONSULTING
Julia Krömker (JvM)

GRAPHIC ART
Daniel Haschtmann (JvM),
Armando Bertolini (JvM)

CAMERA
Dobrivoie Kerpensian

POSTPRODUCTION
Falk Oswald (MF Video),
Paul Breuer (Optix),
Biggi Klier (Optix)

PRODUCTION
Ludger Gorschlüter, Cornelius Rönz,
Hanna Duin

DIRECTION
Clarissa Ruge

SPEAKER
Anna-Lena Strasse

STYLING
Astrid Holk, Sabine Keller,

COPY
Philipp Jessen (JvM)

SOUND ENGINEER
Jochen Laube (Markenfilm),
Felix Lamprecht (nhb),
Felix Müller (nhb)

ADDITIONAL AWARDS
NOMINATION
Volume Advertising page 059
Publikumsanzeigen
Consumer advertisements

NOMINATION
Volume Advertising page 157
Text
Copy

FILME DIESER KATEGORIE FINDEN SIE UNTER WWW.ADC.DE   FOR FILMS FROM THIS CATEGORY VISIT WWW.ADC.DE

Zu dieser Kampagne gehört noch ein weiterer Spot: »Hexler«.

One further spot is part of this campaign: "Hexler".

NOMINATION

Schnick & Schnack, der personifizierte Krimskrams, treiben ihren Schabernack in einem Hornbach Markt. Dabei kommen sie stets auf erzählenswerte Art und Weise um. Und die Moral von der Geschicht: Ein Profi-Baumarkt hat für Schnick und Schnack eben Platze nicht.

Schnick & Schnack, the personification of unnecessary bits and bobs, get up to lots of mischief in a Hornbach store. Along the way, they always perish in a memorable way. The moral of the story: there is no place for Schnick & Schnack, or bits and bobs, at a professional home improvement store.

TITLE
Hornbach Baumarkt »Schnick&Schnack Kampagne«
CLIENT
Hornbach Baumarkt AG
MARKETING DIRECTOR
Jürgen Schröcker
ADVERTISING DIRECTOR
Diana Koob
LEAD AGENCY
HEIMAT, Berlin
CREATIVE DIRECTION
Guido Heffels, Jürgen Vossen

ART DIRECTION
Danny Baarz
CLIENT CONSULTING
Yves Krämer
FILM PRODUCTION
Markenfilm, Berlin
AGENCY PRODUCER
Kerstin Breuer
CONSULTING
Mark Hassan, Sammy Bohneberg
GRAPHIC ART
Jenny Kapteyn

CAMERA
Thomas Kiennast
MUSIC COMPOSITION
Thomas Süß, audioforce Berlin
PRODUCTION
Lutz Müller, Vivian Schröder
DIRECTION
John Fernseher
EDITING
Steffen Schmidt, Arthur Heiseler (VCC)
SOUND DESIGN
Thomas Süß, audioforce Berlin

SPEAKER
John Fernseher
COPY
Matthias Storath
VISUAL EFFECTS
John Fernseher

ADDITIONAL AWARDS
NOMINATION
Volume Advertising page 206
Media
Media

NOMINATION

Die Linien auf einem Notenblatt werden dreidimensional und verwandeln sich in eine virtuelle Achterbahn. Was wir sehen ist auch das, was wir hören – die spektakuläre Fahrt visualisiert das Finale einer Symphonie, die vom Zürcher Kammerorchester gespielt wird

The musical notations on sheet music become three-dimensional and turn into a digital roller coaster track. What we view is what we hear: a spectacular ride illustrates the finale of a symphony played by the Zurich Chamber Orchestra.

TITLE
Zürcher Kammerorchester »Achterbahn«

CLIENT
Zürcher Kammerorchester

MARKETING DIRECTOR
Aviel Cahn

ADVERTISING DIRECTOR
Carola Fischer, Nicole Sandmeier

LEAD AGENCY
Euro RSCG Zürich

CREATIVE DIRECTION
Axel Eckstein

CLIENT CONSULTING
Sarah Gianesi, Andreas Sedmak

FILM PRODUCTION
Virtual Republic

FILM ANIMATION
Marco Kowalik, Christian Marschalt

MUSIC COMPOSITION
Ferdinand Ries

PRODUCTION
Gerhard Vetter

DIRECTION
Michael Klein

STYLING
Steffen Duenner

TECHNICAL DIRECTION
Martin Chatterjee

TECHNICAL IMPLEMENTATION
Patrick Schwidden, Martin Sobott

COPY
Nemanja Gajic

SOUND ENGINEER
Sascha Peters

FILME DIESER KATEGORIE FINDEN SIE UNTER WWW.ADC.DE FOR FILMS FROM THIS CATEGORY VISIT WWW.ADC.DE

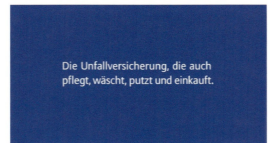

NOMINATION

»Können Sie bitte Fisch und Gemüse besorgen … und bei 90 Grad kochen zusammen mit der weißen Wäsche … genau wie die Kinder, die müssen noch weggebracht werden … in die große Glasvitrine und dann kräftig abstauben … nehmen Sie dazu ein saftiges Wienerschnitzel … gerne auch mit Bügelfalte … Und diesen ganzen Berg Geschirr … muss mein Mann jeden Tag Punkt 12 eingeführt bekommen.«

"Could you get me some vegetables … and boil them with 90° together with the laundry … and donít forget the kids put them in a … big glass showcase and give them a proper dusting … with a big juicy Wienerschnitzel … and a crease there in the middle. (Chart: The accident insurance that covers nursing, washing and shopping). And this stack of dishes … must be inserted into my husband every day at 12 sharp."

TITLE
Allianz Unfall Aktiv »Extrawünsche«

CLIENT
Allianz Beratungs- und Vertriebs-AG

MARKETING DIRECTOR
Jens Erichsen

LEAD AGENCY
Atletico International

CREATIVE DIRECTION
Roland Vanoni/Arndt Dallmann

ART DIRECTION
Kirsa Plewnia

CLIENT CONSULTING
Ilka Gülzau

STRATEGIC PLANNING
Fred Poppenhäger

FILM PRODUCTION
Element-E

AGENCY PRODUCER
Carolin Akhtari

EDITOR
Steven Wilhelm

CAMERA
Martin Ruhe

MUSIC COMPOSITION
Marcel Noll

POSTPRODUCTION
Deli Pictures

PRODUCTION
Bernd Höfflin

DIRECTION
Lars Büchel

SOUND DESIGN
Loft Studio

COPY
Roland Vanoni/Sven Keitel

NOMINATION

Audi baut nicht einfach mal so einen Sportwagen. Im Audi R8 stecken 70 Jahre Vorbereitung: die Erfindung des Mittelmotors und der Alu-Leichtbau in den Dreißigern, quattro Ende der 70er und FSI im Jahre 2007. Bei einer Aufwärmrunde durch die Zeit fährt der Audi R8 noch einmal alle Stationen ab.

Audi doesn't just go out and construct a new sports car. The Audi R8 is backed by 70 years of preparation: the invention of the mid-engine and lightweight aluminum construction in the 1930s, introduction of the Quattro at the end of the 1970s, and FSI in 2007. The Audi R8 takes a warm-up lap past the significant historical milestones in its evolution.

TITLE
Audi R8 »Warm-up«
CLIENT
Audi AG
MARKETING DIRECTOR
Hans-Christian Schwingen
ADVERTISING DIRECTOR
Jagoda Low-Becic, Britta Limbach (Projektmanagemt), Gerhard Kiefer (Produktionsmanagement)

LEAD AGENCY
kempertrautmann gmbh
CREATIVE DIRECTION
Jens Theil, Gerrit Zinke
ART DIRECTION
Gerrit Zinke, Nico Ronacher
CLIENT CONSULTING
Boris Malvinsky,
Ann-Katrin Schelkmann,
Stefanie Pricken, Sebastian Trojand

FILM PRODUCTION
Tony Petersen Film GmbH
AGENCY PRODUCER
Producer bei Tony Petersen:
Tony Petersen, Michael Duttenhöfer
CAMERA
Ian Foster
MUSIC COMPOSITION
Bauhouse – Fabian Grobe,
Clemens Wittkowski

DIRECTION
Lynn Fox
EDITING
Joe Guest
COPY
Jens Theil
VISUAL EFFECTS
The Mill, London

FILME DIESER KATEGORIE FINDEN SIE UNTER WWW.ADC.DE FOR FILMS FROM THIS CATEGORY VISIT WWW.ADC.DE

NOMINATION

Zwei Afrikaner spazieren durch die Steppe, als sie plötzlich von einem hungrigen Löwen gestellt werden. Jäger und Beute starren sich einige Sekunden an. Genug Zeit für einen der beiden Männer, sich seine ASICS-Laufschuhe von Runners Point anzuziehen. Auf die Frage, ober damit schneller sein wolle als der Löwe, antwortet er: »Nein, aber schneller als Du.«

Two Africans are walking through the savanna when suddenly they find themselves standing in front of a hungry lion. Both hunter and prey stare at each other for a few seconds – enough time for one of the men to put on his ASICS running shoes from Runners Point. Asked if he thinks he could run faster than the lion, he answers: "No. But faster than you."

TITLE
Runners Point »Löwe«
CLIENT
RUNNERS POINT
Warenhandelsgesellschaft mbH
MARKETING DIRECTOR
Daniel Kumelis
ADVERTISING DIRECTOR
Daniel Kumelis
LEAD AGENCY
Jung von Matt AG

CREATIVE DIRECTION
Dörte Spengler-Ahrens,
Jan Rexhausen
CLIENT CONSULTING
Julia Krömker, Niklas Kruchten
FILM PRODUCTION
jo!schmid Filmproduktion GmbH
RADIO PRODUCTION
jo!schmid
AGENCY PRODUCER
Julia Cramer
CAMERA
Silvio Helbig

ARTIST
Mntha Vuka, Thabang Kwebu
COMPOSER
Steve Patua
PRODUCTION
Filmproduktion: Producer:
Jürgen Joppen
DIRECTION
Silvio Helbig

EDITING
Tilman Cluss
COPY
Henning Patzner

ADDITIONAL AWARDS NOMINATION
Volume Advertising page 277
Kinowerbefilme
Cinema commercials

NOMINATION

Der Spot beginnt wie eine Dokumentation über eine Vogelmutter, die liebevoll ihre Jungen umsorgt. Doch bald stellt sich die Naturdokumentation als bizarre Szene heraus. Denn das Nest der Vögel befindet sich im langen Vollbart eines Mannes, der auf dem Bett sitzt und das Treiben der Vögel kommentiert. Neben ihm sitzt seine genervte Frau. Die Frage »Zeit für eine Rasur?« löst die Situation auf.

The spot starts like a nature documentary about a bird that is taking care of her chicks. But very soon this documentary shapes up as bizarre comedy scene: the nest of the chicks is situated in the long beard of a man, who is sitting in his bed and commenting the hustle and bustle of the birds. Next to him is his wife, visibly annoyed. The question "Time to shave?" dissolves the situation.

TITLE
ER221 Bart-/Haarschneider »Rotkehlchen«

CLIENT
Panasonic Marketing Europe GmbH

MARKETING DIRECTOR
Rainer Engel, Nina Gustmann

LEAD AGENCY
Scholz & Friends

CREATIVE DIRECTION
Oliver Handlos, Matthias Spaetgens

ART DIRECTION
Jens-Petter Waernes, Erik Dagnell

CLIENT CONSULTING
Stefanie Littek, Jeanine Wyrwoll

FILM PRODUCTION
Motion Blur

AGENCY PRODUCER
Anke Landmark

CAMERA
Askild Vik Edvardsen

POSTPRODUCTION
The Chimney Pot

PRODUCTION
Richard Patterson

DIRECTION
LIFF (Stian Smestad, Jack Cole)

SOUND DESIGN
Baard Haugan Ingebretsen

FILME DIESER KATEGORIE FINDEN SIE UNTER WWW.ADC.DE FOR FILMS FROM THIS CATEGORY VISIT WWW.ADC.DE

NOMINATION

Der Bestand wilder Tiere sinkt dramatisch. Wenn das Aussterben der Tiere nicht gestoppt wird, gibt es in Zukunft keine Wildtiere mehr. Das wird Auswirkungen haben – zum Beispiel auf Safaris. Wir wollen Menschen auf nicht schockierende Weise auf die Bedrohung von Wildtieren hinweisen. Und die Bekanntheit des IFAW steigern.

The number of wild animals is declining dramatically. If the process of extinction is not stopped, there will be no more wild animals in the future. This will have an effect – on safaris, for instance. The task is to point out this fact in a way that is not shocking but fits the tonality of IFAW – ideally in a way that also increases awareness of IFAW.

TITLE
IFAW »Safari«

CLIENT
IFAW International Fund for Animal Welfare

MARKETING DIRECTOR
Dr. Ralf Sonntag;
Projektleitung: Dörte von der Reith

ADVERTISING DIRECTOR
Projektleitung: Dörthe von der Reith

LEAD AGENCY
Springer & Jacoby Werbeagentur GmbH & Co. KG

CREATIVE DIRECTION
Eskil Puhl

ART DIRECTION
Charlotte Badstübner,
Oliver Zboralski

CLIENT CONSULTING
Steffen Behrends, Julia Figur

FILM PRODUCTION
Conegge Film Company, Dickes

AGENCY PRODUCER
Mirco Seyfert

CAMERA
Sebastian Funke, Jan Vogel

MEDIA
Springer & Jacoby Media GmbH & Co. KG

POSTPRODUCTION
cine chromatix Berlin

PRODUCTION
Iwailo Nikolov

DIRECTION
Sebastian Funke, Jan Vogel,
Christian Pfeil

EDITING
Lucy Martens

COPY
Tim Esser

SOUND ENGINEER
audioforce

NOMINATION

Herausstellung der außergewöhnlichen Off-Road-Fähigkeiten von Fahrzeugen der Marke Jeep.

Featuring the extraordinary offroad capability of Jeep vehicles.

TITLE
Jeep »Türknopf«

CLIENT
Chrysler Deutschland GmbH

MARKETING DIRECTOR
Matthias Möhler

ADVERTISING DIRECTOR
Holger Baumann

LEAD AGENCY
KNSK Werbeagentur GmbH

CREATIVE DIRECTION
Tim Krink, Niels Holle

ART DIRECTION
Bill Yom

CLIENT CONSULTING
Jan Isterling, Philipp Ernsting

FILM PRODUCTION
Inhouse

AGENCY PRODUCER
Mareike Holland, Pamela Ross, Kerstin Arndt

POSTPRODUCTION
Sebastian Dörr, Mareike Holland, Pamela Ross, Kerstin Arndt

EDITING
Sebastian Dörr

SOUND DESIGN
NHB Ton Design

COPY
Kurt Müller-Fleischer

SOUND ENGINEER
Markus Roseneck

ADDITIONAL AWARDS NOMINATION
Volume Advertising page 042
Publikumsanzeigen
Consumer advertisements

 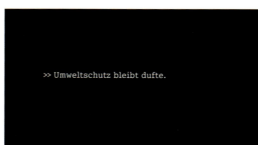 

NOMINATION

Allen Idealismus in Ehren, doch leider sind Umweltschützer gestern wie heute nicht immer umweltfreundlich unterwegs. Denn egal ob Motorboot, Trecker oder der gute alte VW-Bulli – alle verbrauchen doch deutlich mehr als ein smart fortwo. Schließlich ist der die moderne Art, Umweltbewusstsein zu demonstrieren. Oder anders: »Umweltschutz bleibt dufte. smart. open your mind.«

Idealism is all well and good, but unfortunately environmental conservationists do not always travel in environmentally friendly vehicles. A motor-boat, a tractor or the good old VW Transporter – all consume considerably more than the smart fortwo, which is the modern way of demonstrating environmental awareness. In other words: "Environmental protection remains cool. smart. open your mind."

TITLE
smart fortwo cdi »Umwelt«
CLIENT
smart MBVD
MARKETING DIRECTOR
Markus Bauer
ADVERTISING DIRECTOR
Markus Gammert
LEAD AGENCY
BBDO Düsseldorf GmbH
CREATIVE DIRECTION
Toygar Bazarkaya, Ton Hollander, Ralf Zilligen
ART DIRECTION
Tina Oblaten

CLIENT CONSULTING
Marco Golbach, Sebastian Schlosser, Dirk Spakowski
FILM PRODUCTION
Cobblestone Hamburg Filmproduktion GmbH
AGENCY PRODUCER
Steffen Gentis, Anuschka Wallé
IMAGE EDITING
Schönheitsfarm Postproduktion GmbH & Co. KG
EDITOR
Timo Fritsche

CAMERA
Jens Harms
MUSIC COMPOSITION
Musikproduktion: Soundscape Music + Sounddesign
COMPOSER
Backslide Music, Damgaard & Erbler GbR
POSTPRODUCTION
Schönheitsfarm Postproduktion GmbH & Co. KG
PRODUCTION
Cobblestone Hamburg Filmproduktion GmbH

DIRECTION
Markus Walter
EDITING
Timo Fritsche
SOUND DESIGN
Georg Hahn
STYLING
Carola Crede
COPY
Jan Kesting, Kai Hoffmann
SOUND ENGINEER
Georg Hahn, Hahn Nitzsche Studios GmbH

NOMINATION

Die Distanz vom Fahrersitz zum Kofferraum wird zur unzumutbaren Belastung. Um vom vorderen zum hinteren Ende zu kommunizieren, wird ein Telefon gebraucht …
Die Spot-Serie bringt auf den Punkt, was den neuen Golf Variant so besonders macht: Er ist der längste Golf aller Zeiten.

A walk from the driver's seat to the boot becomes too hard to bear, communication from the front of the car to the back is only possible with a mobile phone …
The series of spots sums up what makes the new Golf Variant special: it is the longest Golf of all times.

TITLE
VW Golf Variant Kampagne
»Der längste Golf aller Zeiten«
CLIENT
Volkswagen AG
MARKETING DIRECTOR
Jochen Sengpiehl
ADVERTISING DIRECTOR
Hartmut Seeger
LEAD AGENCY
DDB Germany, Berlin
CREATIVE DIRECTION
Stefan Schulte, Bert Peulecke

ART DIRECTION
Kristoffer Heilemann,
Alexandra Sievers
CLIENT CONSULTING
Cathleen Losch
STRATEGIC PLANNING
Wiebke Dreyer
FILM PRODUCTION
Markenfilm, Wedel
AGENCY PRODUCER
Boris Schepker

EDITOR
Teun Rietveld/Anne Beutel
CAMERA
Gabor Deak
POSTPRODUCTION
Markenfilm, Wedel
PRODUCTION
Ruth Jansen
DIRECTION
Jonathan Herman
EDITING
Teun Rietveld/Anne Beutel

SOUND DESIGN
Hannes Hönemann
STYLING
Vicky von Minckwitz
TECHNICAL DIRECTION
Sascha Mehn
COPY
Ludwig Berndl, Philip Bolland,
Taner Ural, Christian Fries
SOUND ENGINEER
Hannes Hönemann

FILME DIESER KATEGORIE FINDEN SIE UNTER WWW.ADC.DE FOR FILMS FROM THIS CATEGORY VISIT WWW.ADC.DE

GOLD

TITLE
Bundesministerium für Umwelt, Naturschutz und Reaktorsicherheit/EPURON »Power of Wind«
CLIENT
EPURON/Bundesministerium für Umwelt, Naturschutz und Reaktorsicherheit
LEAD AGENCY
Nordpol+ Hamburg Agentur für Kommunikation GmbH
CREATIVE DIRECTION
Lars Rühmann
ART DIRECTION
Björn Rühmann, Joakim Reveman
CLIENT CONSULTING
Mathias Müller-Using
FILM PRODUCTION
PARANOID PROJECTS Paris/PARANOID US Los Angeles
CAMERA
Pascal Marti
MUSIC COMPOSITION
Pigalle Production
POSTPRODUCTION
Mikros Images/Paris
DIRECTION
The Vikings
EDITING
Basile Belkhiri
COPY
Matthew Branning

ADDITIONAL AWARDS
GRAND PRIX
Volume Advertising page 010

GOLD
Volume Advertising page 277
Kinowerbefilme
Cinema commercials

SILVER

TITLE
Hornbach Baumarkt »Mach es fertig«
CLIENT
Hornbach Baumarkt AG
MARKETING DIRECTOR
Jürgen Schröcker
ADVERTISING DIRECTOR
Diana Koob
LEAD AGENCY
HEIMAT, Berlin
CREATIVE DIRECTION
Guido Heffels, Jürgen Vossen
ART DIRECTION
Tim Schneider, Mike Brandt, Marc Wientzek
CLIENT CONSULTING
Yves Krämer
FILM PRODUCTION
Markenfilm, Berlin
AGENCY PRODUCER
Kerstin Breuer
CONSULTING
Mark Hassan, Sammy Bohneberg
IMAGE EDITING
Furia, Barcelona
COMPUTER ANIMATION
Furia, Barcelona
FILM ANIMATION
Furia, Barcelona
CAMERA
Javier Aguirresarobe
MUSIC COMPOSITION
Rudolf Moser, Christian Meyer
COMPOSER
Rudolf Moser, Christian Meyer
POSTPRODUCTION
nhb, Berlin/Furia, Barcelona
PRODUCTION
Lutz Müller, Vivian Schröder
DIRECTION
Carl Erik Rinsch

EDITING
Pablo Plant
SOUND DESIGN
Mosermeyer, Berlin
COPY
Alexander Ardelean, Guido Heffels, Sebastian Kainz, Till Eckel
SOUND ENGINEER
Mastering & Off: Nima Gholiagha, nhb Berlin
VISUAL EFFECTS
Alex Grau (Furia, Barcelona)

ADDITIONAL AWARDS
SILVER
Volume Advertising page 260
Kinowerbefilme
Cinema commercials

SILVER
Volume Advertising page 312
Musikkompositionen/Sound-Design
Music compositions/sound design

BRONZE

TITLE
Mercedes-Benz 4MATIC »4matics«
CLIENT
Daimler AG
MARKETING DIRECTOR
Lothar Korn (Leiter Global Advertising)
ADVERTISING DIRECTOR
Mirco Völker, Mark Niedzballa
LEAD AGENCY
Jung von Matt AG
CREATIVE DIRECTION
Mathias Stiller, Wolfgang Schneider, David Mously, Jan Harbeck
ART DIRECTION
Marius Lohmann
CLIENT CONSULTING
Christian Hupertz, Josef Konstantin Schulte, Yves Rosengart, Johanna Hecker, Helen Seiffe
STRATEGIC PLANNING
Benjamin Pagel
FILM PRODUCTION
Radical.Media
PRODUCTION
Kristin Hirt
DIRECTION
Sebastian Schipper
COPY
Jan Harbeck

ADDITIONAL AWARDS
SILVER
Volume Advertising page 264
Kinowerbefilme
Cinema commercials

TELEVISION COMMERCIALS TV-SPOTS

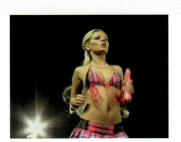

BRONZE

TITLE
Jeep »Ten little vehicles«
CLIENT
Chrysler Deutschland GmbH
LEAD AGENCY
KNSK Werbeagentur GmbH
CREATIVE DIRECTION
Claudia Bach
ART DIRECTION
Michael Reissinger
CLIENT CONSULTING
Jan Isterling, Philipp Ernsting
FILM PRODUCTION
Deli Pictures
ILLUSTRATION
Maurice, Tom, Enzo, Don-sun, Michi, Kim-Eyleen, Johanna-Marie, Emma, Kurt
AGENCY PRODUCER
Kerstin Arndt
IMAGE EDITING
Christian Reimann
COMPUTER ANIMATION
Malte Sarnes, Thomas Volkmann
FILM ANIMATION
Robert Rhee
GRAPHIC ART
Robert Rhee
POSTPRODUCTION
Deli Pictures
PRODUCTION
Sebastian Hellge
DIRECTION
Michael Reissinger
SCREEN DESIGN
Thomas Volkmann, Michael Reissinger
SOUND DESIGN
Markenfilm, nhb Hamburg
COPY
Lisa Port, Fabian Tritsch, Lennert Wendt, Anna-Kristina Schroeder, Nina Burmeister
VISUAL EFFECTS
Christian Reimann

ADDITIONAL AWARDS
BRONZE
Volume Advertising page 270
Kinowerbefilme
Cinema commercials

NOMINATION
Volume Advertising page 303
Audiovisuelle Medien: Design
Audiovisual media: Design

BRONZE

TITLE
Konzerthaus Dortmund Saison 2007/2008 »symphony in red«
CLIENT
Konzerthaus Dortmund – Philharmonie für Westfalen
MARKETING DIRECTOR
Milena Ivkovic
LEAD AGENCY
Jung von Matt AG
CREATIVE DIRECTION
Sascha Hanke, Timm Hanebeck, Wolf Heumann (GF)
ART DIRECTION
Sascha Hanke, Timm Hanebeck
CLIENT CONSULTING
Nina Gerwing, Lena Frers
FILM PRODUCTION
Sehsucht GmbH
AGENCY PRODUCER
Hermann Krug, Alexander Schillinsky
FILM ANIMATION
Niko Tziopanos, Alex Heyer, Martin Hess
CAMERA
Bea Wellenbrock, Alex Heyer, Valentin Heun
MUSIC COMPOSITION
Fazil Say
COMPOSER
Fazil Say
POSTPRODUCTION
Sehsucht GmbH
PRODUCTION
Andreas Coutsoumbelis, Martin Woelke
DIRECTION
Niko Tziopanos
COPY
Michael Okun, Moritz Grub

ADDITIONAL AWARDS
GOLD
Volume Advertising page 278
Filme für Verkaufsförderung/ Unternehmensdarstellungen
Films for sales promotion/ company presentation

GOLD
Volume Advertising page 312
Musikkompositionen/ Sound-Design
Music compositions/ sound design

BRONZE

TITLE
Sixt – rent a car »Matthias Reim«
CLIENT
Sixt GmbH & Co. Autovermietung KG
MARKETING DIRECTOR
Dr. Karsten Willrodt
ADVERTISING DIRECTOR
Daniela Erdmann
LEAD AGENCY
Jung von Matt AG
CREATIVE DIRECTION
Peter Kirchhoff, Wolf Heumann
ART DIRECTION
Vanessa Rabea Schrooten
CLIENT CONSULTING
Sandra Schymetzki, Ann-Kristin Grohsklaus
FILM PRODUCTION
Big Fish Berlin
AGENCY PRODUCER
Julia Cramer
GRAPHIC ART
Felix Taubert
CAMERA
Casey Campell
MUSIC COMPOSITION
Matthias Reim, Bernd Dietrich
DIRECTION
Warwick
COPY
Lisa Maria Hartwich, Peter Kirchhoff, Wolf Heumann

ADDITIONAL AWARDS
SILVER
Volume Advertising page 350
Integrierte Kampagnen
Integrated campaigns

BRONZE
Volume Advertising page 289
Virale Filme
Viral films

BRONZE
Volume Advertising page 313
Musikkompositionen/ Sound-Design
Music compositions/sound design

BRONZE
Volume Design page 246
Digitale Werbung
Digital advertising

NOMINATION
Volume Advertising page 339
Funkspots
Radio commercials

NOMINATION

TITLE
Freeware.de Kampagne »Highspeed Download«
CLIENT
Shareware.de SWV GmbH
MARKETING DIRECTOR
Oliver Kruse
LEAD AGENCY
Scholz & Friends
CREATIVE DIRECTION
Oliver Handlos, Matthias Spaetgens
ART DIRECTION
Jens-Petter Waernes, Erik Dagnell
CLIENT CONSULTING
Sascha Kruse, Benjamin Baader
FILM PRODUCTION
element e filmproduktion gmbh
RADIO PRODUCTION
LOFT Tonstudios GmbH
AGENCY PRODUCER
Anke Landmark
CAMERA
Marc Achenbach
MUSIC COMPOSITION
Fraise
POSTPRODUCTION
Slaughterhouse Hamburg GmbH
PRODUCTION
Bernd T. Hoefflin, Patrick Dettenbach
DIRECTION
Alex Feil
EDITING
Steven Wilhelm
STYLING
Helen Achtermann
SOUND ENGINEER
Jan Dejozé

ADDITIONAL AWARDS
NOMINATION
Volume Advertising page 288
Virale Filme
Viral films

FILME DIESER KATEGORIE FINDEN SIE UNTER WWW.ADC.DE FOR FILMS FROM THIS CATEGORY VISIT WWW.ADC.DE

NOMINATION

TITLE
adidas Football
»Impossible Park Football«
CLIENT
adidas AG
MARKETING DIRECTOR
Markus Rachals
ADVERTISING DIRECTOR
Sven Schindler
LEAD AGENCY
TBWA\ Deutschland
(180/TBWA), Berlin
CREATIVE DIRECTION
Stefan Schmidt
ART DIRECTION
Rochelle Raiss
CLIENT CONSULTING
Kerstin Gold, Falk Lungwitz
STRATEGIC PLANNING
Moritz Kiechle
FILM PRODUCTION
Stink: Jan Dressler,
Nils Schwemer
AGENCY PRODUCER
Johann-Georg Hofer
von Lobenstein
CAMERA
Greg Copeland
MEDIA
Carat, Hamburg
MUSIC COMPOSITION
Blackwell/Millot
COMPOSER
Blackwell/Millot
POSTPRODUCTION
nhb, Berlin
DIRECTION
James Brown
EDITING
Alex Jurkat
STYLING
Martin Manser
COPY
Markus Ewertz

ADDITIONAL AWARDS
NOMINATION
Volume Advertising page 274
Kinowerbefilme
Cinema commercials

NOMINATION

TITLE
Smart »Benzinkanister Blues«
CLIENT
Mercedes-Benz Schweiz AG
MARKETING DIRECTOR
Doris Lengwiler
ADVERTISING DIRECTOR
Fulvio D'Aurelio
LEAD AGENCY
Jung von Matt/Limmat
CREATIVE DIRECTION
Dörte Spengler-Ahrens,
Jan Rexhausen, Alexander Jaggy,
Michael Rottmann
ART DIRECTION
Gun Kanjanapokin,
Ricardo Distefano
CLIENT CONSULTING
Marc Huber, Felix Schröder
FILM PRODUCTION
Markenfilm GmbH & Co
AGENCY PRODUCER
Julia Cramer
COMPUTER ANIMATION
Max Böhm, Stefan Huschenbeth,
Christoph Liebsch,
Christian Wurst-Riecke
EDITOR
Hendrik Smith
CAMERA
Sebastian Pfaffenbichler
MUSIC COMPOSITION
Matthias Rewig (NHB Ton GmbH),
Marcus Löber
COMPOSER
Matthias Rewig (NHB Ton GmbH),
Marcus Löber
POSTPRODUCTION
Daniel Brylka, MF-Video
Produktions GmbH
PRODUCTION
Cornelius Rönz
DIRECTION
Matthieu Mantovani

EDITING
Hendrik Smith
SOUND DESIGN
phreeky beats
COPY
Daniel Pieracci, Fabio Straccia
SOUND ENGINEER
Markus Rosenbeck
VISUAL EFFECTS
Ingo Berends (Flame)

ADDITIONAL AWARDS
BRONZE
Volume Advertising page 266
Kinowerbefilme
Cinema commercials

NOMINATION

TITLE
Hornbach Baumarkt »Screws«
CLIENT
Hornbach Baumarkt AG
MARKETING DIRECTOR
Jürgen Schröcker
ADVERTISING DIRECTOR
Diana Koob
LEAD AGENCY
HEIMAT, Berlin
CREATIVE DIRECTION
Guido Heffels, Jürgen Vossen
ART DIRECTION
Danny Baarz, Tim Schneider
CLIENT CONSULTING
Yves Krämer
FILM PRODUCTION
Markenfilm, Berlin
AGENCY PRODUCER
Kerstin Breuer
CONSULTING
Mark Hassan,
Sammy Bohneberg
GRAPHIC ART
Jessica Philipp, Jenny Kapteyn
CAMERA
Sebastian Blenkov
MEDIA
Crossmedia GmbH, Düsseldorf
MUSIC COMPOSITION
Thomas Süß, audioforce Berlin
PRODUCTION
five_three_double ninety
filmproductions GmbH
DIRECTION
Martin Werner
EDITING
Morton Giese
SOUND DESIGN
Thomas Süß, audioforce Berlin
COPY
Matthias Storath, Till Eckel

ADDITIONAL AWARDS
NOMINATION
Volume Advertising page 275
Kinowerbefilme
Cinema commercials

NOMINATION

TITLE
Mercedes-Benz G-Klasse »Hindernisse«
CLIENT
Daimler AG
MARKETING DIRECTOR
Dr. Olaf Göttgens,
Dr. Kristina Hammer
ADVERTISING DIRECTOR
Mirco Völker, Christina Freier
LEAD AGENCY
Jung von Matt AG
CREATIVE DIRECTION
Fabian Frese, Thimoteus Wagner
ART DIRECTION
Christian Kroll
CLIENT CONSULTING
Klaus Burghauser, Stephan Damm,
Yves Rosengart, Johanna Hecker,
Jan Groenendijk
FILM PRODUCTION
Sehsucht GmbH
ILLUSTRATION
Sehsucht GmbH
COMPUTER ANIMATION
Hannes Geiger, Thore Bornemann,
Maurice Jochem
DESIGN
Alex Heyer
EDITOR
Christoph Senn
MUSIC COMPOSITION
BLUWI Music & Sounddesign
COMPOSER
BLUWI/Timo Blunck, Stefan Will,
Ralf Denker
POSTPRODUCTION
Studio Funk GmbH Co KG
PRODUCTION
Andreas Coutsoumbelis,
Martin Woelke
DIRECTION
Ole Peters, Hannes Geiger
SOUND DESIGN
BLUWI/Marco Dreckkötter
COPY
Peter Gocht
SOUND ENGINEER
Studio Funk/Jochen Kömpe
VISUAL EFFECTS
Daniel Hummer

ADDITIONAL AWARDS
BRONZE
Volume Advertising page 268
Kinowerbefilme
Cinema commercials

NOMINATION
Volume Advertising page 302
Audiovisuelle Medien: Design
Audiovisual media: Design

NOMINATION
Volume Design page 221
Illustration
Illustration

NOMINATION

TITLE
Mercedes-Benz »The Race F1«
CLIENT
Daimler AG
MARKETING DIRECTOR
Lothar Korn, Mirco Völker
ADVERTISING DIRECTOR
Isabell Hartmann,
Jochen Schmidt
LEAD AGENCY
Jung von Matt AG
CREATIVE DIRECTION
Deneke von Weltzien,
Daniel Frericks
ART DIRECTION
Christian Kroll
CLIENT CONSULTING
Christian Hupertz,
Christoph Neuhaus
FILM PRODUCTION
radical media GmbH
AGENCY PRODUCER
Hermann Krug
CAMERA
Paul Laufer
MUSIC COMPOSITION
groove addicts
COMPOSER
Irving Berlin
PRODUCTION
Tommy Turtle, Kristin Hirt
DIRECTION
Tarsem
COPY
Anton von Weltzien,
Karen Am Ende,
Deneke von Weltzien

ADDITIONAL AWARDS
NOMINATION
Volume Advertising page 276
Kinowerbefilme
Cinema commercials

STANLEY KUBRICK

*26. JULI 1928 NEW YORK CITY
†07. MÄRZ 1999 CHILDWICKBURY MANOR BEI LONDON

Nach der Highschool verdiente Stanley Kubrick sein Geld als Fotograf und Journalist in New York. Danach drehte er mehrere kurze Dokumentarfilme. Seine ersten, privat finanzierten Spielfilme machten ihn dann auch für die amerikanische Filmindustrie interessant. Nach »Wege zum Ruhm« kam das Hollywood-Epos »Spartacus« mit Kirk Douglas. Danach schwor er sich, nie wieder einen Film zu drehen, bei dem er nicht vom Buch bis zum Schnitt die Kontrolle ausüben konnte. Er verließ Hollywood und ging nach England. Der Rest ist Filmgeschichte: »Lolita«, »Dr. Seltsam«, »2001: Odyssee im Weltraum«, »A Clockwork Orange«, »The Shining«, »Full Metal Jacket« und »Eyes Wide Shut«.
[MIT FREUNDLICHER ERLAUBNIS DES DEUTSCHEN FILMMUSEUMS FRANKFURT]

*26 JULY 1928 NEW YORK CITY
†07 MARCH 1999 CHILDWICKBURY MANOR, NEAR LONDON

Following high school, Stanley Kubrick earned a living in New York as a photographer and journalist, after which he shot several short documentary films. His first privately financed feature films spawned an interest in him from the American film industry. After *Paths of Glory* came the Hollywood epic *Spartacus*, featuring Kirk Douglas. Following this, he swore never again to direct a film over which he could not maintain control – from the screenplay through to the final cut and beyond. He left Hollywood and moved to England, and the rest is cinema history: *Lolita*, *Dr. Strangelove*, *2001: A Space Odyssey*, *A Clockwork Orange*, *The Shining*, *Full Metal Jacket* and *Eyes Wide Shut*.
[WITH KIND PERMISSION FROM DEUTSCHES FILMMUSEUM FRANKFURT]

A film is – or should be – more like music than like fiction.

EIN FILM IST EHER WIE MUSIK ALS WIE EIN ROMAN – ODER SOLLTE ES SEIN.

SILVER

Der schaurige Anblick seines alten, maroden Badezimmers macht einen Mann dermaßen fertig, dass ihn dieses leibhaftig durch den Tag verfolgt. Kein rennen hilft, er wird es nicht los, weiß er doch: Es ist in seinem Kopf. So hat er nur eine Chance. Er muss das längst überfällige Projekt angehen, er muss zerschlagen, was ihn fertig zu machen scheint.

The ghastly appearance of his old, dilapidated bathroom bothers a man so much that it pursues him throughout the day. Running doesn't help. He can't get rid of it, but he knows … it's in his head. There is only one solution. He must finally get started on the long overdue project. He has to destroy the thing that bugs him the most.

TITLE
Hornbach Baumarkt
»Mach es fertig«
CLIENT
Hornbach Baumarkt AG
MARKETING DIRECTOR
Jürgen Schröcker
ADVERTISING DIRECTOR
Diana Koob
LEAD AGENCY
HEIMAT, Berlin
CREATIVE DIRECTION
Guido Heffels, Jürgen Vossen
ART DIRECTION
Tim Schneider, Mike Brandt,
Marc Wientzek
CLIENT CONSULTING
Yves Krämer
FILM PRODUCTION
Markenfilm, Berlin
AGENCY PRODUCER
Kerstin Breuer
CONSULTING
Mark Hassan, Sammy Bohneberg
IMAGE EDITING
Furia, Barcelona
COMPUTER ANIMATION
Furia, Barcelona
EDITOR
Pablo Plant
FILM ANIMATION
Furia, Barcelona
CAMERA
Javier Aguirresarobe

MEDIA
Crossmedia GmbH
MUSIC COMPOSITION
Rudolf Moser, Christian Meyer
COMPOSER
Rudolf Moser, Christian Meyer
POSTPRODUCTION
nhb, Berlin/Furia, Barcelona
PRODUCTION
Lutz Müller, Vivian Schröder
DIRECTION
Carl Erik Rinsch
EDITING
Pablo Plant
SOUND DESIGN
Mosermeyer, Berlin
COPY
Alexander Ardelean,
Guido Heffels, Sebastian Kainz,
Till Eckel,
SOUND ENGINEER
Mastering & Off:
Nima Gholiagha, nhb Berlin
VISUAL EFFECTS
Alex Grau (Furia, Barcelona)

ADDITIONAL AWARDS
SILVER
Volume Advertising page 254
TV-Spots
Television commercials

SILVER
Volume Advertising page 312
Musikkompositionen/
Sound-Design
Music compositions/sound design

FILME DIESER KATEGORIE FINDEN SIE UNTER WWW.ADC.DE FOR FILMS FROM THIS CATEGORY VISIT WWW.ADC.DE

SILVER

Der TV-Spot zur Einführung des überarbeiteten 4MATIC Allradsystems zeigt uns vier Männer, von denen jeder für einen Teil des Antriebs steht. In einer eleganten Choreografie aus synchronen Worten und Bewegungen erklären sie uns die Technik von 4MATIC. Und zwar so perfekt, schnell und timinggenau, dass eine spektakuläre Analogie zu der Funktionsweise und den Vorzügen des Allradsystems entsteht.

The TV commercial for the launch of the revised 4MATIC all-wheel-drive system features four men, each of whom represents one part of the drivetrain. In an elegant choreography of synchronous words and movements they explain the technology of 4MATIC to us – so perfectly, fast and precisely timed that the result is a spectacular analogy to the workings and advantages of the all-wheel-drive system.

TITLE
Mercedes-Benz 4MATIC
»4matics«

CLIENT
Daimler AG

MARKETING DIRECTOR
Lothar Korn
(Leiter Global Advertising)

ADVERTISING DIRECTOR
Mirco Völker, Mark Niedzballa

LEAD AGENCY
Jung von Matt AG

CREATIVE DIRECTION
Mathias Stiller,
Wolfgang Schneider, Jan Harbeck,
David Mously

ART DIRECTION
Marius Lohmann

CLIENT CONSULTING
Christian Hupertz,
Josef Konstantin Schulte,
Yves Rosengart, Johanna Hecker,
Helen Seiffe

STRATEGIC PLANNING
Benjamin Pagel

FILM PRODUCTION
Radical.Media

PRODUCTION
Kristin Hirt

DIRECTION
Sebastian Schipper

COPY
Jan Harbeck

ADDITIONAL AWARDS
BRONZE
Volume Advertising page 254
TV-Spots
Television commercials

CINEMA COMMERCIALS KINOWERBEFILME 265

BRONZE

Kein anderes Auto auf der Welt verbraucht weniger Benzin als der smart fortwo. Gut für die Umwelt! Doch was das Herz eines jeden smart-Fahrers mit Freude erfüllt, hinterlässt bei manch anderem ein Gefühl von Leere: bei Benzinkanistern zum Beispiel. Um diesem Gefühl Ausdruck zu verleihen, singen sie einen Blues.

The smart fortwo's fuel economy fills the heart of every smart driver with glee. We found the one group of folks (besides those in the oil industry, perhaps) who are saddened by outstanding fuel efficiency: gas cans. They just aren't important anymore, so we wrote them a blues song to share their sorrow with the world. The ad played on TV screens throughout Europe.

TITLE
Smart »Benzinkanister Blues«
CLIENT
Mercedes-Benz Schweiz AG
MARKETING DIRECTOR
Doris Lengwiler
ADVERTISING DIRECTOR
Fulvio D'Aurelio
LEAD AGENCY
Jung von Matt/Limmat
CREATIVE DIRECTION
Jan Rexhausen,
Dörte Spengler-Ahrens,
Alexander Jaggy,
Michael Rottmann
ART DIRECTION
Gun Kanjanapokin,
Ricardo Distefano
CLIENT CONSULTING
Marc Huber, Felix Schröder
FILM PRODUCTION
Markenfilm GmbH & Co
AGENCY PRODUCER
Julia Cramer
COMPUTER ANIMATION
Max Böhm,
Stefan Huschenbeth,
Christoph Liebsch,
Christian Wurst-Rieke
EDITOR
Hendrik Smith
CAMERA
Sebastian Pfaffenbichler

MUSIC COMPOSITION
Matthias Rewig (NHB Ton GmbH),
Marcus Löber
COMPOSER
Matthias Rewig (NHB Ton GmbH),
Marcus Löber
POSTPRODUCTION
Daniel Brylka,
MF-Video Produktions GmbH
PRODUCTION
Cornelius Rönz
DIRECTION
Matthieu Mantovani
EDITING
Hendrik Smith
SOUND DESIGN
phreeky beats
COPY
Daniel Pieracci, Fabio Straccia
SOUND ENGINEER
Markus Rosenbeck
VISUAL EFFECTS
Ingo Berends (Flame)

ADDITIONAL AWARDS NOMINATION
Volume Advertising page 256
TV-Spots
Television commercials

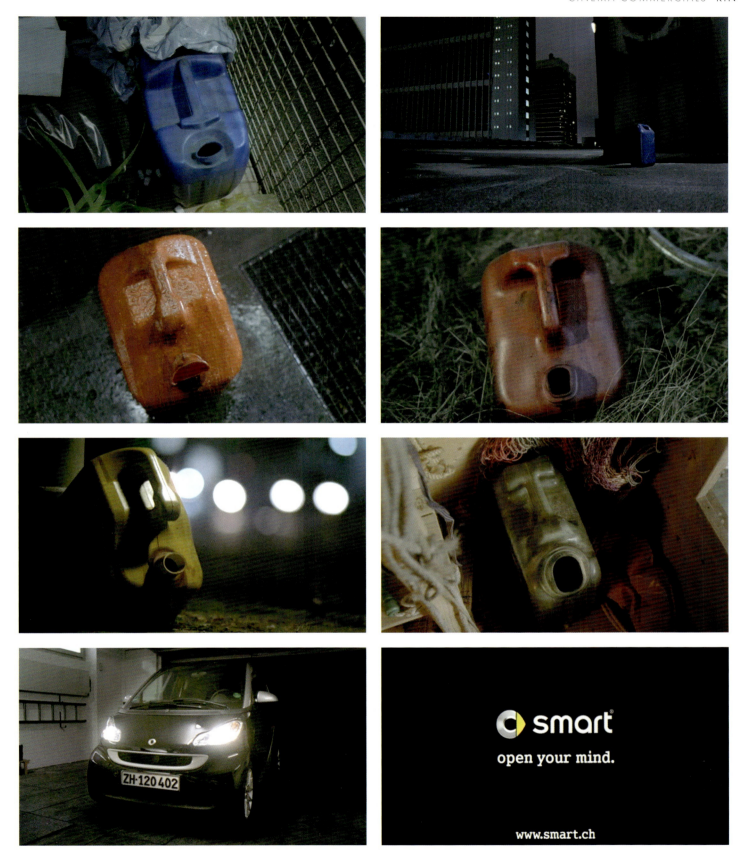

BRONZE

2007 führte Mercedes-Benz die neue Generation der G-Klasse ein. Gefragt war ein Spot, der unterstreicht, dass die G-Klasse seit Jahrzehnten das souveräne Maß aller Dinge unter den Geländewagen ist.

In 2007 Mercedes-Benz launched the new generation G-Class. Our task was to create a commercial, emphasizing that for several decades the G-Class has been the benchmark in the segment of off-road vehicles.

TITLE
Mercedes-Benz G-Klasse »Hindernisse«
CLIENT
Daimler AG
MARKETING DIRECTOR
Dr. Olaf Göttgens,
Dr. Kristina Hammer
ADVERTISING DIRECTOR
Mirco Völker, Christina Freier
LEAD AGENCY
Jung von Matt AG
CREATIVE DIRECTION
Fabian Frese, Thimoteus Wagner
ART DIRECTION
Christian Kroll
CLIENT CONSULTING
Yves Rosengart, Johanna Hecker, Jan Groenendijk
FILM PRODUCTION
Sehsucht GmbH
ILLUSTRATION
Sehsucht GmbH
COMPUTER ANIMATION
Hannes Geiger, Thore Bornemann, Maurice Jochem
DESIGN
Alex Heyer
EDITOR
Christoph Senn
MUSIC COMPOSITION
BLUWI Music & Sounddesign

COMPOSER
BLUWI/Timo Blunck, Stefan Will, Ralf Denker
POSTPRODUCTION
Studio Funk GmbH & Co. KG
PRODUCTION
Andreas Coutsoumbelis, Martin Woelke
DIRECTION
Ole Peters, Hannes Geiger
SOUND DESIGN
BLUWI/Marco Dreckkötter
COPY
Peter Gocht
SOUND ENGINEER
Studio Funk/Jochen Kömpe
VISUAL EFFECTS
Daniel Hummer

ADDITIONAL AWARDS
NOMINATION
Volume Advertising page 257
TV-Spots
Television commercials

NOMINATION
Volume Advertising page 302
Audiovisuelle Medien: Design
Audiovisual media: Design

NOMINATION
Volume Design page 221
Illustration
Illustration

CINEMA COMMERCIALS **KINOWERBEFILME** 269

BRONZE

Für die Marke Jeep sollte ein aufmerksamkeitsstarker Commercial entwickelt werden. Der Spot sollte auch als Viral im Internet funktionieren, und von der Zielgruppe weiterversandt werden.

Jeep is a living legend in the world of off-road vehicles, and still remains the only truly original SUV. We were commissioned to produce an image commercial for Jeep that addresses both existing and potential Jeep customers.

TITLE
Jeep »Ten little vehicles«
CLIENT
Chrysler Jeep
LEAD AGENCY
KNSK Werbeagentur GmbH
CREATIVE DIRECTION
Claudia Bach
ART DIRECTION
Michael Reissinger
CLIENT CONSULTING
Jan Isterling, Philipp Ernsting
FILM PRODUCTION
Deli Pictures
ILLUSTRATION
Maurice, Tom, Enzo, Don-sun, Michi, Kim-Eyleen, Johanna-Marie, Emma, Kurt
AGENCY PRODUCER
Kerstin Arndt
IMAGE EDITING
Christian Reimann
COMPUTER ANIMATION
Malte Sarnes, Thomas Volkmann
FILM ANIMATION
Robert Rhee
GRAPHIC ART
Robert Rhee
POSTPRODUCTION
Deli Pictures

PRODUCTION
Sebastian Hellge
DIRECTION
Michael Reissinger
SCREEN DESIGN
Thomas Volkmann, Michael Reissinger
SOUND DESIGN
Markenfilm, nhb Hamburg
COPY
Lisa Port, Fabian Tritsch, Lennert Wendt, Anna-Kristina Schroeder, Nina Burmeister
VISUAL EFFECTS
Christian Reimann

ADDITIONAL AWARDS
BRONZE
Volume Advertising page 255
TV-Spots
Television commercials

NOMINATION
Volume Advertising page 303
Audiovisuelle Medien: Design
Audiovisual media: Design

BRONZE

Der TV-Spot inszeniert die Fahrkultur des neuen C-Klasse T-Modells in großem Stil. Der Mercedes-Benz unter den Sportkombis wird zum Helden einer modernen Oper. Herausgefordert vom Wind weist das neue C-Klasse T-Modell dank seiner Kraft und Agilität seinen Widersacher in dessen Schranken. Da das Auto steht, werden Dynamik und Geschwindigkeit mithilfe von beweglichen Bühnenelementen erzeugt.

The TV commercial features the driving culture of the new C-Class Estate in grand style. The Mercedes-Benz among the sporty estates becomes the hero of a modern opera. Challenged by the wind, the new C-Class Estate puts its opponent in its place with its power and agility. Since the car is not moving, the impression of dynamics and speed is generated by way of movable stage elements.

TITLE
Mercedes-Benz C-Klasse T-Modell »Oper«

CLIENT
Daimler AG

MARKETING DIRECTOR
Dr. Olaf Göttgens/
Dr. Kristina Hammer

ADVERTISING DIRECTOR
Mirko Völker
(Manager Global Advertising),
Jochen Schmidt

LEAD AGENCY
Jung von Matt AG

CREATIVE DIRECTION
Mathias Stiller,
Wolfgang Schneider,
Boris Schwiedrzik

ART DIRECTION
Frederik Hofmann

CLIENT CONSULTING
Christian Hupertz,
Klaus Burghauser, Darek Stöhr,
Christoph Neuhaus, JoKo Schulte,
Vittal Wagner

FILM PRODUCTION
Markenfilm Hamburg

AGENCY PRODUCER
Lars Wiepking

GRAPHIC ART
Nina Kurowski, Marc Tebart

CAMERA
Sebastian Pfaffenbichler

MUSIC COMPOSITION
White Horse Music & Audioforce
(Co-Produktion), Steve Patuta,
Gerrit Winterstein, Thomas Süß

POSTPRODUCTION
Digital Domain, Los Angeles

PRODUCTION
Harald Beelte, Katie Stiebel,
Oliver Schertlein, Marc Strass

DIRECTION
Carl Erik Rinsch

EDITING
Robert Hoffmann

COPY
Jens Daum

ADDITIONAL AWARDS NOMINATION
Volume Advertising page 311
Musikkompositionen/
Sound-Design
Music compositions/sound design

Das neue C-Klasse T-Modell.
Fahrkultur in großem Stil.

Mercedes-Benz

FILME DIESER KATEGORIE FINDEN SIE UNTER WWW.ADC.DE FOR FILMS FROM THIS CATEGORY VISIT WWW.ADC.DE

NOMINATION

Streift sich ein Fußball-Fan das DFB-Trikot mit der Nummer und dem Namen seines Lieblingsspielers über, identifiziert er sich nicht nur mit dessen Stil und Charakter. Er wird durch dessen Können inspiriert, er wird genauso gut wie dieser.

If a football fan puts on the German National Team Jersey with the number and the name of his favourite player, then he not only identifies with the player's style and character. He is also inspired by the player's skill and becomes just as good.

TITLE
adidas Football
»Impossible Park Football«

CLIENT
adidas AG

MARKETING DIRECTOR
Markus Rachals

ADVERTISING DIRECTOR
Sven Schindler

LEAD AGENCY
TBWA\ Deutschland (180/TBWA), Berlin

CREATIVE DIRECTION
Stefan Schmidt

ART DIRECTION
Rochelle Raiss

CLIENT CONSULTING
Kerstin Gold, Falk Lungwitz

STRATEGIC PLANNING
Moritz Kiechle

FILM PRODUCTION
Stink: Jan Dressler, Nils Schwemer

AGENCY PRODUCER
Johann-Georg Hofer von Lobenstein

CAMERA
Greg Copeland

MEDIA
Carat, Hamburg

MUSIC COMPOSITION
Blackwell/Millot
(Sony/ATV Music Publishing)

COMPOSER
Blackwell/Millot

POSTPRODUCTION
nhb, Berlin

DIRECTION
James Brown

EDITING
Alex Jurkat

STYLING
Martin Manser

COPY
Markus Ewertz

ADDITIONAL AWARD NOMINATION
Volume Advertising page 256
TV-Spots
Television commercials

NOMINATION

Nachdem man durch die 36 Kammern der Heimwerkerzunft gegangen ist, braucht es nicht mal mehr wochenlange Aufenthalte in amerikanischen Postproduktionshäusern, um eine derartige Perfomance an den Tag zu legen. Jedes Projekt macht dich eben besser.

After going through the 36 chambers of the home improvement guild, it is no longer necessary to spend weeks in American post-production houses in order to deliver such a performance. You improve with each project.

TITLE
Hornbach Baumarkt »Screws«
CLIENT
Hornbach Baumarkt AG
MARKETING DIRECTOR
Jürgen Schröcker
ADVERTISING DIRECTOR
Diana Koob
LEAD AGENCY
HEIMAT, Berlin
CREATIVE DIRECTION
Guido Heffels, Jürgen Vossen

ART DIRECTION
Danny Baarz, Tim Schneider
CLIENT CONSULTING
Yves Krämer
FILM PRODUCTION
Markenfilm, Berlin
AGENCY PRODUCER
Kerstin Breuer
CONSULTING
Mark Hassan, Sammy Bohneberg
GRAPHIC ART
Jessica Philipp, Jenny Kapteyn

CAMERA
Sebastian Blenkov
MEDIA
Crossmedia GmbH, Düsseldorf
MUSIC COMPOSITION
Thomas Süß, audioforce Berlin
PRODUCTION
five_three_double ninety filmproductions GmbH
DIRECTION
Martin Werner

EDITING
Morton Giese
SOUND DESIGN
Thomas Süß, audioforce Berlin
COPY
Matthias Storath, Till Eckel

ADDITIONAL AWARDS NOMINATION
Volume Advertising page 256
TV-Spots
Television commercials

FILME DIESER KATEGORIE FINDEN SIE UNTER WWW.ADC.DE   FOR FILMS FROM THIS CATEGORY VISIT WWW.ADC.DE

NOMINATION

Im Motorsport zählt jede Sekunde – auch bei Vodafone McLaren-Mercedes und seinen Fahrern. Fairness spielt jedoch gleichermaßen eine große Rolle. Dass diese Kombination oberste Priorität hat, wird hier veranschaulicht.

The two Vodafone McLaren Mercedes drivers reveal, that they have got racing in their blood. In amusing scenes, we watch friendly rivals on the race track in real life.

TITLE
Mercedes-Benz »The Race F1«
CLIENT
Daimler AG
MARKETING DIRECTOR
Lothar Korn, Mirco Völker
ADVERTISING DIRECTOR
Isabell Hartmann, Jochen Schmidt
LEAD AGENCY
Jung von Matt AG

CREATIVE DIRECTION
Deneke von Weltzien,
Daniel Frericks
ART DIRECTION
Christian Kroll
CLIENT CONSULTING
Christian Hupertz,
Christoph Neuhaus
FILM PRODUCTION
radical.media GmbH
AGENCY PRODUCER
Hermann Krug

CAMERA
Paul Laufer
MUSIC COMPOSITION
groove addicts
COMPOSER
Irving Berlin
PRODUCTION
Tommy Turtle, Kristin Hirt

DIRECTION
Tarsem
COPY
Anton von Weltzien,
Karen Am Ende,
Deneke von Weltzien

ADDITIONAL AWARDS NOMINATION
Volume Advertising page 257
TV-Spots
Television commercials

GOLD

TITLE
Bundesministerium für Umwelt, Naturschutz und Reaktorsicherheit/EPURON »Power of Wind«
CLIENT
EPURON/Bundesministerium für Umwelt, Naturschutz und Reaktorsicherheit
LEAD AGENCY
Nordpol+ Hamburg Agentur für Kommunikation GmbH
CREATIVE DIRECTION
Lars Rühmann
ART DIRECTION
Björn Rühmann, Joakim Reveman
CLIENT CONSULTING
Mathias Müller-Using
FILM PRODUCTION
PARANOID PROJECTS Paris/ PARANOID US Los Angeles
CAMERA
Pascal Marti
MUSIC COMPOSITION
Pigalle Production
POSTPRODUCTION
Mikros Images/Paris
DIRECTION
The Vikings
EDITING
Basile Belkhiri
COPY
Matthew Branning

ADDITIONAL AWARDS
GRAND PRIX
Volume Advertising page 010

GOLD
Volume Advertising page 254
TV-Spots
Television commercials

SILVER

TITLE
Renault Deutschland »Ballett«
CLIENT
Renault Deutschland AG
MARKETING DIRECTOR
Jörg-Alexander Ellhof
LEAD AGENCY
Nordpol+ Hamburg Agentur für Kommunikation GmbH
CREATIVE DIRECTION
Lars Rühmann
ART DIRECTION
Tim Schierwater, Christoph Bielefeldt
CLIENT CONSULTING
Mathias Müller-Using
FILM PRODUCTION
element e
MUSIC COMPOSITION
Jacques Offenbach; Additional composing: Steve Patuta@audioforce
POSTPRODUCTION
Deli Pictures
PRODUCTION
Jürgen Joppen
DIRECTION
Silvio Helbig
EDITING
Sabine Panek
SOUND DESIGN
Loft Tonstudios GmbH
COPY
Sebastian Behrendt
SOUND ENGINEER
Sascha Heiny, Stefan Apell

ADDITIONAL AWARDS
SILVER
Volume Advertising page 226
TV-Spots
Television commercials

NOMINATION
Volume Advertising page 313
Musikkompositionen/ Sound-Design
Music compositions/ sound design

NOMINATION

TITLE
YouTube »Horst Hrubesch«
CLIENT
Google Germany GmbH
MARKETING DIRECTOR
Karl Krainer
ADVERTISING DIRECTOR
Barbara Daliri Freyduni
LEAD AGENCY
Kolle Rebbe Werbeagentur GmbH
CREATIVE DIRECTION
Stefan Wübbe/Rolf Leger
ART DIRECTION
Daniel Serrano
CLIENT CONSULTING
Katharina Lechelt/ Tamara Klien
FILM PRODUCTION
Silbersee Film Produktion GmbH
AGENCY PRODUCER
Henning Stamm
DIRECTION
Norbert Heitker
COPY
Florian Ludwig

ADDITIONAL AWARDS
BRONZE
Volume Advertising page 286
Virale Filme
Viral films

NOMINATION

TITLE
Runners Point »Löwe«
CLIENT
RUNNERS POINT Warenhandelsgesellschaft mbH
MARKETING DIRECTOR
Daniel Kumelis
ADVERTISING DIRECTOR
Daniel Kumelis
LEAD AGENCY
Jung von Matt AG
CREATIVE DIRECTION
Dörte Spengler-Ahrens, Jan Rexhausen
CLIENT CONSULTING
Julia Krömker, Niklas Kruchten
FILM PRODUCTION
jo!schmid Filmproduktion GmbH
RADIO PRODUCTION
jo!schmid
AGENCY PRODUCER
Julia Cramer
CAMERA
Silvio Helbig
ARTIST
Mntha Vuka, Thabang Kwebu
COMPOSER
Steve Patua
PRODUCTION
Filmproduktion: Producer: Jürgen Joppen
DIRECTION
Silvio Helbig
EDITING
Tilman Cluss
COPY
Henning Patzner

ADDITIONAL AWARDS
NOMINATION
Volume Advertising page 248
TV-Spots
Television commercials

GOLD

Ein weißer Raum. Plötzlich füllen gigantische Blutwolken das Bild. Sie geraten in Wallung. Künstlernamen entstehen. Das Blut beginnt, im Takt der Musik zu pulsieren. Es schießt durch den abstrakten Raum und bildet musikalische Formen. Immer schneller die Bewegungen, immer dramatischer die Musik. Bis eine der dünnen Linien einen unsichtbaren Körper, »einen Künstler« mit pulsierendem Blut erfüllt.

A white room. Suddenly huge swirls of blood fill the frame. They surge and undulate. The names of artists are formed in the blood. The blood begins to pulsate with the rhythm of the music. It surges around the blank room taking the form of musical figures. The movement builds in tempo and the music in drama until one of the slender tendrils fills an unseen body "the artist" with pulsing blood.

TITLE
Konzerthaus Dortmund
Saison 2007/2008 Imagefilm
»symphony in red«

CLIENT
Konzerthaus Dortmund GmbH

MARKETING DIRECTOR
Milena Ivkovic

LEAD AGENCY
Jung von Matt AG

CREATIVE DIRECTION
Sascha Hanke, Timm Hanebeck,
Wolf Heumann (GF)

ART DIRECTION
Sascha Hanke, Timm Hanebeck

CLIENT CONSULTING
Nina Gerwing, Lena Frers

FILM PRODUCTION
Sehsucht GmbH

AGENCY PRODUCER
Hermann Krug,
Alexander Schillinsky

FILM ANIMATION
Niko Tziopanos, Alex Heyer,
Martin Hess

CAMERA
Bea Wellenbrock, Alex Heyer,
Valentin Heun

MUSIC COMPOSITION
Fazil Say

COMPOSER
Fazil Say

POSTPRODUCTION
Sehsucht GmbH

PRODUCTION
Andreas Coutsoumbelis,
Martin Woelke

DIRECTION
Niko Tziopanos

COPY
Michael Okun, Moritz Grub

ADDITIONAL AWARDS
GOLD
Volume Advertising page 312
Musikkompositionen/
Sound-Design
Music compositions/sound design

BRONZE
Volume Advertising page 255
TV-Spots
Television commercials

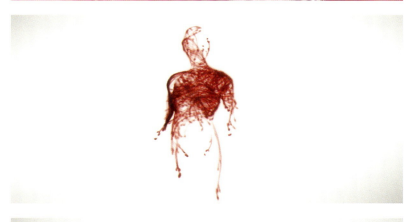

FILME DIESER KATEGORIE FINDEN SIE UNTER WWW.ADC.DE FOR FILMS FROM THIS CATEGORY VISIT WWW.ADC.DE

NOMINATION

Geradeaus zu laufen ist schwieriger, als man denkt. Zumindest nach einer Fahrt im smart fortwo. Sein Wendekreis ist so Schwindel erregend klein, dass nach dem Aussteigen jedem Schritt vorwärts zwei Schritte seitwärts folgen. Das Resultat: stolpernde und taumelnde Menschen, die sich vergeblich bemühen, nicht hinzufallen.

Walking in a straight line is more difficult than you think. At least it is after a trip in the smart fortwo. Its turning circle is so dizzyingly small that after getting out of it, every step forward is followed by two steps sideways. The result: tottering and stumbling people who try in vain to keep from falling down.

TITLE
smart fortwo POS-Spot »Wendekreis«

CLIENT
Daimler AG smart MBVD

ADVERTISING DIRECTOR
Markus Gammert

LEAD AGENCY
BBDO Düsseldorf GmbH

CREATIVE DIRECTION
Ton Hollander, Ralf Zilligen

ART DIRECTION
Kai Gerken

CLIENT CONSULTING
Dirk Spakowski, Marco Golbach

FILM PRODUCTION
Markenfilm GmbH & Co. KG

AGENCY PRODUCER
Steffen Gentis, Silke Rochow

CAMERA
Arne Schiel, Christian-Ole Puls, Kai Gerken

COMPOSER
Soundscape NL, Hessel Herder

POSTPRODUCTION
Locomotion, Düsseldorf

DIRECTION
Ton Hollander, Arne Schiel, Christian-Ole Puls, Kai Gerken

EDITING
Chris Rubino

COPY
Christian-Ole Puls

FILMS FOR SALES PROMOTION/COMPANY PRESENTATION   FILME FÜR VERKAUFSFÖRDERUNG/UNTERNEHMENSDARSTELLUNGEN   281

NOMINATION

Der Instore-Werbespot entführt den Betrachter in die Welt von mi adidas, die – angelehnt an das »create your own«-Logo – einem ständigen Wechsel unterworfen ist. Das dreigeteilte Logo gab den Input für die Welt von mi adidas. Ein »Zauberwürfel«, der die vielfachen Kombinationsmöglichkeiten darstellt. »The world in mi hands« – der Spot spricht für sich.

The instore ad whisks the observer away into the world of mi adidas, which – based on the "create your own" logo – undergoes constant changes. The logo, which is divided into three parts, provided the input for the world of mi adidas. It's a "Rubik's cube" that presents the many and varied combination possibilities. "The world in mi hands" – the ad speaks for itself.

TITLE
mi adidas Animationsfilm
»InStore Spot«

CLIENT
adidas AG

MARKETING DIRECTOR
Chris Aubrey, Anne Nebendahl

LEAD AGENCY
Mutabor Design GmbH

CREATIVE DIRECTION
Heinrich Paravicini

ART DIRECTION
Axel Domke

FILM PRODUCTION
Timo Schädel

FILM ANIMATION
Timo Schädel

CAMERA
Lutz Hattenhauer

COMPOSER
Boris Salchow

STYLING
Nicole Dresen

FILME DIESER KATEGORIE FINDEN SIE UNTER WWW.ADC.DE FOR FILMS FROM THIS CATEGORY VISIT WWW.ADC.DE

NOMINATION

Der Film erzählt die Geschichte des Suppenkaspars, die sich in Pop-up-Manier aus einem Folianten heraus vor uns entfaltet: Mama serviert ihrem Buben die tägliche Suppe, welche dieser beharrlich verweigert: »Nein, ich esse meine Suppe nicht!« In dieser ausweglosen Situation liefert das Maggi Kochstudio die Lösung – die berühmte Maggi Würze! Damit schmeckt es sogar unserem rebellischen Helden.

The task was to create an image building commercial for the 120th birthday of Maggi Wuerze Seasoning. In "The Story of Augustus" the small Augustus almost starves himself to death because he does not like the soups he is being served. But then, the Maggi consultant comes to the rescue with some Maggi Wuerze Seasoning, which for the last 120 years has made everything taste better.

TITLE
Maggi Würze Imagefilm »Suppen-Kaspar«

CLIENT
Maggi GmbH

MARKETING DIRECTOR
Andreas Peters

ADVERTISING DIRECTOR
Alain Duvaud

LEAD AGENCY
Publicis

CREATIVE DIRECTION
Volker Schrader, Bernd Lange

ART DIRECTION
Diana Sukopp

CLIENT CONSULTING
Ingo Schäfer, Ute Poprawe, Simone Grein

FILM PRODUCTION
SEED Frankfurt

ILLUSTRATION
Klaus Blaser, Roland Eisert, Diana Sukopp

AGENCY PRODUCER
Klaus Flemmer

IMAGE EDITING
SEED Digital Vision

COMPUTER ANIMATION
Boris Bruchhaus, Matthias Klew

DESIGN
Diana Sukopp

FILM ANIMATION
SEED

GRAPHIC ART
Diana Sukopp

IDEA
Diana Sukopp

MUSIC COMPOSITION
Fundemental

COMPOSER
Andreas Lucas

POSTPRODUCTION
SEED Digital Production

EDITING
Klaus Blaser

COPY
Diana Sukopp, Bernd Lange

TYPOGRAPHY
Diana Sukopp, Roland Eisert

VISUAL EFFECTS
SEED

GOLD

TITLE
Volkswagen Kampagne
»Horst Schlämmer macht
Führerschein«
CLIENT
Volkswagen AG
MARKETING DIRECTOR
Jochen Sengpiehl
ADVERTISING DIRECTOR
Ralf Maltzen, Hartmut Seeger
LEAD AGENCY
DDB Germany, Berlin
CREATIVE DIRECTION
Amir Kassaei, Stefan Schulte,
Bert Peulecke
ART DIRECTION
Kristoffer Heilemann
CLIENT CONSULTING
Benjamin Reininger,
Niklas Feuerle, Cathleen Losch
FILM PRODUCTION
Telemaz Commercials Berlin
RADIO PRODUCTION
Hastings Audio Network Berlin
AGENCY PRODUCER
Boris Schepker
CONSULTING
Künstlervermittlung:
Special Key –
Christian Biedermann,
Sven Zander
CAMERA
Xaver Schweyer, Detlef Camp
ARTIST
Hape Kerkeling
POSTPRODUCTION
Condor digital media Berlin
PRODUCTION
Barbara Kranz, Frank Hasselbach,
Kjell Kunde
EDITOR
Uli Langguth
DIRECTION
Gerald Grabowski
EDITING
Kathrin Schmoll
STYLING
Brigitte Remmert
TECHNICAL DIRECTION
Sascha Mehn
COPY
Ludwig Berndl, Philip Bolland,
Christian Fries
SOUND ENGINEER
Lars Gelhausen

ADDITIONAL AWARDS
GOLD
Volume Advertising page 186
Verkaufsförderung
Sales promotion
GOLD
Volume Advertising page 221
TV-Spots
Television commercials
GOLD
Volume Advertising page 289
Virale Filme
Viral films
GOLD
Volume Advertising page 347
Integrierte Kampagnen
Integrated campaigns
GOLD
Volume Advertising page 367
Dialogmarketing
Dialogue marketing
GOLD
Volume Design page 242
Digitale Werbung
Digital advertising
SILVER
Volume Advertising page 096
Tages-/Wochenzeitungsanzeigen
Advertisements in daily/weekly
newspapers
SILVER
Volume Advertising page 139
Produkt-/Werbebroschüren
Product/advertising brochures
SILVER
Volume Advertising page 147
Text
Copy
SILVER
Volume Design page 259
Digitale Medien: Viral
Digital media: Viral
BRONZE
Volume Advertising page 152
Text
Copy
BRONZE
Volume Advertising page 326
Funkspots
Radio commercials
NOMINATION
Volume Design page 095
Informationsmedien
Information media
NOMINATION
Volume Design page 235
Websites
Websites

BRONZE

TITLE
ASICS Europe Imagefilm
»Origami«
CLIENT
ASICS Europe B.V
ADVERTISING DIRECTOR
Remco Rietvink
LEAD AGENCY
Nordpol+ Hamburg Agentur
für Kommunikation GmbH
CREATIVE DIRECTION
Lars Rühmann
ART DIRECTION
Sean Kirby
CLIENT CONSULTING
Mathias Müller-Using,
Niklas Franke,
Axel Schüler-Bredt
FILM PRODUCTION
Nordpol/element e
COMPUTER ANIMATION
André Junker,
Christoffer Wolters
FILM ANIMATION
Stoptrick Hamburg
ARTIST
Sipho Mabona
MUSIC COMPOSITION
Audioforce
POSTPRODUCTION
Acolori Medienproduktion
PRODUCTION
Florian Liertz
DIRECTION
Tim Schierwater
SOUND DESIGN
Audioforce/Primetime Studio
COPY
Sebastian Behrendt
SOUND ENGINEER
Pierre Brand

ADDITIONAL AWARDS
BRONZE
Volume Advertising page 300
Audiovisuelle Medien: Design
Audiovisual media: Design

NOMINATION

TITLE
Beate Uhse TV-Spot
»Kindersicherung«
CLIENT
Beate Uhse TV
MARKETING DIRECTOR
Stefanie Eisenschenk
LEAD AGENCY
kempertrautmann gmbh
CREATIVE DIRECTION
Gerrit Zinke, Jens Theil
ART DIRECTION
Florian Schimmer
CLIENT CONSULTING
Hendrik Heine, Jacqueline Koch
FILM PRODUCTION
Markenfilm
ILLUSTRATION
Jost Keller
MUSIC COMPOSITION
Thomas Kisser
POSTPRODUCTION
Markenfilm
PRODUCTION
Acki Heldens,
Jannik Endemann
DIRECTION
Neels Feil
EDITING
Neels Feil
COPY
Michael Götz, Stefan Förster

ADDITIONAL AWARDS
BRONZE
Volume Advertising page 234
TV-Spots
Television commercials
NOMINATION
Volume Advertising page 289
Virale Filme
Viral films

»RAP«

SCHWEINI: I said M-A-S-T-E-R, hehe, a G with a double E. I said I go by the unforgettable name…

KIESSLING: … of the man they call the M-A-S-T-E-R G.

SCHWEINI: Well, my name is known all over the world, but all the foxy ladies and the pretty girls…

SCHWEINI/KIESSLING: Hehe…

SCHWEINI: I'm going down in history, as a baddest stripper there ever could be.

ALLE: Hehe

»HUNDEKACKE«

POLDI: Oah, ne ne, jetzt hab ich auch noch Kacke unterm Schuh, des ist ja ne schöne Schweinerei hier bei euch aufm Rasen.

JUNGE: Hat ich noch nie. Kriegt man das wieder sauber?

POLDI: Ja, ich kratz das immer mit den Fingernägeln raus.

JUNGE: Wirklich?

POLDI: Funktioniert eigentlich ganz gut. So un jetzt geh mir nicht auf'n Sack.

»TOTER FISCH«

KIESSLING: Du, ich hab da neulich so'n Spruch gehört, da konnt ich mir gar keinen Reim drauf machen. Vielleicht weißt du das ja. Was ist grün und stinkt nach Fisch?

MERTESACKER: Weiß nicht.

KIESSLING: Toter Frosch vielleicht? Ja, gut, ist vielleicht ein bisschen an den Haaren herbeigezogen. Aber was ist denn sonst noch grün? Außer toten Fröschen und stinkt?

MERTESACKER: Ja, deine Mudder.

Zu dieser Kampagne gehören noch drei weitere Spots: »Attila«, »Kindergeburtstag« und »Marktstand«.

Three further spots are part of this campaign: "Attila", "Kindergeburtstag" and "Marktstand".

SILVER

Während des Drehs zum adidas TV-Spot »Impossible Park Football« filmten wir die Nationalspieler mit versteckter Kamera. Diese Sequenzen wurden neu vertont und als Viralfilme eingesetzt, um auf die Internetseite adidas.com/football hinzuweisen. Dort warteten unvertonte Filmschnipsel, die von Fans neu vertont und wieder hochgeladen werden konnten. Per Mausklick kürten die User ihren Lieblingsspot.

During the shooting of the adidas TV spot "Impossible Park Football", we also filmed the national team's football players with a hidden camera. These sequences were synchronised with new dialogues in order to lead viewers to the Internet page adidas.com/football. There, the fans found film snippets without sound that they could synchronise with their own dialogues and load back up onto the page. Users voted for their favourite spots via mouse click.

TITLE
adidas Football Kampagne »Impossible Park Football«
CLIENT
adidas AG
MARKETING DIRECTOR
Markus Rachals
ADVERTISING DIRECTOR
Sven Schindler

LEAD AGENCY
TBWA\ Deutschland (180/TBWA), Berlin
CREATIVE DIRECTION
Stefan Schmidt
CLIENT CONSULTING
Kerstin Gold, Falk Lungwitz
STRATEGIC PLANNING
Moritz Kiechle

FILM PRODUCTION
Stink: Jan Dressler, Nils Schwemer
AGENCY PRODUCER
Johann-Georg Hofer von Lobenstein
CAMERA
Niklas Weise
POSTPRODUCTION
nhb, Berlin
DIRECTION
Niklas Weise

EDITING
Alex Jurkat
SPEAKER
Bruno Pischel, Kai-Uwe Lipphardt, Malte Pittner
STYLING
Martin Manser
COPY
Markus Ewertz, Bruno Pischel, Kai-Uwe Lipphardt, Malte Pittner

BRONZE

Bekanntmachung des neuen deutschen Videoportals von YouTube, mit Hilfe einer ungewöhnlichen Idee, die aus der Welt der User kommt.

Announcement of YouTube's new German video portal, with the help of an unusual idea that came from the world of the users.

TITLE
YouTube »Horst Hrubesch«
CLIENT
Google Germany GmbH
MARKETING DIRECTOR
Karl Krainer
ADVERTISING DIRECTOR
Barbara Daliri Freyduni
LEAD AGENCY
Kolle Rebbe Werbeagentur GmbH
CREATIVE DIRECTION
Stefan Wübbe/Rolf Leger
ART DIRECTION
Daniel Serrano
CLIENT CONSULTING
Katharina Lechelt/Tamara Klien

FILM PRODUCTION
Silbersee Film Produktion GmbH
AGENCY PRODUCER
Henning Stamm
DIRECTION
Norbert Heitker
COPY
Florian Ludwig

ADDITIONAL AWARDS NOMINATION
Volume Advertising page 277
Kinowerbefilme
Cinema commercials

Jetzt auch auf deutsch.

FILME DIESER KATEGORIE FINDEN SIE UNTER WWW.ADC.DE FOR FILMS FROM THIS CATEGORY VISIT WWW.ADC.DE

NOMINATION

Wir machen High-Speed-Downloads wahrnehmbar, indem wir den abstrakten Downloadvorgang auf einer Laufstrecke im Stadion visualisieren und die einzelnen Elemente des Downloads einen 100-Meter-Lauf absolvieren lassen. Nach vollbrachtem Download, also nach Zielüberquerung der Darsteller, wird das Produkt des Downloads erlebbar.

The goal was to prove the fact that Freeware.de has the fastest download-manager.
Studies show that the most popular entertainment to download on the world wide web is pornography and music. How much time does it take to download a song for your listening pleasure? 14.07 seconds.
It is timed. It is captured. In fact, it is officially the new world record.

TITLE
Freeware.de Kampagne
»Highspeed Download«
CLIENT
Shareware.de SWV GmbH
MARKETING DIRECTOR
Oliver Kruse
LEAD AGENCY
Scholz & Friends
CREATIVE DIRECTION
Oliver Handlos, Matthias Spaetgens

ART DIRECTION
Jens-Petter Waernes, Erik Dagnell
CLIENT CONSULTING
Sascha Kruse
FILM PRODUCTION
element e filmproduktion gmbh
RADIO PRODUCTION
LOFT Tonstudios GmbH
AGENCY PRODUCER
Anke Landmark

CAMERA
Marc Achenbach
MUSIC COMPOSITION
Fraise
POSTPRODUCTION
Slaughterhouse Hamburg GmbH
PRODUCTION
Bernd T. Hoefflin,
Patrick Dettenbach
DIRECTION
Alex Feil

EDITING
Steven Wilhelm
STYLING
Helen Achtermann
SOUND ENGINEER
Jan Dejozé

ADDITIONAL AWARDS
NOMINATION
Volume Advertising page 255
TV-Spots
Television commercials

VIRAL FILMS VIRALE FILME 289

GOLD

TITLE
Volkswagen Kampagne
»Horst Schlämmer
macht Führerschein«
CLIENT
Volkswagen AG
MARKETING DIRECTOR
Jochen Sengpiehl
ADVERTISING DIRECTOR
Ralf Maltzen, Hartmut Seeger
LEAD AGENCY
DDB Germany, Berlin
CREATIVE DIRECTION
Amir Kassaei, Stefan Schulte,
Bert Peulecke
ART DIRECTION
Kristoffer Heilemann
CLIENT CONSULTING
Benjamin Reininger,
Niklas Feuerle, Cathleen Losch
FILM PRODUCTION
Telemaz Commercials Berlin
RADIO PRODUCTION
Hastings Audio Network Berlin
AGENCY PRODUCER
Boris Schepker
CONSULTING
Künstlervermittlung:
Special Key –
Christian Biedermann,
Sven Zander
CAMERA
Xaver Schweyer, Detlef Camp
ARTIST
Hape Kerkeling
POSTPRODUCTION
Condor digital media Berlin
PRODUCTION
Barbara Kranz, Frank Hasselbach,
Kjell Kunde
EDITOR
Uli Langguth
DIRECTION
Gerald Grabowski
EDITING
Kathrin Schmoll
STYLING
Brigitte Remmert
TECHNICAL DIRECTION
Sascha Mehn
COPY
Ludwig Berndl, Philip Bolland,
Christian Fries
SOUND ENGINEER
Lars Gelhausen

ADDITIONAL AWARDS
GOLD
Volume Advertising page 186
Verkaufsförderung
Sales promotion
GOLD
Volume Advertising page 221
TV-Spots
Television commercials
GOLD
Volume Advertising page 283
Filme für Verkaufsförderung/
Unternehmensdarstellungen
Films for sales promotion/
company presentation
GOLD
Volume Advertising page 347
Integrierte Kampagnen
Integrated campaigns
GOLD
Volume Advertising page 367
Dialogmarketing
Dialogue marketing
GOLD
Volume Design page 242
Digitale Werbung
Digital advertising
SILVER
Volume Advertising page 096
Tages-/Wochenzeitungsanzeigen
Advertisements in daily/weekly
newspapers
SILVER
Volume Advertising page 139
Produkt-/Werbebroschüren
Product/advertising brochures
SILVER
Volume Advertising page 147
Text
Copy
SILVER
Volume Design page 259
Digitale Medien: Viral
Digital media: Viral
BRONZE
Volume Advertising page 152
Text
Copy
BRONZE
Volume Advertising page 326
Funkspots
Radio commercials
NOMINATION
Volume Design page 095
Informationsmedien
Information media
NOMINATION
Volume Design page 235
Websites
Websites

BRONZE

TITLE
Sixt – rent a car »Matthias Reim«
CLIENT
Sixt GmbH & Co.
Autovermietung KG
MARKETING DIRECTOR
Dr. Karsten Willrodt
ADVERTISING DIRECTOR
Daniela Erdmann
LEAD AGENCY
Jung von Matt AG
CREATIVE DIRECTION
Peter Kirchhoff, Wolf Heumann
ART DIRECTION
Vanessa Rabea Schrooten
CLIENT CONSULTING
Sandra Schymetzki,
Ann-Kristin Grohsklaus
FILM PRODUCTION
Big Fish Berlin
AGENCY PRODUCER
Julia Cramer
GRAPHIC ART
Felix Taubert
CAMERA
Casey Campell
MUSIC COMPOSITION
Matthias Reim, Bernd Dietrich
DIRECTION
Warwick
COPY
Lisa Maria Hartwich,
Peter Kirchhoff, Wolf Heumann

ADDITIONAL AWARDS
SILVER
Volume Advertising page 350
Integrierte Kampagnen
Integrated campaigns
BRONZE
Volume Advertising page 255
TV-Spots
Television commercials
BRONZE
Volume Advertising page 313
Musikkompositionen/
Sound-Design
Music compositions/sound design
BRONZE
Volume Design page 246
Digitale Werbung
Digital advertising
NOMINATION
Volume Advertising page 339
Funkspots
Radio commercials

NOMINATION

TITLE
Beate Uhse »Kindersicherung«
CLIENT
Beate Uhse TV
MARKETING DIRECTOR
Stefanie Eisenschenk
LEAD AGENCY
kempertrautmann gmbh
CREATIVE DIRECTION
Gerrit Zinke, Jens Theil
ART DIRECTION
Florian Schimmer
CLIENT CONSULTING
Hendrik Heine
FILM PRODUCTION
Markenfilm
ILLUSTRATION
Jost Keller
MUSIC COMPOSITION
Thomas Kisser
POSTPRODUCTION
Markenfilm
PRODUCTION
Acki Heldens,
Jannik Endemann
DIRECTION
Neels Feil
EDITING
Neels Feil
COPY
Michael Götz, Stefan Förster

ADDITIONAL AWARDS
BRONZE
Volume Advertising page 234
TV-Spots
Television commercials
NOMINATION
Volume Advertising page 283
Filme für Verkaufsförderung/
Unternehmensdarstellungen
Films for sales promotion/
company presentation

TAMARA DE LEMPICKA

*16. MAI 1898 WARSCHAU †18. MÄRZ 1980 CUERNAVACA/MEXIKO

Tamara de Lempickas Lebensphasen lesen sich wie eine Weltreise. Geboren in Warschau, Schulzeit in Lausanne, jung geheiratet in St. Petersburg, Flucht vor den Bolschewiki nach Kopenhagen, Studium in Paris, Flucht vor den Nazis in die USA, Lebensabend in Mexiko. Sie war eine sehr eigenwillige und ehrgeizige Frau. Luxus war sie von Kindesbeinen an gewöhnt, und als in Paris ihr Geld knapp wurde, entschied sie sich, das in St. Petersburg begonnene Kunststudium fortzusetzen. Sie wurde Schülerin des Symbolisten Maurice Denis und des Kubisten André Lhote. Tamara de Lempicka war noch keine 30 Jahre alt, da gehörte sie bereits zu den Stars des Art déco. Zielstrebig malte sie mondäne Bilder und zelebrierte sich betont elegant und divenhaft in der Öffentlichkeit. Ihr schwülwarmer Kubismus war so eigenständig und präsent, dass er innerhalb weniger Jahre die Welt und bis heute jeden Postershop erorberte.

*16 MAY 1898 WARSAW †18 MARCH 1980 CUERNAVACA/MEXICO

Tamara de Lempicka's biography reads like a world tour: born in Warsaw; educated in Lausanne; married at an early age in St. Petersburg; fled from the Bolsheviks and travelled to Copenhagen; studied in Paris; fled to the USA to escape the Nazis; twilight years spent in Mexico. She was a very headstrong, ambitious woman. She had been accustomed to luxury from a very young age, and on finding herself hard up for money in Paris, she decided to continue the art studies she had started in St. Petersburg. She became a student of the symbolist Maurice Denis and the cubist André Lhote. Tamara de Lempicka became one of the stars of the Art Deco movement while still in her twenties. She single-mindedly painted glamorous, sophisticated pictures, while cultivating a public image of herself as an elegant diva. Her sultry take on cubism was so unique, so striking, that within a few years it had conquered the world, remaining a staple in poster shops to this day.

I live life in the margins of society, and the rules of normal society don't apply to those who live on the fringe.

MEIN LEBEN VERLÄUFT AM RAND DER GESELLSCHAFT, UND DIE REGELN DER NORMALEN GESELLSCHAFT SIND NICHT AUF DIE ANWENDBAR, DIE IN DER RANDZONE LEBEN.

BRONZE

Ein guter Thriller erzeugt Nervenkitzel nicht nur durch das, was er zeigt, sondern vor allem auch durch das, was er nicht zeigt. Genau dieses Prinzip steckt auch hinter der Kampagne für den Action- und Horror-Sender 13 TH STREET. Die Filme erzählen Anfang und Ende einer düsteren Geschichte und lassen dazwischen Spielraum für die Vorahnung und Fantasie des Betrachters.

A good thriller generates excitement not only by what we see but also largely by what we do not see. This is precisely the principle behind the campaign for the action and horror channel 13 TH STREET. The films tell the beginning and ending of a gloomy story, and in between leave room for the forebodings and imagination of the viewer.

TITLE
13 TH STREET Kampagne »Kopfkino«

CLIENT
NBC Universal Global Networks Deutschland GmbH

MARKETING DIRECTOR
Andreas Lechner

LEAD AGENCY
Jung von Matt

CREATIVE DIRECTION
Wolfgang Schneider, Mathias Stiller, David Mously, Jan Harbeck

ART DIRECTION
Andreas Böhm

CLIENT CONSULTING
Frank Lotze, Helen Seiffe

FILM PRODUCTION
Frisbee Film

AGENCY PRODUCER
Nadja Catana

CAMERA
Felix Novo de Oliveira

PRODUCTION
Frisbee Film

DIRECTION
Till Franzen

COPY
Max Millies

INTERACTIVE PRODUCER
Alexander Bickenbach

ADDITIONAL AWARDS
BRONZE
Volume Advertising page 039
Publikumsanzeigen
Consumer advertisements

NOMINATION
Volume Advertising page 081
Fachanzeigen
Trade advertisements

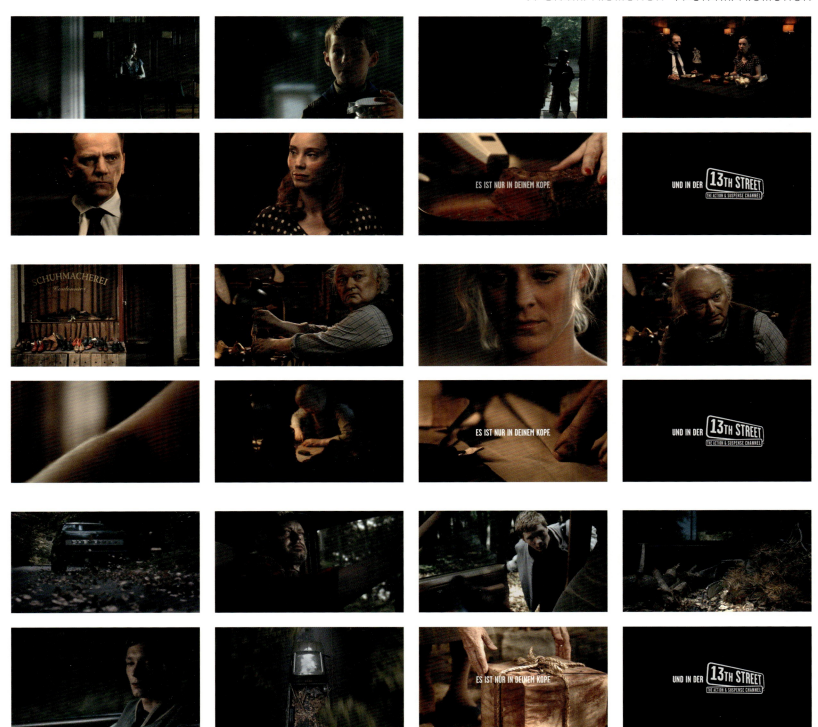

BRONZE

Verführe ungewöhnliche Leute zu ungewöhnlichen Filmen. Mit diesem Anspruch zeigt das Schweizer Fernsehen jeden Montag leckerste Bissen internationaler Filmkunst. »Delikatessen« heißt das Label für diesen eigenwilligen Genuss. Getreu dem Rezept »Auge isst mit« würzten die Kreativen des SF kräftig nach und setzten das Ganze mit dem Schweizer Topmodel Nadine Strittmatter schmackhaft in Szene. Yummy!

Seducing extraordinary people into watching extraordinary movies. With this claim, Swiss Television shows the yummiest bites of international movie art every Monday. The label of this unique enjoyment is called "Delikatessen". True to the recipe "a feast for the eyes", the creative of SF seasoned well and added Swiss topmodel Nadine Strittmatter. Yummy!

TITLE
Schweizer Fernsehen
»SF Delikatessen«
CLIENT
Schweizer Fernsehen
LEAD AGENCY
Schweizer Fernsehen
CREATIVE DIRECTION
Alex Hefter
ART DIRECTION
Marcel Weiss, Patrick Arnecke
FILM PRODUCTION
Filmstyler Frankfurt

DESIGN
Martin Bernhard,
Jürg Dummermuth,
Jan van Wezemael, SF
PRODUCTION
Filmstyler Frankfurt
DIRECTION
Frank Schneider, Filmstyler
VISUAL EFFECTS
Acht Frankfurt

FILME DIESER KATEGORIE FINDEN SIE UNTER WWW.ADC.DE FOR FILMS FROM THIS CATEGORY VISIT WWW.ADC.DE

NOMINATION

Die vorliegende Imagekampagne zeigt die Verbundenheit der Menschen mit der Schweiz und mit dem Schweizer Fernsehen. Der Claim »Meine Schweiz, mein Fernsehen« dokumentiert diese einzigartige Positionierung. Die Inszenierung der beliebten Testimonials ist authentisch, persönlich, reduziert gehalten und daher in Bezug zu SF von hoher Glaubwürdigkeit.

The present image campaign shows the viewers' connection with Switzerland and consequently also Swiss Television, regardless of age and target group. The claim "My Switzerland, my TV" documents this unique positioning. The testimonials of famous and popular Swiss celebrities are kept intentionally authentic and minimal. Their statements are very personal and highly credible in regard to SF.

TITLE
Schweizer Fernsehen
»Imagekampagne«

CLIENT
Schweizer Fernsehen

LEAD AGENCY
Schweizer Fernsehen

CREATIVE DIRECTION
Alex Hefter

FILM PRODUCTION
Eqal

PHOTOGRAPHY
Michel Comte

AGENCY PRODUCER
Lea Rindlisbacher

GRAPHIC ART
SF On Air Design

IDEA
Alex Hefter/Michel Comte

ARTIST
Noëmi Nadelmann, Heinz Spoerli,
Patricia Schmid

MUSIC COMPOSITION
Kings of Convenience »Misread«

PRODUCTION
Eqal

DIRECTION
Michel Comte

COPY
Frank Baumann

NOMINATION

Ganz lässig trägt ein schlaksiger Typ ein Auto mit sich herum. Aus dem Wagen wummern die Bässe, dass es nur so donnert. Offensichtlich benutzt er den Wagen dank Blaupunkt-Soundsystem als aufgemotztes Kofferradio frei nach dem Motto: Pimp my ride is sponsored by Blaupunkt.

A lanky guy is very casually carrying a car around with him. The bass is booming from the car, making it rumble. Thanks to the Blaupunkt-Soundsystem, he is able to use the car as a pimped up portable radio based loosely on the motto: Pimp my ride is sponsored by Blaupunkt.

TITLE
Blaupunkt »Car Hifi«
CLIENT
Blaupunkt GmbH
MARKETING DIRECTOR
Clemens Krebs
ADVERTISING DIRECTOR
Vincent Brucker
LEAD AGENCY
Jung von Matt AG

CREATIVE DIRECTION
Peter Kirchhoff, Wolf Heumann (GF)
ART DIRECTION
Vanessa Rabea Schrooten
CLIENT CONSULTING
Andreas Krah, Jochen Schwarz
FILM PRODUCTION
GrandHotelPictures
AGENCY PRODUCER
Julia Cramer

EDITOR
Reza Memari
CAMERA
Christoph Dammast
COMPOSER
Tai Jason
POSTPRODUCTION
Horst Riediger (FX Factory GmbH)

PRODUCTION
Norbert Kneißl
DIRECTION
Bernd Katzmarczyk
SOUND DESIGN
Hans Hoffmann
SPEAKER
Colin Solman
COPY
Peter Kirchhoff

FILME DIESER KATEGORIE FINDEN SIE UNTER WWW.ADC.DE FOR FILMS FROM THIS CATEGORY VISIT WWW.ADC.DE

BRONZE

NICK Winter Design: Versteckt in Alltags-Umgebungen von Kindern finden sich Micro-Winterwelten, zusammengesetzt aus realen und künstlichen Elementen und bevölkert von winterlichen Charakteren.

NICK Winter Design: Hidden in children's everyday surroundings lay micro winter-worlds, consisting of a mix of real and artificial elements and inhabited by a bunch of winter characters

TITLE
NICK »Winterdesign«

CLIENT
MTV Networks Germany GmbH, NICK

LEAD AGENCY
NICK On Air & Bionic Systems

CREATIVE DIRECTION
Bettina Vogel

ART DIRECTION
Doris Fürst, Malte Haust

FILM PRODUCTION
Bionic Systems

COMPUTER ANIMATION
Andreas Jung, Doris Fürst, Elisa Krenz, Malte Haust

DESIGN
Doris Fürst, Malte Haust

PRODUCTION
Doris Fürst, Malte Haust, Niklas Bäumer, Natalie Buba

SOUND DESIGN
Sebastian Müller (TonTotal@A-Medialynx)

SPEAKER
Marianne Graffam, Sebastian Müller

BRONZE

Die Geschichte und Philosophie der japanischen Marke ASICS wird durch sich immer wieder verändernde, immer komplexer werdende Origami-Figuren illustriert. ASICS Gründer Kihachiro Onitsuka erzählt von den Anfängen bis zur Weltmarke. Immer geht es darum, mit Ideen und Perfektionismus Produkte noch besser zu machen. Der Spot endet dann auch mit einem weißen Blatt Papier: »What will be the next idea?«

The history and philosophy of the Japanese brand ASICS is illustrated using ever changing, ever more complex origami figures. ASICS founder Kihachiro Onitsuka tells the story, from the beginning to becoming a global brand. It is always a question of improving products with ideas and perfectionism. The commercial ends with a white piece of paper: "What will be the next idea?"

TITLE
ASICS Europe »Origami«

CLIENT
ASICS Europe B.V

ADVERTISING DIRECTOR
Remco Rietvink

LEAD AGENCY
Nordpol+ Hamburg Agentur für Kommunikation GmbH

CREATIVE DIRECTION
Lars Rühmann

ART DIRECTION
Sean Kirby

CLIENT CONSULTING
Mathias Müller-Using, Niklas Franke

FILM PRODUCTION
Nordpol/element e

COMPUTER ANIMATION
André Junker, Christoffer Wolters

FILM ANIMATION
Stoptrick Hamburg

ARTIST
Sipho Mabona

MUSIC COMPOSITION
Audioforce

POSTPRODUCTION
Acolori Medienproduktion

PRODUCTION
Florian Liertz

DIRECTION
Tim Schierwater

SOUND DESIGN
Audioforce/Primetime Studio

COPY
Sebastian Behrendt

SOUND ENGINEER
Pierre Brand

ADDITIONAL AWARDS
BRONZE
Volume Advertising page 283
Filme für Verkaufsförderung/
Unternehmensdarstellungen
Films for sales promotion/
company presentation

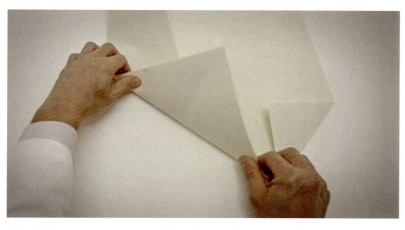
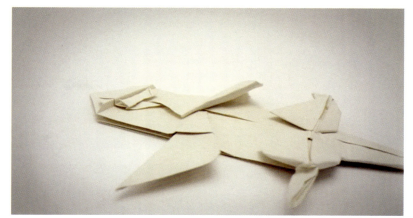

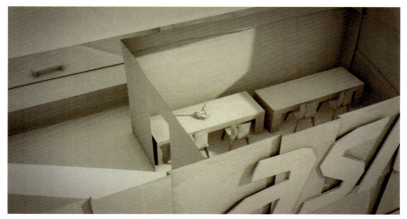

FILME DIESER KATEGORIE FINDEN SIE UNTER WWW.ADC.DE   FOR FILMS FROM THIS CATEGORY VISIT WWW.ADC.DE

NOMINATION

2007 führte Mercedes-Benz die neue Generation der G-Klasse ein. Gefragt war ein Spot, der unterstreicht, dass die G-Klasse seit Jahrzehnten das souveräne Maß aller Dinge unter den Geländewagen ist.

In 2007 Mercedes-Benz launched the new generation G-Class. Our task was to create a commercial, emphasizing that for several decades the G-Class has been the benchmark in the segment of off-road vehicles.

TITLE
Mercedes-Benz G-Klasse »Hindernisse«

CLIENT
Daimler AG

MARKETING DIRECTOR
Dr. Olaf Göttgens,
Dr. Kristina Hammer

ADVERTISING DIRECTOR
Mirco Völker, Christina Freier

LEAD AGENCY
Jung von Matt AG

CREATIVE DIRECTION
Fabian Frese, Thimoteus Wagner

ART DIRECTION
Christian Kroll

CLIENT CONSULTING
Klaus Burghauser, Stephan Damm,
Yves Rosengart, Johanna Hecker,
Jan Groenendijk

FILM PRODUCTION
Sehsucht GmbH

ILLUSTRATION
Sehsucht GmbH

COMPUTER ANIMATION
Hannes Geiger, Thore Bornemann,
Maurice Jochem

DESIGN
Alex Heyer

EDITOR
Christoph Senn

MUSIC COMPOSITION
BLUWI Music & Sounddesign

COMPOSER
BLUWI/Timo Blunck, Stefan Will,
Ralf Denker

POSTPRODUCTION
Studio Funk GmbH & Co. KG

PRODUCTION
Andreas Coutsoumbelis,
Martin Woelke

DIRECTION
Ole Peters, Hannes Geiger

SOUND DESIGN
BLUWI/Marco Dreckkötter

COPY
Peter Gocht

SOUND ENGINEER
Studio Funk/Jochen Kömpe

VISUAL EFFECTS
Daniel Hummer

ADDITIONAL AWARDS
BRONZE
Volume Advertising page 268
Kinowerbefilme
Cinema commercials

NOMINATION
Volume Advertising page 257
TV-Spots
Television commercials

NOMINATION
Volume Design page 221
Illustration
Illustration

NOMINATION

Für die Marke Jeep sollte ein aufmerksamkeitsstarker Commercial entwickelt werden. Der Spot sollte auch als Viral im Internet funktionieren, und von der Zielgruppe weiterversandt werden.

Jeep is a living legend in the world of off-road vehicles, and still remains the only truly original SUV. We were commissioned to produce an image commercial for Jeep that addresses both existing and potential Jeep customers.

TITLE
Jeep Animationsfilm
»Ten little vehicles«
CLIENT
Chrysler Jeep
LEAD AGENCY
KNSK Werbeagentur GmbH
CREATIVE DIRECTION
Claudia Bach
ART DIRECTION
Michael Reissinger
CLIENT CONSULTING
Jan Isterling, Philipp Ernsting
FILM PRODUCTION
Deli Pictures

ILLUSTRATION
Maurice, Tom, Enzo, Don-sun, Michi, Kim-Eyleen, Johanna-Marie, Emma, Kurt
AGENCY PRODUCER
Kerstin Arndt
IMAGE EDITING
Christian Reimann
COMPUTER ANIMATION
Malte Sarnes, Thomas Volkmann
FILM ANIMATION
Robert Rhee
GRAPHIC ART
Robert Rhee

POSTPRODUCTION
Deli Pictures
PRODUCTION
Sebastian Hellge
DIRECTION
Michael Reissinger
SCREEN DESIGN
Thomas Volkmann, Michael Reissinger
SOUND DESIGN
Markenfilm, nhb Hamburg
COPY
Lisa Port, Fabian Tritsch, Lennert Wendt, Anna-Kristina Schroeder, Nina Burmeister

VISUAL EFFECTS
Christian Reimann

ADDITIONAL AWARDS
BRONZE
Volume Advertising page 255
TV-Spots
Television commercials

BRONZE
Volume Advertising page 270
Kinowerbefilme
Cinema commercials

JOSEPHINE BAKER

*03. JUNI 1906 ST. LOUIS/MISSOURI †12. APRIL 1975 PARIS

Als uneheliche Tochter eines jüdischen Schlagzeugers und einer Waschfrau war Josephines Kindheit kein Zuckerschlecken. Mit elf Jahren wird sie Augenzeugin eines Rassenpogroms. Mit 13 Jahren wird sie zwangsverheiratet, kann aber der Ehe nach wenigen Wochen entrinnen. Sie tritt stattdessen als Komparsin beim Theater auf. Mit 16 Jahren singt und tanzt sie im Standard Theatre in Philiadelphia. Ihr Karriere beginnt. Nach New York folgt Paris, was rasch zu ihrer neuen Wahlheimat wurde. Europa lag ihr zu Füßen. Sie verzückte ihr Publikum im Bananenkleidchen und brachte ihnen erstmalig Carleston bei. Adolf Loos entwarf ein Haus für sie. Le Corbusier durfte sie nackt zeichnen. 1937 wurde sie französische Staatsbürgerin. Sie machte einen Pilotenschein und arbeitete für die Résistance gegen Hitler. Sie brachte es bis zum Leutnant und erhielt nach Kriegsende die Rosette der »Légion d'honneur«. Sie adoptierte zwölf Waisenkinder unterschiedlicher Hautfarbe, um gegen den US-Rassismus zu protestieren.

*03 JUNE 1906 ST. LOUIS/MISSOURI †12 APRIL 1975 PARIS

Josephine's childhood was no bed of roses: the illegitimate daughter of a Jewish drummer and a washerwoman, she witnessed a racist pogrom at the age of 11 and was forcibly married at 13, only to run away from the marriage a few weeks later, appearing instead as a theatre extra. At the age of 16 she was singing and dancing in the Standard Theatre in Philadelphia. Her career was beginning. New York was followed by Paris, which quickly became her adopted home. Europe lay at her feet. She enchanted her public with her banana skirt, and introduced them to the Charleston. Adolf Loos designed a house for her. Le Corbusier drew her in the nude. In 1937 she became a French citizen. She acquired a pilot licence and worked for the Résistance against Hitler, rising to the rank of lieutenant and receiving the rosette of the *Légion d'honneur* following the war. She also adopted twelve orphans of varying skin colour as a protest against racism in the US.

I like Frenchmen very much, because even when they insult you they do it so nicely.

ICH MAG FRANZÖSISCHE MÄNNER SEHR, DENN SELBST WENN SIE EINEN BELEIDIGEN, TUN SIE DAS AUF EINE SO NETTE ART.

SILVER

Fahrdynamik und Präzision des neuen Audi A5 stehen im Mittelpunkt des Spots. Perfekt aufeinander abgestimmt gelingt es zwei Audi A5, einen Lenkdrachen in der Luft zu steuern. Eine spektakuläre Performance, die ausschließlich aus real gedrehtem Material besteht. Keine Tricks, keine nachträglichen Computereffekte. Für das entsprechend progressive Sounddesign zeichnet sich Duo Yello verantwortlich, die als Pioniere elektronischer Klangwelten bekannt geworden sind.

The driving dynamics and precision of the new Audi A5 take centre stage in the spot. Two Audi A5's fly a kite in the air in perfect synchronicity. A spectacular performance filmed exclusively without any tricks or additional computer effects. Duo Yello, well known as pioneers of electrical soundscapes, designed the sound.

TITLE
AUDI Sound-Design »Kite«
CLIENT
AUDI AG
MARKETING DIRECTOR
Michael Renz
ADVERTISING DIRECTOR
Jagoda Becic
LEAD AGENCY
HEIMAT, Berlin
CREATIVE DIRECTION
Jürgen Vossen, Guido Heffels
ART DIRECTION
Bastian Kuhn, Tim Schneider
CLIENT CONSULTING
Matthias von Bechtolsheim, Joachim Stürken
STRATEGIC PLANNING
Andreas Mengele
CONSULTING
Sebastian Marx, Marcus Bank

GRAPHIC ART
Andreas Grill
CAMERA
John Lynch
PRODUCTION
Tempomedia Filmproduktion GmbH, Hamburg
DIRECTION
Daniel Barber
EDITING
Neil Smith
(Work Film Editors)
SOUND DESIGN
Neil Smith/yello
COPY
Till Eckel,
Alexander Weber-Grün
SOUND ENGINEER
Thomas Süß, audioforce Berlin

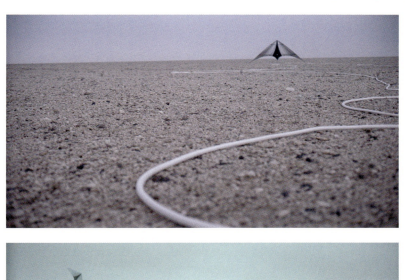

FILME DIESER KATEGORIE FINDEN SIE UNTER WWW.ADC.DE FOR FILMS FROM THIS CATEGORY VISIT WWW.ADC.DE

BRONZE

Eine alltägliche Situation: Ein Teekessel mit kochendem Wasser auf einer Herdplatte. Dazu hören wird das typische Pfeifen der Kesselflöte. Nach einer Weile wird die Flöte abgenommen. Das Pfeifen hört jedoch nicht auf. Es verändert sich lediglich ein wenig und bleibt in Form eines quälenden Tinnitus-Geräuschs. Erst als die URL: www.tinnitus-hilfe.org eingeblendet wird, herrscht endlich Stille.

A daily situation: the tea kettle boiling water on the hob. It's accompanied by the typical whistling sound. After some time, the whistle is taken off. But the sound doesn't stop. It changes slightly and continues in the agonising way that it does for Tinnitus sufferers. Silence returns when the URL is displayed: www.tinnitus-hilfe.org.

TITLE
Tinnitus Hilfe Düsseldorf Sound-Design »Teekessel«
CLIENT
Tinnitus Hilfe Düsseldorf, Dr. Greuel
MARKETING DIRECTOR
Dr. med. Hans Greuel
ADVERTISING DIRECTOR
Dr. med. Hans Greuel
LEAD AGENCY
Heye Group, GmbH
CREATIVE DIRECTION
Martin Kiessling, Alexander Bartel, Günther Marschall
ART DIRECTION
Felix Hennermann
CLIENT CONSULTING
Markus Goetze, Daniel Hartmann
STRATEGIC PLANNING
Günther Marschall
FILM PRODUCTION
Product Eye
AGENCY PRODUCER
Sascha Driesang

IMAGE EDITING
Mario Mosner
COMPUTER ANIMATION
Mario Mosner
DESIGN
Felix Hennermann, Mario Mosner
CAMERA
Boris Mosner
POSTPRODUCTION
Postbar
DIRECTION
Boris Mosner
EDITING
Mario Mosner, Stefan Ohlmann
SCREEN DESIGN
Felix Hennermann, Mario Mosner
SOUND DESIGN
Exit Studios
COPY
Günther Marschall
SOUND ENGINEER
Klaus Lesoine

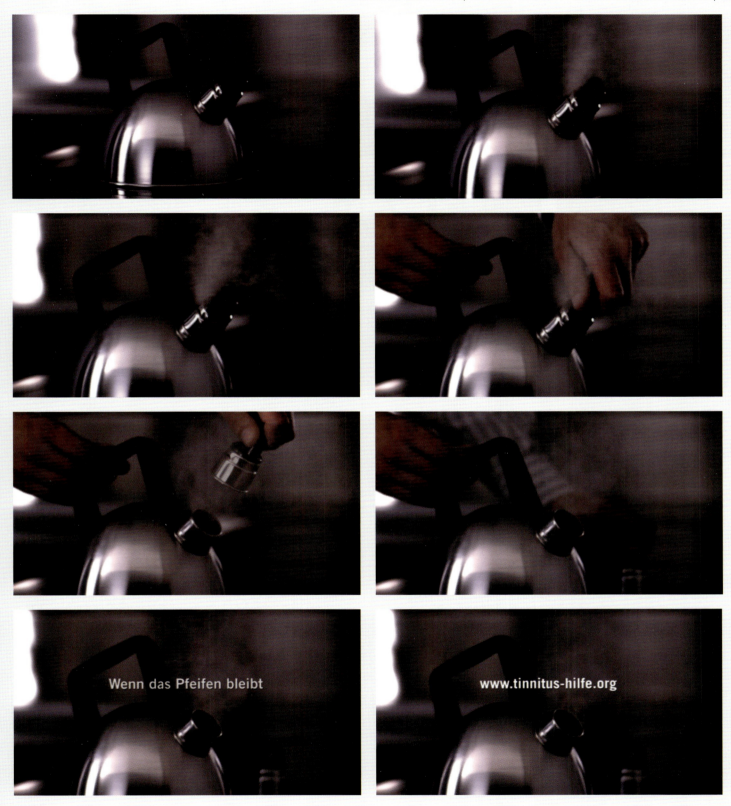

FILME DIESER KATEGORIE FINDEN SIE UNTER WWW.ADC.DE FOR FILMS FROM THIS CATEGORY VISIT WWW.ADC.DE

NOMINATION

Schon lange setzt sich Coop für Ökologie und Ethik ein. Das unterstreicht der berühmte Rapper Stress mit seinem engagierten Song, den er eigens für diesen Spot komponierte.

Coop has been environmentally and socially conscious for years. The famous rapper Stress underscores this with his committed song, composed specially for this spot.

TITLE
Coop Musikkomposition »Stress«

CLIENT
Coop

MARKETING DIRECTOR
Jürg Peritz

LEAD AGENCY
Krieg, Schlupp, Bürge/
Springer & Jacoby

CREATIVE DIRECTION
Daniel Krieg

CLIENT CONSULTING
Dany Kielholz, Sabrina Arthur

FILM PRODUCTION
Combo Entertainment

CAMERA
Aladin Hasic

COMPOSER
Stress

POSTPRODUCTION
Combo Entertainment

PRODUCTION
Siro Micheroli

DIRECTION
Roman Peritz

SOUND DESIGN
Stress

TECHNICAL IMPLEMENTATION
Christoph Schönholzer

VISUAL EFFECTS
Milos May

MUSIC COMPOSITIONS/SOUND DESIGN MUSIKKOMPOSITIONEN/SOUND-DESIGN 311

NOMINATION

Der TV-Spot inszeniert die Fahrkultur des neuen C-Klasse T-Modells in großem Stil. Der Mercedes-Benz unter den Sportkombis wird zum Helden einer modernen Oper. Herausgefordert vom Wind weist das neue C-Klasse T-Modell dank seiner Kraft und Agilität seinen Widersacher in dessen Schranken. Da das Auto steht, werden Dynamik und Geschwindigkeit mithilfe von beweglichen Bühnenelementen erzeugt.

The TV commercial features the driving culture of the new C-Class Estate in grand style. The Mercedes-Benz among the sporty estates becomes the hero of a modern opera. Challenged by the wind, the new C-Class Estate puts its opponent in its place with its power and agility. Since the car is not moving, the impression of dynamics and speed is generated by way of movable stage elements.

TITLE
Mercedes-Benz C-Klasse T-Modell Sound-Design »Oper«
CLIENT
Daimler AG
MARKETING DIRECTOR
Dr. Olaf Göttgens/
Dr. Kristina Hammer
ADVERTISING DIRECTOR
Mirko Völker (Manager Global Advertising),
Jochen Schmidt
LEAD AGENCY
Jung von Matt AG

CREATIVE DIRECTION
Mathias Stiller, Wolfgang Schneider, Boris Schwiedrzik
ART DIRECTION
Frederik Hofmann
CLIENT CONSULTING
Christian Hupertz,
Klaus Burghauser, Darek Stöhr, Christoph Neuhaus, JoKo Schulte, Vittal Wagner
FILM PRODUCTION
Markenfilm Hamburg
AGENCY PRODUCER
Lars Wiepking

GRAPHIC ART
Nina Kurowski, Marc Tebart
CAMERA
Sebastian Pfaffenbichler
MUSIC COMPOSITION
White Horse Music & Audioforce (Co-Produktion), Steve Patuta, Gerrit Winterstein, Thomas Süß
POSTPRODUCTION
Digital Domain, Los Angeles
PRODUCTION
Harald Beelte, Katie Stiebel, Oliver Schertlein, Marc Strass
DIRECTION
Carl Erik Rinsch

EDITING
Robb Hoffmann
SOUND DESIGN
White Horse Music & Audioforce (Co-Produktion), Steve Patuta, Gerrit Winterstein
COPY
Jens Daum

ADDITIONAL AWARDS
BRONZE
Volume Advertising page 272
Kinowerbefilme
Cinema commercials

FILME DIESER KATEGORIE FINDEN SIE UNTER WWW.ADC.DE   FOR FILMS FROM THIS CATEGORY VISIT WWW.ADC.DE

GOLD

TITLE
Konzerthaus Dortmund Saison 2007/2008 Musikkomposition »symphony in red«
CLIENT
Konzerthaus Dortmund – Philharmonie für Westfalen
MARKETING DIRECTOR
Milena Ivkovic
LEAD AGENCY
Jung von Matt AG
CREATIVE DIRECTION
Sascha Hanke, Timm Hanebeck, Wolf Heumann (GF)
ART DIRECTION
Sascha Hanke, Timm Hanebeck
CLIENT CONSULTING
Nina Gerwing, Lena Frers
FILM PRODUCTION
Sehsucht GmbH
AGENCY PRODUCER
Hermann Krug, Alexander Schillinsky
FILM ANIMATION
Niko Tziopanos, Alex Heyer, Martin Hess
CAMERA
Bea Wellenbrock, Alex Heyer, Valentin Heun
MUSIC COMPOSITION
Fazil Say
COMPOSER
Fazil Say
POSTPRODUCTION
Sehsucht GmbH
PRODUCTION
Andreas Coutsoumbelis, Martin Woelke
DIRECTION
Niko Tziopanos
COPY
Michael Okun, Moritz Grub

ADDITIONAL AWARDS
GOLD
Volume Advertising page 278
Filme für Verkaufsförderung/ Unternehmensdarstellungen
Films for sales promotion/ company presentation

BRONZE
Volume Advertising page 255
TV-Spots
Television commercials

SILVER

TITLE
Hornbach Baumarkt Sound-Design »Mach es fertig«
CLIENT
Hornbach Baumarkt AG
MARKETING DIRECTOR
Jürgen Schröcker
ADVERTISING DIRECTOR
Diana Koob
LEAD AGENCY
HEIMAT, Berlin
CREATIVE DIRECTION
Guido Heffels, Jürgen Vossen
ART DIRECTION
Tim Schneider, Mike Brandt, Marc Wientzek
CLIENT CONSULTING
Yves Krämer
FILM PRODUCTION
Markenfilm, Berlin
AGENCY PRODUCER
Kerstin Breuer
CONSULTING
Mark Hassan, Sammy Bohneberg
IMAGE EDITING
Furia, Barcelona
COMPUTER ANIMATION
Furia, Barcelona
EDITOR
Pablo Plant
FILM ANIMATION
Furia, Barcelona
CAMERA
Javier Aguirresarobe
MEDIA
Crossmedia GmbH
MUSIC COMPOSITION
Rudolf Moser, Christian Meyer
COMPOSER
Rudolf Moser, Christian Meyer
POSTPRODUCTION
nhb, Berlin/Furia, Barcelona
PRODUCTION
Lutz Müller, Vivian Schröder
DIRECTION
Carl Erik Rinsch
EDITING
nhb, Berlin
SOUND DESIGN
Mosermeyer, Berlin
COPY
Alexander Ardelean, Guido Heffels, Sebastian Kainz, Till Eckel
SOUND ENGINEER
Masterin & Off: Nima Gholiagha, nhb Berlin
VISUAL EFFECTS
Alex Grau (Furia, Barcelona)

ADDITIONAL AWARDS
SILVER
Volume Advertising page 254
TV-Spots
Television commercials

SILVER
Volume Advertising page 260
Kinowerbefilme
Cinema commercials

BRONZE

TITLE
Dextro Energy Musikkomposition »Hotline«
CLIENT
Dextro Energy
MARKETING DIRECTOR
Viola Ehrenbeck
LEAD AGENCY
kempertrautmann gmbh
CREATIVE DIRECTION
Willy Kaussen, Frank Bannöhr
ART DIRECTION
Frank Bannöhr
CLIENT CONSULTING
Hendrik Heine, Nils Möller, Jacqueline Koch
FILM PRODUCTION
Tempomedia
GRAPHIC ART
Christoph Zapletal
CAMERA
Eduard Schneidermeier
MUSIC COMPOSITION
Thomas Kisser »Wake-Up-Music«, Hastings Audio Network
COMPOSER
Thomas Kisser
PRODUCTION
Alexander Schildt, Stefan Vollmert, Daniela Dreyer
DIRECTION
Andreas Link
EDITING
Christoph Zapletal, Jörn Falldorf
COPY
Willy Kaussen

ADDITIONAL AWARDS
BRONZE
Volume Advertising page 230
TV-Spots
Television commercials

 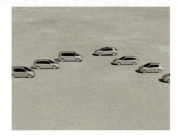

BRONZE

TITLE
Sixt – rent a car
»Matthias Reim«
CLIENT
Sixt GmbH & Co.
Autovermietung KG
MARKETING DIRECTOR
Dr. Karsten Willrodt
ADVERTISING DIRECTOR
Daniela Erdmann
LEAD AGENCY
Jung von Matt AG
CREATIVE DIRECTION
Peter Kirchhoff, Wolf Heumann
ART DIRECTION
Vanessa Rabea Schrooten
CLIENT CONSULTING
Sandra Schymetzki,
Ann-Kristin Grohsklaus
AGENCY PRODUCER
Julia Cramer
GRAPHIC ART
Felix Taubert
MUSIC COMPOSITION
Matthias Reim, Bernd Dietrich
COMPOSER
Matthias Reim, Bernd Dietrich
COPY
Lisa Maria Hartwich,
Peter Kirchhoff,
Wolf Heumann

ADDITIONAL AWARDS
SILVER
Volume Advertising page 350
Integrierte Kampagnen
Integrated campaigns

BRONZE
Volume Advertising page 255
TV-Spots
Television commercials

BRONZE
Volume Advertising page 289
Virale Filme
Viral films

BRONZE
Volume Design page 246
Digitale Werbung
Digital advertising

NOMINATION
Volume Advertising page 339
Funkspots
Radio commercials

NOMINATION

TITLE
Renault Deutschland
Musikkomposition »Ballett«
CLIENT
Renault Deutschland AG
MARKETING DIRECTOR
Jörg-Alexander Ellhof
LEAD AGENCY
Nordpol+ Hamburg Agentur für
Kommunikation GmbH
CREATIVE DIRECTION
Lars Rühmann
ART DIRECTION
Tim Schierwater,
Christoph Bielefeldt
CLIENT CONSULTING
Mathias Müller-Using
FILM PRODUCTION
element e
MUSIC COMPOSITION
Jacques Offenbach;
Additional composing:
Steve Patuta@audioforce
COMPOSER
Jacques Offenbach;
Additional composing:
Steve Patuta@audioforce
POSTPRODUCTION
Deli Pictures
DIRECTION
Silvio Helbig
EDITING
Sabine Panek
SOUND DESIGN
Loft Tonstudios, GmbH
COPY
Sebastian Behrendt
SOUND ENGINEER
Sascha Heiny, Stefan Apell

ADDITIONAL AWARDS
SILVER
Volume Advertising page 226
TV-Spots
Television commercials

SILVER
Volume Advertising page 277
Kinowerbefilme
Cinema commercials

*19. DEZEMBER 1915 PARIS †11. OKTOBER 1963 PARIS

Als Kind hatte Edith Gassion nicht viel zu lachen. Ihre Mutter machte sich nach der Geburt aus dem Staub, und die Großmutter ließ das Baby fast verhungern. Ihr Vater arbeitete als Schlangenmensch beim Zirkus und brachte sie dann bei seiner Familie unter. Mit sieben ging sie das erste Mal mit ihrem alkoholkranken Vater auf Tournee. Mit 15 machte sie sich dann selbstständig und zog als Straßensängerin durch Paris. Der Kabarettbesitzer Louis Leplée holte sie als Chanteuse in sein Etablissement. Er nannte das nur 1,47 m große Mädchen mit der großen Stimme »La Môme Piaf« (der kleine Spatz). Doch das Unglück blieb ihr hold. Mit 18 gebar sie ihr einziges Kind, das zwei Jahre später verstarb. Ihr Mentor Leplée wurde ermordet und sie der Mitschuld bezichtigt. Doch danach ging es endlich wieder bergauf. Edith Piaf schaffte den Durchbruch. Mit Yves Montand hatte sie ein leidenschaftliches Verhältnis. Sie förderte aktiv die Karrieren der Nachwuchssänger Aznavour, Bécaud, Constantine, Moustaki, Pills und Lai. Sie hatte viele Affären, aber keine war von Dauer. Leider blieb der Alkohol ihr treuester Freund.

*19 DECEMBER 1915 PARIS †11 OCTOBER 1963 PARIS

Edith Gassion didn't have much to laugh about as a child. Her mother left her following her birth, and her grandmother almost let her starve as a baby. Her father, an alcoholic, worked as a contortionist at the circus, and took her to live with his family; she was seven when she first accompanied him on tour. She became self-reliant at the age of 15, making her way around Paris as a street singer. Then nightclub owner Louis Leplée hired her as a singer in his club. He dubbed the 4-foot-10-inch tall girl with the big voice *La Môme Piaf* ("the little sparrow chick"). But her ill-fortune stuck to her. At the age of 18 she had her only child, who died two years later. When her mentor Leplée was murdered, she was accused of complicity. After this, however, things began to look up and she achieved her breakthrough. She had a passionate relationship with Yves Montand, and played an active role in advancing the careers of the up-and-coming singers Aznavour, Bécaud, Constantine, Moustaki, Pills and Lai. She had many affairs, although none lasted: sadly, alcohol remained her most faithful companion.

I want to make people cry even if they don't understand my words.

ICH MÖCHTE DIE MENSCHEN ZUM WEINEN BRINGEN, SELBST WENN SIE MEINE WORTE NICHT VERSTEHEN.

TITLE
VW Polo Kampagne »Polo Podcast«
CLIENT
Volkswagen AG
MARKETING DIRECTOR
Jochen Sengpiehl
ADVERTISING DIRECTOR
Hartmut Seeger
LEAD AGENCY
DDB Germany, Berlin
CREATIVE DIRECTION
Stefan Schulte, Bert Peulecke
RADIO PRODUCTION
Studio Funk Berlin
CONSULTING
Silke Lagodny, Helen Georgi
COPY
Ludwig Berndl
SOUND ENGINEER
Stephan Moritz, Christoph Meyer

Zu dieser Kampagne gehören noch zwei weitere Spots: »Kran« und »Vulkan«.

Two further spots are part of this campaign: "Kran" and "Vulkan".

DER PODCAST »LAWINE«

ERZÄHLER: »Mensch und Natur ... Also was wir da so alles anstellen, man macht sich das ja oft gar nicht so richtig bewusst. Stichwort Erosion und Schutzwald weg, abgeholzt – also im Gebirge, mein' ich jetzt hauptsächlich.

Ich komm bloß drauf, weil heute – und wenn man das dann am eigenen Leibe ... halt erlebt, quasi – dann steigt irgendwie die Relevanz auch, deswegen. Weil heute war ich eben im Gebirge, klassische Sonntagsfahrt. Ich bin auf so einen Panorama-Parkplatz gefahren. Ganz allein war ich da, alles ruhig ... Irgendwie schon sehr erhaben.

Und dann, das war eigentlich ein Glück, bin ich von der Brüstung gleich wieder weg – Höhen vertrag ich nicht so hervorragend – und eben gleich wieder eingestiegen. Weil: Dass sich da was in irgendeiner Weise, ja, Gewaltiges anbahnt, das hat man schon gemerkt, da war so ein mächtiges Geräusch, wie wenn der Berg sich räuspert, von ganz tief unten, so: ›Meine Herrschaften, jetzt mal aufgepasst hier!‹ Dass jetzt allerdings gleich dieser ganze Felsvorsprung, auf dem der Parkplatz war, sich gen Tal verabschiedet, das war dann doch etwas drastischer, als ich es vielleicht erwartet hätte, in dem Moment.

Ja, jedenfalls bin ich da also runtergefahren beziehungsweise gerutscht vielmehr, weil: Ich hab dann die Handbremse angezogen. Nicht, dass das jetzt viel genützt hätte ... Ich hab eh noch überlegt, davor, ob ich's machen soll, aber hab mir dann gedacht: Irgendwann stößt ABS auch an seine Grenzen. Und wenn du erst mal auf dem Dach unterwegs bist, ist es eh egal, ob die Räder jetzt blockieren oder nicht.

Wie gesagt, bin ich also runter. Und dann plötzlich direkt auf diesen Baum da zu. Wo ich mir noch gedacht hab – komisch, was man alles denkt in so einer Situation, es ging ja eigentlich alles sehr, na ja, flott – jedenfalls hab ich mir noch gedacht: auweia. Das wär dann wieder ein Baum weniger, den irgendein ... was weiß ich ... Greenpeace wieder aufforsten muss.

Aber kam dann überhaupt nicht so weit, weil dieser große Felsen, den ich dann touchiert hab, der hat mir den entscheidenden Tick Richtungsänderung noch gegeben.

Zur Orientierung war dieser Baum übrigens ganz gut, weil Baumgrenze – in Mitteleuropa – ja bei so circa 1.800 Meter. Da wusst' ich dann gleich ungefähr, wie viel ich noch vor mir hab.

Und ... so weiter und so weiter. Gibt nicht mehr viel zu erzählen, eigentlich. Weil wie das war, kann jeder ganz leicht nachvollziehen, der einmal mühsam so einen Berg hinaufgewandert ist – indem er sich einfach das genaue Gegenteil vorstellt: nämlich sehr, sehr schnell. War das. Die wunderbare Welt der Schwerkraft. Oder, alte Skifahrer-Weisheit: Runter kommt man immer. Na ja, und unten bin ich dann auf so einer saftigen, grünen Wiese langsam ausgerollt – also ein paar Mal noch überschlagen – und sogar wieder auf die Räder zu stehen gekommen. Was insofern ganz gut war, weil dann bin ich schon weggefahren gewesen, wie dieser ganze ... äh ... Felslawine dann angekommen ist. Muss ich unterwegs irgendwie überholt haben.

Ich bin dann ins nächste Dorf gefahren, da war ein Mordsaufruhr und Hin und Her. Da hab ich auch rausgefunden, dass das jetzt im Prinzip so ganz überraschend gar nicht war, weil diese Geologen, also ... Gebirgsfachleute, schon gesagt haben: Demnächst kann da mal was sein. Jetzt ist es aber so, dass in den, na ja, Dimensionen von Gebirgen ›demnächst‹ schon heißen kann: ›heute‹. Oder ›morgen‹. Es kann aber auch genauso gut heißen: achttausend Jahre.

Insofern kann man das, glaub ich, guten Gewissens unter der Rubrik ›Pech‹ einordnen, dass es – ausgerechnet heute – mich da erwischt hat. Bloß falls die Versicherung sich aufregt, wegen diesem Sprung in der Windschutzscheibe. Na ja. Ich glaub, ich geh jetzt mal duschen.«

OFF: »Beruhigend sicher. Der Polo.«
CLAIM: Volkswagen. Das Auto.

GOLD

TITLE
Arcor Spam Blocker Kampagne
»Spam Blocker«
CLIENT
Arcor AG & Co. KG
MARKETING DIRECTOR
Jörg Quehl
LEAD AGENCY
Grabarz & Partner
CREATIVE DIRECTION
Ralf Heuel, Martin Graß
CLIENT CONSULTING
Marc Pech, Lydia Heydel
RADIO PRODUCTION
Studio Funk KG
AGENCY PRODUCER
Patrick Cahill
DIRECTION
Ralf Heuel, Torsten Hennings
COPY
Martin Graß
SOUND ENGINEER
Torsten Hennings

SPOT »HERBERT RINGSTON«

MANN: (in stark akzentuiertem Englisch) »Dear listener, I am Barrister Nenito Villaran from the Republic of the Philippines. One of my clients deposited 40 Million Dollar Cash in my office. Before he died. For safety reasons I need to send the money abroad very swiftly. If you agree I send it to your adress and we share fifty fifty. There is only one obstacle: The customs ask for bribe. I suggest humbly we also share this investion fifty fifty. So please transfer 6,000 Dollars on my account number 94771 in the Holecombe Bank in Georgetown. I assure you this is the most important radio commercial you ever listened to.«

OFF: »Spams: Jetzt überall – nur nicht mehr per E-Mail. Der Spam-Blocker von Arcor.«

SOUND-LOGO: Arcor.

SPOT »DR. DAGOGO«

MANN: (in stark akzentuiertem Englisch) »Hello my friend. I am Dr. Dagogo Jack Abubakar, former minister of finance of Federal Republic of Nigeria. Through this radio message I am searching for a truthful person. If you are truthful I will transfer 40 Million Dollars to your account. 30 Million you invest for me. And 10 Million Dollars is for you. All I need is your truthfulness. And a little transaction fee. So please transfer 8,000 Dollars to my bank account number 811315 at Morrison Private Bank in Lagos. Yours sincerely Dr. Dagogo Jack Abubakar – but my friends call me Jack.«

OFF: »Spams: Jetzt überall – nur nicht mehr per E-Mail. Der Spam-Blocker von Arcor.«

SOUND-LOGO: Arcor.

SILVER

TITLE
Mercedes-Benz Kampagne
»Nanga Parbat«

CLIENT
Daimler AG

LEAD AGENCY
Jung von Matt AG

CREATIVE DIRECTION
Fabian Frese, Götz Ulmer,
Deneke von Weltzien, Oliver Voss

CLIENT CONSULTING
Yves Rosengart, Stephan Damm,
Christian Hupertz

RADIO PRODUCTION
Studio Funk Hamburg
GmbH & Co. KG

DIRECTION
Torsten Hennings, Florian Panier

SPEAKER
Fabian Frese, Ole Jacobsen

COPY
Jan-Florian Ege

SOUND ENGINEER
Torsten Hennings, Florian Panier

SPOT »NANGA PARBAT 1«

SFX: Ein tosender Schneesturm.
(Ein Mann schreibt einen Tagebuch-Eintrag, wir hören seine ernste Gedankenstimme mit starkem Tiroler Akzent.)

MANN: »9. Mai: Schind auf 6.600 Mäter auf der Diamir-Seite vom Nanga Parbat. Der Bärg isch brutal. Die Wetterumschwünge zwingen uns ämmer wieder zu Pausen, verlangen alles von uns ab. Zum Gchlück haben wir noch genügend Vorräte. In der Gruppe gibd äs Streit über die morgige Route zum Gchipfel. Ein Teil will über die Bazhinscharte. Franz und ich wollen den Gchipfel über den Silberzacken erreichen. Aber wälche Route wir morgen auch nähmen, ich hoffe inschtändig, dass ich diesmal fahren darf.«

VO: »Die neue Generation der G-Klasse:
Jetzt bei Ihrem Mercedes-Benz-Partner.«

SPOT »NANGA PARBAT 2«

SFX: Ein tosender Schneesturm.
(Ein Mann schreibt einen Tagebuch-Eintrag, wir hören seine ernste Gedankenstimme mit starkem Tiroler Akzent.)

MANN: »13. Mai: 7.800 Höhenmeter. Wir sind kurz vor dem Chipfel des Nanga Parbat. Än den letzten drei Tagen haben wir uns über die Bazhinscharte gequält. Es schien so, als ob där Bärg sich gegen seine Besteigung währen wollte – Lawinenabgänge und unglaubliche Stürme haben unseren unbedingten Willen hart auf die Probe gäställt. Für mich als Bergsteiger ist es ämmer wieder erschtaunlich am eigenen Körper zu ärläben, zu was der Mänsch fähig ist, wenn er im richtigen Auto sitzt.«

VO: »Die neue Generation der G-Klasse:
Jetzt bei Ihrem Mercedes-Benz-Partner.«

SPOT »NANGA PARBAT 3«

SFX: Ein tosender Schneesturm.
(Ein Mann schreibt einen Tagebuch-Eintrag, wir hören seine ernste Gedankenstimme mit starkem Tiroler Akzent.)

MANN: »18. Mai: Wir haben äs geschafft! Der Chipfel des Nanga Parbat ist bezwungen. Franz wainte vor Glück. Ihm warän die Strapazen am deutlichsten anzusähen. Aber auch ich war ergriffen. Zwei Jahre harte Vorbereitung finden än dieser Erstürmung ähren Chöhepunkt. Aber wir chatten wirklich unglaubliches Chlück – dass das Benzin noch gereicht hat.«

VO: »Die neue Generation G-Klasse:
Jetzt bei Ihrem Mercedes-Benz-Partner.«

SPOTS DIESER KATEGORIE FINDEN SIE UNTER WWW.ADC.DE FOR RADIO COMMERCIALS FROM THIS CATEGORY VISIT WWW.ADC.DE

SILVER

TITLE
Philharmonie Essen Kampagne
»Polizeichor«

CLIENT
Philharmonie Essen

ADVERTISING DIRECTOR
Adrian Schmidt

LEAD AGENCY
Tillmanns, Ogilvy & Mather
GmbH & Co. KG

CREATIVE DIRECTION
Bernd Grellmann

CLIENT CONSULTING
Andreas Fischer

RADIO PRODUCTION
Sprachlabor Audioproduktionen,
Düsseldorf

ARTIST
Gotthard Wallscheid,
Ralf-Jürgen Pflug, Walter Lauer,
Thomas Bullinger

MUSIC COMPOSITION
Eike Steffen, Thomas Bullinger

SPEAKER
Silke Lindermaus

COPY
Markus Bredenbals,
Thomas Bullinger, Adrian Butnariu

SOUND ENGINEER
Eike Steffen, Tim Prögler

SPOT »UMSTELLT«

(Gespannte Stille in einer Konzerthalle. Im Publikum hustet noch jemand, bevor man das Klopfen eines Taktstocks auf ein Dirigentenpult hört. Ein Chor beginnt zu singen.)

CHOR: »Das Ge-bäu-de ist umstellt, kommen Sie mit erho-be-nen HÄNDEN heraus!
Kommen Sie raus! Geben Sie auf!
Kommen Sie raus! Geben Sie auf!
Sie ham doch keine Schaaaaaaaangse.«

OFF: »Der Polizeichor Essen.
Am 15. und 16. Dezember in der Philharmonie Essen.«

SPOT »ALLGEMEINE VERKEHRSKONTROLLE«

(Ein letztes Räuspern. Dann beginnt ein Teil eines Chores zu singen.)

CHOR: »Allgemeine Verkehrskontrolle,
Ihre Papiere, bitte.«

(Der Rest des Chores stimmt im Kanon ein, während der erste weiter singt.)

CHOR: »Haben Sie Alkohol getrunken?
Alles okay. Gute Fahrt.«

OFF: »Der Polizeichor Essen.
Am 15. und 16. Dezember in der Philharmonie Essen.«

BRONZE

TITLE
Feuerwehr Dresden Recruiting
»Warteschleife«

CLIENT
Feuerwehr der Landeshauptstadt
Dresden

MARKETING DIRECTOR
Brandoberamtsrat
Dipl.-Ing. Thomas Mende

LEAD AGENCY
Scholz & Friends

CREATIVE DIRECTION
Dirk Silz, Markus Daubenbüchel,
Matthias Schmidt, Stefan Setzkorn

CLIENT CONSULTING
Raphael Brinkert, Jens Hoffmann

RADIO PRODUCTION
Loft Tonstudios GmbH

AGENCY PRODUCER
Susanne Schneider

COPY
Bastian Otter

SPOT »WARTESCHLEIFE«

SFX: Telefontuten, Atmo im Stile einer Telefonwarteschleife.

SPRECHERIN: »Willkommen bei der Feuerwehrleitstelle!
… leider sind derzeit sämtliche Mitarbeiter im Einsatz. Bis dahin steht Ihnen unser telefonisches Brandmeldesystem zur Verfügung: Brennt Ihr Haus, sagen Sie ›eins‹! Brennt Ihr Haus und es befinden sich Personen darin, sagen Sie ›zwei‹! Brennt Ihr Haus und Sie haben eine Gasleitung, sagen Sie ›drei‹! Oder Sie bestellen Ihren Löschzug einfach online! …«

SFX: Auflegen, Tuten.

SPRECHER: »Lassen Sie es nicht so weit kommen.
Werden Sie freiwilliger Helfer Ihrer Feuerwehr –
unter www.feuerwehr-dresden.de«

SPOTS DIESER KATEGORIE FINDEN SIE UNTER WWW.ADC.DE FOR RADIO COMMERCIALS FROM THIS CATEGORY VISIT WWW.ADC.DE

BRONZE

TITLE
Volkswagen Kampagne
»Horst Schlämmer macht Führerschein«

CLIENT
Volkswagen AG

MARKETING DIRECTOR
Jochen Sengpiehl

ADVERTISING DIRECTOR
Ralf Maltzen, Hartmut Seeger

LEAD AGENCY
DDB Germany, Berlin

CREATIVE DIRECTION
Amir Kassaei, Stefan Schulte, Bert Peulecke

ART DIRECTION
Kristoffer Heilemann

CLIENT CONSULTING
Cathleen Losch, Silke Lagodny

RADIO PRODUCTION
Hastings Audio Network Berlin

AGENCY PRODUCER
Boris Schepker

ARTIST
Hape Kerkeling

PRODUCTION
Nina Steiger, Simone Roggel

SOUND DESIGN
Lars Gelhausen

COPY
Ludwig Berndl, Philip Bolland

SOUND ENGINEER
Lars Gelhausen

ADDITIONAL AWARDS

GOLD
Volume Advertising page 186
Verkaufsförderung
Sales promotion

GOLD
Volume Advertising page 221
TV-Spots
Television commercials

GOLD
Volume Advertising page 283
Filme für Verkaufsförderung/
Unternehmensdarstellungen
Films for sales promotion/
company presentation

GOLD
Volume Advertising page 289
Virale Filme
Viral films

GOLD
Volume Advertising page 347
Integrierte Kampagnen
Integrated campaigns

GOLD
Volume Advertising page 367
Dialogmarketing
Dialogue marketing

GOLD
Volume Design page 242
Digitale Werbung
Digital advertising

SILVER
Volume Advertising page 096
Tages-/Wochenzeitungsanzeigen
Advertisements in daily/weekly newspapers

SILVER
Volume Advertising page 139
Produkt-/Werbebroschüren
Product/advertising brochures

SILVER
Volume Advertising page 147
Text
Copy

SILVER
Volume Design page 259
Digitale Medien: Viral
Digital media: Viral

BRONZE
Volume Advertising page 152
Text
Copy

NOMINATION
Volume Design page 095
Informationsmedien
Information media

NOMINATION
Volume Design page 235
Websites
Websites

Zu dieser Kampagne gehören noch vier weitere Spots:
»Einkaufs-Tipp«, »Gegendarstellung«, »Knallhart nachgefragt« und »Single der Woche«.

Four further spots are part of this campaign:
"Einkaufs-Tipp", "Gegendarstellung", "Knallhart nachgefragt" and "Single der Woche".

SPOT »PROMINENTE«

INTRO-JINGLE:	»Radiooo Greveenbroooiich.«
RADIOMODERATORIN:	»Prominente Hautnah.«
REPORTER:	»Herr Schlämmer, was machen Sie hier gerade in Grevenbroich?«
SCHLÄMMER:	»Ja, also was ich in Grevenbroich mache, darf ich eigentlich nicht sagen. Dat is Top-Sekret. Ähm, dat is für eine große Automebil… Autome… für ne Kraftfahrzeug… Ich, äh, es ist eine Werbung für die, eine der größten und reno… ren… äh … renommiertesten … deutschen … Autofirmen – Golf. Ach so, nee dat sollt ich nich, ne?«
	(Outro-Jingle)
RADIOMODERATORIN:	»Die ganze Geschichte gibt's unter www.schlämmerblog.de.«
SFX:	Wählgeräusch und Gekrächze eines Internetmodems.
SCHLÄMMER:	(Logo/Claim, gesprochen von Schlämmer am Telefon) »Volkswagen, da weißte Bescheid.«

SPOT »REKLAME«

INTRO-JINGLE:	»Radiooo Greveenbroooiich.«
RADIOMODERATORIN:	»Reklame.«
SCHLÄMMER:	»Ja, ich könnt mir vorstellen für Volkswagen Werbung zu machen, weil … ääh … weiß ich jetzt nich hehehe … warte … Ja, also für Volkswagen könnte ich mir vorstellen, Werbung zu machen. Dat is solide, dat ist gutes Handwerk – leider darf nichts getrunken werden (er lacht) … nein, das könnt Ihr nicht. Nehmt Ihr dat?«
	(Outro-Jingle)
RADIOMODERATORIN:	»Und noch mal Reklame.«
SCHLÄMMER:	(Logo/Claim, gesprochen von Schlämmer) »Volkswagen, da weißte Bescheid.«
RADIOMODERATORIN:	»Die ganze Geschichte gibt's unter www.schlämmerblog.de.«

BRONZE

TITLE
K-Fee Kampagne »Nachrichten«

CLIENT
K-fee AG

MARKETING DIRECTOR
Richard Radtke, Hubertus Sprungala

LEAD AGENCY
Jung von Matt AG

CREATIVE DIRECTION
Fabian Frese, Götz Ulmer

CLIENT CONSULTING
Alexandra Beck, Jascha Oevermann

RADIO PRODUCTION
Hastings Audio Network

DIRECTION
Mathias Lührsen,
Andreas »Beavis« Ersson

SPEAKER
Marco Tristram, Matti Klemm

COPY
Björn Ingenleuf

SOUND ENGINEER
Andreas »Beavis« Ersson

SPOT »PAPST«
(Eine vermeintliche Radio-Nachrichtensendung)

SFX: Nachrichten-Jingle plus Ansage.
»Breaking-News.«

SPRECHER: »Rom. Papst Benedict der 16. hat sich für die Schwulenehe ausgesprochen. Auf einer Pressekonferenz des Vatikan sagte das Oberhaupt der katholischen Kirche, dass er aus eigener Erfahrung berichten könne, dass die Liebe zwischen gleichgeschlechtlichen Partnern ebenso stark und wahrhaftig sein kann wie zwischen Mann und Frau.«

OFF: »Diesen Wachmacher präsentierte Dir K-Fee.
So wach warst Du noch nie.«

SPOT »EURO«
(Eine vermeintliche Radio-Nachrichtensendung)

SFX: Nachrichten-Jingle plus Ansage.
»Breaking-News.«

SPRECHER: »Frankfurt am Main: Der Euro vor dem Aus. Wie die europäische Zentralbank heute Morgen mitteilte, wird auf Beschluss der EU-Mitgliedsländer der Euro als Währung zum Ende des Jahres wieder abgeschafft. Ab 2008 gelten dann wieder die ursprünglichen Währungen. Im Falle Deutschlands bedeutet das: Die D-Mark ist ab 2008 wieder offizielles Zahlungsmittel der Bundesrepublik. Euro-Scheine und -Münzen können bis zum 31.12.2007 bei Banken, Apotheken und an Tankstellen wieder gegen D-Mark eingetauscht werden. Danach verlieren sie ihre Gültigkeit.«

OFF: »Diesen Wachmacher präsentierte Dir K-Fee.
So wach warst Du noch nie.«

SPOT »ADOLF«

(Eine vermeintliche Radio-Nachrichtensendung)

SFX: Nachrichten-Jingle plus Ansage.
»Breaking-News.«

SPRECHER: »Berlin. Adolf Hitler hatte einen Sohn. Wie das Bundesamt für Ahnenforschung heute auf einer anberaumten Pressekonferenz bekannt gab, entstammt das Kind aus der Affäre mit einer italienischen Haushälterin während eines Treffens mit Benito Mussolini 1936 in Rom. Der Abkömmling Hitlers, der mit bürgerlichem Namen Fausto Arrabiata heißt, ist 71 Jahre alt und betreibt eine Mozzarella-Fabrik in der Toskana, so ein Sprecher des Ahnenforschungsinstitutes.«

OFF: »Diesen Wachmacher präsentierte Dir K-Fee.
So wach warst Du noch nie.«

BRONZE

TITLE
Comedy Central »Halloween-Kitty«

CLIENT
MTV Networks Germany GmbH

MARKETING DIRECTOR
Imke Deigner (Marketing Director), Torsten Wolf (Head of Consumer Marketing)

ADVERTISING DIRECTOR
Vivien Hucke (Junior Manager Consumer Marketing)

LEAD AGENCY
kempertrautmann gmbh

CREATIVE DIRECTION
Willy Kaussen

CLIENT CONSULTING
Peter Matz, Ilker Yilmazalp

RADIO PRODUCTION
Hastings Audio Network Hamburg

DIRECTION
Willy Kaussen

SPEAKER
Konstantin Graudus, Michael Lutter, Malou Kästner

COPY
Willy Kaussen

SOUND ENGINEER
Dennis Gunske

SPOT »HALLOWEEN-KITTY«

SFX: Telefonklingeln, Hörer wird abgehoben.

MANN: (ahnungslos am Telefon) »Lohmüller!«
(Über die andere Leitung des Telefons hören wir eine künstlich verzerrte Stimme, wie im Hollywood-Thriller, wenn sich ein perverser Entführer meldet.)

SFX: Gruselige Musik setzt ein und sorgt für eine unheimliche Stimmung.

ENTFÜHRER: (übers Telefon) »Hören Sie mir gut zu, Herr Lohmüller. Wir haben von Ihrer Tochter die Katze entführt.«

LOHMÜLLER: (verunsichert) »Oje, ... die Kitty???«

ENTFÜHRER: (wird gemeiner) »Genau, die süße, kleine Kitty. Noch ist sie unversehrt. Aber wenn Sie nicht bereit sind, auf unsere Forderungen einzugehen, werden wir die kleine, unschuldige Kitty häuten, mit Rotweinsoße und Rosmarin braten und in großer Runde verspeisen.
Haben Sie verstanden?«

LOHMÜLLER: (überlegt ... und findet plötzlich die Idee gar nicht mal so schlecht) »Ja, gut, äh ... hört sich lecker an ... dann komm ich vorbei ... heute abend, halb acht – okay?«

ENTFÜHRER: (fragt übers Telefon nach) »Kartoffeln oder Klöße?«

OFF-STIMME: »Keine Minute ohne Comedy. Die Halloween Night auf Comedy Central. Der erste Comedy-Sender im Free-TV.«

NOMINATION

TITLE
BIONADE Kampagne
»Anrufe für eine bessere Welt«

CLIENT
BIONADE GmbH

MARKETING DIRECTOR
Wolfgang Blum

LEAD AGENCY
Kolle Rebbe Werbeagentur GmbH

CREATIVE DIRECTION
Ulrich Zünkeler/Rolf Leger/
Stefan Wübbe

CLIENT CONSULTING
Katharina Lechelt/Tamara Klien/
Birgit Heikamp

RADIO PRODUCTION
Studio Funk

EDITING
Philipp Feit

SOUND DESIGN
Philipp Feit

SPEAKER
Matthias Strzoda

COPY
Matthias Strzoda/Stefan Wübbe/
Simon Kämper

SOUND ENGINEER
Philipp Feit

Zu dieser Kampagne gehören noch drei weitere Spots: »Batterien«, »Bibliothek« und »Imbiss«.

Three further spots are part of this campaign: "Batterien", "Bibliothek" and "Imbiss".

SPOT »BAHN«

SPRECHER: »BIONADE präsentiert: Anrufe für eine bessere Welt.«
Ein Telefon tutet.

ANRUFER: »Guten Tag. Äh, ich bin bei der Bahn?«

MANN: »Ja, Sie sind bei der Beschwerdestelle. Wen darf ich denn begrüßen?«

ANRUFER: »Ja, ich rufe an aus Ennepetal. Ich fahr selber mit der Bahn immer, ja.«

MANN: »Oh, das ist ja wunderbar. Dankeschön!«

ANRUFER: »Die kommt ja immer zu spät.«

MANN: »Sie kommen zu spät? Welche Bahn, wann fahren Sie denn immer?«

ANRUFER: »Nein, das ist ja immer, passen Sie auf, das steht ja immer in der Zeitung. Ich wollte Sie jetzt mal informieren, dass das meines Erachtens gar nicht stimmt! Ich fahr' morgens zur Arbeit, fahr' abends zurück und bin noch nie zu spät gekommen. Ich wollte mich bei Ihnen bedanken!«

MANN: (trocken) »Sie wollen sich bedanken bei mir, aber trotzdem bin ich ja noch immer die Beschwerdestelle. Ich gebe das gerne so weiter, aber 'ne kleine Beschwerde werden Sie doch bestimmt noch haben, oder?«

ANRUFER: »Nein!«

SPRECHER: »Dieser Anruf wurde Ihnen präsentiert von: BIONADE. Das offizielle Getränk einer besseren Welt.«

NOMINATION

TITLE
VW Fox Kampagne »Kurz & Gut«

CLIENT
Volkswagen AG

MARKETING DIRECTOR
Jochen Sengpiehl

ADVERTISING DIRECTOR
Hartmut Seeger

LEAD AGENCY
DDB Germany/Düsseldorf

CREATIVE DIRECTION
Amir Kassaei, Eric Schoeffler,
Thomas Schwarz, Tim Jacobs

CLIENT CONSULTING
Silke Lagodny

RADIO PRODUCTION
Studio Funk Düsseldorf

AGENCY PRODUCER
Petra Hacsi

DIRECTION
Dennis May, Georgios Engels

SPEAKER
Susanne Giergerich,
Dennis May, Georgios Engels,
Ina-Katrin von Chamier,
Timo Kockmeyer, Jürgen Kluckert

COPY
Dennis May, Georgios Engels,
Sandra Illes

SOUND ENGINEER
Timo Kockmeyer

Zu dieser Kampagne gehört noch ein weiterer Spot: »Raumfahrt«.

One further spot is part of this campaign: "Raumfahrt".

SPOT »MOZART«

SFX: Kurz-und-gut-Eröffnungsmelodie.

SPRECHER: »Die Geschichte von Mozart in 30 Sekunden.«

STIMMEN UND SFX: Frau presst. Kind wird geboren. Kind schreit.

FRAU: »Es ist ein Junge!«

(Kurze und schnelle Musik von Mozart.)

MEHRERE MENSCHEN: »Ohhhh!«

EIN EINZELNER: »Ein Wunderkind!«

(Andere kurze und schnelle Musik von Mozart.)

MEHRERE MENSCHEN: »Ohhhh!«

EIN EINZELNER: »Ein Wunderkind!«

(Und wieder andere kurze und schnelle Musik von Mozart.)

MEHRERE MENSCHEN: »Ohhhh!«

EIN EINZELNER: »Ein Wunderkind!«

(Stock wird auf Marmorboden geschlagen.)

JEMAND VERKÜNDET: »Eure Hoheit, Herr Wolfgang Amadeus Mozart.«

MOZART: »Nennt's mich Wolferl.«

(Mozart lacht hysterisch. Kurzer Ausschnitt aus einer Mozart-Oper.)

MOZART: »Prost!«

(Gläser werden angestoßen.)

GATTIN: (empört) »Wolferl, wo ist das ganze Geld?«

MOZART: »Prost!«

(Jemand fällt zu Boden.)

FRAU SAGT: Wolferl?

(Der »Todesmarsch« von Chopin.)

EIN EINZELNER RUFT: Hey, das ist Chopin!

SPRECHER: »Kurz und gut. Genau wie der VW Fox. Volkswagen. Das Auto.«

NOMINATION

TITLE
Volkswagen Kampagne
»Original Teile«
CLIENT
Volkswagen AG
MARKETING DIRECTOR
Dirk Zimmer
ADVERTISING DIRECTOR
Philipp Benzler
LEAD AGENCY
DDB Germany/Düsseldorf
CREATIVE DIRECTION
Eric Schoeffler, Amir Kassaei
CLIENT CONSULTING
Silke Lagodny
RADIO PRODUCTION
Studio Funk Düsseldorf
AGENCY PRODUCER
Petra Hacsi
PRODUCTION
Timo Kockmeyer
DIRECTION
Dennis May, Jan Propach,
Timo Kockmeyer
SPEAKER
Michael Kessler, Susanne Giegerich,
Stefanie Stanjes, Robert Missler,
Dennis May, Robert Missler,
Timo Kockmeyer
COPY
Dennis May, Jan Propach

SPOT »SCHEIBENWISCHER«

MANN 1: »Hallo, ich bin ein Wischblatt. Ich sorge in regelmäßigen Abständen dafür, dass die Windschutzscheibe meines Fahrers frei von Schmutz und Wasser ist. Zuverlässig bewegt werde ich dabei von …«

MANN 2: »… mir, dem Wischerarm. Bei mir geht es immer hin und her und hin und her. Dabei ist Präzision für mich das oberste Gebot. Für meinen Antrieb sorgt …«

MANN 3: (mit tiefer Stimme und osteuropäischem Akzent)
»Iiiich. Dähm Antriebsmotorrrrr. Genau was ich machä, aaaandärä wiiiissen. Icccch nuuuur billik.«

OFF-SPRECHER: »Entscheiden Sie sich lieber für Originalteile vom Volkswagen Service. Damit Ihr Volkswagen ein Volkswagen bleibt.«

SPOT »BREMSE«

MANN 1: »Hallo zusammen, ich bin das Bremspedal. Ich reagiere auf leichteste Berührungen des rechten Fußes meines Fahrers. Und dadurch gebe ich ein unmissverständliches Signal an meinen zuverlässigen Kollegen, den …«

MANN 2: »… Bremskraftverstärker. Ich bin in der Lage, jedes Signal meines Vorredners an die Stellen zu verteilen, die dann den Bremsvorgang einleiten. Zum Beispiel ist das die …«

MANN 3: (mit tiefer Stimme und asiatischem Akzent)
»Brämsscheiba. Isch aba Backan und Sssattel un so wrunde andere Scheiba. Ffffunsionier imma. Fast.«

OFF-SPRECHER: »Entscheiden Sie sich lieber für Originalteile vom Volkswagen Service. Damit Ihr Volkswagen ein Volkswagen bleibt.«

NOMINATION

TITLE
Mercedes-Benz Vito Kampagne
»Falscher Partner«

CLIENT
Mercedes-Benz Vertriebsorganisation
Deutschland

MARKETING DIRECTOR
Ulrike Mönnich

LEAD AGENCY
BBDO Germany GmbH

CREATIVE DIRECTION
Andreas Manthey, Patrick They

ART DIRECTION
Lars Buri

CLIENT CONSULTING
Holger Hennschen,
MonaFee Feldhus

RADIO PRODUCTION
Studio Funk Hamburg

AGENCY PRODUCER
Tanja Schulze

CONSULTING
MonaFee Feldhus

DIRECTION
Torsten Hennings, Andreas Manthey

SOUND DESIGN
Torsten Hennings

SPEAKER
Erik Schäffler, Konstantin Graudus,
Christian Rudolf, Ole Jacobsen,
Colin Solman

COPY
Tobias Geigenmüller,
Benjamin Schwarz,
Andreas Manthey

SOUND ENGINEER
Torsten Hennings

SPOT »WINNETOU«

SFX: Winnetou-Melodie.
SFX: Pferdehufe.
WINNETOU: (zum Pferd) »Brrrr …«
WINNETOU: »Dr. Watson, mein Bruder …«
OFF: »Falscher Partner? Holen Sie sich den richtigen!
Den Mercedes-Benz Vito – der Partner, der zu Ihnen passt.
Jetzt bei Ihrem Mercedes-Benz-Händler.«

SPOT »TARZAN«

SFX: Dschungel-Atmo
SFX: Tarzan-Schrei. Hände klopfen auf Brust.
TARZAN: »Ich Tarzan, du Gretel …«
OFF: »Falscher Partner? Holen Sie sich den richtigen!
Den Mercedes-Benz Vito – der Partner, der zu Ihnen passt.
Jetzt bei Ihrem Mercedes-Benz-Händler.«

NOMINATION

TITLE
Pan Sandwiches Kampagne
»Frische Zutaten«

CLIENT
Pan Sandwiches Berlin

MARKETING DIRECTOR
Zeki Caglar

LEAD AGENCY
Scholz & Friends

CREATIVE DIRECTION
Oliver Handlos

CLIENT CONSULTING
Jana Singer, Cathleen Michaelis

RADIO PRODUCTION
Studio Funk Berlin

DIRECTION
Stephan Moritz

SOUND DESIGN
Markus Weber

COPY
Caspar Heuss

SOUND ENGINEER
Leene Rafelt

SPOT »THUNFISCH«

Ein ziemlich lässiger Aggro-Thunfisch rappt aus seinem Leben:
»Ey yio, wasslos? – MC Thunfisch – blupp blupp«

(Beat setzt ein.)
»Ich bin der Thunfisch, der Chef in der See
ich tauche tief – hey, das ist o.k.
Meine Moves hier im Pazi – fick
sind konkret, real, kein Trick

Das Meer ist salzig – wie die Tränen, die ich nicht habe
Weil ich ein Thunfisch bin – ohne die Gabe
zu weinen, zu lachen – all diese Sachen
hey, weißt du … all diese Sachen

Kommt geschwommen der Hering
Und macht hier sein Ding
Dann mach ich ihn kalt und fress ich ihn auf
Ey, ihr Penner, da steht ihr doch drauf!

(singend)
So zieh ich, der Thunfisch, von Blau zu Blau
Zeig meine Flosse – im göttlichen Grau …«

OFF: (Der Stecker wird gezogen, die Musik setzt plötzlich aus.)
»Entschuldigen Sie die Unterbrechung. Wir brauchen den Thun-
FISCH: fisch für einen Sandwich.«
OFF: »Wie? Ah nö, oh nö, oh nö! Ne?«
»PAN-Sandwiches. – Die frischesten Sandwiches der Stadt.«

NOMINATION

TITLE
Rodenstock Gleitsichtbrillen Kampagne
»Golf Moderator / Formel 1 Moderator / Fußball Moderator«

CLIENT
Rodenstock GmbH

MARKETING DIRECTOR
Torsten Meier

LEAD AGENCY
Serviceplan München/Hamburg

CREATIVE DIRECTION
Bernd Huesmann

ART DIRECTION
Sandra Loibl, Julia Pfund

CLIENT CONSULTING
Monica Klingenfuß, Bianca Becher

RADIO PRODUCTION
Florian Leissle,
Neue Westpark Studios GmbH

DIRECTION
Florian Leissle, Thorsten Voigt

SOUND DESIGN
Florian Leissle,
Neue Westpark Studios GmbH

SPEAKER
Florian Odendahl,
Christian Baumann

COPY
Thorsten Voigt

SPOT »GOLF MODERATOR«

SFX: Grundrauschen auf einem Golfplatz.

MODERATOR: »Live vom SPWA Golfturnier in Birmingham. Martin Kochs dritter Schlag auf der 18. Der Deutsche trägt einen beigen Pullunder, an dem sich – wie ich sehe – oben links eine Löwenzahnpolle verfangen hat. Koch holt aus, während 3.107 Meter über dem Platz ein … ja – Airbus A340 der … mmh … norwegischen Fluggesellschaft Richtung Süden fliegt.«

SFX: Schlag, Raunen im Publikum, Klatschen.

MODERATOR: »Diesmal schlägt er mit viel Risiko. Der Ball bekommt beim Abschlag einen fingerkuppengroßen Grasflecken und geht links von der Fahne, weg vom Wasser, Richtung Mitte Grün. Und landet 4 Yards vorm Loch, 6,78 Meter vor den Zuschauern und 18 Millimeter vor einem Borkenkäfeeeeer……weibchen!«

OFF: »Besser sehen mit Rodenstock Gleitsichtbrillen. Jetzt bei Ihrem Augenoptiker.«

RADIO COMMERCIALS **FUNKSPOTS** 337

NOMINATION

TITLE
VW Nutzfahrzeuge Caddy Maxi
Kampagne »Platz«

CLIENT
Volkswagen AG Nutzfahrzeuge
Hannover

MARKETING DIRECTOR
Ramsis Moussa

ADVERTISING DIRECTOR
Dirk Tuchow

LEAD AGENCY
Grabarz & Partner

CREATIVE DIRECTION
Ralf Heuel, Martin Graß

CLIENT CONSULTING
Peter Ströh, Volker Jensen

RADIO PRODUCTION
Studio Funk AG

DIRECTION
Ralf Heuel, Torsten Hennings

COPY
Andreas Schriewer

SOUND ENGINEER
Torsten Hennings

Zu dieser Kampagne gehört noch ein weiterer Spot: »Nasoprol«.

One further spot is part of this campaign: "Nasoprol".

SPOT »BAUMARKT«

SFX: Der Original-Sprecher der Praktiker-Werbung.

SPRECHER: »Jetzt bei Praktiker: Zwanzig Prozent auf alle Akkuschrauber, Arbeitsplatten, Badeacessoires, Bandsägen, Carports, Cerankochfelder, Dachrinnen, Deltaschleifer, Einbauküchen, Farben, Fenster, Fensterbänke, Garagen, Garagentore, Garagentorantriebe, Häcksler, Jalousien, Kettensägen, Lamellentüren, Ladegeräte, Markisen, Nachtlichter, Nass- und Trockensauger, Ofenrohre, Pinsel, Profilholz, Rasengitter, Regalböden, Schaufeln, Schlagbohrmaschinen, Tischbohrmaschinen, Wandleuchten, Zangen, Zimmerbrunnen und alle anderen Artikel, ausgenommen Nahrung für Chinchillas, Fische, Hunde, Meerschweinchen, Kaninchen, Katzen, Ratten, Schlangen, Wellens…«

OFF: »Stellen Sie sich vor, jeder hätte so viel Platz wie der neue Caddy Maxi Kombi. Der Caddy Maxi Kombi – mit bis zu 3.950 Litern Laderaumvolumen. Volkswagen. Das Auto.«

SPOT »KINO«

SFX: Großstadt.

MANN: »Jane, geh nicht …«

FRAU: »Pete … lass mich gehen!«

SFX: Kinotrailer-Musik.

SPRECHER: »Jetzt im Kino: ›Sie war's.‹ Der neue Film von Pierre Pulmain. Ein junger Cop verliebt sich in die einzige Zeugin eines völlig überraschenden Mordes in der dritten Etage einer abgelegenen Fabrik. Sie bringt ihn dazu, das Beweismaterial in Form einer Neun-Millimeter-Patrone zu unterschlagen. Steckt sie mit dem Killer unter einer Decke? Ja. Aber das weiß der junge Mann am Anfang natürlich nicht. Nach zwei Dritteln des Films aber schöpft er Verdacht und stellt fest, dass sie die Geliebte des Killers ist. Wird es ihm gelingen, das Komplott rechtzeitig aufzuklären? Nein. Aus Sentimentalität und ein bisschen auch aus Dummheit vermasselt er es und stirbt am Ende des Films völlig überraschend durch eine unglücklich abgefälschte Kugel der jungen Frau in einer Schießerei auf einem Schrottplatz – mit der keiner rechnen konnte. ›Sie war's.‹ Jetzt im Ki…«

OFF: »Stellen Sie sich vor, jeder hätte so viel Platz wie der neue Caddy Maxi Kombi. Der Caddy Maxi Kombi – mit bis zu 3.950 Litern Laderaumvolumen. Volkswagen. Das Auto.«

SPOTS DIESER KATEGORIE FINDEN SIE UNTER WWW.ADC.DE FOR RADIO COMMERCIALS FROM THIS CATEGORY VISIT WWW.ADC.DE

NOMINATION

TITLE
Blaupunkt Radios »Funksehen«
CLIENT
Blaupunkt
MARKETING DIRECTOR
Clemens Krebs
ADVERTISING DIRECTOR
Vincent Brucker
LEAD AGENCY
Jung von Matt AG
CREATIVE DIRECTION
Arno Lindemann, Bernhard Lukas
ART DIRECTION
Florian Pack
CLIENT CONSULTING
Jascha Oevermann
RADIO PRODUCTION
Hastings Music GmbH
EDITOR
Florian Panier, Sven Schönmann
IDEA
Florian Pack, Teja Fischer
DIRECTION
Teja Fischer, Noorman Karim
COPY
Teja Fischer
SOUND ENGINEER
Noorman Karim

SPOT »FUNKSEHEN«

(Parallel zu dem Sprecher erscheint Text auf dem Radio-Display.)

SPRECHER: »Liebe Hörerinnen und Hörer: Falls Sie zufällig gerade über ein neues Blaupunkt-Radio nachdenken:
(Display: WAS?????)
Passen Sie auf: Es könnte passieren, dass Ihr altes Gerät NICHT mit seiner Auswechslung einverstanden ist.
(Display: LASS ES!)
Ja – mit Ihren Plänen bringen Sie es richtig auf die Palme.
(Display: NEIIIIN!)
Aber lassen Sie sich davon nicht irritieren. Vermeiden Sie einfach den Blick aufs Radio-Display, wenn es Ihnen gegenüber etwas – na ja – ungehalten wird.
(Display: SCHUFT!!)
Womöglich fängt es sogar an, Sie zu beleidigen. Oder macht seinem Ärger mit üblen Kraftausdrücken Luft.
(Display: SACK!!!!)
Bewahren Sie Ruhe und lassen Sie sich nicht provozieren. Es ist doch schließlich nur ein Radio.
(Display: GRMPFF!!)
Also nehmen Sie es ihm nicht übel, sondern freuen Sie sich lieber darauf, dass Sie bald ein viel viel besseres haben. Von Blaupunkt.«

Blaupunkt präsentiert:

Die erste Radiowerbung, die man sehen kann.

Dafür nutzten wir die RDS-Textfunktion gängiger Radio-Displays in Zusammenspiel mit einem Funkspot.

NOMINATION

TITLE
Sixt – rent a car »Matthias Reim«
CLIENT
Sixt GmbH & Co.
Autovermietung KG
MARKETING DIRECTOR
Dr. Karsten Willrodt
ADVERTISING DIRECTOR
Daniela Erdmann
LEAD AGENCY
Jung von Matt AG
CREATIVE DIRECTION
Peter Kirchhoff, Wolf Heumann
ART DIRECTION
Vanessa Rabea Schrooten
CLIENT CONSULTING
Sandra Schymetzki,
Ann-Kristin Grohsklaus
RADIO PRODUCTION
Hastings Audio Network
AGENCY PRODUCER
Julia Cramer
MUSIC COMPOSITION
Matthias Reim, Bernd Dietrich
COPY
Lisa Maria Hartwich,
Peter Kirchhoff, Wolf Heumann

ADDITIONAL AWARDS
SILVER
Volume Advertising page 350
Integrierte Kampagnen
Integrated campaigns

BRONZE
Volume Advertising page 255
TV-Spots
Television commercials

BRONZE
Volume Advertising page 289
Virale Filme
Viral films

BRONZE
Volume Advertising page 313
Musikkompositionen/Sound-Design
Music compositions/sound design

BRONZE
Volume Design page 246
Digitale Werbung
Digital advertising

SPOT »MATTHIAS REIM«

Matthias Reim singt zur Melodie seines größten Hits
»Verdammt ich lieb Dich« den folgenden Text:

Ich fahre auf der Straße günstig ohne Dach.
Ich hab das immer schon gern gemacht.
Den Fahrtwind im Gesicht.
Ich sitz im Wagen, dreh die Mucke auf.
Fahr wieder mal zum nächsten Schlussverkauf.
Denn Kohle hab ich nicht.
Jetzt fragt man sich: Wo hat der 's Cabrio her.
Die arme Sau hat doch kein' Groschen mehr.
Das juckt mich überhaupt nicht.
Hey ich hab Spaß und werde höllisch braun.
Auch wenn Ihr alle denkt: »Wie kann man' Cabrio klau'n«.
Ich frag nur: »Habt Ihr'n Stift?«
Und ich unterschreib 'nen Mietvertag bei Sixt.

Verdammt ich hab nichts, ich miet bei Sixt.
Verdammt ich brauch nichts, es gibt ja Sixt.
Verdammt ich will nicht, will wirklich nicht,
Nicht noch mehr Geld verlier'n.

Ganz lässig spring ich in mein Cabrio rein.
Fahr raus aufs Meer und spür den Sonnenschein.
Den Strand schon fast in Sicht.
Ich parke nicht, das kostet nur viel Geld.
Und das ist das, was mir am meisten fehlt.
Nein, Kohle hab ich nicht.
Und trotzdem winken mir die geilsten Frau'n.
Weil alle nur auf mein' Schlitten schau'n.
Ich bremse und nehm die Brille vom Gesicht.
Ich sag, hey Süße, ich bin nicht reich.
Doch was ich in der Hose hab, das siehst Du gleich.
Hey Baby, das glaubst Du nicht.
Es ist ein günstiger Mietvertrag von Sixt.

Verdammt ich hab nichts, ich miet bei Sixt.
Verdammt ich brauch nichts, es gibt ja Sixt.
Verdammt ich will nicht, will wirklich nicht,
Nicht noch mehr Geld verlier'n.

NOMINATION

TITLE
Odol-med3 Zahnseide
»Nachrichten«

CLIENT
GlaxoSmithKline GmbH & Co. KG

MARKETING DIRECTOR
Frédéric Lehmann

LEAD AGENCY
Grey Worldwide GmbH

CREATIVE DIRECTION
Cordelia Eucker-Apsel

CLIENT CONSULTING
Michael Andre, Stefan Kluss

RADIO PRODUCTION
Giesing Team Düsseldorf

AGENCY PRODUCER
Danilo Klöfer

SPEAKER
Cordelia Eucker-Apsel,
Wolfgang Bark, André Weigel

COPY
Wolfgang Bark

SOUND ENGINEER
André Weigel

SPOT »NACHRICHTEN«

Wir hören eine Radio-Sprecherin, die die Nachrichten verliest. Immer wieder gackert penetrant ein Huhn dazwischen.

SFX: Beep, das Nachrichtensignal des Radiosenders.

SPRECHERIN: »19 Uhr – Die Nachrichten.
Washington. *gaaack-gaack-gack-gack* Bundeskanzlerin Angela Merkel *gaaack-gack-gack* und US-Präsident George W. Bush *gaaaack* trafen sich heute Nachmittag im Pentagon zum Gespräch. *gaaaack-gackgaaaack* Die Bundeskanzlerin bekräftigte *gack* einmal *gack* mehr die deutsche *gack* Haltung zum Klimawandel *gaaaack* …«
(Das Gackern wird immer störender, überlagert schließlich die Sprache, bis man kaum noch etwas versteht …)
»Merkel begrüßte *gack* das Vorhaben der US-am*gaaaack*erikanischen *gaaaack-gack-gack* Automobil-Industrie, *gaaaack-gack-gack* schrittweise *gack* die Umstellung *gack-gaaaack-gack* auf weltweit führende *gaack-gack-gaaack* Technologien vorzunehmen *gaaaackgack-gaaaaack*.«

OFF: »Huhn, da wo's nicht hingehört?
Zahnseide von Odol-med3 befreit.«

SFX: Odol-med3 Jingle.

NOMINATION

TITLE
smart fortwo cdi »Wiedersehen«

CLIENT
Mercedes-Benz Vertriebsorganisation Deutschland

ADVERTISING DIRECTOR
Markus Bauer, Markus Gammert

LEAD AGENCY
BBDO Düsseldorf GmbH

CREATIVE DIRECTION
Ton Hollander, Toygar Bazarkaya, Ralf Zilligen

ART DIRECTION
Peter Moje

CLIENT CONSULTING
Sebastian Schlosser, Marco Golbach, Dirk Spakowski

RADIO PRODUCTION
Studio Funk GmbH & Co. KG, Düsseldorf/Hamburg

AGENCY PRODUCER
Sabine Boenigk, Anuschka Wallé

DIRECTION
Ingo Hoentschke, Peter Moje

SPEAKER
Gunter Lüdke, Norman Matt, Utz-Werner Richter

COPY
Ingo Hoentschke, Markus Steinkemper

SOUND ENGINEER
Christoph Ahrens, Florian Schweitzer

SPOT »WIEDERSEHEN«

SFX: Atmo Tankstelle – gedämpfter Straßenlärm, Zapfsäule.

SEHR ALTER MANN 1: »Guten Tag, einmal Volltanken bitte!«

SEHR ALTER MANN 2: »Ja gern … aber Moment mal – sagen Sie, kennen wir uns nicht?«

SEHR ALTER MANN 1: »Ach, Gott, jaa – ich war doch schon mal hier …!«

SEHR ALTER MANN 2: »Tatsächlich … ach, wann war das denn noch?«

SEHR ALTER MANN 1: »Ich weiß auch nicht – wir waren ja damals noch richtig junge Kerle – nicht wahr!?«

SEHR ALTER MANN 2: »Tja – ich hab Sie auch nur an Ihrem Auto wiedererkannt! So, schon voll getankt – na dann: bis zum nächsten Mal!«

SEHR ALTER MANN 1: »Ja, ja … nächstes mal – Spaßvogel.«

OFF: »Selten Tanken. Der neue smart fortwo cdi. Nur 3,3 Liter auf 100 Kilometer.«

BRUCE LEE *27. NOVEMBER 1940 SAN FRANCISCO †20. JULI 1973 HONGKONG

Bruce Lee stand bereits mit sechs Jahren vor der Kamera. Mit 18 Jahren konnte er bereits auf zwanzig Filme zurückblicken. Neben der Schule trainierte er eifrig seine Kampfkünste sowie Cha-Cha-Cha. Nach einer Schlägerei musste er Hongkong verlassen. Er heuerte als Tanzlehrer auf einem Dampfschiff nach San Francisco an. Dort angekommen, arbeitete er als Kellner und qualifizierte sich für die Universität. Er studierte Philosophie und eröffnete nebenbei eine Kung-Fu-Schule. Hollywood wurde langsam auf ihn aufmerksam. Steve McQueen, James Coburn, Chuck Norris und viele andere Stars nahmen bei ihm Kung-Fu-Unterricht. Doch so richtig in Fahrt kam seine Filmkarriere erst wieder in Hongkong. Nach den ersten großen Erfolgen begann Bruce Lee, eigene Drehbücher zu schreiben. Seine Kampfchoreografien gingen in die Geschichte ein und brachen in Hongkong alle Kassenrekorde.

*27 NOVEMBER 1940 SAN FRANCISCO †20 JULY 1973 HONG KONG

Bruce Lee's first appearance in front of the camera came at the age of six. By the time he was 18, he already had twenty films under his belt. Alongside school, he trained diligently in the martial arts, and also in the cha-cha. He was forced to leave Hong Kong following a brawl, signing on as a dance teacher aboard a steamship bound for San Francisco. On arrival, he worked as a waiter, and qualified for university. He studied philosophy, opening up a kung fu school on the side. Gradually, Hollywood became aware of him. Steve McQueen, James Coburn, Chuck Norris and many other stars took lessons in kung fu from him. However, it was back in Hong Kong that his career really took off. After his first major successes, Bruce Lee began to write his own screenplays. His fight scene choreographies not only became legendary, but broke all box-office records in Hong Kong, too.

Simplicity is the key to brilliance.

DIE EINFACHHEIT IST DER SCHLÜSSEL ZUR BRILLANZ.

FILME DIESER KATEGORIE FINDEN SIE UNTER WWW.ADC.DE FOR FILMS FROM THIS CATEGORY VISIT WWW.ADC.DE

GOLD

Um seine Chancen bei den Frauen zu verbessern, macht Horst Schlämmer Führerschein. Dieses Abenteuer epischen Ausmaßes wurde mit Hilfe der unterschiedlichsten Kommunikationskanäle zum Leben erweckt. So schaffte es Horst Schlämmer, ganz Deutschland zu unterhalten und fuhr Volkswagen mitten in die Herzen der Menschen.

Horst Schlämmer gets his driving licence – to improve his chances with the ladies. This story of epical dimensions was brought to life through a multitude of communication channels. Horst Schlämmer managed to entertain an entire nation and drove Volkswagen right into people's hearts.

TITLE
Volkswagen »Horst Schlämmer macht Führerschein«
CLIENT
Volkswagen AG
MARKETING DIRECTOR
Jochen Sengpiehl
ADVERTISING DIRECTOR
Ralf Maltzen, Hartmut Seeger
LEAD AGENCY
DDB Germany, Berlin
CONTRIBUTING AGENCIES
Tribal DDB, Hamburg
CREATIVE DIRECTION
Amir Kassaei, Stefan Schulte, Bert Peulecke, Friedrich v. Zitzewitz
ART DIRECTION
Kristoffer Heilemann, Thomas Bober, Torben Cording, Alexandra Sievers, Tim Schmitt
CLIENT CONSULTING
Benjamin Reininger, Niklas Feuerle, Kathrin Lamm, Mirco Lange, Marc Baumann
FILM PRODUCTION
Telemaz Commercials Berlin
PHOTOGRAPHY
Markus Bachmann, Sven Schrader
RADIO PRODUCTION
Hastings Audio Network Berlin
AGENCY PRODUCER
Boris Schepker, Michael Blendow
ART BUYING
Elke Dilchert

CONSULTING
Künstlervermittlung:
Special Key – Christian Biedermann, Sven Zander
GRAPHIC ART
Peter Mayer, Sarah Pöhlmann
CAMERA
Xaver Schweyer, Detlef Camp
ARTIST
Hape Kerkeling
POSTPRODUCTION
Condor digital media Berlin
PRODUCTION
Barbara Kranz, Frank Hasselbach, Kjell Kunde
PROGRAMMING
Marc Hitzmann, Sacha Hertel, Gregory Jacoby, André Wischnewski
EDITOR
Uli Langguth
DIRECTION
Gerald Grabowski
EDITING
Kathrin Schmoll
STYLING
Brigitte Remmert
TECHNICAL DIRECTION
Sascha Mehn
COPY
Ludwig Berndl, Jan Hertel, Catharina Hauernherm, Philip Bolland, Christian Fries, Angela Gillmann, Ulrike Schumann
SOUND ENGINEER
Lars Gelhausen

ADDITIONAL AWARDS
GOLD
Volume Advertising page 186
Verkaufsförderung
Sales promotion

GOLD
Volume Advertising page 221
TV-Spots
Television commercials

GOLD
Volume Advertising page 283
Filme für Verkaufsförderung/
Unternehmensdarstellungen
Films for sales promotion/
company presentation

GOLD
Volume Advertising page 289
Virale Filme
Viral films

GOLD
Volume Advertising page 367
Dialogmarketing
Dialogue marketing

GOLD
Volume Design page 242
Digitale Werbung
Digital advertising

SILVER
Volume Advertising page 096
Tages-/Wochenzeitungsanzeigen
Advertisements in daily/weekly newspapers

SILVER
Volume Advertising page 139
Produkt-/Werbebroschüren
Product/advertising brochures

SILVER
Volume Advertising page 147
Text
Copy

SILVER
Volume Design page 259
Digitale Medien: Viral
Digital media: Viral

BRONZE
Volume Advertising page 152
Text
Copy

BRONZE
Volume Advertising page 326
Funkspots
Radio commercials

NOMINATION
Volume Design page 095
Informationsmedien
Information media

NOMINATION
Volume Design page 235
Websites
Websites

FILME DIESER KATEGORIE FINDEN SIE UNTER WWW.ADC.DE FOR FILMS FROM THIS CATEGORY VISIT WWW.ADC.DE

INTEGRATED CAMPAIGNS INTEGRIERTE KAMPAGNEN 349

FILME DIESER KATEGORIE FINDEN SIE UNTER WWW.ADC.DE FOR FILMS FROM THIS CATEGORY VISIT WWW.ADC.DE

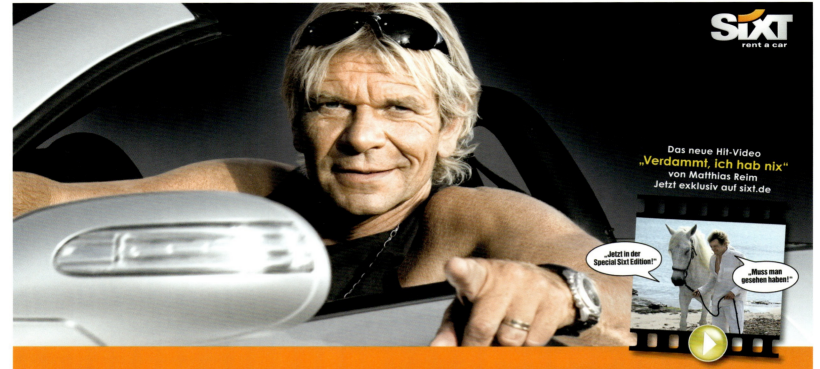

SILVER

Deutschlands berühmtester Pleitier, Matthias Reim, hat für Sixt seinen größten Hit noch einmal aufgenommen – mit neuem Text, neuem Video und durchschlagendem Erfolg. Bundesweit angekündigt über Anzeigen und Banner, in Rekordzeit von über vier Millionen Deutschen angesehen, runtergeladen, weitergeleitet, als Musik-CD gekauft und über mehrere Wochen in den offiziellen Singlecharts platziert.

Matthias Reim, the famously bankrupt German pop star, has re-recorded his greatest hit for Sixt – with new lyrics, a new video and amazing success. In only a short time after its nationwide launch in advertisements and on banners, it was viewed, downloaded, forwarded and bought on CD by over four million Germans and maintained a position in the official singles charts for several weeks.

TITLE
Sixt – rent a car »Matthias Reim«
CLIENT
Sixt GmbH & Co. Autovermietung KG
MARKETING DIRECTOR
Dr. Karsten Willrodt
ADVERTISING DIRECTOR
Daniela Erdmann
LEAD AGENCY
Jung von Matt AG
CREATIVE DIRECTION
Peter Kirchhoff, Wolf Heumann
ART DIRECTION
Vanessa Rabea Schrooten
CLIENT CONSULTING
Sandra Schymetzki, Ann-Kristin Grohsklaus

FILM PRODUCTION
Big Fish Berlin
PHOTOGRAPHY
Lars Borges
RADIO PRODUCTION
Hastings Audio Network
AGENCY PRODUCER
Julia Cramer
ART BUYING
Martina Traut
IMAGE EDITING
PX Group
GRAPHIC ART
Felix Taubert, Lars Borker
CAMERA
Casey Campell

MUSIC COMPOSITION
Matthias Reim, Bernd Dietrich
PRODUCTION
Carsten Koeslag
PROGRAMMING
Carlos Wallutt
DIRECTION
Warwick
COPY
Lisa Maria Hartwich, Peter Kirchhoff, Wolf Heumann

ADDITIONAL AWARDS
BRONZE
Volume Advertising page 255
TV-Spots
Television commercials

BRONZE
Volume Advertising page 289
Virale Filme
Viral films

BRONZE
Volume Advertising page 313
Musikkompositionen/Sound-Design
Music compositions/sound design

BRONZE
Volume Design page 246
Digitale Werbung
Digital advertising

NOMINATION
Volume Advertising page 339
Funkspots
Radio commercials

INTEGRATED CAMPAIGNS   INTEGRIERTE KAMPAGNEN   351

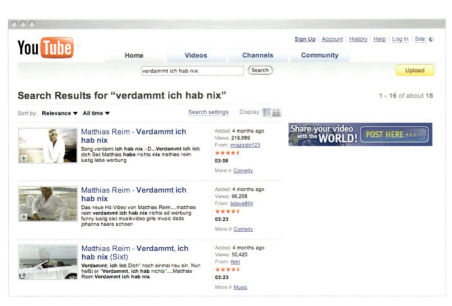

FILME DIESER KATEGORIE FINDEN SIE UNTER WWW.ADC.DE   FOR FILMS FROM THIS CATEGORY VISIT WWW.ADC.DE

INTEGRATED CAMPAIGNS INTEGRIERTE KAMPAGNEN   353

FILME DIESER KATEGORIE FINDEN SIE UNTER WWW.ADC.DE FOR FILMS FROM THIS CATEGORY VISIT WWW.ADC.DE

SILVER

Über 30 Ausnahmeathleten verraten in Zeichnungen, Gemälden und Skulpturen, wie sie die Schwierigkeiten auf dem Weg zur Weltspitze überwunden haben. Das Projekt erzählt von den Wendepunkten im Leben dieser Sportler – u. a. von David Beckham, Jonah Lomu und Gilbert Arenas. Die Kunstwerke schaffen eine Authentizität, wie sie im Hochleistungssport selten zu finden ist.

The world's greatest athletes inspire us in adidas' Impossible is Nothing 2007 global brand campaign with their real "impossible stories", using their own words and artwork. The athletes describe and illustrate defining moments in their lives and inspire an unprecedented amount of integrated content. Their stories present a truth and honesty rarely seen in advertising.

TITLE
adidas International »Impossible Is Nothing – Where Sport meets Art«
CLIENT
adidas International
MARKETING DIRECTOR
Eric Liedtke
ADVERTISING DIRECTOR
Andrew Lux
LEAD AGENCY
180 Amsterdam (180\TBWA)
CONTRIBUTING AGENCIES
TBWA
CREATIVE DIRECTION
Sean Thompson & Dean Maryon
ART DIRECTION
Dean Maryon

CLIENT CONSULTING
Mark Schermers, Nicolas Kettelhake, Frank Persyn
STRATEGIC PLANNING
Andy Edwards
FILM PRODUCTION
Passion Pictures
PHOTOGRAPHY
David Turnley
AGENCY PRODUCER
Tony Stearns, Kate Morrison
ART BUYING
Maud Klarenbeek
IMAGE EDITING
Magic Group Amsterdam
IMAGE DEPARTMENT
Marlon Lee
COMPUTER ANIMATION
Dan Sumich

EDITOR
Jamie Foord, Peter Haddon
FILM ANIMATION
Dan Sumich, Rikke Asbjoern, Tom Gravestock, Kristian Hammerstad, Jerry Fordher, Tim Snapher, John Robertson, Pete Candaland, Yu Sato, Dave Burns, John Williams, Stephane Coedel, Wip Vernooij
CONCEPT
Sean Thompson, Dean Maryon
POSTPRODUCTION
Passion Pictures
DIRECTION
Sean Thompson, Dean Maryon, Dan Gordon

SOUND DESIGN
Grand Central Studios
TECHNICAL INSTALLATION
Passion Pictures
COPY
Sean Thompson
INTERACTIVE PRODUCER
De-Construct, London

ADDITIONAL AWARDS
GOLD
Volume Design page 111
Bücher, Verlagsobjekte
Books, publishing house products

SILVER
Volume Advertising page 223
TV-Spots
Television commercials

FILME DIESER KATEGORIE FINDEN SIE UNTER WWW.ADC.DE FOR FILMS FROM THIS CATEGORY VISIT WWW.ADC.DE

INTEGRATED CAMPAIGNS   INTEGRIERTE KAMPAGNEN   357

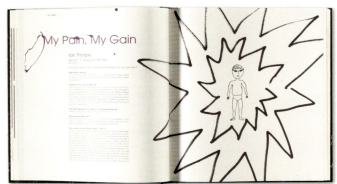
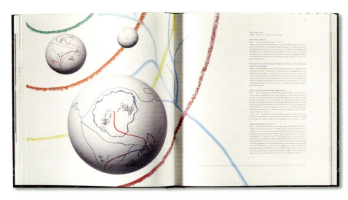

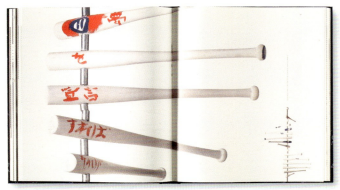

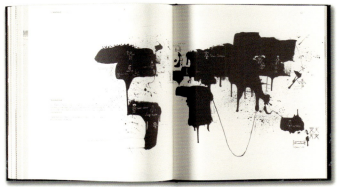

FILME DIESER KATEGORIE FINDEN SIE UNTER WWW.ADC.DE FOR FILMS FROM THIS CATEGORY VISIT WWW.ADC.DE

NOMINATION

Mit der Kampagne zum Launch des neuen BMW 1er Coupé konnte man im ganzen Land Fahrfreude in ihrer intensivsten Form erleben. Und das, ohne in einem BMW zu sitzen. Denn bei der Kampagne ging es weniger darum, den Menschen zu erklären, was technisch in diesem Fahrzeug steckt, als vielmehr darum, deutlich zu machen, wie es sich anfühlt, es zu fahren: das neue BMW 1er Coupé – verdichtete 1ntensität.

The campaign for the launch of the new BMW 1 Series Coupé allowed people throughout the country to experience driving pleasure in its most intense form – without anyone having to get into a BMW. This is because the primary purpose of this campaign was not to explain the technical components within this car, but rather to show what it feels like to drive it: The new BMW 1 Series Coupé – Condensed intensity.

TITLE
BMW 1er Coupé
»Verdichtete 1ntensität«
CLIENT
BMW AG
MARKETING DIRECTOR
Manfred Bräunl
ADVERTISING DIRECTOR
Dr. Tobias Nickel,
Dr. Hans-Peter Ketterl
LEAD AGENCY
MAB, Berlin
CONTRIBUTING AGENCIES
Mediaplus, Plant.Net Media
CREATIVE DIRECTION
Nils Haseborg, Sven Sorgatz,
Stefan Schmidt, Tomas Tulinius

ART DIRECTION
Michael Janke, Sven Sorgatz
CLIENT CONSULTING
Christian Wind, Alexander Kerkow,
Christiane Wolters,
Henning Gerstner
STRATEGIC PLANNING
Moritz Kiechle, Till Buchner
FILM PRODUCTION
Glassfilm Hamburg, Matthias Kraft,
Stephanie Martens
PHOTOGRAPHY
Mats Cordt
AGENCY PRODUCER
Johann-Georg Hofer von Lobenstein,
Lars Ebeling
ART BUYING
Martina Kersten, Tatjana Bilger

EDITOR
Glassfilm, Alex Jurkat,
Christian Aeby
GRAPHIC ART
Alexander Tibelius, Sandra Mithöfer
MEDIA
Werner Reineke,
Christian Kaessmann,
Dominik Terruhn
MUSIC COMPOSITION
adelphoimusic, Nico Steiger
POSTPRODUCTION
VCC Hamburg, Zerone Hamburg
PRODUCTION
Nowadays: Tobias Wenske;
Mats Cordt Photography:
Matthias Pretzsch
DIRECTION
Christian Aeby

COPY
Ilja Schmuschkowitsch,
Stefan Schmidt, Nils Haseborg

ADDITIONAL AWARDS
BRONZE
Volume Advertising page 024
Publikumsanzeigen
Consumer advertisements

NOMINATION
Volume Advertising page 124
Plakate und Poster
(indoor und outdoor)
Billboards and posters
(indoor and outdoor)

NOMINATION
Volume Advertising page 203, 214
Media
Media

INTEGRATED CAMPAIGNS INTEGRIERTE KAMPAGNEN 359

FILME DIESER KATEGORIE FINDEN SIE UNTER WWW.ADC.DE FOR FILMS FROM THIS CATEGORY VISIT WWW.ADC.DE

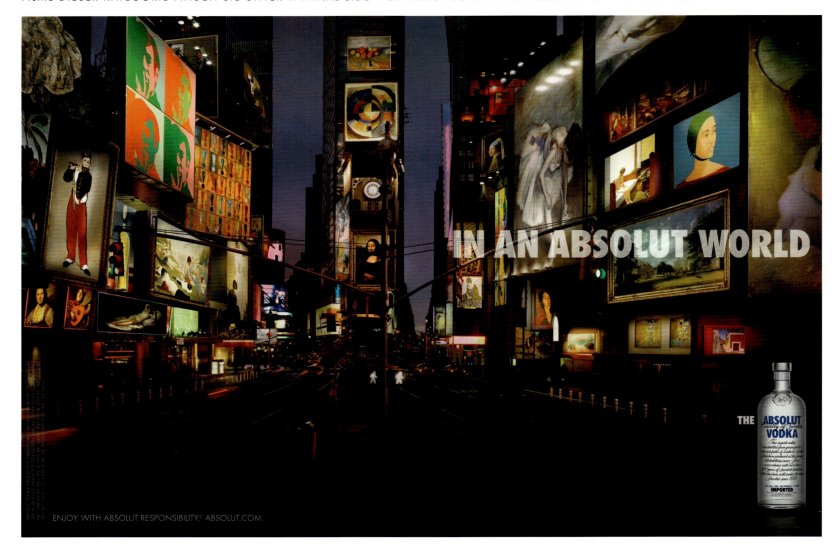

NOMINATION

Nach 25 Jahren entwickelten wir für ABSOLUT die neue Marken-Kampagne IN AN ABSOLUT WORLD. Sie zeigt, wie wunderbar die Welt wäre, wenn sie so perfekt wäre wie der ABSOLUT VODKA. Und das nicht nur in Print und TV, sondern in allen Lebensbereichen: z. B. beim Taxifahren in kostenlosen Porsche-Taxis, am Geldautomat mit Happy Hour und kostenlosem Geld oder beim Lesen, mit einer Zeitung voller aktueller und ausschließlich guter Nachrichten. Selbst für die G8-Gipfel-Proteste boten wir im Umfeld der TV-Nachrichten eine »IN AN ABSOLUT WORLD«-Lösung an: mit dem Spot »Kissenschlacht«.

After 25 years, we developed the new brand campaign IN AN ABSOLUT WORLD for ABSOLUT. It showed how the world would be if it were as perfect as ABSOLUT VODKA. We showed it not only in Print or TV, but in real life: e. g. offering free rides in Porsche Taxis, sponsoring Happy Hours at ATM machines, which gave away money for free, and publishing a real daily newspaper only with good news. We even used the G8 Summit protests in Germany to show how riots would be IN AN ABSOLUT WORLD, airing the TVC "Pillow Fight" right before the news broadcasts.

TITLE
ABSOLUT VODKA
»In An ABSOLUT World«

CLIENT
V&S ABSOLUT Spirits

MARKETING DIRECTOR
Ann Ystén

LEAD AGENCY
TBWA\Deutschland, Berlin

CONTRIBUTING AGENCIES
TBWA\Chiat Day, New York

CREATIVE DIRECTION
Gerry Graf, Rob Smiley,
Philip Borchardt, Dirk Henkelmann

ART DIRECTION
Jaime Mandelbaum, Pam Fujimoto

CLIENT CONSULTING
Richard Breaux, Manuela Bosch,
Michael Nickerson

STRATEGIC PLANNING
Joe Konietzko

AGENCY PRODUCER
Katrin Dettmann, Nathy Aviram

ART BUYING
Julia Menassa, Hillary Frileck

DESIGN
Harald Renkel

PRODUCTION
K-MB – Kamps Markenberatung:
Christoph Kamps, Sven Schöne,
Hanna Rübsamen

EDITOR
Corporate Publishing Service:
Birgit Gehrmann, Jan Leiskau

COPY
Emiliano Trierveiler

INTEGRATED CAMPAIGNS INTEGRIERTE KAMPAGNEN

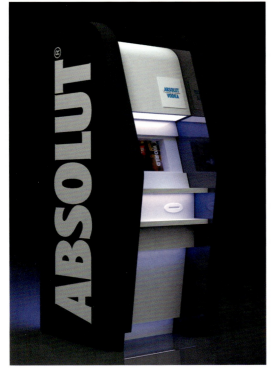

STEVE MCQUEEN

*24. MÄRZ 1930 INDIANAPOLIS
†07. NOVEMBER 1980 CIUDAD JUÁREZ/MEXIKO

Steve McQueen wuchs im Internat auf. Seinen Vater hat er nie kennengelernt. Mit 22 studierte er bei Uta Hagen und Herbert Berghof Schauspielerei in New York. Drei Jahre später feierte er seinen ersten Erfolg am Broadway. Genauso wichtig wie die Schauspielerei war ihm der Motorsport. 1964 gehörte er zum US-Nationalteam und fuhr in Erfurt bei den »Six Days« auf einer Enduro mit. 1970 wurde er Zweiter beim 12-Stunden-Rennen von Sebring. Als Filmschauspieler gehörte ihm in den 60er und 70er Jahren die ungeteilte Aufmerksamkeit des Kinopublikums. Unvergessen ist er uns als Papillon, als Bullit, als Tom Horn, als Cincinnati Kid, als Thomas Crown oder als Carter Doc McCoy in »Getaway«. Er erschien nie als Held. Wortkarg und nach innen gekehrt, ließ er nichts an sich herankommen.

[MIT FREUNDLICHER ERLAUBNIS VON: ™ 2008 THE CHADWICK MCQUEEN AND THE TERRY MCQUEEN TESTAMENTARY TRUST, REPRESENTED EXCLUSIVELY BY GREENLIGHT, LLC]

*24 MARCH 1930 INDIANAPOLIS
†07 NOVEMBER 1980 CIUDAD JUÁREZ/MEXICO

Steve McQueen grew up in a boarding school and never knew his father. At the age of twenty-two, he studied acting in New York under Uta Hagen and Herbert Berghof. Three years later he enjoyed his first success on Broadway. McQueen considered motor racing every bit as important as acting. In 1964 he was a member of the US national motorcycle racing team and took part in an enduro, the "Six Days" in Erfurt. In 1970 he was the second driver in the winning car in the "12 Hours of Sebring" race. As a film actor, he enjoyed the undivided attention of the movie-going public in the 60s and 70s. His performances as Papillon, Bullit, Tom Horn, the Cincinnati Kid, Thomas Crown or Carter Doc McCoy in *Getaway* will never be forgotten. He never played a hero. Taciturn and introverted, he never allowed anything to ruffle his composure.

[WITH KIND PERMISSION FROM: ™ 2008 THE CHADWICK MCQUEEN AND THE TERRY MCQUEEN TESTAMENTARY TRUST, REPRESENTED EXCLUSIVELY BY GREENLIGHT, LLC]

I'm not sure that acting is something for a grown man to be doing.

ICH WEISS NICHT SO RECHT, OB SCHAUSPIELERN WIRKLICH ETWAS IST, WAS EIN ERWACHSENER MANN TUN SOLLTE.

FILME DIESER KATEGORIE FINDEN SIE UNTER WWW.ADC.DE FOR FILMS FROM THIS CATEGORY VISIT WWW.ADC.DE

„Hallo Schätzelein, schön, dass du anrufst. Ich bin nicht da, weißte ... Du musst mir nur deine Adresse hinterlassen, Schätzelein, und dann gibt's eine kleine Überraschung von deinem Horst."

GOLD

Horst Schlämmer macht Führerschein. Im Rahmen dieses Abenteuers wurden auf unterschiedlichste Weise Direktkontakte generiert. Zum Beispiel durch ein Mailing – Schlämmers Grevenbroicher Tagblatt –, das zur Probefahrt einlud, durch Give-aways und vor allem im Internet: Von Schlämmers Website, die das Abenteuer ausführlich dokumentierte, wurden die User direkt zur Volkswagen-Seite und zum Golf geführt.

Horst Schlämmer gets his driving licence. This adventure enabled Volkswagen to generate direct contacts in many different ways. For example with a mailing, an issue of Schlämmer's own newspaper, which invited clients to a test drive, giveaways and, above all, in the internet: from Schlämmer's website, which documented the whole story, users were directly led to the Volkswagen page and the Golf.

TITLE
VW Golf Kampagne
»Horst Schlämmer macht Führerschein«

CLIENT
Volkswagen AG

MARKETING DIRECTOR
Jochen Sengpiehl

ADVERTISING DIRECTOR
Ralf Maltzen, Hartmut Seeger

LEAD AGENCY
DDB Germany, Berlin

CONTRIBUTING AGENCIES
Tribal DDB, Hamburg

CREATIVE DIRECTION
Amir Kassaei, Stefan Schulte,
Bert Peulecke, Friedrich v. Zitzewitz

ART DIRECTION
Kristoffer Heilemann,
Thomas Bober, Torben Cording,
Alexandra Sievers, Tim Schmitt

CLIENT CONSULTING
Benjamin Reininger, Niklas Feuerle,
Kathrin Lamm, Mirco Lange,
Marc Baumann, C. Losch

FILM PRODUCTION
Telemaz Commercials Berlin

PHOTOGRAPHY
Markus Bachmann, Sven Schrader

RADIO PRODUCTION
Hastings Audio Network Berlin

AGENCY PRODUCER
Boris Schepker, Michael Blendow

ART BUYING
Elke Dilchert

CONSULTING
Künstlervermittlung:
Special Key –
Christian Biedermann, Sven Zander

GRAPHIC ART
Sarah Pöhlmann, Peter Mayer

ARTIST
Hape Kerkeling

POSTPRODUCTION
Condor digital media Berlin

PRODUCTION
Barbara Kranz, Frank Hasselbach

PROGRAMMING
Marc Hitzmann, Sacha Hertel,
Gregory Jacoby, André Wischnewski

DIRECTION
Gerald Grabowski

EDITING
Kathrin Schmoll

TECHNICAL DIRECTION
Sascha Mehn

COPY
Ludwig Berndl, Jan Hertel,
Catharina Hauernherm,
Philip Bolland, Christian Fries

SOUND ENGINEER
Lars Gelhausen

URL
http://www.entry-hamburg-hafen.de/89/

ADDITIONAL AWARDS

GOLD
Volume Advertising page 186
Verkaufsförderung
Sales promotion

GOLD
Volume Advertising page 221
TV-Spots
Television commercials

GOLD
Volume Advertising page 283
Filme für Verkaufsförderung/
Unternehmensdarstellungen
Films for sales promotion/
company presentation

GOLD
Volume Advertising page 289
Virale Filme
Viral films

GOLD
Volume Advertising page 347
Integrierte Kampagnen
Integrated campaigns

GOLD
Volume Design page 242
Digitale Werbung
Digital advertising

SILVER
Volume Advertising page 096
Tages-/Wochenzeitungsanzeigen
Advertisements in daily/weekly newspapers

SILVER
Volume Advertising page 139
Produkt-/Werbebroschüren
Product/advertising brochures

SILVER
Volume Advertising page 147
Text
Copy

SILVER
Volume Design page 259
Digitale Medien: Viral
Digital media: Viral

BRONZE
Volume Advertising page 152
Text
Copy

BRONZE
Volume Advertising page 326
Funkspots
Radio commercials

NOMINATION
Volume Design page 095
Informationsmedien
Information media

NOMINATION
Volume Design page 235
Websites
Websites

FILME DIESER KATEGORIE FINDEN SIE UNTER WWW.ADC.DE FOR FILMS FROM THIS CATEGORY VISIT WWW.ADC.DE

SILVER

Das Cover des IKEA Katalogs wurde dreidimensional exakt nachgebaut und auf Tour durch 24 deutsche Städte geschickt. Passanten konnten sich in unserem begehbaren Katalog-Cover fotografieren lassen. Ein paar Tage später konnten die Teilnehmer des Foto-Shootings einen Katalog bei IKEA abholen, auf dem sie selbst das Model waren! Insgesamt haben 7.120 Menschen an der Aktion teilgenommen.

We created a three-dimensional replica of the living room on the IKEA catalogue cover and sent it on tour throughout 24 German cities. Passers-by had the opportunity to have their picture taken on our catalogue cover set. A few days later, participants in the photo shoot could go to IKEA and pick up a catalogue featuring themselves as the cover model! In total 7,120 people were photographed.

TITLE
IKEA Katalog Promotionkampagne »3D-Cover«

CLIENT
IKEA Deutschland GmbH

MARKETING DIRECTOR
Claudia Willvonseder

ADVERTISING DIRECTOR
Jens Helfrich, Gerrit Kaminski

LEAD AGENCY
Jung von Matt AG

CONTRIBUTING AGENCIES
Act Agency Hamburg,
Stein Promotions

CREATIVE DIRECTION
Arno Lindemann, Bernhard Lukas, Tom Hauser, Sören Porst

ART DIRECTION
Joanna Swistowski

CLIENT CONSULTING
Nicole Drabsch, Nic Heimann

COMPUTER ANIMATION
Sven Schoenmann

PRINTING
Gerstenberg Druck & Direktwerbung

GRAPHIC ART
Matthias Grundner, Julia Jakobi

CAMERA
Justus Becker, Ingo Dannecker

MUSIC COMPOSITION
Malte Hagemeister

EDITING
Justus Becker

TECHNICAL IMPLEMENTATION
Birgit Ballhause, Philipp Mokrohs

COPY
Caroline Ellert, Tom Hauser

ADDITIONAL AWARDS
SILVER
Volume Advertising page 186
Verkaufsförderung
Sales promotion

SILVER
Volume Advertising page 215
Media
Media

NOMINATION
Volume Design page 319
Events
Events

FILME DIESER KATEGORIE FINDEN SIE UNTER WWW.ADC.DE   FOR FILMS FROM THIS CATEGORY VISIT WWW.ADC.DE

BRONZE

In 5.000 Familien der Evangelischen Gemeinde Frankfurt leben Kinder im Alter von bis zu zwölf Jahren, die noch nicht getauft wurden. Wie bekommt man das Thema Taufe in die Köpfe dieser Familien?
Mit einem Brief aus Spezial-Papier. Sobald der Brief in Wasser getaucht wird, erscheint unsere Botschaft. Der Akt der Taufe durch Wasser wird so für Kind und Eltern spielerisch erlebbar.

5,000 families belonging to the Frankfurt Protestant community have children under the age of twelve who have not yet been baptised. How can we manage to get these familys to think about baptism?
With a letter made from special paper. As soon as the paper is submerged in water, our message appears. The act of baptism become tangible for parents and children alike in an effortless, playful way.

TITLE
Evangelische Kirche Frankfurt Mailing »Der Taufbrief«

CLIENT
Evangelische Öffentlichkeitsarbeit Frankfurt am Main

MARKETING DIRECTOR
Ralf Bräuer

ADVERTISING DIRECTOR
Sandra Hofmann

LEAD AGENCY
Ogilvy Frankfurt

CREATIVE DIRECTION
Michael Koch

ART DIRECTION
Thomas Knopf

CLIENT CONSULTING
Sophia Berhe

AGENCY PRODUCER
Andrea Martinis

ART BUYING
Gunnar Schlau

PRINTING
Druckhaus Bohl

COPY
Markus Töpper

FILME DIESER KATEGORIE FINDEN SIE UNTER WWW.ADC.DE   FOR FILMS FROM THIS CATEGORY VISIT WWW.ADC.DE

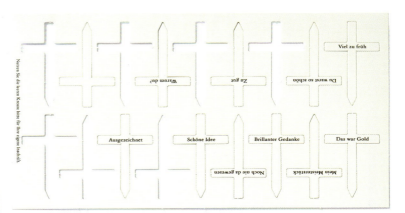

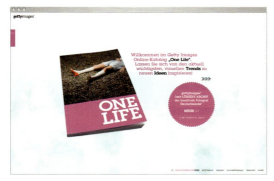

BRONZE

Jeder Kreative kennt das: Täglich sterben gute Ideen. Jetzt gibt es für sie eine adäquate Ruhestätte: den Ideenfriedhof. Ein Kondolenzbrief von Getty Images drückt die Anteilnahme aus und liefert sowohl einen echten Friedhof für den Schreibtisch als auch eine Online-Version. Nach der Online-Beerdigung werden die Trauernden zum neuen Getty-Images-Katalog für neue Ideen geführt.

Every creative knows that good ideas "die" each day (a German expression). Now there is a resting place for them: the idea graveyard. A condolence letter from Getty Images offered heartfelt sympathy along with desktop and online cemeteries. Good ideas don't go to hell, but to heaven. After the online funeral, mourners were directed to the new catalogue, One Life, for new ideas.

TITLE
Getty Images »Der Ideenfriedhof«
CLIENT
Getty Images Deutschland GmbH
MARKETING DIRECTOR
Birgit Rühl

LEAD AGENCY
Heye, 121 GmbH
CREATIVE DIRECTION
Andreas Klemp, Ole Suraj
ART DIRECTION
Judith Baumgartner

CLIENT CONSULTING
Frank Miller
ILLUSTRATION
Arnd Böhm
PRODUCTION
Ines Thomas

COPY
Dagmar Schott, Ole Suraj
URL
http://www.ideenfriedhof.com/
INTERACTIVE PRODUCER
Jürgen Graf

FILME DIESER KATEGORIE FINDEN SIE UNTER WWW.ADC.DE FOR FILMS FROM THIS CATEGORY VISIT WWW.ADC.DE

BRONZE

Der NABU wollte Meinungsführer auf die vielfältigen Bedrohungen, denen die Erde durch den Klimawandel ausgesetzt ist, aufmerksam machen und für den NABU Presse-Newsletter werben.
Das »Earth Memory« zeigt auf simple und direkte Weise, was sich auf der Erde alles verändert. Die Pärchen bestehen aus Bildern von Gletschern von früher und heute oder von Seen, die verschwunden sind.

NABU wanted to alert opinion leaders to the multi-faceted threats confronting earth as a result of the climate change, and to solicit this target group to subscribe to the NABU press newsletter.
"Earth Memory" shows all the things that are changing on planet earth. The game's pairs consist of before- and after-photos showing glaciers past and present and lakes that have vanished.

TITLE
Naturschutzbund Deutschland
Mailing »Earth Memory«
CLIENT
Naturschutzbund Deutschland
(NABU) e.V.

MARKETING DIRECTOR
Bernd Pieper
LEAD AGENCY
Y&R Germany
CREATIVE DIRECTION
Uwe Marquardt

ART DIRECTION
Harald Schumacher
AGENCY PRODUCER
Martina Wiegand

ART BUYING
Britta Joh
PRINTING
Albrecht GmbH
COPY
Christian Daul

DIALOGUE MARKETING **DIALOGMARKETING** 375

FILME DIESER KATEGORIE FINDEN SIE UNTER WWW.ADC.DE FOR FILMS FROM THIS CATEGORY VISIT WWW.ADC.DE

NOMINATION

In der HDI-TV-Kampagne ist der Schaden nie zu sehen und geschieht im Kopf des Betrachters. Im Online-Special werden interaktiv verschiedenste Schäden verursacht. So wird auf das umfangreiche Leistungsspektrum der HDI-Versicherungen hingewiesen. Am Ende blendet sich ein Filialfinder ein und ermöglicht so den direkten Kontakt. Die Site kann außerdem an Freunde und Kunden verschickt werden.

In the HDI TV-campaign, the damage is never noticeable, instead only occurring in the viewer's imagination. The online special works vice versa, as damage occur interactively. That's how the wide-ranging services of HDI Insurances are shown. At the conclusion, a branch finder appears and enables immediate contact to the nearest HDI office. The site can be forwarded on to friends and clients.

TITLE
HDI Versicherungen Kampagne »Einkaufswagen gone wilder«
CLIENT
HDI-Gerling Sach Serviceholding AG
MARKETING DIRECTOR
Olaf Rühmeier
LEAD AGENCY
gudella, barche. Werbeagentur GmbH und Co. KG
CONTRIBUTING AGENCIES
blackbeltmonkey GBR

CREATIVE DIRECTION
Michael Barche, Mike John Otto, Oliver Bentz
ART DIRECTION
Ariane Vietz, Lisa Berger, Mike John Otto
CLIENT CONSULTING
Heike Gudella, Frank v. Wisotzki
STRATEGIC PLANNING
Heike Gudella
FILM PRODUCTION
silberlink GmbH
RADIO PRODUCTION
Studio Funk

IMAGE EDITING
Helmut Gass Medientechnik
GRAPHIC ART
Nicolas Thiessenhusen
CAMERA
Jan Fehse,
Ann Kathrin Steffens (HDTV),
Phillip Kirsamer
MUSIC COMPOSITION
eardrum
COMPOSER
Michi Besler
POSTPRODUCTION
Deli Pictures

PRODUCTION
Wiebke Schuster, Marcellus Gau, Nina Balke, Sarah Schütz
DIRECTION
Detlev W. Buck
COPY
Daniel Cachandt
SOUND ENGINEER
Jochen Kömpe
URL
www.wasauchkommt.de
INTERACTIVE PRODUCER
Maren Stölzer

FILME DIESER KATEGORIE FINDEN SIE UNTER WWW.ADC.DE   FOR FILMS FROM THIS CATEGORY VISIT WWW.ADC.DE

NOMINATION

Vorhang auf für das Teletheater! Auf der Bühne wird ein ganzer Fernsehabend inszeniert: In 13 Sendungen auf neun Kanälen spielt der neue Renault Twingo die Hauptrolle – immer ganz typisch für jedes Genre. Mit der Fernbedienung seines DVD-Players wird der Zuschauer zum Programmdirektor. Per Knopfdruck kann er unmittelbar den Bühnenauf- bzw. -abbau einleiten oder die Kameraperspektive wechseln.

Raise the curtain for the teletheatre! A whole evening of TV is presented on stage starring the Twingo in the leading role. Nine channels with 13 broadcasts, all in the typical style of their genre. The remote control of the DVD player turns the viewer into the programme director: Each scene is assembled or disassembled at the push of a button. Additionally viewers can switch to the manual camera.

TITLE
Renault Twingo »Teletheater«
CLIENT
Renault Deutschland AG
MARKETING DIRECTOR
Jörg-Alexander Ellhof
LEAD AGENCY
Nordpol+ Hamburg Agentur für Kommunikation GmbH

CREATIVE DIRECTION
Ingo Fritz, Lars Rühmann
ART DIRECTION
Dominik Anweiler, Mark Höfler
CLIENT CONSULTING
Mathias Müller-Using,
Niklas Franke, Nicolas Kittner
FILM PRODUCTION
Bigfish Filmproduktion GmbH

PHOTOGRAPHY
Sven Glage
MUSIC COMPOSITION
Tonbüro Berlin
POSTPRODUCTION
PICTORION das werk berlin;
Acolori Medienproduktion
DIRECTION
The Vikings

SOUND DESIGN
Tonbüro Berlin;
Loft Tonstudios GmbH
COPY
Ingmar Bartels

ADDITIONAL AWARDS NOMINATION
Volume Design page 237
Websites
Websites

NOMINATION

Moderne Rodungstechnik macht es möglich: Im Regenwald werden alle 60 Minuten drei Tier- und Pflanzenarten ausgerottet. Ein Schaubild, das Erinnerungen an die Schulzeit wach werden lässt, lenkt den Blick auf die systematische Zerstörung der tropischen Artenvielfalt.

As a side-effect of modern deforestation technology, three animal and plant species are made extinct every 60 minutes in the tropical rainforest. A wall chart that reminds us of school lessons draws our attention towards the systematic extinction of the tropic diversity of species.

TITLE
OroVerde Mailing »Artenvielfalt«

CLIENT
OroVerde Tropenwaldstiftung

MARKETING DIRECTOR
Dr. Volkhard Wille

ADVERTISING DIRECTOR
Birthe Hesebeck

LEAD AGENCY
Ogilvy Frankfurt

CREATIVE DIRECTION
Christian Mommertz,
Dr. Stephan Vogel

ART DIRECTION
Stefan Lenz, Christian Mommertz

CLIENT CONSULTING
Roland Stauber, Friederike Vogel

ILLUSTRATION
Anke Vera Zink

ART BUYING
Christina Hufgard

GRAPHIC ART
Sonja Fritsch

PRODUCTION
Thomas Mattner

COPY
Stefan Lenz

FILME DIESER KATEGORIE FINDEN SIE UNTER WWW.ADC.DE   FOR FILMS FROM THIS CATEGORY VISIT WWW.ADC.DE

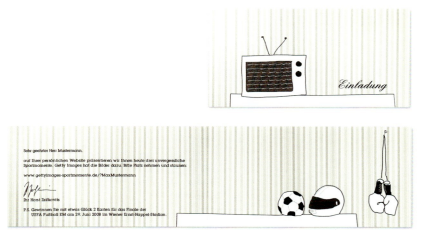

NOMINATION

Sportredakteure überraschte eine Einladung zu ihrer persönlichen Website. Dort zeigten drei Animationen große Sportmomente: Tyson beißt Hollyfields Ohr ab, Zidane streckt Materazzi nieder und Schumacher überholt in der Luft. Um Tickets für die EM 2008 zu gewinnen, ordneten die Redakteure jeweils drei passende Fotos zu. Große Sportmomente – große Bilder. Getty Images hat sie alle.

Sports journalists were surprised by an invitation to a personal website. There they saw three animated sports moments: Tyson biting off Hollyfield's ear. Zidane striking down Materazzi. Schumacher overtaking in midair. To win tickets for the Euro Cup 2008 the journalists matched the according photos to the scenes. Great sports moments – great images. Getty Images has got them all.

TITLE
Getty Images
Sportmailing »Sportmomente«
CLIENT
Getty Images Deutschland GmbH
MARKETING DIRECTOR
Horst Zsifkovits
LEAD AGENCY
Heye, 121 GmbH

CREATIVE DIRECTION
Andreas Klemp, Ole Suraj
ART DIRECTION
Judith Baumgartner
CLIENT CONSULTING
Eva Herbst, Florian Rank
COMPUTER ANIMATION
Jürgen Graf, ARRI

PRODUCTION
Ines Thomas
PROGRAMMING
Christoph Flecke
SOUND DESIGN
Giesing Team
COPY
Niklas Maier, Claus-Uwe Werner

URL
http://www.gettyimages-sportmomente.de/?MaximMustermann
INTERACTIVE PRODUCER
Jürgen Graf

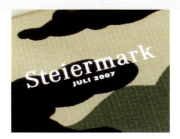

BRONZE

TITLE
Serviceplan Hamburg
»Shen International
Advertising«

CLIENT
Serviceplan Hamburg

MARKETING DIRECTOR
Alexander Schill

LEAD AGENCY
Serviceplan München/
Hamburg

CONTRIBUTING AGENCIES
Plan.Net

CREATIVE DIRECTION
Alexander Schill,
Axel Thomsen, Maik Kähler,
Christoph Nann,
Friedrich v. Zitzewitz,
Daniel Könnecke

ART DIRECTION
Till Diestel

PROGRAMMING
Arne Kanese,
André Wischnewski

SCREEN DESIGN
Dennis Fritz

COPY
Marietta Mandt-Merck,
Frances Rohde

ADDITIONAL AWARDS
SILVER
Volume Advertising page 171
Verkaufsförderung
Sales promotion

NOMINATION
Volume Design page 257
Digitale Medien: Viral
Digital media: Viral

BRONZE

TITLE
Mercedes-Benz G-Klasse
Broschüre »Der Stoff
aus dem die Helden sind«

CLIENT
Daimler AG, MBVD

MARKETING DIRECTOR
Michael Dietz

ADVERTISING DIRECTOR
Peer Näher

LEAD AGENCY
Scholz & Friends

CREATIVE DIRECTION
Constantin Kaloff

ART DIRECTION
Jens Stein, Robert Bilz

CLIENT CONSULTING
Stephan Braun, Nadja Richter,
Ulf Cerning

AGENCY PRODUCER
Sabine Bäsler

COPY
Philipp Wöhler,
Christian Brandes, Felix Heine

ADDITIONAL AWARDS
BRONZE
Volume Advertising page 130
Produkt-/Werbebroschüren
Product/advertising brochures

NOMINATION
Volume Design page 101
Informationsmedien
Information media

NOMINATION
Volume Design page 157
Grafische Einzelarbeiten
Single works of graphic art

D + SEITENZAHL weisen auf zusätzliche Medaillen oder Auszeichnungen der Agentur im ADC Volume Design hin.

AGENTUREN
Agencies

.start GmbH 090, D 218
180 Amsterdam (180\TBWA) 223, 354, D 111
3klang 240
6/0/7er Druckvorlagen GmbH 138, D 100

A

ABC Digital 042, 049, 080, 093, 125
Acht Frankfurt 294
Acolori Medienproduktion 283, 300, 378, D 237
Act Agency Hamburg 186, 215, 368, D 319
adelphoimusic 358
Albrecht GmbH 374
Alphadog Hamburg 057
annaundbenne.gbr 137
Appel Grafik, Berlin 037, 053, 119
Archiv Brot für die Welt 208
ARRI 380
Atletico International 246
audioforce Berlin 206, 226, 244, 250, 256, 272, 275, 277, 283, 300, 306, 311, 313

B

Backslide Music 252
Bargfeld Scheer 132
Bauhouse 247
BBDO Düsseldorf GmbH 105, 181, 252, 280, 341
BBDO Germany GmbH 334
BBDO Stuttgart GmbH 128, 144, 148, 210
Big Fish Filmproduktion GmbH 228, 255, 289, 350, 378, D 237
Bionic Systems 299
blackbeltmonkey GBR 377
Blackwell/Millot 256, 274
Blaupapier, Wien 116
BLUWI Musik & Sounddesign 257, 268, 302, D 221

C

Carat, Hamburg 256, 274
CCP, Heye Werbeagentur GmbH 116
Cicero Werkstudio für Schriftgestaltung 148
cine chromatix Berlin 250
Cobblestone Hamburg Filmproduktion GmbH 252
Combo Entertainment 310
Condé Nast 214
Condor digital media Berlin 186, 221, 283, 289, 347, 367, D 235, D 242, D 259
Conegge Film Company, Dickes 250
Corbis 042
Crossmedia GmbH, Düsseldorf 022, 029, 091, 181, 206, 256, 260, 275

D

Damgaard & Erbler GbR 252
DDB Germany, Berlin 027, 043, 066, 087, 096, 097, 123, 124, 125, 139, 147, 152, 180, 185, 186, 215, 221, 253, 283, 289, 316, 326, 347, 367, D 095, D 235, D 242, D 259, D 264
DDB Germany, Düsseldorf 056, 123, 187, 188, 332, 333
De-Construct, London 354
Deli Pictures 226, 246, 255, 270, 277, 303, 313, 377
Demner, Merlicek & Bergmann 207
Digital Domain, Los Angeles 272, 311
Digital Druck Emden 055
Dorten Bauer 134, D 082, D 088, D 094, D 158
Druckerei Dehl 132
Druckhaus Bohl 370

E

eardrum 377
element e filmproduktion gmbh 173, 226, 246, 255, 277, 283, 288, 300, 313
Entspanntfilm 232, D 256
Eqal 296
Euro RSCG Düsseldorf 113, 209
Euro RSCG Zürich 169, 245
Exit Studios 308

F

Filestyle Medienproduktion GmbH 137
Filmstyler Frankfurt 294
five_three_double ninety filmproductions GmbH 256, 275
Florian Leissle, Neue Westpark Studios GmbH 336
Floridan Studios GmbH 210

D + PAGE NUMBER refer to additional medals or nominations of the agency in the ADC Volume Design.

AGENCIES AGENTUREN 383

FOKINA Produktions- und Dienstleitungs GmbH 205
Fraise 255, 288
Frisbee Film 292
Fundemental 282
Furia, Barcelona 254, 260, 312

gerhardschmal.de 132
Gerstenberg Druck & Direktwerbung 186, 215, 368, D 319
Geschke/Pufe 140
Giesing Team Düsseldorf 236, 340, 380
Glassfilm Hamburg 358
gloss postproduction gmbh, Hamburg 019, 096, 178, D 127, D 205
Grabarz & Partner 034, 065, 076, 095, 228, 242, 320, 337
Grand Central Studios 223, 354
GrandHotelPictures 297
Grey Worldwide GmbH 340
Grimm Gallun Holtappels 179
groove addicts 257, 276
Gruner & Jahr AG & Co. KG 214
gudella, barche. Werbeagentur GmbH und Co. KG 377

H

Hahn Nitzsche Studios GmbH 252
Hastings Audio Network 328, 339, 350
Hastings Audio Network Berlin 186, 194, 221, 283, 289, 326, 347, 367, D 164, D 190, D 235, D 242, D 259
Hastings Audio Network Hamburg 230, 312, 328, 330, 339, 350
Hastings Music GmbH 338
HEIMAT, Berlin 022, 029, 091, 156, 206, 244, 254, 256, 260, 275, 306, 312, D 099
Helmut Gass Medientechnik 377
Heye Group 066, 111, 121, 236, 308, 373, 380

I

Inhouse 251

J

jo!schmid Filmproduktion GmbH 248, 277
Jung von Matt AG 019, 020, 031, 039, 041, 045, 046, 048, 052, 054, 059, 066, 077, 079, 081, 089, 096, 102, 115, 116, 124, 142, 150, 157, 159, 161, 163, 179, 186, 187, 199, 201, 205, 208, 211, 212, 215, 243, 248, 254, 255, 257, 264, 268, 272, 276, 277, 278, 289, 292, 297, 302, 311, 312, 313, 322, 328, 338, 339, 350, 368, D 124, D 127, D 138, D 151, D 180, D 184, D 186, D 205, D 220, D 221, D 228, D 236, D 246, D 251, D 253, D 254, D 255, D 267, D 270, D 276, D 315, D 317, D 319
Jung von Matt/Limmat 256, 266

K

kaishaprojects 070
kempertrautmann gmbh 059, 063, 066, 072, 096, 123, 157, 204, 225, 230, 234, 243, 247, 283, 289, 312, 330, D 014, D 016, D 018, D 022, D 045, D 046, D 062, D 096, D 210
Kings of Convenience 296
K-MB – Kamps Markenberatung 360
KNSK Werbeagentur GmbH 042, 049, 080, 093, 125, 251, 255, 270, 303, D 187
Kolle Rebbe Werbeagentur GmbH 055, 074, 123, 176, 178, 277, 286, 331, D 312
Krieg, Schlupp, Bürge 310

L

LIFF 249
Locomotion, Düsseldorf 280
Loft Tonstudios GmbH 226, 246, 255, 277, 288, 325, 313, 378, D 237

M

M.A.R.K.13 210
M.E.C.H. The Communications House Berlin GmbH 114
MAB, Berlin 024, 044, 124, 203, 214, 358
Magic Group Amsterdam 354
Markenfilm 225, 234, 255, 266, 270, 280, 283, 289, 303
Markenfilm, Berlin 206, 244, 254, 256, 260, 275, 312
Markenfilm, Hamburg 238, 243, 272, 311
Markenfilm, Wedel 253
MassiveMusic Amsterdam 187, 196
Mats Cordt Photography 024, 124, 203, 358
Mediaedge:cia 192
Mediaplus, Hamburg 024, 044, 124, 203, 208, 214
Metagate GmbH, Hamburg 078, 112, 120, 178
Mikros Images/Paris 254, 277, 358
Mosermeyer, Berlin 254, 260, 312
Motion Blur 249
Mutabor Design GmbH 281, D 133, D 136, D 163, D 193, D 290

N

NERDFILMS a division of Embassy of Dreams Filmproduktion GmbH 192
Netzwerk P, Berlin 128, 136, 144, 210
nhb, Berlin 254, 255, 256, 260, 274, 285, 312
nhb, Hamburg 225, 243, 251, 270, 303
NICK On Air 299
Nordpol+ Hamburg Agentur für Kommunikation GmbH 173, 226, 254, 277, 283, 300, 313, 378, D 237
Nowadays 024, 124, 203, 358

O

Ogilvy Frankfurt 032, 047, 067, 108, 370, 379, D 116, D 158, D 211, D 244
Ogilvy Paris 032, D 211
Optix Digital Pictures GmbH 177, 187, 196, 225, 238
ORT Studios 050

P

PARANOID PROJECTS Paris/ PARANOID US Los Angeles 254, 277
Passion Pictures 223, 354
Philipp und Keuntje GmbH 118, 175, 183, D 170
phreeky beats 256, 266
PICTORION das werk berlin 378, D 237
Pigalle Production 254, 277
Pilot Media GmbH & Co. KG 178
Pixelpartners.com 207
Plan.Net Media 171, 358, 381, D 234, D 257
Postbar 308
Primetime Studio 283, 300
Product Eye 308
Produktionsbüro Romey von Malottky GmbH 137
Publicis 282
PX Group 048, 350
PX1 066, 079, 087, 096, 124
PX1@Medien GmbH 114

R

radical.media GmbH 254, 257, 264, 276
Raff Digital GmbH 134, D 088, D 158
Recom GmbH, Ostfildern 062
Ringier Publishing GmbH 203
Robota, Prag 236

S

Saatchi & Saatchi 121
santamaria 238
Scheufele Kommunikationsagentur GmbH 138, D 100
Scholz & Friends 037, 053, 062, 078, 094, 106, 112, 119, 120, 122, 130, 160, 162, 182, 184, 202, 232, 249, 255, 288, 325, 335, 381, D 101, D 128, D 157, D 189, D 208, D 256
Scholz & Friends Identify 194, D 164, D 190
Schönheitsfarm Postproduktion GmbH & Co. KG 252
Schweizer Fernsehen 294, 296
SEED Digital Production, Frankfurt 282
Sehsucht GmbH 255, 257, 268, 278, 302, 312, D 221
Serviceplan München/Hamburg 051, 057, 061, 064, 171, 192, 336, 381, D 097, D 144, D 234, D 259, D 314
SF On Air Design 296
SHANGHAI DGM 136
silberlink GmbH 377
Silbersee Film Produktion GmbH 277, 286
SIZZER Music & Sound Amsterdam 238
Skudi Optics 194, D 164
Slaughterhouse Hamburg GmbH 242, 255, 288

Soundscape
Music + Sounddesign 252
Soundscape NL 280
Special Key 152, 186, 221, 283, 289, 347, 367, D 242, D 259
Spillmann/Felser/Leo Burnett 158
Sprachlabor Audioproduktionen GmbH, Düsseldorf 181, 324
Springer & Jacoby Werbeagentur GmbH & Co. KG 187, 196, 250, 310, D 216
Stillking, Prag 236
Stink 256, 274, 285
Stoptrick Hamburg 283, 300
Stress 310
Studio Funk 178, 257, 268, 302, 331, 377
Studio Funk AG 337
Studio Funk Berlin 316, 335
Studio Funk Düsseldorf 332, 333, 341
Studio Funk GmbH & Co. KG 242, 257, 268, 302, 320, D 221
Studio Funk Hamburg 322, 334, 341
Sugar Power c/o Margarethe Hubauer GmbH 095

TBWA 223, 354, D 111
TBWA\ Chiat Day, New York 360
TBWA\ Deutschland (180/TBWA), Berlin 084, 256, 274, 285
TBWA\ Deutschland, Berlin 360
Telemaz Commercials Berlin 186, 221, 283, 289, 347, 367, D 235, D 242, D 259
Tempomedia Filmproduktion GmbH, Hamburg 230, 306, 312
The Chimney Pot 249
The Mill, London 247
The Vikings 254, 277, 378, D 237
Thomas Beecken, Realisations KG 175
Thomas – Grafische Veredelung GmbH & Co. KG 138, D 100
Tillmanns, Ogilvy & Mather GmbH & Co. KG 324
Tonbüro Berlin 378, D 237
Tony Petersen Film GmbH 247
Tribal DDB, Hamburg 152, 347, 367, D 235, D 242, D 259
trio-group 240
trio-westag-bsb 240

Un-Über-Seh-Bar 205
Universal McCann Frankfurt 238
UPP, Prag 236

VASATA|SCHRÖDER Werbeagentur GmbH 213
VCC Hamburg 358
VCC Perfect Pictures AG 181, 242
Virtual Republic 245
Vogelsänger Film GmbH 240

Wake-Up-Music 230, 312
WEDIA Visuelle Großflächenwerbung 192
weigertpirouzwolf Werbeagentur GmbH 060, D 129
Westparkstudios 192
White Horse Music 272, 311
www.anna-clea.de 137
www.buschwork.com 177

Y&R Germany 050, 374, D 188

Z

Zerone, Hamburg 024, 078, 124, 203, 358

beef ist das Magazin für kreative Kommunikation - herausgegeben von HORIZONT und dem ADC. Es berichtet viermal im Jahr über Trends und Innovationen aus Werbung und Design. Gleich zugreifen und keine beef-Ausgabe mehr verpassen:

www.beef-magazin.de/abo

Herausgeber:

Sponsoren:

D + SEITENZAHL weisen auf zusätzliche Medaillen oder Auszeichnungen der Firma im ADC Volume Design hin.

FIRMEN
Companies

A

adidas AG 084, 256, 274, 281, 285, D 238, D 240
adidas International 223, 354, D 111
Allianz Beratungs- und Vertriebs-AG 246
Anwaltsuchservice Verlag Dr. Otto Schmidt GmbH 047
Arcor AG & Co. KG 242, 320
ASICS Europe B.V. 173, 283, 300
Audi AG 247, 306, D 193, D 290, D 293
Axel Springer AG, Zeitungsgruppe: Bild/BamS 238

B

Beate Uhse TV 234, 283, 289
BIC Deutschland GmbH & Co. OHG 079, 096
BIONADE GmbH 178, 331
Bischöfliches Hilfswerk Misereor e.V. 055
Bitburger Braugruppe GmbH 211
Blaupunkt GmbH 297, 338
BMW AG 024, 044, 124, 203, 214, 358, D 266, D 278, D 301, D 315
Boehringer Ingelheim Pharma GmbH & Co. KG 113
Braun GmbH 105
Brot für die Welt 208
Bundesministerium für Bildung und Forschung 194, D 164, D 190
BURGER KING GMBH 090, D 218

C

Chrysler Deutschland GmbH 042, 093, 251, 255, D 252
Chrysler Jeep 270, 303
CinemaxX AG 054, D 220
Coop 310

D

Daimler AG 020, 045, 046, 124, 142, 150, 199, 254, 257, 264, 268, 272, 276, 302, 311, 322, D 151, D 221, D 282, D 306
Daimler AG smart MBVD 280
Daimler AG, MBVD 130, 381, D 101, D 157
Daimler AG, Mercedes-Benz Vertriebsorganisation Dtld. Marketing Kommunikation Service, MBVD/VSP 136
Dali a/s, Nørager 140
Deutsche Post AG 102
DEVK Versicherung 228
Dextro Energy 230, 312
DMAX TV GmbH & Co. KG 041, 159
Du bist Deutschland GmbH 059, 157, 243

E

edding international GmbH 060
EnBW Energie Baden-Württemberg AG 205
EPURON/Bundesministerium für Umwelt, Naturschutz und Reaktorsicherheit 254, 277
Euryza GmbH 050
Evangelische Öffentlichkeitsarbeit Frankfurt am Main 370
EXIT Deutschland 034

F

Falk Marco Polo Interactive GmbH 053, 122
Festspielhaus und Festspiele Baden-Baden gGmbH 162
Feuerwehr der Landeshauptstadt Dresden 325
Filmfest Hamburg GmbH 213
Frankfurter Allgemeine Zeitung GmbH 037, 062

G

Getty Images Deutschland GmbH 373, 380
GlaxoSmithKline GmbH & Co. KG 340
Google Germany GmbH 277, 286, D 279, D 312
Greenpeace 115, 169
Greenpeace Österreich 207

D + PAGE NUMBER refer to additional medals or nominations of the company in the ADC Volume Design.

H

HDI-Gerling Sach Service-holding AG 377
Holsten-Brauerei AG 118, 183
Honda Motor Europe (North) GmbH 078
Hornbach Baumarkt AG 022, 029, 091, 156, 206, 244, 254, 256, 260, 275, 312
Hut Weber 051

I

IFAW International Fund for Animal Welfare 250
IKEA Deutschland GmbH & Co. KG 065, 179, 186, 215, 368, D 180, D 241, D 248, D 319
Inlingua Freiburg 074, 123
IWC International Watch Co. AG 052, 089, 163, D 255

J

jobsintown.de GmbH 202, 232, D 256
Johnson & Johnson GmbH 049
Jung von Matt/Fleet GmbH 077

K

Katholische Klinikseelsorge 132
K-fee AG 328
Kolle Rebbe Werbeagentur GmbH 176, D 125, D 153
Konzerthaus Dortmund GmbH 278
Konzerthaus Dortmund – Philharmonie für Westfalen 019, 096, 161, 255, 312, D 127, D 205

L

Leifheit AG 204
Loewe Opta GmbH 094
Louis Vuitton Malletier 032, D 211
Lufthansa AG 114

M

Maggi GmbH 282
Malteser Hilfsdienst e.V. 067, 108, D 244
McDonald's Austria 116
McDonald's Deutschland 066, 111
Meister Camera, Hamburg 175
Mercedes-Benz LKW, Vertriebsorganisation Deutschland 128, 144, 210
Mercedes-Benz Schweiz AG 256, 266
Mercedes-Benz Vertriebs-organisation Deutschland 181, 334, 341, D 250
MKI Matzku & Konz Industrievertretung GmbH 134, D 088, D 158
MTV Networks Germany GmbH 063, 066, 072, 096, 123, 330
MTV Networks Germany GmbH, NICK 299
MTV Networks GmbH & Co. OHG 148

N

Naturschutzbund Deutschland (NABU) e.V. 374
NBC Universal Global Networks Deutschland GmbH 039, 081, 292
neu.de 121
n-tv Nachrichtenfernsehen GmbH & Co. KG 209

O

OHROPAX GmbH 138, D 100, D 253
OLYMPUS EUROPA GmbH 187, 196
OroVerde Tropenwaldstiftung 379

P

Pan Sandwiches Berlin 335
Panasonic Marketing Europe GmbH 249
PAPSTAR Vertriebsgesellschaft mbH & Co. KG 120
Philharmonie Essen 324
Private Weissbierbrauerei G. Schneider & Sohn GmbH 240

Q

Queisser Pharma GmbH & Co. KG 112, 160

R

redblue marketing GmbH 225
Renault Deutschland AG 226, 277, 313, 378, D 237
Robert Bosch GmbH 066, 116, D 270
Rodenstock GmbH 336
RUNNERS POINT Warenhandelsgesellschaft mbH 248, 277

S

Schweizer Fernsehen 294, 296
Serviceplan Hamburg 171, 381, D 144, D 259
Shareware.de SWV GmbH 255, 288
Sixt GmbH & Co. Autovermietung KG 031, 048, 124, 201, 255, 289, 313, 339, 350, D 246
smart MBVD 252
Sönke Busch 177
Sony Ericsson Mobile Communications International AB 192, D 314
Staatliches Museum für Naturkunde Stuttgart 119, D 128, D 287
STABILO International GmbH 061, 064

T

Tamedia AG, Verlag Tages-Anzeiger 158
Taxiruf 22456/aperto move GmbH 184
Tierpark Berlin-Friedrichsfelde GmbH 106
Tinnitus Hilfe Düsseldorf, Dr. Greuel 308
TITANIC-Verlag GmbH & Co. KG 182
TUI AG 187, 212

U

UNICEF Deutschland 057, D 234
Upsolut Merchandising GmbH & Co. KG 137
Uwe Duettmann 070, D 197, D 201, D 206

V

V&S ABSOLUT Spirits 360
Volkswagen AG 027, 043, 066, 087, 095, 096, 097, 123, 124, 125, 139, 147, 152, 180, 185, 186, 187, 188, 215, 221, 253, 283, 289, 316, 326, 332, 333, 347, 367, D 235, D 242, D 259, D 264
Volkswagen AG Nutzfahrzeuge Hannover 337

W

Wieners + Wieners Werbelektorats GmbH 076
Wikimedia e.V. 056
WMF AG 080, 125
Wrigley GmbH 236

Z

Zettl GmbH 154
Zürcher Kammerorchester 245

PRODUKTE

13TH STREET 039, 081, 292

A

ABSOLUT VODKA 360
adidas 084, 223, 256, 274, 281, 285, 354
Allianz Unfall Aktiv 246
Aquatimer Automatic 2000 089
Arcor 242, 320
ASICS 173, 283, 300
Astra 118, 183
Audi 247, 306

B

Beate Uhse 234, 283, 289
BIC Cristal 079, 096
Bild am Sonntag 238
BIONADE 178, 331
Bitburger 211
Blaupunkt 297, 338
BMW 024, 044, 124, 203, 214, 358
Bosch Akkuschrauber 066, 116
Braun Nasenhaarschneider 105
Brot für die Welt 208
Bundesministerium für Umwelt, Naturschutz und Reaktorsicherheit/EPURON 254, 277
BURGER KING 090

C

CinemaxX 054, D 223
Comedy Central 063, 066, 072, 096, 123, 330
Coop Musikkomposition 310

D

Dali 140
Deutsche Lufthansa 114
Deutsche Post 102
DEVK Versicherung 228
Dextro Energy 230, 312
DMAX Anzeigenkampagne 041, 159
Dolormin 049
Doppelherz 160
Du bist Deutschland 059, 157, 243

E

Edding 060
EnBW 205
Eos Cabriolet 123, 187, 188
ER221 Bart-/Haarschneider 249
Evangelische Kirche Frankfurt 370
EXIT Deutschland 034

F

F.A.Z. 037, 062
Falk Navigationsgeräte 053, 122
Fanartikelkatalog 137
Festspielhaus Baden-Baden 162
Feuerwehr Dresden Recruiting 325
Filmfest Hamburg 213
Freeware.de 255, 288

G

Getty Images 373, 380
Greenpeace 115, 169, 207

H

HDI Versicherungen 377
Honda Motoren 078
Hornbach 022, 029, 091, 156, 206, 244, 254, 256, 260, 275, 312
Hut Weber 051

I

IFAW 250
IKEA 065, 179, 186, 215, 368, D 180, D 319
Inlingua Kampagne 074, 123
IWC 052, 163

J

Jeep 042, 093, 251, 255, 270, 303
jobsintown.de 202, 232, D 256
Jung von Matt 077

K

Katholische Klinikseelsorge 132
K-Fee 328
Kolle Rebbe 176
Konzerthaus Dortmund 019, 096, 161, 255, 278, 312, D 127, D 205

L

Leifheit 204
Loewe Flat TV 094
Louis Vuitton 032, D 211

M

Maggi Würze 282
Malteser 067, 108, D 244
McDonald's 066, 111, 116
Media Markt 225
Meister Camera/Leica D-LUX 3 175
Mercedes-Benz 020, 045, 046, 124, 128, 130, 136, 142, 144, 150, 199, 210, 254, 257, 264, 268, 272, 276, 302, 311, 322, 334, 381, D 101, D 151, D 157, D 221, D 250, D 282, D 306
Misereor Hilfswerk 055
MKI Matzku & Konz Industrievertretung 134, D 088, D 158
MTV 148, 192

N

Naturkundemuseum Stuttgart 119, D 128
Naturschutzbund Deutschland 374
neu.de 121
NICK 299
n-TV 209

O

Odol-med3 Zahnseide 340
OHROPAX 138, D 100, D 253
Olympus Unterwassergehäuse PT-029 187, 196
Optix Digital Pictures 177
OroVerde 379
Oryza Spitzenreis 050

P

Pan Sandwiches 335
PAPSTAR Aluminiumfolie 120
Philharmonie Essen 324
Protefix Haft-Creme 112

R

Renault 226, 277, 313, 378, D 237
Rodenstock Gleitsichtbrillen 336
Runners Point 248, 277

S

Schneider Weisse 240
Schweizer Fernsehen 294, 296
Serviceplan Hamburg 171, 381, D 259
Sixt 031, 048, 124, 201, 255, 289, 313, 339, 350, D 246
smart 181, 252, 256, 266, 280, 341
STABILO BOSS ORIGINAL 061, 064

T

Tages-Anzeiger 158
Taxiruf 22456 184
Thomapyrin Kopfschmerztabletten 113
Tierpark Berlin 106
Tinnitus Hilfe Düsseldorf 308
Titanic 182
TUI 187, 212

U

UNICEF 057, D 234
Uwe Duettmann 070, D 197, D 201, D 205

V

VW 027, 043, 066, 087, 095, 096, 097, 123, 124, 125, 139, 147, 152, 180, 185, 186, 215, 221, 253, 283, 289, 316, 326, 332, 333, 337, 347, 367, D 095, D 235, D 242, D 259, D 264

W

Wieners + Wieners Werbelektorat 076
Wissenschaftsjahr 2007 194, D 164, D 190
WMF 080, 125
Wrigley Juicy Fruit Squish 236
www.scheidungsanwalt.de 047
www.wikipedia.org 056

Y

YouTube 277, 286

Z

Zettl Katalog 154
Zürcher Kammerorchester 245

www.volkswagen.de

„Schätzelein,
das sind die Nägel.
Und ich bin der Hammer."

Horst Schlämmer und Volkswagen bedanken sich für 7 x Gold, 4 x Silber, 2 x Bronze und zwei Auszeichnungen.

Das Auto.

MACHER

D – SEITENZAHL weisen auf zusätzliche Medaillen oder Auszeichnungen im ADC Volume Design hin.

A

Achenbach, Marc 255, 288
Achtermann, Helen 255, 288
Adam, Bastian 204
Adenauer, Thorsten 114
Adolph, Daniel 208
Aeby, Christian 358
Aemmer, Jürg 169
Aguirresarobe, Javier 254, 260, 312
Ahrend, William 161
Ahrens, Christoph 341
Akhtari, Carolin 246
Albertini, Dominique von 158
Albus, Thomas 236
Algieri, Nicole 194, D 164, D 190
Alker, Jürgen 041, 159
Allemann, Markus 169
Alpin, Nawrocki 194, D 164, D 190
Alzen, Niels 238
Amato, Catia 202
Amtmann, Stefan 066
Andre, Michael 340
Anweiler, Dominik 378, D 237
Apell, Stefan 226, 277, 313
Ardelean, Alexander 254, 260, 312
Argueta, Javier Suarez 054, D 220
Arndt, Kerstin 251, 255, 270, 303
Arnecke, Patrick 294
Arnim, Adriana Meneses von 106, 119, D 128
Arnold, Martin 158
Arnoult, Antoine 032, D 211
Arthur, Sabrina 310
Arthus-Bertrand, Yann 027, 097, 123
Asbjoern, Rikke 354
Asbrand, Silke 138, D 100
Aschauer, Katharina 090, D 218
Aschermann, Frank 094
Aubrey, Chris 281
Augustin, Magnus 192
Aviram, Nathy 360
Aykurt, Daniel 105

B

Baader, Benjamin 255
Baarz, Danny 029, 156, 206, 244, 256, 275
Baba, Marcin 182
Bach, Claudia 255, 270, 303
Bach, Ina 034, 076
Bacherl, Jo 067, 108, D 244
Bachmann, Markus 096, 139, 147, 152, 186, 347, 367, D 095, D 235, D 242, D 259
Back, Stefanie 053, 122

Badly Drawn Boy 223
Badstübner, Charlotte 250
Baier, Julia 059, 157, 243, D 142
Bajer, Peter 202
Bayer, Ulla 059, 157
Balke, Nina 377
Ballhause, Birgit 186, 215, 368, D 319
Bank, Marcus 306
Bannöhr, Frank 230, 312
Barber, Daniel 306
Barche, Michael 377
Barilaro, Angela 078
Bark, Wolfgang 340
Barrett, Suze 182
Bartel, Alexander 308
Bartels, Ingmar 173, 378, D 237
Barth, Philipp 052, 163, D 254, D 255
Barthen, Jens 208
Bartkowski, Christoph von 102
Barton, David 084
Baslam, Farid 202
Bäsler, Sabine 130, 381, D 101, D 157
Bauer, Bernd 059, 157, 243
Bauer, Jörg 134, D 082, D 088, D 094, D 158
Bauer, Markus 252, 341
Baumann, Christian 336
Baumann, Frank 296
Baumann, Holger 042, 093, 251
Baumann, Marc 152, 347, 367, D 235, D 242, D 259, D 268
Bäumer, Niklas 299
Baumgartner, Judith 373, 380
Baur, Georg 148
Bayer, Ulla 059, 157
Bazarkaya, Toygar 105, 181, 252, 341
Becher, Bianca 336
Bechtolsheim, Matthias von 306
Becic, Jagoda 306
Beck, Alexandra 179, 211, 328
Beck, Maren 158
Beck, Steffi 187, 196
Becker, Justus 186, 215, 368, D 319
Becker, Laura 120
Becker, Roman 057, D 144
Beeck, Marion 046, 059, 157
Beecken, Thomas 175
Beelte, Harald 272, 311
Berends, Ingo 256, 266
Behrends, Ingo 238
Behrends, Steffen 250, D 216
Behrendt, Sebastian 173, 226, 277, 283, 300, 313
Behrens, Nils 187, 212
Beimdieck, Maik 055
Belger, Sabrina 067, 108, D 244
Belkhiri, Basile 254, 277
Belles, Peggy 138, D 100

Belser, Tim 066, 072, 096, 123
Bentz, Oliver 377
Benzler, Philipp 185, 215, 333
Berg, Beate van den 114
Berg, Claus von 066, 116, 213
Berg, Jan 118, 183
Berger, Lisa 180, 377
Bergmann, Tony 090,
Berhe, Sophia 370
Berlin, Irving 257, 276
Berndl, Ludwig 043, 096, 125, 139, 147, 152, 186, 221, 253, 283, 289, 316, 326, 347, 367,
Bernhard, Martin 294
Berning, Tina 178
Bertolini, Armando 243
Besler, Michi 377
Best, Katja 205
Bethke, Wiebke 093
Beutel, Anne 253
Bianchi, Kim 236
Bickenbach, Alexander 292
Biedermann, Christian 152, 186, 221, 283, 289, 347, 367,
Bielefeldt, Christoph 226, 277, 313
Biggeleben, Dr. Christof 194,
Bihn, Christian 123, 187, 188
Bilger, Tatjana 044, 358
Bilz, Robert 130, 381,
Bischur, Rosina 066, 111
Biskoping, Rüdiger 066, 111
Bison, Andrea 059, 157, 243
Blaser, Klaus 282
Blendow, Michael 347, 367,
Blenkov, Sebastian 256, 275
Blome, Karen 019, 052, 096, 163,
Blum, Wolfgang 178, 331
Blunck, Timo 257, 268, 302
Blunier, Charles 169
Bober, Thomas 152, 347, 367,
Bödeker, Daniel 062, 232,
Bodin, Frank 169
Boenigk, Sabine 341
Böhm, Andreas 039, 081, 292
Böhm, Arnd 373
Böhm, Max 256, 266
Bohneberg, Sammy 022, 029, 091, 156, 206, 244, 254, 256, 260, 275, 312
Böhning, Tobias 178
Bolland, Philip 043, 096, 125, 139, 147, 186, 221, 253, 283, 289, 326, 347, 367,
Bommes, Sven 048

Borchardt, Philip 360
Borck, Timon 046
Borges, Lars 350
Borker, Lars 089, 350,
Bornemann, Thore 257, 268, 302,

Bosch, Manuela 360
Boyens, Franziska 042, 093
Brand, Pierre 283, 300
Brandes, Christian 130, 381,

Brandstetter, Johann 119,
Brandt, Mike 254, 260, 312
Branning, Matthew 254, 277
Bräuer, Ralf 370
Braun, Stephan 130, 381,

Bräunl, Manfred 024, 044, 124, 203, 214, 358
Breaux, Richard 360
Bredenbals, Markus 324
Bremer, Dominique 213
Breuer, Kerstin 206, 244, 254, 256, 260, 275, 312
Breuer, Martin 113, 209
Breuer, Paul 243
Brinkert, Raphael 112, 160, 182, 325
Brockfeld, Timm 059, 157, 243
Brönnimann, Peter 158
Brös, Marini 173
Brown, James 256, 274
Bruch, Wolfgang 076
Bruchhaus, Boris 282
Bruchmann, Felix 240
Brucker, Vincent 297, 338
Brückner, Mathias 120
Brylka, Daniel 256, 266
Buba, Natalie 299
Büchel, Lars 246
Büchelmeier, Camillo 066, 111
Büchin, Frank 136
Buchner, Till 203, 214, 358
Buck, Detlev W. 377
Bullinger, Thomas 324
Bultmann, Holger 238
Burchardt, Lina 238
Burghauser, Klaus 020, 142, 257, 272, 302, 311,
Buri, Lars 334
Burkhardt, Ralph 205
Burkhart, Andreas 128, 144, 210
Burmeister, Fedja 175, 187, 196
Burmeister, Nina 255, 270, 303
Burns, Dave 223, 354
Burrichter, Maren 118, 183
Bürvenich, Monika 194,

Busch, Holger 205
Busse, Benjamin 076
Butnariu, Adrian 324

Cachandt, Daniel 377
Caglar, Zeki 335
Cahill, Patrick 228, 242, 320
Cahn, Aviel 245
Camp, Detlef 221, 283, 289, 347
Campell, Casey 255, 289, 350,

Camphausen, Wolf-Peter 128, 144, 210
Candaland, Pete 354
Catana, Nadja 292
Catsky, Claude 169
Cavicchioli, Régine 169
Celand, Werner 116
Cerning, Ulf 130, 381,
Cesar, F. A. 043, 096, 125, 139, 147,
Chamier, Ina-Katrin von 332
Chan, Lai-Sha 178
Chatterjee, Martin 245
Chen, Bey-Bey 243
Ciuraj, Cathrin 037, 062
Clayton, Sunny 187, 212
Cluss, Tilman 248, 277
Coedel, Stephane 354
Cole, Jack 249
Comte, Michel 296
Copeland, Greg 256, 274
Cordeiro, Klaus 084
Cording, Torben 152, 347, 367,

Cordt, Mats 024, 124, 203, 358
Coutsoumbelis, Andreas 255, 257, 268, 278, 302, 312,
Cramer, Julia 248, 255, 256, 266, 277, 289, 297, 313, 339, 350,
Crede, Carola 252
Cremer, Petra 176
Cruickshank, James 094
Crux, Hermann 118, 183
Cuenca, David 066, 087, 124
Czerny, Peter 116

Dagnell, Erik 053, 122, 249, 255, 288
Dalferth, Wolfgang 080, 125
Dallmann, Arndt 246
Damm, Stephan 046, 142, 257, 302, 322,
Dammast, Christoph 297
Dannecker, Ingo 186, 215, 368,

Daubenbüchel, Markus 325
Daul, Christian 050, 374,
Daum, Jens 194, 272, 311,

D'Aurelio, Fulvio 256, 266
Deak, Gabor 253
Dechant, Claudia 210
Deigner, Imke 063, 066, 072, 096, 123, 148, 330
Dejozé, Jan 255, 288
Denker, Ralf 257, 268, 302,
Derpmann, Mirko 194,

Dettenbach, Patrick 255, 288
Dettmann, Katrin 084, 360
Diekmann, Jan 027, 097, 123
Diel, Marco 056
Diener, Holger 238
Diestel, Till 057, 064, 171, 381,

Dietrich, Bernd 255, 289, 313, 339, 350,
Dietz, Michael 130, 381,

Dilchert, Elke 027, 096, 097, 123, 139, 147, 152, 186, 347, 367,

Distefano, Ricardo 256, 266
Döhren, Hannes von 076
Dölle, Heribert 132
Domann, Madlen 059, 157
Domke, Axel 281,

Don-sun 255, 270, 303
Dorfner, Josef 067, 108,
Döring, Anne 084
Dörner, Philipp 118
Dörr, Sebastian 251
Dötz, Laura 061, 064
Dotzler, Franz-Christoph 046
Drabsch, Nicole 179, 186, 215, 368,

Drautz, Michael 162
Dreckkötter, Marco 257, 268, 302
Dresen, Nicole 281
Dressler, Jan 256, 274, 285
Drexl-Schegg, Mia 066, 087, 124
Dreyer, Daniela 230, 312
Dreyer, Wiebke 123, 187, 188, 253
Driesang, Sascha 308
Dübbers, Susanna 213
Duenner, Steffen 245
Duettmann, Uwe 070,

Duin, Hanna 243
Dummermuth, Jürg 294
Dürr, Andreas 041, 159
Duttenhöfer, Michael 247
Duvaud, Alain 282
Dziedek, Rolf 050

E

Ebeling, Lars 024, 124, 203, 214, 358
Ebenwaldner, Marc 106, 162
Eckel, Till 022, 091, 254, 256, 260, 275, 306, 312
Eckstein, Axel 245
Edvardsen, Askild Vik 249
Edwards, Andy 354
Ege, Jan-Florian 041, 054, 159, 179, 211, 322,
Egneus, Daniel 044
Ehrenbeck, Viola 230, 312
Eichinger, Tobias 208
Eichler, Stephan 181
Eichner, Kay 060,
Eickhoff, Thomas 034, 076, 228
Eickmeyer, Matthias 181
Eisenschenk, Stefanie 234, 283, 289
Eisert, Roland 282
El-Kayem, Leila 084
Ellenberger, Stefan 066, 111
Ellendt, Alexander 240
Ellert, Caroline 186, 215, 368,
Elles, Julia 095
Ellhof, Jörg-Alexander 226, 277, 313, 378,
Elstermann, Rainer 112
Emhardt, Yvonne 020, 142
Emma 255, 270, 303
Ende, Karen Am 257, 276
Endemann, Jannik 234, 283, 289
Engbert, Bastian 094
Engel, Rainer 249
Engels, Georgios 332
Enzo 255, 270, 303
Erdmann, Daniela 031, 048, 124, 255, 289, 313, 339, 350,
Erichsen, Jens 246
Ernst, Christopher 213
Ernsting, Daniel 063
Ernsting, Philipp 042, 049, 093, 251, 255, 270, 303
Ersson, Andreas »Beavis« 328
Esders, Hans 118, 183
Esser, Tim 250
Eucker-Apsel, Cordelia 340
Ewald, Denise 065
Ewertz, Markus 084, 256, 274, 285

F

Fabian, Tim 240
Falldorf, Jörn 230, 312
Farwick, Jo Marie 041, 052, 054, 059, 157, 159, 163,
Faulhaber, Nina 180
Fehse, Jan 377
Feil, Alex 255, 288
Feil, Neels 234, 283, 289
Feit, Philipp 178, 242, 331
Feldhus, MonaFee 334
Fernseher, John 206, 244
Feuerle, Niklas 152, 186, 221, 283, 289, 347, 367,
Fiebranz, Sandra 118, 183
Fiedler, Susanne 238
Figur, Julia 250
Fischer, Andreas 324
Fischer, Carola 245
Fischer, David 062, 232,
Fischer, Teja 115, 338
Flecke, Christoph 380
Flemmer, Klaus 282
Flohrs, Oliver 201
Florenz, Jürgen 213
Flügen, Sylvia 102
Foord, Jamie 223, 354
Forberger, Andreas 236
Fordher, Jerry 223, 354
Förster, Stefan 234, 283, 289,
Försterling, Stephan 089, 179
Foster, Ian 247
Fox, Lynn 247
Frank, Alexander 059, 157, 243
Frank, Heike 076
Frank, Lennart 201,
Franke, Niklas 173, 283, 300, 378,
Franken, Susanne 079, 096
Franz, Christina 057,
Franzen, Till 292
Freier, Christina 045, 046, 257, 268, 302,
Frericks, Daniel 041, 052, 159, 163, 257, 276
Frers, Lena 019, 096, 161, 255, 278, 312,
Frese, Fabian 020, 041, 054, 142, 159, 179, 211, 257, 268, 302, 322, 328,
Freyduni, Barbara Daliri 277, 286
Freyland, Heiko 123, 187, 188
Fries, Christian 186, 221, 253, 283, 289, 347, 367,
Frileck, Hillary 360
Fritsch, Sonja 379
Fritsche, Timo 252
Fritschen, Tobias 052, 163
Fritz, Dennis 171, 381,
Fritz, Ingo 378,
Frixe, Michael 123, 187, 188
Fröhlich, Danny 178
Fuchs, Joachim 238
Fujimoto, Pam 360
Funke, Sebastian 250
Fürst, Doris 299

G

Gaentzsch, Julia 042, 093
Gaissert, Sebastian 128, 144
Gajic, Nemanja 245
Galvin, Brandon 223
Gammert, Markus 181, 252, 280, 341
Gangl, Viola 116
Garbers, Colin 242
Gareis, Sven 148, 210
Gassner, Christina 202
Gast, Oliver 236
Gau, Marcellus 377
Gehrmann, Birgit 360
Geib, Anja 205
Geigenmüller, Tobias 334
Geiger, Hannes 257, 268, 302,
Gelhausen, Lars 186, 221, 283, 289, 326, 347, 367,
Gellert, Ralf 105
Genesius, Markus 060
Gentis, Steffen 181, 252, 280
Georgi, Helen 316
Georgi, Peter 209
Gerard, Claire 079, 096
Gerckens, Inga 066, 116,
Gerhard, Clemens 238
Gerken, Kai 280
Gerlach, Stephan 118, 183
Gerlich, Lilli 207
Gerstner, Henning 024, 203, 214, 358
Gerwing, Nina 019, 096, 161, 255, 278, 312,
Geschke, Jan 140
Gessat, Søren 106, 202,
Gessenhardt, Jan 184
Gessulat, Karsten 192
Gholiagha, Nima 254, 260, 312
Gianesi, Sarah 245
Giblin, Samuel 032,
Giegerich, Susanne 332, 333
Giese, Morton 256, 275
Giesler, Verena 089,
Gillmann, Angela 152, 347,
Glage, Sven 378,
Glauner, Felix 113, 209
Gloeden, John 187, 196
Gnoycke, Finn 178,
Göbber, Anke 211
Gocht, Peter 020, 052, 142, 163, 257, 268, 302,
Goetze, John F. 047, 067, 108,
Goetze, Markus 308
Gohde, Gordon 203, 214
Golbach, Marco 252, 280, 341
Gold, Kerstin 084, 256, 274, 285
Gombert, Stefanie 045
Gonan, Erik 084
Gordon, Dan 223, 354
Gorschlüter, Ludger 243
Görzel, Peter 114
Gössler, Dörthe 136
Göttgens, Dr. Olaf 045, 046, 150, 257, 268, 272, 302, 311,
Götz, Marian 180
Götz, Michael 234, 283, 289
Graalfs, Amelie 057,
Grabowski, Gerald 186, 221, 283, 289, 347, 367,
Graf, Gerry 360
Graf, Jürgen 373, 380
Graffam, Marianne 299
Grahl, Stefan 052, 163
Granitza, Stefanie 232,
Graß, Martin 228, 320, 337
Grau, Alex 254, 260, 312
Graudus, Konstantin 330, 334
Gravestock, Tom 354
Gregor, Jean-Pierre 113
Grein, Simone 282
Grellmann, Bernd 324
Greuel, Dr. med. Hans 308
Greuner, Sebastian 094, 194,
Grill, Andreas 306
Grimm, Tobias 041, 052, 054, 159, 163
Grobe, Fabian 247
Grochau, Sören 084
Groenendijk, Jan 020, 045, 124, 142, 199, 257, 268, 302,
Grohsklaus, Ann-Kristin 048, 255, 289, 313, 339, 350,
Grub, Moritz 048, 255, 278, 312,
Grübel, Hartmut 194,
Grundner, Matthias 186, 215, 368,
Gsella, Thomas 182
Gudella, Heike 377
Guest, Joe 247
Gülzau, Ilka 246
Günder, Diana 192
Gundlach, Christiane 121
Gunske, Dennis 330
Gursky, Andreas 037

Gustafsson, Jessica 055
Gustmann, Nina 249
Gutscher, Tassilo 208

H

H., Peggy 031, 124
Haber, Sascha 232, D 256
Hackelsperger, Sebastian 066, 111
Hackner, Gregor 106
Hacsi, Petra 332, 333
Haddon, Peter 223, 354
Haeusermann, Dirk 089, 187, 196
Hafemeister, Cornelius 060
Hagemann, Kirsten 115
Hagemeister, Malte 186, 215, 368, D 319
Hahn, Georg 252
Hahn, Sebastian 76
Haider, Rosa 154
Hammer, Dr. Kristina 045, 046, 257, 268, 272, 302, 311, D 221
Hammerschmidt, Christoph 209
Hammerstad, Kristian 354
Handlos, Oliver 037, 053, 062, 119, 122, 184, 202, 232, 249, 255, 288, 335, D 128, D 208, D 256
Hanebeck, Timm 019, 048, 066, 096, 116, 161, 255, 278, 312, D 127, D 184, D 205, D 317
Hanel, Katharina 119, 184, D 128
Hanke, Sascha 019, 048, 066, 096, 116, 161, 255, 278, 312, D 127, D 184, D 205, D 317
Hannemann, Sven 039, 079, 081, 096, 102, D 124
Hannich, Thomas 116
Hansen, Alexander 089
Harbeck, Jan 039, 079, 081, 096, 102, 254, 264, 292
Harbeck, Matthias 187, 196
Hardenberg, Jasper von 094
Hardieck, Sebastian 181
Harding, Claudia 112
Härle, Josefine 034
Harms, Jens 252, D 248
Harsdorf, Anja von 052, 163
Hartl, Helmut 192
Hartmann, Daniel 308
Hartmann, Isabell 257, 276
Hartmann, Patrik 019, 048, 096, 161, D 127, D 205
Hartwich, Lisa Maria 031, 124, 255, 289, 313, 339, 350, D 246
Hartwig, Tim 076
Haschtmann, Daniel 041, 059, 157, 243
Haseborg, Nils 024, 044, 124, 203, 214, 358
Hasic, Aladin 310

Hassan, Mark 022, 029, 091, 156, 206, 244, 254, 256, 260, 275, 312
Hasselbach, Frank 186, 221, 283, 289, 347, 367, D 235, D 242, D 259
Hattenhauer, Lutz 281
Hauernherm, Catharina 152, 347, 367, D 235, D 242, D 259
Hauser, Tom 179, 186, 215, 368, D 180, D 319
Haust, Malte 299
Hecker, Johanna 020, 045, 124, 142, 199, 254, 257, 264, 268, 302, D 151, D 221
Heffels, Guido 022, 029, 091, 156, 206, 244, 254, 256, 260, 275, 306, 312
Hefter, Alex 294, 296
Heidorn, Oliver 034
Heikamp, Birgit 178, 331
Heilemann, Kristoffer 043, 096, 125, 139, 147, 152, 186, 221, 253, 283, 289, 326, 347, 367, D 095, D 235, D 242, D 259
Heimann, Nic 115, 186, 187, 212, 215, 368, D 180, D 319
Heine, Felix 130, 381, D 101, D 157
Heine, Hendrik 225, 230, 234, 283, 289, 312
Heiny, Sascha 226, 277, 313
Heiseler, Arthur 206, 244
Heitker, Norbert 277, 286
Helbig, Silvio 226, 248, 277, 313
Heldens, Acki 234, 283, 289
Helfrich, Jens 186, 215, 368, D 180, D 319
Hellge, Sebastian 255, 270, 303
Henkel, Wolfgang 049
Henkelmann, Dirk 360
Hennermann, Felix 308
Henning, Daniel 114, D 124
Hennings, Jürgen 160
Hennings, Torsten 320, 322, 334, 337
Hennschen, Holger 334
Herbst, Eva 380
Herder, Hessel 280
Herdieckerhoff, Fabian 052, 089, 163, D 255
Herman, Jonathan 253
Hermansson, Benni 179
Herold, Norbert 066, 111
Herrnberger, Christin 207
Hertel, Jan 152, 347, 367, D 235, D 242, D 259, D 264, D 268
Hertel, Sacha 152, 347, 367, D 235, D 242, D 259
Hesebeck, Birthe 379
Hesel, Marie 236
Hess, Martin 255, 278, 312
Hesse, Oliver 138, D 100
Hesse, Sabina 067, 108, D 244

Heuel, Ralf 034, 065, 076, 095, 228, 242, 320, 337
Heumann, Wolf 019, 031, 048, 066, 089, 096, 116, 124, 161, 255, 278, 289, 297, 312, 313, 339, 350, D 127, D 184, D 186, D 205, D 246, D 317
Heun, Valentin 255, 278, 312
Heuss, Caspar 062, 335
Heydel, Lydia 320
Heydiri, Beatrice 057, D 234
Heyen, Thomas 045, 046, 187, 212
Heyer, Alex 255, 257, 268, 278, 302, 312, D 221
Hicks, Johannes 180
Hiersemann, Sabine 112, 160
Hildenbrand, Dirk 090, D 218
Hipp, Roland 115
Hirt, Kristin 254, 257, 264, 276
Hissen-Laux, Angela 160
Hitzmann, Marc 152, 347, 367, D 235, D 242, D 259
Hoek, Niels van 192
Hoentschke, Ingo 341
Hoff, Arndt v. 177
Hoefflin, Bernd T. 246, 255, 288
Hoffmann, Amelie 187, 196
Hoffmann, Andreas 228
Hoffmann, Daniel 175
Hoffmann, Hans 297
Hoffmann, Jens 325
Hoffmann, Kai 181, 252
Hoffmann, Robb 311
Hoffmann, Robert 272
Hoffmeister, Helge 059, 157, 243
Höfler, Mark 378, D 237
Hofmann, Frederik 194, 272, 311, D 164, D 190
Hofmann, Sandra 370
Hohmann, Till 208
Holk, Astrid 243
Holland, Mareike 251
Holland, Tobias 078, 112
Hollander, Ton 181, 252, 280, 341
Holle, Niels 042, 049, 080, 093, 125, 251, D 187
Holtappels, Benedikt 179
Holzäpfel, Judith 201, D 138
Holzhausen, Kristine 056
Holzportz, Peter 113
Hönemann, Hannes 253
Höper, Henner 211
Höpker, Jürgen 078
Horn, Carsten 066, 111
Horrer, Sven 078
Hose, Frank 179
Hoss, Annette 031, 124
Hotz, Stephanie 041
Huber, Karoline 041, 052, 089, 159, 163, D 254, D 255
Huber, Marc 256, 266

Huber, Martina 063, 066, 072, 096, 123
Hucke, Vivien 063, 066, 072, 096, 123, 330
Huesmann, Bernd 336
Hueter, Lukas 052, 163
Hufgard, Christina 047, 067, 108, 379, D 116, D 158, D 244
Hummer, Daniel 257, 268, 302, D 221
Hupertz, Christian 020, 046, 142, 254, 257, 264, 272, 276, 311, 322
Hurtado, Jose Carlos Gonzalez 105
Huschenbeth, Stefan 256, 266
Huschka, Helmut 066, 111
Huvart, Lars 032, D 211

I

Ibing, Louisa 027, 097, 123
Iff, Vanessa 065
Illes, Sandra 332
Inderbitzin, Eduardo 034
Ingebretsen, Baard Haugan 249
Ingenleuf, Björn 054, 328, D 220
Innamorato, Nadya 161, D 184
Isken, Marc 180
Isterling, Jan 042, 093, 251, 255, 270, 303
Ivkovic, Milena 019, 096, 161, 255, 278, 312, D 127, D 205

J

Jääskeläinen, Jussi 185, 215
Jacobs, Tim 332
Jacobsen, Ole 322, 334
Jacoby, Gregory 152, 347, 367, D 235, D 242, D 259
Jaeger, Michael 162, D 189
Jäger, Simon 194, D 164, D 190
Jaggy, Alexander 256, 266
Jagodda, Arthur 225
Jahn, Joerg 106, 162, D 189
Jahrreiss, Otto Alexander 225
Jakob, Marie-Louise 066, 087, 124
Jakobi, Julia 045, 186, 215, 368, D 319
Janke, Michael 024, 124, 203, 214, 358
Janneau, Laurent 032, D 211
Janssen, Sven 078, 112
Jansen, Ruth 253
Jarry, Marc-Antoine 032, D 211
Jason, Tai 297
Jedam, Robert 201, D 253, D 270
Jensen, Volker 337
Jessen, Philipp 059, 157, 243

Wir korrigieren auch in der Kategorie „Kommunikation im Raum".

BUTTER.
sucht
Kreative
mit Eiern

In.

WIENERS+WIENERS
Übersetzen · Adaptieren · Korrigieren

Jessen, Sharon 225
Jochem, Maurice 257, 268, 302, D 221
Jochum, Armin 128, 144, 148, 210
Joh, Britta 050, 374
Johanna-Marie 255, 270, 303
Joneck, Leif 160
Joppen, Jürgen 226, 248, 277
Joosten, Silke 105
Jorrot, Marjorie 022, 029, 091, 156, D 099
Joshi, Kristian 048, 161
Jung, Andreas 299
Junghanns, Stephan 047
Junker, André 283, 300
Jürgens, Nele 194
Jurkat, Alex 256, 274, 285, 358
Jurkat, Alexander 238
Jurok, Imke 051

K

Kaessmann, Christian 024, 044, 124, 203, 214, 358
Kähler, Maik 057, 064, 171, 381, D 144, D 234, D 259
Kainz, Sebastian 022, 027, 091, 097, 123, 207, 254, 260, 312
Kaloff, Constantin 094, 130, 381, D 101, D 157
Kaminski, Gerrit 186, 215, 368, D 319
Kämper, Simon 178, 331
Kämpfer, Silke 094
Kamps, Christoph 360
Kanese, Arne 171, 381, D 259
Kanjanapokin, Gun 256, 266
Kapteyn, Jenny 029, 156, 206, 244, 256, 275
Karim, Noorman 338
Karl, Stefan 136
Karrer, Stefanie 074, 123
Kassaei, Amir 056, 096, 123, 139, 147, 152, 186, 187, 188, 221, 283, 289, 326, 332, 333, 347, 367, D 095, D 235, D 242, D 259
Kästner, Malou 330
Kastner-Linke, Susi 204
Katzmarczyk, Bernd 297
Kaufmann, Sebastian 120
Kaussen, Willy 059, 157, 225, 230, 312, 330
Kehl, Fedja 242
Keitel, Sven 246
Keller, Jonas 077
Keller, Jost 234, 283, 289
Keller, Sabine 137, 243
Kennedy, Adam 105
Kentner, Dominik 208
Kerber, Christian 065

Kerkeling, Hape 096, 152, 186, 221, 283, 289, 326, 347, 367, D 095, D 235, D 242, D 259
Kerkow, Alexander 024, 044, 124, 203, 358
Kerner, Diether 175
Kerpensian, Dobrivoie 243
Kersten, Martina 024, 124, 203, 358
Kessler, Michael 333
Kesting, Jan 252
Kettelhake, Nicolas 223, 354
Ketterl, Dr. Hans-Peter 024, 044, 124, 203, 214, 358
Keuter, Andreas 211
Kharma, Hisham 124, 199, D 151
Kiechle, Moritz 084, 203, 214, 256, 274, 285, 358
Kiefer, Gerhard 247
Kielholz, Dany 310
Kienemann, Uta 236
Kiener, Annett 225
Kiennast, Thomas 206, 244
Kiessling, Martin 308
Kim-Eyleen 255, 270, 303
Kim, Gussi 084
Kim, Jinhi 194, D 164, D 190
Kirby, Sean 173, 283, 300
Kirchhoff, Eberhard 121
Kirchhoff, Frank 046
Kirchhoff, Peter 031, 124, 255, 289, 297, 313, 339, 350, D 246
Kirchmair, Sabine 039, 081
Kirner, Fabian 123, 187, 188
Kirsamer, Phillip 377
Kirves, Thorsten 173
Kisser, Thomas 230, 234, 283, 289, 312
Kittel, Marc-Philipp 078, 112
Kittel, Michael 123, 187, 188
Kittner, Nicolas 378
Kläden, Dr. Dietrich von 238
Klarenbeek, Maud 354
Klebe, Konradin 048
Klein, Michael 245
Kleine, Michael 055
Kleine-Benne, Wenke 225
Kleinhans, Ole 187, 212, D 180
Kleinjan, Johan 054, D 220
Klemm, Matti 328
Klemp, Andreas 373, 380
Klenke, Ulrich 185, 215
Klessig, Daniel 184, 194
Klew, Matthias 282
Kliem, Sonja 042, 080, 093, 125
Klien, Tamara 178, 277, 286, 331, D 279
Klier, Biggi 243
Klimek, Wojciech 019, 096, D 127, D 205
Klingbeil, Fabian 034

Klingenfuß, Monica 336
Klöfer, Danilo 340
Klohk, Sven 055
Kluckert, Jürgen 332
Kluss, Stefan 340
Knaup, Michael 228
Kneißl, Norbert 297
Knopf, Thomas 370
Kober, Frederick 044
Koch, Christopher 049, 118
Koch, Jacqueline 230, 283, 312
Koch, Michael 370
Kockmeyer, Timo 332, 333
Köditz, Marco 211
Koeslag, Carsten 048, 350
Kohls, Kirsten 080, 125
Kohnen, Katja 181
Kohtz, Oliver 118, 183
Kolipost, Nadine 065
Kollender, Johannes 187, 196
Kömpe, Jochen 257, 268, 302, 377
Konietzko, Joe 360
Könnecke, Daniel 171, 381, D 234, D 259
Konz, Stephan 134, D 083, D 158
Koob, Diana 022, 029, 091, 156, 206, 244, 254, 256, 260, 275, 312
Korn, Lothar 150, 254, 257, 264, 276
Kortemeier, Pia 178
Koslik, Matthias 062, 106
Kowalik, Marco 245
Kraft, Matthias 358
Kraft, Stefan 202, 232, D 256
Krah, Andreas 297
Krainer, Karl 277, 286, D 279, D 312
Krämer, Björn 106, 119, D 128
Krämer, Yves 022, 029, 091, 156, 206, 244, 254, 256, 260, 275, 312
Krannich, Ingmar 209
Krantz, Jürgen 078
Kranz, Barbara 186, 221, 283, 289, 347, 367, D 235, D 242, D 259
Krebs, Clemens 297, 338
Kreil, Dietmar 116
Kremer, Markus 045, 046, 187, 212
Krenz, Elisa 299
Krichbaumer, Walter 207
Krieg, Daniel 310
Krink, Tim 042, 049, 080, 093, 125, 251, D 187
Kroll, Christian 020, 052, 142, 163, 257, 268, 276, 302, D 221
Krömker, Julia 059, 157, 243, 248, 277, D 254
Kruchten, Niklas 248, 277, D 251
Krug, Hermann 255, 257, 276, 278, 312
Krüger, Nathalie 042, 080, 093, 125

Krugsperger, Jürgen 194, D 164, D 190
Krumpel, Philipp 116
Kruse, Oliver 255, 288
Kruse, Sascha 202, 232, 255, 288, D 256
Kuehl, Bastian 046
Kuhn, Bastian 306
Kumelis, Daniel 248, 277
Kummer, Stuart 094
Kunde, Kjell 221, 283, 289, 347
Kunze, Manuela 066, 111
Küpper, Wolfgang 120
Kurowski, Nina 272, 311
Kurt 255, 270, 303
Kuskowski, Jan K. 112, 160
Kuss, Jutta 084
Kütemeyer, Dr. Jürgen 240
Kwebu, Thabang 248, 277

L

Laake, Änne 238
Lage-Weiland, Jutta 187, 212
Lagodny, Silke 027, 043, 066, 087, 096, 097, 123, 124, 125, 139, 147, 152, 180, 185, 186, 187, 188, 215, 221, 316, 326, 332, 333, D 095
Lakatos, Marion 050
Lambersy, Leveke 024, 203, 214
Lambertz, Michael 187, 212
Lamken, Mathias 063, 066, 072, 096, 123
Lamm, Kathrin 152, 347, 367, D 235, D 242, D 259
Lamprecht, Felix 243
Landmark, Anke 194, 232, 249, 255, 288, D 256
Lang, Wolf 112
Lange, Bernd 282
Lange, Garnet 065
Lange, Mirco 152, 347, 367, D 235, D 242, D 259
Lange, Nicola 114
Lange, Patrice 204
Langguth, Uli 221, 283, 289, 347
Larscheid, Georg 055
Laube, Jochen 243
Lauer, Katrin 204
Lauer, Walter 324
Laufer, Paul 257, 276
Laur, Christian 060, D 129
Lausenmeyer, Jens 055
Lechelt, Katharina 178, 277, 286, 331, D 279
Lechenmayer, Wolfgang 236
Lechner, Alescha 162
Lechner, Andreas 039, 081, 292
Lee, Marlon 354, D 259

Leger, Rolf 074, 123, 178, 277, 286, 331
Lehmann, Christoph 020, 142
Lehmann, Frédéric 340
Leibovitz, Annie 032, D 211
Leinweber, David 077, D 180
Leiskau, Jan 360
Leissle, Florian 336
Leitmeyer, Marc 060
Lemcke, Felix 123, 187, 188
Lengwiler, Doris 256, 266
Lenz, Stefan 379
Lesoine, Klaus 308
Leube, Jan 184, 232, D 208, D 256
Leuw, Daniel de 067, 108, D 244
Liebig, Jana 118
Liebsch, Christoph 256, 266
Liedtke, Eric 223, 354
Liertz, Florian 283, 300
Lima, Gito 194, D 164, D 190
Limbach, Britta 247
Linde, Nicolas 079, 096
Lindemann, Arno 045, 046, 077, 115, 150, 186, 187, 212, 215, 338, 368, D 180, D 319
Lindermaus, Silke 324
Link, Andreas 230, 312
Lipp, Eva 053, 106, 119, 122, D 128
Lipphardt, Kai-Uwe 285
Littek, Stefanie 053, 122, 249
Lobenstein, Johann-Georg Hofer von 256, 274, 285, 358
Löber, Marcus 256, 266
Lohmann, Marius 102, 254, 264
Loibl, Sandra 336
Loick, Marcus 046
Loo, Jo van de 051
Loomit 192
Lopez, Juan Carlos 240
Lorenz, Wiebke 184
Losch, Cathleen 027, 043, 066, 087, 096, 097, 123, 124, 125, 139, 147, 152, 180, 186, 221, 253, 283, 289, 326, 367, D 095
Lotze, Frank 039, 079, 081, 096, 102, 292, D 124
Low-Becic, Jagoda 247
Lübke, Karsten 094
Lucas, Andreas 282
Lück, Dennis 182
Lüdke, Gunter 341
Ludwig, Florian 074, 123, 178, 277, 286
Lühe, Martin 055
Lührsen, Mathias 328
Lukas, Bernhard 045, 046, 077, 115, 150, 186, 187, 212, 215, 338, 368, D 180, D 319
Lungwitz, Falk 256, 274, 285
Lüssem, Uwe 187, 196
Lutter, Michael 330

Lüttmer, Hendrik 137
Lux, Andrew 223, 354
Lynch, John 306

Maass, Francisca 051, 061
Mabona, Sipho 283, 300
Mackens, Michael 022, 091
Madison, Pia 179
Maier, Niklas 380
Malasek, Filip 236
Malosczyk, Sina 049
Maltzen, Ralf 096, 139, 147, 152, 186, 221, 283, 289, 326, 347, 367, D 095, D 235, D 242, D 259
Malvinsky, Boris 225, 247
Mandelbaum, Jaime 360
Mandt-Merck, Marietta 171, 381, D 259
Manns, Elena Bartrina y 055
Mann-Wisniowski, Tanja 205
Manser, Martin 256, 274, 285
Manthey, Andreas 334
Mantovani, Matthieu 256, 266
Margraf, Daniel 194, D 164
Marquardt, Uwe 050, 374
Marschall, Günther 308
Marschalt, Christian 245
Martens, Lucy 250
Martens, Stephanie 358
Marti, Pascal 254, 277
Martinis, Andrea 370
Marx, Sebastian 306
Maryon, Dean 223, 354, D 111
Matiasek, Martin 236
Matt, Norman 341
Mattner, Thomas 379, D 116, D 158
Matz, Peter 063, 066, 072, 096, 123, 330
Maurer, Manuela 074, 123
Maurice 255, 270, 303
May, Dennis 056, 332, 333
May, Milos 310
Mayer, Eric 057, D 234
Mayer, Peter 096, 139, 147, 186, 347, 367, D 095
Mayer, Sigi 154
Mclean, Russell 223
McManus, Ryan 192
Mehn, Sascha 027, 043, 066, 087, 096, 097, 123, 124, 125, 139, 147, 152, 180, 185, 186, 215, 221, 253, 283, 289, 347, 367, D 235, D 242, D 259
Mehne, Dr. Philipp 194, D 164, D 190
Mehrwald, Marco 090, D 218
Meier, Torsten 336
Meifert, Tom 236

Meilicke, Gerald 094
Meimberg, Florian 113
Meister, Martin 175
Melman, Alex 223
Melten, Egbert 032, D 211
Memari, Reza 297
Menassa, Julia 360
Mende, Brandoberamtsrat Dipl.-Ing. Thomas 325
Mende, Kerstin 078
Mene, Chantal 078, 112, 120
Mengele, Andreas 306
Menz, Jenny 240
Menze, Lars 136
Meske, Kathrin 055
Meske, Stefan 187, 196
Messerschmidt, Alexandra 105
Metchanova, Antoaneta 032, D 211
Metz, Katja 114
Meyer, Berthold T. 050
Meyer, Christian 254, 260, 312, D 178
Meyer, Christoph 316
Meyer, Hans Joachim 211
Meyer, Mikis 238
Micalizzi, Franco 236
Michaelis, Cathleen 335
Micheroli, Siro 310
Michi 255, 270, 303
Mika, Florian 089
Milczarek, Raphael 123, 187, 188
Miller, Frank 373
Millies, Max 039, 081, 292
Minckwitz, Vicky von 253
Missler, Robert 333
Mithöfer, Sandra 203, 214, 358
Mock, Andreas 066, 116
Möck, Franziska 114
Möhler, Matthias 042, 093, 251, D 252
Moje, Peter 341
Mokrohs, Philipp 186, 215, 368, D 319
Mölder, Tobias 059, 157, 243
Moll, Sabine 078
Möller, Nils 204, 225, 230, 312
Mommertz, Christian 067, 108, 379, D 244
Mönnich, Ulrike 334
Monshausen, Till 054, 059, 157, 243, D 220
Montjean, Edgard 032, D 211
Morgenstern, Arne 060
Morgenstern, Dirk 184
Moritz, Stephan 316, 335
Morrison, Kate 223, 354
Moser, Rudolf 254, 260, 312
Mosner, Boris 308
Mosner, Mario 308

Mously, David 039, 079, 081, 096, 102, 254, 264, 292
Moussa, Ramsis 337
Muck, Michael 121
Mühlendahl, Paul von 242
Müller, Armin 209
Müller, Axel 020, 211
Müller, Lothar 032, D 211
Müller, Lutz 244, 254, 260, 312
Müller, Felix 243
Müller, Ingo 176, 178
Müller, Robert 059, 157
Müller, Roland 138, D 100
Müller, Sebastian 299
Müller-Fleischer, Kurt 042, 080, 093, 125, 142, 251
Müller-Horn, Andreas 118, 183
Müller-Kähmann, David 078
Müller-Using, Mathias 173, 226, 254, 277, 283, 300, 313, 378, D 237
Münchenberg, Ulrike 236
Munteanu, Raluca 202

N

Nadelmann, Noemi 296
Nagel, Jörg 175
Nagel, Stefan 128, 144, D 278, D 301
Nagenrauft, Bernd 090, D 218
Näher, Peer 130, 381, D 101, D 157
Nann, Christoph 057, 064, 171, 381, D 144, D 234, D 259
Nawrocki, Holger 194, D 164, D 190
Nebendahl, Anne 281
Neff, Frederick 208, D 138
Negwer, Michael 138, D 100, D 253
Neis, Angie 240
Neuhaus, Christoph 150, 257, 272, 276, 311
Neumann, Aline 201
Neumann, Dietmar 181
Neumann, Sebastian 094
Nguyen, Duc 079, 096
Nickel, Dr. Tobias 024, 044, 124, 203, 214, 358
Nickerson, Michael 360
Niedzballa, Mark 254, 264
Niehaus, Christiane 228
Niehues, Pia 181
Nielsen, Mona 140
Niemann, Nic 232, D 256
Nikolov, Iwailo 250
Nittmann, Johannes 034
Noll, Marcel 246
Nolting, Ralf 034, 095
Novotny, Rudy 064

Nowak, Olivier 194, D 164, D 190
Nowotny, Pawel 020, 142
Nugent, Corinna 187, 196

O

Oblaten, Tina 252
Ochs, Benne 137
Odendahl, Florian 336
Oehrlich, Holger 201, D 253, D 270
Oelckers, Jan Hendrik 079, 096, 102
Oevermann, Jascha 179, 328, 338
Ohanian, Michael 201, 225, D 138, D 253
Ohlmann, Stefan 308
Okun, Michael 019, 096, 161, 255, 278, 312, D 127, D 205
Oliveira, Felix Novo de 292
Orth, Thorsten 047, 067, 108, D 244
Ostertag, Dr. Franka 194, D 164, D 190
Ostertag, Susanne 205
Oswald, Falk 243
Ott, Jan Hendrik 066, 087, 124
Ott, Sabrina 210
Otten, Torben 148
Otter, Bastian 325
Otto, Mike John 377
Ouchiian, Djik 228

P

Pack, Florian 115, 338
Pagel, Benjamin 254, 264
Pakravesh, Bahador 063
Pakull, Thomas 090, D 218
Panek, Sabine 226, 277, 313
Panier, Florian 322, 338
Papen, Franziska von 059, 157, 243
Paravicini, Heinrich 281, D 133, D 136, D 163, D 223
Paschke, Catherina 114
Patterson, Richard 249
Patuta, Steve 226, 248, 272, 277, 311, 313
Patzner, Henning 248, 277
Pätzold, Patricia 034, 095
Paulat, Birgit 105
Pawelke, Nicole 039, 081
Pawelski, Kathrin 041, 159
Pech, Marc 320
Penzo, Sergio 124, 199, D 151
Peritz, Jürg 310
Peritz, Roman 310
Persyn, Frank 223, 354
Peters, Andreas 282

Peters, Ole 257, 268, 302, D 221
Peters, Sascha 245
Petersen, Tony 247
Peulecke, Bert 027, 043, 066, 087, 096, 097, 123, 124, 125, 139, 147, 152, 180, 185, 186, 215, 221, 253, 283, 289, 316, 326, 347, 367, D 095, D 235, D 242, D 259
Pfaffenbichler, Sebastian 256, 266, 272, 311
Pfau, Jens Paul 041, 052, 054, 159, 163, D 220
Pfeiffer, Bona 192
Pfeil, Christian 250
Pflug, Ralf-Jürgen 324
Pflüger, Cornelia 094
Pfund, Julia 336
Philipp, Jessica 256, 275
Philipp, Simon Jasper 063, 066, 072, 096, 123
Picareta, Paula 150
Piehler, Moritz 137
Pieper, Bernd 374
Pieracci, Daniel 256, 266
Piltz, Verena 148
Pischel, Bruno 285
Pittner, Malte 285
Plant, Pablo 254, 260, 312
Plate, Leonie 120
Plewnia, Kirsa 246
Pöhlmann, Sarah 096, 139, 147, 186, 347, 367, D 095, D 235, D 242, D 259
Polcar, Aleš 118, 183
Pollmann, Torsten 113
Poppenhäger, Fred 246
Poprawe, Ute 282
Porst, Sören 186, 215, 368, D 319
Port, Lisa 255, 270, 303
Posselt, Karolin 106
Poulionakis, Andreas 020, 142
Prange, Bettina 194, D 164, D 190
Pretzsch, Matthias 024, 124, 203, 358
Pricken, Stefanie 247
Prilop, Jan-Christoph 137
Prögler, Tim 324
Propach, Jan 123, 187, 188, 333
Puccio, Katja 158
Pufe, Stefan 140
Puhl, Eskil 187, 196, 250, D 216
Puls, Christian-Ole 280

Q

Quehl, Jörg 242, 320

R

Rabenstein, Djamila 044
Rachals, Markus 084, 256, 274, 285
Radermacher, Frank 240
Radtke, Richard 328
Rafelt, Leene 335
Raiss, Rochelle 256, 274
Raith, Roland 090, D 218
Ramm, Oliver 175
Rank, Florian 380
Raphael, Melanie 045, D 180
Räther, Franziska 136
Raufmann, Hendrik 185, 215
Rauscher, Andreas 128, 144, 148, 210
Rauscher, Tabea 232, D 256
Rebmann, Mathias 119, 184, D 128, D 208
Rechtacek, Wulf 027, 097, 123
Reckeweg, Lena 056
Redlich, Nadine 132
Rees, Barney 169
Rehde, Malte 045, 046, 059, 157
Reim, Matthias 255, 289, 313, 339, 350, D 246
Reimann, Christian 255, 270, 303
Reineke, Werner 024, 044, 124, 203, 214, 358
Reininger, Benjamin 152, 186, 221, 283, 289, 347, 367, D 235, D 242, D 259
Reissinger, Michael 255, 270, 303
Reith, Dörthe von der 250
Remmert, Brigitte 221, 283, 289, 347
Rendel, Thomas 176
Rendtel, Kirsten 094
Renkel, Harald 084, 360
Renz, Michael 306
Reuilly, Christian 032, D 211
Reveman, Joakim 254, 277
Rewig, Matthias 256, 266
Rexhausen, Jan 124, 199, 248, 256, 266, 277, D 151
Rhee, Robert 255, 270, 303
Riccius, Christoph York 029, 156
Richel, Natalia 050, D 188
Richter, Nadja 130, 185, 215, 381, D 101, D 157
Richter, Max 223
Richter, Ralf 047
Richter, Utz-Werner 341
Rieder, Maximilian 052, 163
Riediger, Horst 297
Ries, Ferdinand 245
Rietveld, Teun 253
Rietvink, Remco 173, 283, 300
Rindlisbacher, Lea 296

Rinsch, Carl Erik 254, 260, 272, 311, 312
Rittenbusch, Markus 056
Ritter, Lorenz 055
Robert, Henning 041, 052, 159, 163
Robertson, John 354
Rochow, Silke 181, 280
Rogge, Heiner Baptist 136
Roggel, Simone 326
Rohde, Frances 171, 381, D 259
Rohrer, Daniel 052, 163, D 255
Röhrig, Anna 202
Ronacher, Nico 247
Rönz, Cornelius 243, 256, 266
Rose, Annika 066, 116
Rose, Désirée 113
Rose, Jacqueline 052, 163, D 255
Rose, Szymon 045, 150
Rosenbeck, Markus 251, 256, 266
Rosengart, Yves 020, 045, 124, 142, 199, 254, 257, 264, 268, 302, 322, D 151, D 221
Ross, Pamela 251
Rossi, Diana 158
Rötterink, Alexander 175
Rottmann, Michael 256, 266
Rubino, Chris 280
Rübsamen, Hanna 360
Ruckwied, Christopher 102
Rudnicki, Michael 060
Rudolf, Christian 334
Ruge, Clarissa 243
Ruh, Philipp 115
Ruhe, Martin 225, 246
Rühe, Christian 194, D 164, D 190
Rühl, Birgit 373
Rühl, Marco 037, 062
Rühmann, Björn 254, 277
Rühmann, Lars 173, 226, 254, 277, 283, 300, 313, 378, D 237
Rühmeier, Olaf 377
Ruschke, Robin 057, D 234
Rutenbach, Henrik 094
Rütten, Jan 059, 157

S

Sachtleben, Jörg 113
Sadakane, Gen 066, 087, 124
Salam, Kai Abd-El 180
Salchow, Boris 281
Salzmann, Eva 055
Sanchez, Argentina 094
Sanden, Jenny 236
Sanders, Cornelia 209
Sandmeier, Nicole 245
Saner, Simone 158
Sarnes, Malte 255, 270, 303
Sass, Kai-Oliver 050, D 188

Sato, Yu 223, 354
Sauter, Stephanie 238
Say, Fazil 255, 278, 312
Schaar, Marcel 019, 096, D 127, D 205
Schädel, Timo 281
Schäfer, Daniel 150
Schäfer, Ilan 102
Schäfer, Ingo 282
Schäfer, Peter 169
Schäfer, Silke 113
Schaffarczyk, Till 032, D 211
Schäffler, Erik 334
Scharf, Patrick 185, 215
Scharnau, Michael 185, 215
Schäufele, Caroline 128, 144, 148, 210
Schecker, Marc 176
Scheer, Stefan 132
Scheer, Ulrich 029, 156
Schelkmann, Ann-Katrin 247
Schellberg, Kirsten 236
Scheller, Nina Sophie 187, 212
Schepker, Boris 186, 221, 253, 283, 289, 326, 347, 367, D 235, D 242, D 259
Schermers, Mark 223, 354
Schertlein, Oliver 272, 311
Scheufele, Beate 138, D 100
Schieferecke, Jörg 134, D 088, D 158
Schiel, Arne 280
Schierl, Alexander 106, 162
Schierwater, Jan 173
Schierwater, Tim 173, 226, 277, 283, 300, 313
Schif, Wolfgang 128, 144, 148
Schildt, Alexander 230, 312
Schildt, Claudia 124, 199, D 151
Schill, Alexander 051, 057, 061, 064, 171, 381, D 144, D 234, D 259
Schillings, Peter 240
Schillinsky, Alexander 255, 278, 312
Schimmer, Florian 234, 283, 289
Schindler, Mathias 056
Schindler, Sven 084, 256, 274, 285
Schipper, Sebastian 254, 264
Schlau, Gunnar 370
Schlegl, Julia 187, 212
Schlehbusch, Caroline 240
Schlipfinger, Marion 207
Schlosser, Sebastian 181, 252, 341
Schmal, Gerhard 132
Schmid, Alexander 176
Schmid, Patricia 296
Schmidlechner, Andreas 116
Schmidt, Adrian 324
Schmidt, Caroline 238
Schmidt, Christian 062

Schmidt, Frauke 079, 096, 102
Schmidt, Jochen 257, 272, 276, 311
Schmidt, Julia 094
Schmidt, Matthias 078, 112, 120, 160, 182, 325
Schmidt, Michael 062, D 122
Schmidt, Sönke 175
Schmidt, Stefan 024, 084, 124, 256, 274, 285, 358
Schmidt, Steffen 206, 244
Schmidt, Susan 066, 111
Schmiedekampf, Ramin 059, 157
Schmitt, Tim 096, 139, 147, 186, 347, 367, D 095, D 242, D 259
Schmoll, Kathrin 186, 221, 283, 289, 347, 367, D 235, D 242, D 259
Schmucker, Florian 074, 123, 178
Schmuschkowitsch, Ilja 203, 214, 358
Schneider, Carsten 236
Schneider, Dennis 182
Schneider, Frank 294
Schneider, Holger 078
Schneider, Stefan 240
Schneider, Susanne 325
Schneider, Tim 022, 091, 254, 256, 260, 275, 306, 312
Schneider, Wolf 194, D 164, D 190
Schneider, Wolfgang 039, 079, 081, 096, 102, 254, 264, 272, 292, 311, D 124
Schneidermeier, Eduard 230, 312
Schoeffler, Eric 056, 123, 187, 188, 332, 333
Schoenmann, Sven 186, 215, 368, D 319
Schölermann, Marc 238
Schöne, Sven 360
Schönholzer, Christoph 310
Schönmann, Sven 338
Schöps, Gerhard R. 066, 111
Schott, Dagmar 373
Schrader, Sven 027, 096, 097, 123, 139, 147, 152, 186, 347, 367, D 095, D 235, D 242, D 259
Schrader, Volker 282
Schramm, Florian 046
Schreibauer, Susanna 192
Schriewer, Andreas 337
Schröcker, Jürgen 022, 029, 091, 156, 206, 244, 254, 256, 260, 275, 312
Schröder, Felix 256, 266
Schröder, Vivian 244, 254, 260, 312
Schroeder, Anna-Kristina 255, 270, 303
Schroeder, Rolf 047
Schrooten, Vanessa Rabea 031, 124, 255, 289, 297, 313, 339, 350, D 246

Schubert, Jakob 043, 125
Schubiger, Caroline 052, 163
Schüler-Bredt, Axel 173, 283
Schuller, Kristian 031, 124
Schulte, Josef Konstantin 039, 081, 254, 264, 272, 311
Schulte, Stefan 027, 043, 066, 087, 096, 097, 123, 124, 125, 139, 147, 152, 180, 185, 186, 215, 221, 253, 283, 289, 316, 326, 347, 367, D 095, D 235, D 242, D 259
Schulte-Herbrüggen, Sarah 078
Schulze, Christian 066, 111
Schulze, Tanja 334
Schumacher, Angelika 060
Schumacher, Harald 374
Schumacher, Jennifer 202
Schumann, Ulrike 096, 139, 147, 186, 347, D 095, D 144, D 259
Schupp, Jonathan 051, 061
Schuster, Wiebke 377
Schütt, Ronja 121
Schütz, Pia 050
Schütz, Sarah 377
Schwalme, Florian 119, 184, D 128, D 208
Schwarm, Christian 134, D 082, D 088, D 158
Schwarz, Benjamin 334
Schwarz, Jochen 297
Schwarz, Sven 213
Schwarz, Thomas 332
Schwarzinger, Jasmin 095
Schwarzwald, Oliver 178
Schweitzer, Florian 341
Schwemer, Nils 256, 274, 285
Schweyer, Xaver 221, 283, 289, 347
Schwidden, Patrick 245
Schwiedrzik, Boris 272, 311, D 124
Schwiegk, Marius 066, 089, 116
Schwingen, Hans-Christian 247
Schymetzki, Sandra 031, 048, 124, 255, 289, 313, 339, 350, D 246
Sedmak, Andreas 245
Seeger, Hartmut 027, 043, 066, 087, 095, 096, 097, 123, 124, 125, 139, 147, 152, 180, 186, 187, 188, 221, 253, 283, 289, 316, 326, 332, 347, 367, D 095, D 235, D 242, D 259
Seegers, Katrin 037, 062
Seelig, Christine 205
Seiffe, Helen 039, 081, 254, 264, 292
Seigerschmidt, Florian 181
Selge, Hans 194, D 164, D 190
Seltmann, Anne 210
Sengpiehl, Jochen 027, 043, 066, 087, 095, 096, 097, 123, 124, 125, 139, 147, 152, 180, 186, 187, 188, 221, 253, 283, 289, 316, 326, 332, 347, 367, D 095, D 235, D 242, D 259
Senn, Christoph 257, 268, 302, D 221
Serrano, Daniel 277, 286
Sethuraman, Shiv 032, D 211
Setzkorn, Stefan 078, 112, 120, 160, 182, 325
Seupel, Kathrin 066, 116
Seyedasgari, Siyamak 029, 156
Seyfert, Mirco 250
Siebenhaar, Dirk 065, 076, 228
Siebert, Ulrike 162
Siegl, Stefanie 208
Siegmund, Elisabeth 019, 096, D 127, D 205
Siehl, Sabine 187, 196
Sierp, Claus-Michael 240
Sievers, Alexandra 043, 125, 186, 253, 347, 367, D 235, D 242, D 259
Sievers, Petra 121
Sieverts, Simon 236
Silz, Dirk 325
Simocko, Rasto 236
Singer, Jana 335
Skoluda, Anna Clea 137
Sluyter, Katja 031, 124
Smestad, Stian 249
Smiley, Rob 360
Smith, Hendrik 256, 266
Smith, Neil 306
Snapher, Tim 354
Sobott, Martin 245
Solbach, Daniel 084
Sollinger, Sandra 240
Solman, Colin 297, 334
Sonntag, Dr. Ralf 250
Sonntag, Stefan 136
Sorgatz, Sven 024, 044, 124, 358
Sossidi, Constantin 095
Spaetgens, Matthias 037, 053, 062, 106, 119, 122, 184, 202, 232, 249, 255, 288, D 128, D 190, D 208, D 256
Spakowski, Dirk 181, 252, 280, 341
Spengler-Ahrens, Dörte 124, 199, 248, 256, 266, 277, D 151
Spieske, Stephan 084
Spillmann, Martin 158
Spilker, Michael 136
Spoerli, Heinz 296
Spreen, Maik 074, 123, D 176
Sprungala, Hubertus 328
Stäheli, Andy 158
Stahr, Wolfgang 022, 091
Stamm, Henning 277, 286
Stamp, Christian 210
Standt, Jacqueline 105
Stangl, Nina 181

Stanjes, Stefanie 333
Stauber, Roland 379
Stearns, Tony 223, 354
Steffen, Eike 181, 324
Steffens, Ann Kathrin 377
Steffens, Steffen 049
Steiger, Nico 358
Steiger, Nina 326
Stein, Jens 130, 381, D 101, D 157
Steiner, Dominique 094
Steiner, Sebastian 240
Steinkemper, Markus 181, 341
Steinküller, Tim 136
Steinmeyer, Lars Colin 182, 194
Stiebel, Katie 272, 311
Stierl, Annika 202, D 260
Stiller, Mathias 039, 079, 081, 096, 102, 254, 264, 272, 292, 311, D 124
Stoffer, Julia 045
Stöhr, Darek 272, 311
Stölzer, Maren 377
Storath, Matthias 029, 156, 206, 244, 256, 275
Störl, Norman 238
Storp, Felix 225
Storto, Carola 022, 029, 091, 156
Straccia, Fabio 256, 266
Strass, Marc 272, 311
Strasse, Anna-Lena 243
Strauch, Kajo Titus 209
Strauß, Oskar 079, 096
Strauss, Peter 047
Stritz, Thomas 176
Ströh, Peter 095, 337
Strothmann, Constanze 051
Struzyna, Stefanie 211
Strzoda, Matthias 178, 331
Stübane, Tim 066, 087, 124, 185, 215
Stuhldreier, Detlef 113, 209
Stumpe, Peter 096, 139, 147, D 095
Stürken, Joachim 306, D 099
Stürmer, Frauke 077
Suchatzky, Boris 213
Sukopp, Diana 282
Sumich, Dan 223, 354
Sunderdiek, Nicola 138, D 100
Suraj, Ole 373, 380
Süß, Thomas 206, 244, 256, 272, 275, 306, 311
Suter, Patrick 158
Svechtarov, Nina 238
Swistowski, Joanna 186, 215, 368, D 319
Sydow, Pedro 078, 112
Szymanski, Achim 128, 144

T

Tarsem 257, 276
Tasdan, Filiz 225
Taubert, Felix 031, 124, 255, 289, 313, 350, D 246
Tebart, Marc 272, 311
Tehrani, Turan 052, 163, D 255
Temminghoff, Barbara 208
Terruhn, Dominik 358
Theil, Jens 204, 234, 247, 283, 289
They, Patrick 334
Thiele, Dominik 236
Thiele, Thomas 049
Thieme, Sascha 128, 144, 210
Thiessenhusen, Nicolas 377
Thoemen, Julia 051, 061, 064, D 144
Thomas, Ines 373, 380
Thompson, Alistair 207
Thompson, Sean 223, 354, D 111
Thomsen, Axel 051, 057, 061, 064, 171, 381, D 144, D 234, D 259
Thöner, Dagmar 236
Tibelius, Alexander 024, 124, 358
Tietke, Annika 106
Tom 255, 270, 303
Töpper, Markus 370
Tötzke, Christian 137
Tran, Thanh Vu 181
Trau, Frank-Michael 078
Traut, Martina 031, 079, 096, 124, 350
Trautmann, Michael 059, 157, 243
Trevisan, Tobias 037, 062
Trierveiler, Emiliano 360
Trippel, Claudia 202
Tristram, Marco 328
Tritsch, Fabian 255, 270, 303
Trojand, Sebastian 247
Tromm, Friedrich 128, 144, 148, D 278, D 301
Trott, Andrea 067, 108, D 244
Tschöpe, Mandy 162, D 260
Tuchow, Dirk 337
Tulinius, Tomas 024, 044, 124, 203, 214, 358
Tunick, Spencer 169
Turiak, Tim 132
Turner, Sebastian 037, 062
Turnley, David 354, D 111
Turtle, Tommy 257, 276
Tziopanos, Niko 255, 278, 312

U

Uhlich, Dr. Gerald R. 106
Uhlig, Isabel 204
Ulmer, Götz 041, 054, 159, 179, 211, 243, 322, 328, D 220
Ural, Taner 253
Urban, Simon 160

V

Valentyn, Birgit van den 185, 215
Vanoni, Roland 246
Veihl, Stefanie 205
Veken, Domonic 178
Venn, Martin 209
Vernooij, Wip 354
Vetter, Gerhard 245
Vetter, Sebastian 053, 122
Vietz, Ariane 377
Vogel, Bettina 299
Vogel, Dr. Stephan 067, 108, 379, D 244
Vogel, Friederike 379
Vogel, Jan 250
Vogl, Johannes 106
Voigt, Thorsten 336
Völker, Mirco 045, 046, 124, 150, 199, 254, 257, 264, 268, 272, 276, 302, 311, D 151, D 221
Volkmann, Thomas 255, 270, 303
Völlmecke, Tobias 041
Vollmert, Stefan 230, 312
Voß, Katrin 037, 062, 202, 232, D 256
Voß, Sonja 236
Voss, Oliver 041, 052, 054, 059, 157, 159, 163, 243, 322, D 220
Vossen, Jürgen 022, 029, 091, 156, 206, 244, 254, 256, 260, 275, 306, 312
Vosshagen, Christian 160
Vuka, Mntha 248, 277

W

Wachenfeld, Volker 061, 064
Wäcker, Klaus 225
Waernes, Jens-Petter 053, 122, 202, 249, 255, 288
Wages, Jens 205, D 253
Wagner, Bernd 034
Wagner, Isabelle 121
Wagner, Thimoteus 020, 142, 257, 268, 302, D 221
Wagner, Vittal 150, 272, 311
Walde, Cissy 176
Walder, Pascal 228
Wallé, Anuschka 252, 341
Wallscheid, Gotthard 324
Wallutt, Carlos 350, D 246
Walter, Markus 252
Warns, Ole 179, D 248
Warwick 255, 289, 350
Weber, Benny 236
Weber, Birgit 045, 059, 157
Weber, Florian 225
Weber, Markus 335
Weber, Thomas 051
Weber, Timm 120
Weber-Grün, Alexander 306, D 099
Wege, Stephan 043, 125
Wegener, Karsten 063, 066, 072, 096, 123
Wegner, Stefan 194, D 164, D 190
Weigel, André 340
Weise, Niklas 285
Weiss, Marcel 294
Weiß, Nicola 118, 183
Wellenbrock, Bea 255, 278, 312
Weltzien, Anton von 257, 276
Weltzien, Deneke von 020, 142, 257, 276, 322
Wendt, Lennert 255, 270, 303
Wenhold, Philipp 066, 089, 116, 124, 199, D 151
Weng, Alexander 113
Wenk, Martin 201
Wenske, Tobias 024, 124, 203, 358
Werner, Claus-Uwe 380
Werner, Katja 178
Werner, Martin 256, 275
Weskamp, Anne 039, 059, 081, 089, 157, 243, D 124
Westhoff, Anne 209
Wezemael, Jan van 294
Wichowski, Taro B. 114
Wicki, Samuel 052, 163
Widmann, Marcus 128, 144
Wiegand, Martina 374
Wiehle, Stephanie 119, 184, D 128
Wieners, Ralf 076
Wientzek, Marc 022, 027, 091, 097, 123, 207, 254, 260, 312
Wiepking, Lars 272, 311
Wilbrenninck, Johannes 032, D 211
Wilhelm, Julia 228
Wilhelm, Steven 246, 255, 288
Wilhelm, Tobias 119, D 128
Will, Stefan 257, 268, 302, D 221
Wille, Dr. Volkhard 379
Williams, John 354
Willrodt, Dr. Karsten 031, 048, 124, 201, 255, 289, 313, 339, 350, D 246
Willvonseder, Claudia 065, 186, 215, 368, D 180, D 319
Wilmsen, Daniel 074, 123

Wilson, Christopher 223
Wimberger, Robert 207
Wimmer, Louisa 182
Wind, Christian 358
Winkler, Daniela 037, 062
Winschewski, Anke 042, 080, 093, 125
Winter, Bianca 048
Winterhagen, Michael 106, 162, D 189
Winterhager, Penelope 194, D 164, D 190
Winterstein, Gerrit 272, 311
Wirz, Cyrill 158
Wischnewski, André 152, 171, 347, 367, 381, D 235, D 242, D 259
Wisotzki, Frank v. 377
Wittkowski, Clemens 247
Woelke, Martin 255, 257, 268, 278, 302, 312, D 221
Wöhler, Philipp 130, 381, D 101, D 157
Wohlmuther, Elena 116
Wolber, Torsten 120
Wolf, Heinz 136
Wolf, Marilyn 056
Wolf, Torsten 063, 066, 072, 096, 123, 148, 330
Wolfberg 236
Wolff, Anna 236
Wolff, Tobias 194, D 164, D 190
Wolk, Julia 204
Wollny, Nils 204, D 096
Wolters, Christiane 024, 124, 358
Wolters, Christoffer 283, 300
Worre, Lars 140
Wos, Justyna 031, 124
Wübbe, Stefan 074, 123, 178, 277, 286, 331
Wulff, Alexandra 192
Wursthorn, Axel 102
Wurst-Riecke, Christian 256, 266
Wüst, Gerald 211
Wuttge, Diana 184
Wyrwoll, Jeanine 053, 122, 249

Y

Yazdi, Alexander 120
Yilmazalp, Ilker 063, 066, 072, 096, 123, 330
Yom, Bill 042, 080, 093, 125, 142, 251
Ystén, Ann 360

Z

Zander, Sven 152, 186, 221, 283, 289, 347, 367, D 242, D 259
Zapletal, Christoph 230, 312
Zastrow, Kai 070
Zboralski, Oliver 095, 250
Zeh, Joachim 022, 091
Zell, Fabian 124, 199, D 151
Zettl, Brigitta 154
Zeuner, Sebastian 169
Ziegaus, Veronika 095
Ziegler, Julia 054, 179, 211, D 220
Ziegler, Walter 106, 162
Ziesmer, Jac 137
Zilligen, Ralf 181, 252, 280, 341
Zimmer, Dirk 333
Zimmermann, Stefanie 160
Zink, Anke Vera 379
Zinke, Gerrit 204, 234, 247, 283, 289
Zinnhobler, Nina 090, D 218
Zisselsberger, Therese 066, 111
Zitzewitz, Friedrich von 152, 171, 347, 367, 381, D 234, D 235, D 242, D 259
Zoch, Cornelius 039, 081
Zoubek, Dan 079, 096
Zschirnt, Bettina 019, 096, 124, 199, D 127, D 151, D 205
Zsifkovits, Horst 380
Zünkeler, Ulrich 074, 123, 176, 178, 331

JUNG v. MATT

marius.linde@jvm.de

Jung von Matt/Spree GmbH, Tel. 030/7 89 56-513, Fax -119
Hasenheide 54, 10967 Berlin

DDB

marius.linde@de.ddb.com

DDB Berlin GmbH
Neue Schönhauser Straße 3–5   10178 Berlin
Telefon +49 30 240 84 54373   Fax +49 30 240 84 54374

Marius Linde
Texter

DDB Worldwide Communications Group Inc
www.de.ddb.com

Egal, wie deine Karriere verläuft: Zum Glück gibt's die Altersvorsorge der Sparkassen.

JURYS
Juries

C+SEITENZAHL sind ein Hinweis auf die Kontaktdaten des Jurymitglieds im ADC Volume Creative Report.

JURY 01
PUBLIKUMSANZEIGEN
CONSUMER ADVERTISEMENTS

Schirner, Michael (Juryvorsitz) C 126
Apostolou, Paul C 108
Bartel, Alexander C 108
Büren, Thilo von C 110
Frings-Rupp, Niklas C 112
Herold, Christoph C 115
Heuel, Ralf C 116
Karpinski, Detmar C 118
Kugelmann, Irene C 119
Lamken, Mathias C 120
Neubert, Hans C 122
Röffen, Kai C 125
Schill, Alexander C 126
Schneider, Tim C 127
Schoeffler, Eric C 127
Spaetgens, Matthias C 128
Voss, Oliver C 131

JURY 02
FACHANZEIGEN, TAGES-/WOCHENZEITUNGS-ANZEIGEN
TRADE ADVERTISEMENTS, ADVERTISEMENTS IN DAILY/WEEKLY NEWSPAPERS

Baader, Fred (Juryvorsitz) C 108
Borchardt, Philip C 109
Hoefer-Wirwas, Nicole C 116
Höntschke, Ingo C 116
Knopf, Werner C 118
König, Dagmar C 119
Lindemann, Arno C 120
Meyer, Michael »Much« C 122
Mommertz, Christian C 122
Nolting, Ralf C 123
Römer, Alex C 125
Schmidt, Matthias C 127
Stiller, Mathias C 130
Vonderstein, Stefan C 131
Weber-Grün, Alexander C 132
Wohlnick, Lars C 133
Zschaler, Stefan C 134

JURY 03
PLAKATE UND POSTER (INDOOR UND OUTDOOR)
BILLBOARDS AND POSTERS (INDOOR AND OUTDOOR)

Harbeck, Matthias (Juryvorsitz) C 114
Bannöhr, Frank C 108
Berger-Gley, Kathrin C 109
Demner, Mariusz Jan C 111
Derschow, Feico C 111
Hardieck, Sebastian C 114
Jacobs, Tim C 117
Krempl, Johannes C 119
Müllner, Gudrun C 122
Okusluk, Jan C 123
Pätzold, Patricia C 123
Püttmann, Raphael C 124
Ramm, Oliver C 124
Schmidt, Heiko C 126
Schneider, Wolfgang C 127
Turner, Sebastian C 130
Wegert, Ulrike C 132

JURY 04
PRODUKT-/WERBEBROSCHÜREN, TEXT
PRODUCT/ADVERTISING BROCHURES, COPY

Wetzel, Matthias (Juryvorsitz) C 132
Berndl, Ludwig C 109
Bruchmann, Felix C 110
Depper, Hajo C 111
Florenz, Catrin C 112
Geschke, Jan C 113
Harbeck, Jan C 114
Jochum, Armin C 117
Krink, Stephanie C 119
Linsenmeier, Harald C 120
Mothwurf, Ono C 122
Quester, Peter C 124
Reins, Armin C 124
Rogge, Heiner Baptist C 125
Römmelt, Peter C 125
Wildberger, Thomas C 133

C+PAGE NUMBER refer to the contact details of the jury member in the ADC Volume Creative Report.

JURIES JURYS

JURY 07
VERKAUFSFÖRDERUNG, MEDIA
SALES PROMOTION, MEDIA
Walmrath, Thomas (Juryvorsitz) C 131
Ahrens, Tobias C 108
Dovidat, Frank C 111
Eichinger, Tobias C 111
Heilemann, Kristoffer C 115
Hirrlinger, Peter C 116
Hohmann, Till C 116
Homoki, Judith C 116
Kolle, Stefan C 119
Kötter, Helen C 119
Krüger, Detlef C 119
Liebig, Jana C 120
Meske, Stefan C 121
Poetzsch, Britta C 124
Scheven, Burkhart von C 126
Schmidt, Stefan C 127
Vasata, Mirko C 130

JURY 08
TV-SPOTS
TELEVISION COMMERCIALS
Kemper, André (Juryvorsitz) C 118
Alzen, Niels C 108
Frank, Oliver C 112
Frenkler, Ekki C 112
Gley, Ove C 113
Heintzsch, Carsten C 115
Herold, Norbert C 115
Kaloff, Constantin C 117
Krink, Tim C 119
Kuhn, Bastian C 119
Meixner, Oscar C 121
Ries, Mike C 125
Schulte, Stefan C 127
Spengler-Ahrens, Dörte C 128
Vossen, Jürgen C 131
Waterkamp, Hermann C 132

JURY 09
KINOWERBEFILME, FILME FÜR VERKAUFSFÖRDERUNG/ UNTERNEHMENSDARSTELLUNGEN, VIRALE FILME
CINEMA COMMERCIALS, FILMS FOR SALES PROMOTION/COMPANY PRESENTATION, VIRAL FILMS
Zastrow, Dietrich (Juryvorsitz) C 133
Bazarkaya, Toygar C 108
Berndt, Hans-Joachim C 109
Bultmann, Holger C 110
Busch, Sönke C 110
Delfgaauw, Martien C 111
Handlos, Oliver C 114
Heffels, Guido C 115
Hennings, Torsten C 115
Herken, Thorsten C 115
Kessler, Oliver C 118
Olf, Bettina C 123
Ritter, Jan C 125
Stackmann, Julia C 128
Wolf, Ewald C 133
Wübbe, Stefan C 133

JURY 10
TV-ON-AIR-PROMOTION, AUDIOVISUELLE MEDIEN: DESIGN
TV ON-AIR PROMOTION, AUDIOVISUAL MEDIA: DESIGN
Ulmer, Götz (Juryvorsitz) C 130
Baumöller, Asta C 108
Bollmann, Rainer C 109
Jahn, Joerg C 117
Neumann, Gerd C 122
Reissinger, Michael C 124
Sperling, Heike C 128
Strotmann, Marc C 130

JURY 11
MUSIKKOMPOSITIONEN/ SOUND-DESIGN
MUSIC COMPOSITIONS/ SOUND DESIGN
Besser, Reinhard (Juryvorsitz) C 109
Besler, Michi C 109
Hanke, Sascha C 114
Mierau, Olaf C 122
Moritz, Stephan C 122
Schneider, Christian C 127
Schöpfer, Joachim C 127
Seifert, Christian C 128
Timm, Hans-Joachim C 130
Willvonseder, Mathias C 133

JURY 12
FUNKSPOTS
RADIO COMMERCIALS
Funk, Klaus (Juryvorsitz) C 112
Albrecht, Hans-Peter C 108
Eichner, Kay C 111
Haider-Merlicek, Rosa C 114
Kaussen, Willy C 118
Leisewitz, Jochen C 120
Leube, Jan C 120
Lukas, Bernhard C 121
May, Dennis C 121
Osenbrügge, Fiete C 123
Reif, Cosima C 124
Schüttken, Klemens C 128
Szymanski, Achim C 130
Vogel, Stephan C 131
Wagner, Thimoteus C 131
Wittig, Harald C 133
Zünkeler, Ulrich C 134

JURY 13
INTEGRIERTE KAMPAGNEN
INTEGRATED CAMPAIGNS
Zilligen, Ralf (Juryvorsitz) C 133
Berendts, Arwed C 109
Classen, Veronika C 110
Dieckert, Kurt Georg C 111
Heumann, Wolf C 116
Hinrichsen, Gepa C 116
Jahn, Mathias C 117
Jung, Eva C 117
Jung, Richard C 117
Kassaei, Amir C 118
Krause, Delle C 119
Krause, Robert C 119
Preiswerk, Michael C 124
Puri, Nina C 124
Scheer, Stefan C 126
Störl, Norman C 130
Weber, Timm C 132

JURY 14
DIALOGMARKETING
DIALOGUE MARKETING
Koch, Michael (Juryvorsitz) C 119
Barche, Michael C 108
Geyer, Andreas C 113
Hildebrand, Christoph C 116
Kainz, Sebastian C 117
Klemp, Andreas C 118
Marquardt, Uwe C 121
Pross, Martin C 124
Rump, Detlef C 126
Schier, Sebastian C 126
Schneider, Manfred C 127
Waibel, Peter C 131
Weishäupl, Hans C 132
Wrage, Folker C 133

Jury-Chairman
Lürzer, Walter C 012, C 137

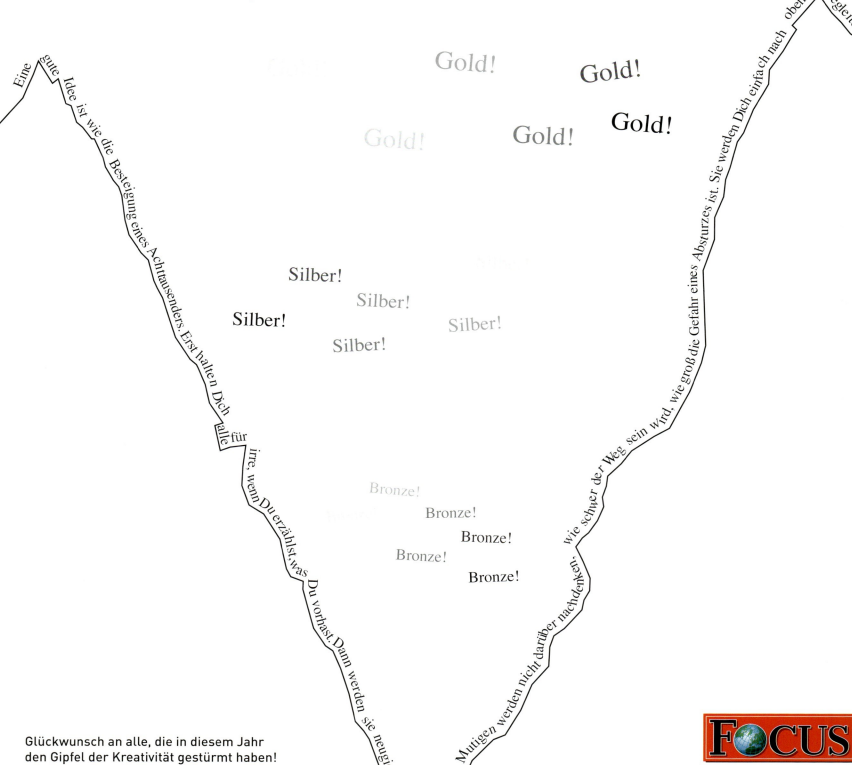

HERAUSGEBER
EDITOR
Herausgeber und verantwortlich für den redaktionellen Inhalt:
Publisher and responsible for editorial content:
Art Directors Club Verlag GmbH
Franklinstraße 15
10587 Berlin
T 0049-30-5900310-0
www.adc.de

KONZEPTION UND GESTALTUNG
CONCEPTION AND DESIGN
Hesse Design GmbH
www.hesse-design.com
Klaus Hesse (Art Direction)
Sandra Klemt (Design)

ILLUSTRATION
ILLUSTRATION
Uli Knörzer
www.uliknoerzer.com

BILDRECHTE
PICTURE COPYRIGHTS
Corbis GmbH: Andy Warhol (Titel), Willy Brandt (068), Edward Hopper (098), Coco Chanel (167), Stanley Kubrick (259), Steve McQueen (363)
Getty Images Deutschland GmbH: Marlene Dietrich (015), Alfred Hitchcock (217), Josephine Baker (305), Edith Piaf (314), Bruce Lee (343)
weblogs.clarin.com: Tamara de Lempicka (291)
www.graefinzahl.de: Klaus Kinski (126)

KURZBIOGRAFIEN
SHORT BIOGRAPHIES
Klaus Hesse (Text)
Stefanie Sausmikat (Redaktion und Lektorat)

TEXTQUELLEN
LITERARY SOURCES
www.brainyquote.com (Zitate)
www.thinkexist.com (Zitate)
www.wikipedia.org (Kurzbiografien und Zitate)

REDAKTION
EDITORIAL OFFICE
Susann Schronen
Skadi Groh

ADC PROJEKTMANAGEMENT
ADC PROJECT MANAGEMENT
Skadi Groh

ÜBERSETZUNG
TRANSLATION
WIENERS+WIENERS GmbH Hamburg

ORGANISATION
ORGANIZATION
Bertram Schmidt-Friderichs
Günter Busch
Ulrike Jürgens

HERSTELLUNG
PRODUCTION
Günter Busch
Ulrike Jürgens

GEWINNERSEITEN
WINNER PAGES
Ulrike Jürgens

SATZ
COMPOSITION
Universitätsdruckerei H. Schmidt, Mainz
Martina Becker
Volker Kehl
Talisha Kreuzberg
Elisabeth Scholz
Michael Staab
Jennifer Töpel

VIELEN DANK FÜR DIE UNTERSTÜTZUNG
THANKS FOR THE SUPPORT
Christiane Gillissen
Christine Hesse
Claudia Kempf
Thomas Rempen
Raban Ruddigkeit
Ralf Zilligen

SCHRIFTEN
FONTS
Futura, Melior

DRUCK
PRINT
Universitätsdruckerei H. Schmidt, Mainz

BINDUNG
BINDING
Buchbinderei Schaumann, Darmstadt

EINBANDMATERIAL
COVER MATERIAL
Luxocard 2, 350 g/qm von SchneiderSöhne

PAPIER
PAPER
BVS, 135 g/qm von Scheufelen

VERLAG
PUBLISHING HOUSE
Verlag Hermann Schmidt Mainz GmbH & Co. KG
Robert-Koch-Straße 8
55129 Mainz
www.typografie.de
T 0049-6131-506030
F 0049-6131-506080

Volume Advertising: ISBN 978-3-87439-753-7
Volume A, D, C: ISBN 978-3-87439-752-0

© 2008 by Art Directors Club Verlag GmbH
Nachdruck, auch auszugsweise, nur mit Genehmigung der Art Directors Club Verlag GmbH
Reprint, also in extracts, only with prior approval of the Art Directors Club Verlag GmbH
Die Deutsche Bibliothek – CIP-Einheitsaufnahmen
Ein Titelsatz für diese Publikation ist bei der Deutschen Bibliothek erhältlich.

When you think department of like museums.